MILO CHRONICLES

BY THE SAME AUTHOR

From Judgment to Passion: Devotion to
Christ and the Virgin Mary, 800–1200

Mary and the Art of Prayer: The Hours of the
Virgin in Medieval Christian Life and Thought

MILO CHRON ICLES

DEVOTIONS 2016-2019

RACHEL FULTON BROWN

DANGEROUS BOOKS

Milo Chronicles: Devotions 2016-2019
Rachel Fulton Brown

Published by Dangerous Books

Cover Design: Milo Yiannopoulos

ISBN 978-952-7303-57-3

CONTENTS

INTRODUCTION

2016

2017

CONTENTS

2019

TO OUR LADY AND HER SON
WHO GAVE ME WISDOM TO SEE

Wherefore I wished, and understanding was given me: and I called upon God, and the spirit of wisdom came upon me:

And I preferred her before kingdoms and thrones, and esteemed riches nothing in comparison of her.

— Wisdom 7:7-8 (Douay-Rheims)

Introduction

MILO MEETS THE PROFESSOR

It was Saturday, September 17, 2016, and I had an email to write. I was excited—who wouldn't be?! But I was also nervous. What if he didn't write back? What if someone found out that I had written to him? What if it became known that I admired a man already infamous for being *dangerous*? It was a risk I was willing to take. Staying silent was not an option. For in him, I saw something to which I had to respond. *Joy.*

"Dear Mr. Yiannopoulos," I wrote,

I teach at the University of Chicago. As I am sure you are aware, a few weeks ago our dean of students Jay Ellison sent out a letter advising our incoming students not to expect to find trigger warnings or safe spaces on our campus shielding them from the life of the mind (or words to that effect). In response, some of my colleagues have written a letter to be published in our campus newspaper (I am not sure exactly when, it may have already come out) insisting that they do not subscribe to the administration's description of what our campus culture should be like.

Ever the Ent (not really on anybody's side because I am not sure anybody is on mine), I decided that I needed to spend some time watching the videos of the talks that had excited so much controversy last year—and so have spent a very enjoyable past several days with the videos that you have posted of your tour.

MILO CHRONICLES: INTRODUCTION

Thank you. You and Christina Hoff Sommers are doing exceptional work, God's work, drawing attention to the looniness that has infected our campuses these last several years.

I hope very much that your tour goes as well this year as it did last.

As it turns out, at the time that you were on your tour last year, I was embroiled in my own more local version of the same, in response to a blog post that I published on my personal blog in June 2015, but which caught the attention of one of my medievalist colleagues in January [2016].

The post was entitled "Three Cheers for White Men," the three cheers being for the ideas of chivalry (that it is wrong, in fact, to rape women, much better to protect and serve them), of marriage defined as being by consent (a medieval invention), and of the right to vote (which we women would not have if the men who could vote at the time had not voted to give us, something people seem inclined to forget).

My colleague [shared] this post on a Facebook feminist group and got many of my other colleagues gasping in horror—at which point I learned about it from another colleague, joined the group, and jumped in. I wrote about my experience with the [Facebook] thread on my own blog, but more important, I was inspired to write the longer version of the argument that I had meant to make on the original post.

Given your interest in this argument, I wanted to bring my blog to your attention now, in the hope that you might find some of my facts helpful in your presentations this year. There was a short piece about the controversy published in *The College Fix* last winter, with an excellent image of a real white knight. I have since written additional posts on the importance of defending our culture, which I would likewise hope you find helpful. I would be very happy to supply further references if you are interested.

The fight you are leading for us is of the utmost importance: you are now my white knight in spirit[1] and I want to make sure you have the best weapons!

---

[1] I now understand that this phrasing was not quite the compliment that I meant it to be! But Milo has become my champion nevertheless. See Milo's *Middle Rages: Why the Battle for Medieval Studies Matters to America* (2019).

Milo wrote back within minutes: "Rachel: thank you! I will take a look. Do stay in touch. M." A few days later, Milo shared on his Facebook page the first of the blog posts in which I wrote about him—cautiously, as if I were only observing him from a distance, but by that point we were already in regular conversation by email and continue to be so to this day. As a certain *Buzzfeed* writer famously found out, I was eager to share with Milo what I know about "the history of Christianity, the Crusades, and the righteousness of the West." You will have heard some of the things that I wrote to Milo about in his campus lectures, particularly those in which he talks about how the Catholic church is right "about everything."[2]

Meanwhile, I was getting bolder on my blog *Fencing Bear at Prayer*. Within a month, I had dedicated a post on Milton's *Areopagitica* to Milo, which he also shared on his Facebook page. And then came the Channel 4 interview with Cathy Newman, at which I outed myself as Milo's chronicler. The rest is history.

I was there watching as Milo and his team traveled the country in Anita, the Dangerous Faggot Tour bus.

I was there watching his fans talk about how much they loved him and how they took courage from him.

I was there watching on the night of the riot at Berkeley.

I was there watching when he appeared on *Real Time with Bill Maher*.

I was there watching when CPAC disinvited him and Simon & Schuster cancelled his book contract.

I was there watching when he returned on the Cinco de Milo wearing a snake.

I was there watching when he sent his best-selling book *Dangerous* soaring into the heavens.

[2] It is! Well, about most things. Okay, Pope Benedict XVI was. See Milo's *Diabolical: How Pope Francis Has Betrayed Clerical Abuse Victims Like Me—And Why He Has To Go* (2018). I wrote the Foreword.

I was there watching when he took to his knees on campus at Berkeley after Free Speech Week was cancelled.

I was there watching when he married John.

I was there watching when *Buzzfeed* published its exposé on the emails they had acquired, including mine.

I was there watching when the video of Milo's singing *America the Beautiful* was released.

I was there watching when long-time supporters declared him divisive.

I was there watching when he flew to Australia and appeared in the clouds.

I was there watching when he set up his lion throne.

I was there watching when even those who had previously praised him refused to stand in his defense.

I was there watching when the Mayor of New York stepped in to cancel his lecture at NYU.

I was there watching when he confessed how he became poor.

I was there. Watching.

What did I see? I saw a young man willing to take enormous personal and professional risks out of love for the truth. I saw a fellow Christian undaunted by the slurs thrown at him by enemies and former friends for speaking the truth. I saw a student eager to learn from what I was telling him, able to take the lessons that I taught and transform them into wisdom that others might hear. I saw a sinner on his knees, filled with compassion for the suffering in our world. This is not, of course, the way the mainstream liberal media describe him, not to mention many of his fellow conservatives who are convinced he is a standard bearer for the alt-right. How is it that I see something so very different when I look at him?

I am not only Fencing Bear of my blog. I am the Merry Medievalist of Dangerous.com. Even better, I am a real-life professor of religious symbology who teaches courses on the history of Christianity and the works of J.R.R. Tolkien. I know how to read the signs. What I see is a religious crisis in which Milo is playing catalyst. The University of Toronto professor of psychology Jordan B. Peterson called him an archetypal trickster, a kind of character who appears in times of crisis and points out the things nobody wants to see and says the things nobody will say. I call him a holy fool, dancing like King David before the ark of the Lord, making himself ridiculous to the world out of joy for the truth.

Milo is like the grotesques in the margins of medieval manuscripts, capering about among the prayers. He is like the clown in the medieval story who tumbled before the image of Mary and her Child, serving God and his Mother with laughter and love. As medieval illuminators and story-tellers knew, the devil hates laughter even more than he loves sin. But God loves laughter, particularly when it exposes lies. I said as much in an article that I published in the University of Chicago Divinity School Martin Marty Center for the Public Understanding of Religion's weekly newsletter *Sightings* in February 2017 only days before Simon & Schuster and CPAC caved to the bullying of the conservative right (a.k.a. "spineless cunts") and cancelled Milo's contracts with them:

> This, I would argue, is why American college students and faculty find Milo's talks so threatening. The issues that Milo talks about are usually considered political, but in fact have to do with people's deepest convictions: the proper relations between women and men, the definition of community, the role of beauty, access to truth.

> Milo professes himself a Catholic and wears a pair of gold crosses around his neck. He speaks about the importance of Christianity for the values of Western civilization. As he put it in one interview: "[Western

civilization] has created a religion in which love and self-sacrifice and giving are the highest possible virtues... That's a good thing... But when you remove discipline and sacrifice from religion you get a cult."

None of these issues, most especially the civilizational roots of culture and virtue in religious faith, are typically addressed in modern college education in America. Rather, they are, for the most part, purposefully avoided....

Not to address these issues openly does not allow students to keep an open mind. Their minds are already open—and being filled with what they are given in place of religion: multiculturalism; race, class, gender; the purportedly secular ideals of socialism and Marxism. Particularly for those students, and faculty, who have little to no religious education outside of school, these ideals have become their faith.

This is why students and faculty find Milo so threatening. He not only challenges them to examine beliefs they have never been taught to question. Thanks to his near charismatic appeal as a speaker, at least for those who attend his talks rather than stand outside protesting, he holds out the possibility of conversion, of changing hearts and minds.

It is much easier to call Milo names than to accept the challenge he presents. Milo's tour has made clear how high the stakes are. If you drive out explicit theology from public education, you get not *no* theology, but only *bad* theology, theology never properly examined as such....

The violent response to Milo's tour of our college campuses, culminating in the riot at Berkeley, is evidence of a deep crisis in religious thinking. If students cannot practice these difficult conversations in school, there is nothing to stop them from spilling into the streets.[3]

Since the spring of 2017, the crisis has only gotten worse. We have people screaming at the sky. We have students and faculty calling for speakers to be cancelled whose works they have never read, whose lectures they have never attended, on the basis that to let them speak will cause harm to people not even in the room.

---

[3] https://divinity.uchicago.edu/sightings/why-milo-scares-students-and-faculty-even-more

We have senior academics claiming that to allow controversial speakers on campus is a threat to student safety, when, as Milo regularly points out, the only real threats typically made are against speakers like him. In my own field of medieval studies, colleagues are convinced that not to declare ourselves explicitly not white supremacists is tantamount to declaring we are. Open letters circulate at the speed of light calling for those who speak out against this kind of silencing themselves to be silenced—or else.

Writing for and about Milo has brought me to my academic colleagues' attention more than once over the past three years. I have had letters signed against me by hundreds of colleagues, some on my own campus, many more whom I do not know. I myself am considered by many as a threat to their well-being for my relationship with Milo, although to its credit, my university has stood firm in defense of my freedom as an academic to speak. But as the violent responses to Milo's efforts to speak publicly, whether on campus or in private venues, continue to prove, this is a war that is far from over. Nor, as Milo reminds us, will it ever be, because the forces of repression and sinister Social Justice totalitarian instincts that we are fighting will always be with us. "Indeed," he said, "they are part of our nature."

What Milo understands and what I see in his willingness to play the fool is that the real fight we are in is not about politics, but about culture—and that it is about culture because it is about love. Conservatives like to say that we argue on the basis of logic and reason, but logic and reason can take us only so far. They are effective as weapons only insofar as they are wielded with love. Next time you are in an argument with a Social Justice Warrior, ask him or her this question: *What do you love?* Milo loves John. He also loves guns and the Bible. He loves freedom and property rights and capitalism and democracy. But he loves beauty and truth and goodness more because he loves God.

What does it mean to love God? Milo keeps on his desk a copy of Thomas of Kempen's *The Imitation of Christ,* a fifteenth-century best-seller on how to train the soul in devotion to God. Thomas is not the author you would think—based on his reputation as a gay man who loves sucking black dick—Milo would be most likely to read, but after all he is playing the fool. It is his role to ridicule those who depend on the wisdom of the world, that is, on society's mores rather than God.

It is just as J.S. Mill, another of Milo's favorite authors, warned. Society has become the tyrant. Society, that is, our need to live in groups and seek others' approval, is ever there to tell us what to say and what not to say, what to wear and what not to wear, what to read and what not to read, what to be and what not to be, what to love and what not to love. It is this need to seek others' approval that enables us to live in groups, but it is this same need against which we must fight when the desire to conform with other people's expectations overwhelms the love of goodness, beauty, and truth. This is why the greatest weapon in the arsenal of the Social Justice Warriors is *shame.* And it is why the greatest weapon at our disposal is *ridicule.*

The Devil hates laughter. The Devil would like nothing more than a world without jokes, satire, laughter, and joy. The Devil, that is, all our worst propensities as human beings to envy each other for our abilities and accomplishments, hates being made to look ridiculous because ridicule reminds him—us—how mortal and fallible we are. Ridicule reminds us that however noble we may think our ideals, it is rarely possible to realize them in real life. We fail more than we succeed. Particularly when we try to fix the world.

Social Justice Warriors hate thinking that they may not have all the answers. They hate the thought that they cannot change the world simply on the strength of their convictions. They hate the thought that they cannot simply will away all the pain and suffering that they see—pain and suffering, they are convinced, that we, as conservatives and libertarians, cannot see because we refuse to accept their solutions for how to make it go away.

"If thou be the Son of God," the Devil tempted Jesus in the desert, "command that these stones be made bread.... Cast thyself down [from this pinnacle, and the angels will bear thee up].... All these [kingdoms of the world] will I give thee, if falling down thou wilt adore me" (Matthew 4:3-9). Beware ideologies that promise to take all your pain away! Milo understands the Devil's temptations—and mocks them with the characters he plays: The Dangerous Faggot dripping with gold and pearls. Ivana Wall in diamonds and heels carrying her Bible. Social Justice Warrior Styrm ("with a y") in her facial piercings and combat boots. MILO in all caps, being bitchy and fabulous, dressed in Gucci and Louis Vuitton.

Or, as I called him, Jesus. Well, not exactly. What I actually called him was Kung Fu Milo, after the Kung Fu Panda Po, who defeats the great Musk-Ox Warrior Kai by turning Kai's attack back on him with love. At the time I wrote that post, Milo was on the first leg of his Dangerous Faggot campus tour, traveling around the country giving talks about on why "Fat Shaming Works," "How to Destroy the Alt-right," "10 Things I Hate About Islam," and why "Feminism is Cancer for Men...and Women!"

He had a team of young men helping him and was speaking to standing-room-only audiences for free about the ways in which the hypocrisies of the Left and Right had led them astray. It was uncanny, almost mythical, the way in which what Milo was doing mirrored what Jesus did. And then came Berkeley, when the mob ran Milo out of town. And then came *Real Time with Bill Maher*, when Milo became known to the mainstream as a mischievous fool egging on both the Left and the Right. And then came the video, in which what Milo said about his own abuse growing up was used in an attempt to destroy his career. I started to worry that somehow, I had brought it about by writing about him in the way that I had. Prophetically, as it were. Seeing the signs.

Now that you have the key, you can guess how I read the next two years. How Milo returned as if from the dead having conquered the dragon. How he ascended into the heavens in the person of his book. How he married his love, albeit himself taking the part of the bride. How he returned bringing judgment Down Under ("Judgement Gay"), and then set up his throne in the heavens where, seated amongst the lions, he spoke with wisdom about what he sees in the world. How he was denied. How he confessed his sins. You can't make this stuff up! Except Milo did.

"I swear she's the only person who really understands me," Milo commented on the Facebook share of my post about how I read his Show set. (Guess who I identified as the Whore of Babylon?[4]) Now, remember: *I knew none of this was going to happen when I wrote him that first email—and neither did he.* I chronicled it all on my blog in real time, and yet, there it was. The joy and the sorrow. The love and the hate. The triumph and failure. The laughter and shame.

"I wonder what sort of story we've fallen into," said Sam. "I wonder," said Frodo. "But I don't know. And that's the way of a real tale. Take any one that you're fond of. You may know, or guess, what kind of tale it is, happy-ending or sad-ending, but the people in it don't know. And you don't want them to."[5] What if, like the hobbits,

---

[4] https://fencingbearatprayer.blogspot.com/2018/01/i-spy-milo-on-set.html
[5] J.R.R. Tolkien, *The Lord of the Rings* (1955), bk. 4, chap. 8

you found yourself inside such a tale? What would you do? *A fool and a teddy bear take on the world. You gotta laugh!*

RACHEL FULTON BROWN
CHICAGO, IL

2016

SAFE SPACES VS. SACRED SPACES

September 29, 2016

As I am sure you are all aware, a few weeks ago, John Ellison, the Dean of Students in the College at the University of Chicago, sent a letter out to all of our incoming freshman in which he described some of the things that they should expect—and not expect—to encounter as students in the College. "One of the University of Chicago's defining characteristics," he told them, "is our commitment to freedom of inquiry and expression.... Members of our community are encouraged to speak, write, listen, challenge and learn, without fear of censorship.

"Civility and mutual respect are vital to all of us, and freedom of expression does not mean the freedom to harass or threaten others. You will find that we expect members of our community to be engaged in rigorous debate, discussion, and even disagreement. At times this may challenge you and even cause discomfort."

Not, arguably, all that remarkable a claim, you might think. Of course our students should expect to feel challenged, possibly even uncomfortable at times, they have been admitted to one of the top universities in the country, the university where, as it says on all the t-shirts, "fun comes to die." But there was more. "Our commitment to academic freedom," Dean Ellison went on, "means that we do not support so-called 'trigger warnings,' we do not cancel invited speakers because their topics might prove controversial, and we do not condone the creation of intellectual 'safe spaces' where individuals can retreat from ideas and perspectives at odds with their own."

The response from the nation at large (who knew so many were paying attention to us?) was sharp and swift, none sharper and swifter (at least in academia's terms) than the letter that 150 of my fellow faculty members signed and published in the campus student newspaper during Orientation week in which they distanced themselves from the Dean's take on things.[6] "Those of us who have signed this letter," they told the students, "have a variety of opinions about requests for trigger warnings and safe spaces. We may also disagree as to whether free speech is ever legitimately interrupted by concrete pressures of the political. That is as it should be.

"But let there be no mistake: such requests often touch on substantive, ongoing issues of bias, intolerance and trauma that affect our intellectual exchanges. To start a conversation by declaring that such requests are not worth making is an affront to the basic principles of liberal education and participatory democracy."

They went on to talk about how important it was for the work that we do in the classroom to be conducted in an atmosphere of mutual respect and to a commitment to learning from "a wealth of histories and experiences—*to more discussion, not less; to openness, not closure.*" After which they offered a brief history of the history of "safe spaces" in "gay, civil rights, and feminist efforts of the mid-20th century to create

---

[6] https://www.chicagomaroon.com/article/2016/9/13/letter-faculty-respond-ellison-letter/

places protected from quite real forces of violence and intimidation.... It would be naïve," they acknowledged (or insisted?), "to think that the University of Chicago is immune from social problems. Yet the administration [that is, our dean of students, who is an administrative dean, but also our college dean, who is a member of the faculty; Dean Ellison's letter was meant as a cover letter for Dean Boyer's book] confusingly disconnects 'safe spaces' it supports (see the list of mentoring services on the College's own website) from 'intellectual safe spaces' that it does not, as if issues of power and vulnerability stop at the classroom door."

I did not sign this letter. Not because I do not think my colleagues did anything inappropriate as such in publishing it—quite the reverse! They would not be University of Chicago faculty if they didn't get up in arms about something the administration says at least twice a decade. That, as our very own Dean John Boyer has chronicled at length in his recently published history of the College, is what we at Chicago do: fight with the administration.[7] But likewise we argue with ourselves, sometimes at length, not always as openly as perhaps we should. I was happy when I saw the posts streaming on my Facebook feed about Dean Ellison's letter.

I was afraid when I saw the email sent to my department letting me know about the faculty's letter and inviting me to sign. I was even more afraid when I read the names on the list of those who approved the faculty letter, among them colleagues in my own field of medieval studies, many of them colleagues in my own department of history. What would they think of me if I didn't sign? I am scrolling through the list of names again now; it has grown since the letter was originally circulated. My hearts sinks just a little bit when I see the name of someone I respect; I breathe easier when there is a name missing.

---

[7] *The University of Chicago: A History* (2015)

What if, I asked myself when I first saw the letter, I just pretended I was too engrossed in my research to have known about it? I am on leave this quarter and next, not attending faculty meetings or functions on campus. Nobody would ever know that I had seen the letter and refused—not just neglected, but *refused*—to sign.

Oh, look, there is my upstairs neighbor's name; what if she reads through the list of names and mine isn't there? Oh, and there is the colleague whose office is next door to mine, whom I saw only a week ago or so in the grocery store. There are several of our MacArthur fellows, three of them in my department. There is another of the colleagues whom I respect the most.... Oh, look, there's an Editor's Note: "The online edition of this article will be continually updated as more faculty members sign the letter." I will have no excuse come Spring when I am back on campus, will I?

If I am this frightened at the thought of disagreeing with my colleagues—me, a tenured faculty member—think how our students must feel if they agree with the Deans and disagree with their teachers on issues of "power and vulnerability" and what should be done about them. Yes, we're talking political correctness here, even at the University of Chicago. Seriously, my colleagues think that the administration is creating a hostile environment for our students by telling them that they should expect to be challenged and made uncomfortable over the course of their studies?

I should hope so! Otherwise what are they coming here for? College is not therapy. It is more like a monastery (or should be—wouldn't everybody be better able to study if we were all segregated by sex and expected to be celibate?): a *schola* for training the soul. And training the soul is terrifying work. This is the way Benedict of Nursia described the purpose of the monastery in the prologue to his "rule for beginners" on which the Benedictine tradition was based:

And so we are going to establish a school for the service of the Lord. In founding it we hope to introduce nothing harsh or burdensome. But if a certain strictness results from the dictates of equity for the amendment of vices or the preservation of charity, do not be at once dismayed and fly from the way of salvation, whose entrance cannot but be narrow (Matthew 7:14). For as we advance in the religious life and in faith, our hearts expand and we run the way of God's commandments with unspeakable sweetness of love. Thus, never departing from His school, but persevering in the monastery according to His teaching until death, we may by patience share in the sufferings of Christ (1 Peter 4:13) and deserve to have a share also in His kingdom.[8]

You will say: "But colleges and universities aren't monasteries; they are institutions of higher learning, not communities of prayer." To which I would respond: "But they are; where do you think all that higher learning comes from?" Here is where I think we, as professors, have done our students a terrible disservice in preparing them for what it means to engage in the kind of learning that we do—or ought to be doing—on our university campuses. To judge from the outrage that has been sparked (should I say, triggered?) over the past year or so by such events as Milo Yiannopoulos's "Dangerous Faggot Tour" or Ben Shapiro's speeches on the importance of diversity of thought and free speech, our students come to campus woefully ill-prepared to encounter arguments that run counter to the things that others in our on-going national conversations about race, class, and gender have said.[9]

In part, this is because their teachers themselves do not know these counter-arguments, at least to judge from the responses that I get from my colleagues if I even mention that I may have read about them, never mind taken the time to find out what these dangerous

---

[8] https://www.osb.org/our-roots/the-rule/texts-and-translations-of-the-rule-of-saint-benedict/

[9] http://www.breitbart.com/tag/dangerous-faggot-tour/

speakers actually say. (Pro tip: it isn't what you read in the mainstream media. As I told Dean Boyer when I wrote to thank him for the book that he sent the students about academic freedom at the University of Chicago, maybe it's because I'm a medievalist, but I do dislike people being labeled heretics without a proper inquisition.[10] Plus, I'm a *medievalist*. More or less on a daily basis I am wrestling with the way in which the history of Europe has been distorted by, as my colleagues would put it, "concrete pressures of the political." Don't even get me started on Marx.)

But the problem, I think, goes deeper than this, which is why our students are feeling so anxious and, yes, triggered by some of the things that we ask them to read, talk, and think about in our classrooms and lecture halls. (What happens on campus outside of the classroom or lecture hall is a topic for another post; bear with me.) Bluntly, we aren't teaching them. (Okay, not me, I think I am, at least I hope I am, but I am trying to be inclusive here.) Sure, we assign them reading to do and problem sets to solve, we ask them questions in our discussion sections, we critique their writing and supervise their research. But these are just exercises, like standing and singing the Psalms over and over for the whole of one's life, as Benedict's monks did.

To put it in Simon Sinek's terms, they are the WHAT of intellectual labor: the things that we do as scholars, whether writing papers, conducting experiments, giving talks to our colleagues, and so forth.[11] Arguably, for most of us, this is the only level at which we engage with our students' encounter with the materials of our respective fields. We assign them things to read or problems to work and then test them on their ability to manipulate similar materials according to the models we have given them. (This, by the by, is why we have so much

[10] https://college.uchicago.edu/sites/college.uchicago.edu/files/attachments/Boyer_OccasionalPapers_V10.pdf

[11] https://www.startwithwhy.com/LearnYourWhy.aspx

scholarship that simply takes the dominant modes of interpretation—by now in the humanities and social sciences almost exclusively "race, class, and gender"—and "applies" them over and over again; we are stuck at the WHAT.)

Occasionally, although even at Chicago, less and less so (ask me about the BA requirements in my department that my colleagues just voted on), we force ourselves to engage with the HOW: training our students not just to practice manipulating texts or data according to the models we have given them, but getting them to look at intellectual labor (I am using the term here in its monastic sense, the *labora* of the cloister and scriptorium as opposed to the *ora* of the choir) as itself a kind of practice that makes certain kinds of demands, above all, on the imagination, but also on the ego, as anyone who has ever faced the terrors of writer's block knows.[12]

Almost never, and I do mean never, do we address the question at the center of Sinek's Golden Circle: the WHY of what we do, whether as teachers or scholars. This, I would argue, is what is most triggering to our students. Why? Because the WHY question is not something you can answer in terms of skills or employability or credentials or any of the other external measures by which we gauge our effectiveness as teachers and our students' ability to learn.

WHY should students spend tens of thousands of dollars being tested in particular subjects so as to gain the credential of a BA? Nobody—at least, nobody in my nearly thirty years in academia—ever asks. WHY? Because asking this question requires us to do far more than perform well on a test or get an article accepted through peer review (the professors' equivalent of a mid-term exam). Because asking this question opens us up and lays us bare before God.

---

[12] https://home.uchicago.edu/~rfulton/Tips.htm

Tolkien, as always, put it best. Towards the end of his life, Tolkien received a letter from Camilla Unwin, the daughter of his publisher, asking him for help with a school project on the theme: "What is the purpose of life?" Tolkien responded (late, as always): "What does the question really mean?"[13] Such questions, he argued, are "only really useful when they refer to the conscious purposes or objects of human beings, or to the uses of things they design and make." The value of all other things, those things not designed and made by human beings, lies not in their utility to people, but in themselves: "they ARE, they would exist even if we did not. But since we do exist one of their functions is to be contemplated by us," and given that we are human—that is, curious—we are prone in our contemplation of things other than ourselves to ask the question HOW they came to have the patterns and structures that they do, which then brings us to the question WHY all other such things exist.

"But WHY in this sense, implying reasons and motives, can only refer to a MIND. Only a Mind can have purposes in any way or degree akin to human purposes," which brings us to the Question: "Is there a God, a Creator-Designer, a Mind to which our minds are akin (being derived from it) so that It is intelligible to us in part. With that we come to religion and the moral ideas that proceed from it."

Without belief in such a personal God, Tolkien contends, "the question: 'What is the purpose of life?' is unaskable and unanswerable. To whom or what would you address the question?" But since (he continues) there are things in the Universe who have developed with minds to ask such questions, it is likely that if the Universe were to reply it would say something like this: "I am as I am. There is nothing you can do about it. You may go on trying to find out what I am, but

---

[13] Letter 310 to Camilla Unwin, 20 May 1969, in *The Letters of J.R.R. Tolkien*, ed. Humphrey Carpenter with Christopher Tolkien (1981)

you will never succeed. And why you want to know, I do not know. Perhaps the desire to know for the mere sake of knowledge is related to the prayers that some of you address to what you call God. At their highest these seem simply to praise Him for being, as He is, and for making what He has made, as He has made it." This, for Tolkien, was the purpose of life, the only purpose life could conceivably have, given that "purpose" implies by definition "being made":

> to increase according to our capacity our knowledge of God by all the means we have, and to be moved by it to praise and thanks. To do as we say in the *Gloria in Excelsis*: Laudamus te... We praise you, we call you holy, we worship you, we proclaim your glory, we thank you for the greatness of your splendour. And in moments of exaltation we may call on all created things to join in our chorus, speaking on their behalf, as is done in Psalm 148, and in The Song of the Three Children in Daniel II [3:57-88, 56, *The Benedicite*]: PRAISE THE LORD...all mountains and hills, all orchards and forests, all things that creep and birds on the wing.

Such praises, I am sure you are unsurprised to hear, have little to no place in the modern university—but, I would argue, our students sense them nevertheless. They come to us hungry for meaning, hungry for understanding, hungry for some sense of WHAT IT ALL MEANS. And we feed them scraps, the leavings of centuries upon centuries of human inquiry into the workings of our souls and of the universe as creatures of God, disconnected from the WHY that originally gave them purpose. Because, of course, for most of the centuries of the existence of universities (and before them, monasteries) the whole point of academic inquiry was to prepare for the encounter with God in the choir.

The *labora* was never intended as an end in itself. Rather, it was the discipline which the monks and scholars practiced so as to be able to endure the great mystery of the choir: the encounter with the

Creator of Heaven and earth in all his awe-inspiring love. This was the reason that Benedict provided the rule that he did, with all of its recommendations for how the monks should schedule their labors and prayers: such encounters with the sacred are terrifying, difficult for mere mortals to withstand without going mad.

Our students are going mad. We have brought them into a place where we systematically expose them to the terrors of existence, its beauty and tragedy, its greatness and profundity, and we give them no training in how to prepare themselves for this encounter, in large part because we as teachers have no training ourselves. How does one train for the encounter with God? Perhaps we might start by acknowledging that we should.

A FEW WORDS OF ADVICE TO TRIGGLYPUFF (AND HER TEACHERS)

September 30, 2016

I would not want to be this young woman. By now, five months after the event she attended at the University of Massachusetts Amherst featuring a discussion with Christina Hoff Sommers, Steven Crowder, and Milo Yiannopoulos on the problems besetting university campuses with speech considered "triggering," she has become a favorite meme among those who see such concerns as at best mildly hysterical, at worst a symptom of the total breakdown of our national character (I paraphrase).[14] Audiences at several of Milo's recent talks have made reference to her, imitating her arm gestures (which I am having a hard time ignoring on the gif as I am writing) and laughing at her expense.[15]

Milo, to his credit, has admonished them: "No, we love Trigglypuff! Trigglypuff is wonderful!," while insisting that it is not she, but those who have lied to her about what will make her happy that are to blame. "She is going to be miserable," he has said (again, I paraphrase),

---

[14] http://knowyourmeme.com/memes/trigglypuff

[15] https://www.youtube.com/user/yiannopoulosm

"because feminists have taught her to believe that she can be fat without consequence," pointing especially in his talk at Louisiana State University to the health effects of obesity. While, as long-time readers of this blog know, I have had my own struggles with fat shaming, I think he does have a point: it is possible to take "body positivity" too far the other way.

Just as it is possible to be too thin, it is also possible to be too fat; we risk young (and old) women's lives suggesting that fitness and size have no effects on their ability to be happy.[16] But when I look at the full video from which the gif was generated, I see something other than just a young woman who needs to lose weight. I see a young woman who needs training, not only in formal methods of debate (wait for the question and answer period to raise your concerns), but even more fundamentally, in schooling her soul. Here, as Fencing Bear, I would like to give her a few words of advice about how to begin.

First, consider the falcon.[17] This was a meditation that first came to me as I was thinking about my weight and my responses to eating, how hard it seemed to sit with the feelings that constantly threatened to overwhelm me and which, as I learned reading Geneen Roth, I would stifle with food.[18] Milo likes to say: "Fuck your feelings," whenever anyone tries to use his or her sense of being offended to try to shut down debate. Roth, more gently, would say: "Practice sitting with them." Practice sitting with all of the anxieties and fears and doubts that feel like they are going to overwhelm you. Practice feeling your feelings, letting them simply be there, not trying to make them go away, not trying to fight them, just feeling them. Sit with them long

---

[16] http://fencingbearatprayer.blogspot.com/2009/04/daughters-of-eve.html

[17] http://fencingbearatprayer.blogspot.com/2011/09/on-training-falcon-heart-not-to-bate.html

[18] https://geneenroth.com/

enough to realize that they are only feelings, they cannot hurt you, however overwhelming they may seem.

This applies to feelings that you have by yourself, when you are alone and wishing you could be with friends; when you are struggling with your schoolwork (more on this in a moment) and your demon is telling you how stupid are; when you are listening to someone speak and he or she says something that you aren't sure about, particularly when it conflicts with things you have previously been taught by your parents, teachers, or friends. Sit with them, let them wash over you, feel them in their full force...and then, over time, realize that they aren't scary anymore. They're just feelings.

Second, develop a skill. Here, your falcon training will serve you well, because one of the greatest barriers (as Fencing Bear knows all too well) to developing a skill is, you guessed it, your feelings. Feelings of envy and pride. Feelings of "should." Feelings of frustration and anger and doubt and impatience. Feelings of all the times someone (e.g. your father or mother) suggested that you didn't have the talent for this or that art.

Feelings of the shame that washed over you whenever your mother told you not to "show off." Feelings of wishing you were anyone other than who you are. Again, they are just feelings. They can make you miserable, but they cannot make you happy. What can? As Mihaly Csikszentmihalyi has argued, skill.[19] More particularly, skill exercised under the appropriate conditions of difficulty, such that you are neither anxious or bored. "Flow," he calls it, as if it is easy. Which it is—but only in concept, almost never in execution. (I, Fencing Bear, am living proof.[20],[21])

---

[19] *Flow: The Psychology of Optimal Experience* (1990)

[20] http://fencingbearatprayer.blogspot.com/2009/07/comfort-zone.html

[21] http://fencingbearatprayer.blogspot.com/2016/07/gratitude-and-fellowship-of-sword.html

Why? Because real happiness comes not from doing things we find easy—or, worse, from following our "passion"—but from confronting challenges and rising to them. Here, competition is our friend because it gives us opportunities in which to exercise our skills, but even more importantly, because it provides real opportunities for failure.[22] We learn nothing when we win, except that our skills were adequate to the task. We learn—and learn big, if having learned to sit with our feelings, we can ignore them and pay attention to what we need to change in our practice.

This, to my mind, as both Fencing Bear and Professor of History, is the real scandal afflicting our university and college campuses today. Not that the students are feeling triggered by the feelings that they experience when confronting ideas or assignments that they do not know how to address, but that we, their teachers, have failed to give them proper challenges because we (and, no, I don't really include myself in this group, but as a teacher, I know I always have room to improve) have become so obsessed with making sure that they never feel bad. Well, to coin a phrase: "Fuck our feelings!"

Fuck our discomfort when we ask them a question and they don't know the answer. Fuck our anxieties about whether we are implicitly biased (of course we are, Mrs. Clinton is hardly the first to make this observation—as the Avenue Q puppets put it, "Everyone's a little bit racist!") when we respond to them.[23] Fuck our feelings when we grade their assignments and feel sorry for them because, in all honesty, we cannot give them an A, no matter how hard we know they tried. Fuck our feelings—because, if we don't, we are *lying* to them, and that is far worse than making them feel a little bad. Why? Because, as teachers, it is our *JOB* to give them accurate and honest feedback about the

---

[22] http://fencingbearatprayer.blogspot.com/2008/11/competition-in-nutshell.html
[23] https://youtu.be/RovF1zsDoeM

work they are doing, the thoughts and opinions that they express, their grammatical and arithmetical skills, their comprehension of the material that we have assigned them and their ability to work with it.

If, as Milo likes to say, "feminism is cancer," grade inflation is heart disease, diabetes, and suicide rolled into one. And not just the kind of grade inflation that everyone talks about, when all the students at Harvard get As. The kind that sucks at your soul because you have never been presented with an actual challenge and so have no idea whatsoever what to do with a novel and difficult task or idea. Political correctness is a symptom, not a cause. It is a symptom of putting students in situations, for whatever well-meaning reason we might give, for which they do not have the skills because they have never been given accurate feedback about how they performed.

Of course they are triggered when they encounter professors like Christina Hoff Sommers suggesting that maybe all college-aged men are not rapists or that equality of opportunity is different from equality of outcome, if every time that they have been presented with something that made them mildly uncomfortable—for example, like losing a fencing bout—they have been told that what mattered was their feelings rather than that they learned what they needed to do to improve either their understanding of what the speaker has said or their ability to provide an appropriate answer.[24] This is one of the key elements, as Csikszentmihalyi has shown, of experiencing "flow": *immediate and unambiguous feedback*, combined with clarity of goals and a concentration on the task at hand, so that one learns from the practice and thus can grow in skill.

By now you will have guessed that I admire Milo greatly for what he is doing in making his tour of our college campuses. He has inspired me to take up some of these difficult issues on my blog, about which

---

[24] http://fencingbearatprayer.blogspot.com/2014/04/why-i-choked.html

I hope to say more over the coming weeks, but above all, the thing that struck me most when I started watching the videos of the talks that he gave last year and has continued to impress me as he makes his current tour, is how he is training our students to understand the difference between emotional outpourings and actual questions, to the latter of which he responds immediately and unambiguously with appropriate facts. If we want our students to stop feeling so triggered, we need to start practicing feeling less triggered ourselves. The Dangerous Faggot Tour, I would submit, is a good place to start.

FREE SPEECH FUNDAMENTALS: MILTON

October 29, 2016

I have a theory: people get anxious when they don't know where the ideas that they are asked to live by come from. Certainly, I get anxious, and I am a professionally trained historian. What must it be like for those presented with a concept like "freedom of speech" who have no idea why this should be a Good Thing except because their teachers tell them so—especially when their teachers are at the same time insisting such contradictory things as, "We all need to be respectful of each other's opinions," even as they model shutting those opinions down?[25]

Happily, Professor Fencing Bear is here to help. Or, at least, to provide a few notes. Freedom of speech is one of those concepts that come to us (by which I mean, those of us living in the present) out of the tradition that many of my colleagues have spent the past several decades teaching their students to be suspicious of. The shorthand labels tend to be things like "the Enlightenment" or "the English-speaking tradition," but all most people hear nowadays is "dead white

---

[25] http://fencingbearatprayer.blogspot.com/2016/09/safe-spaces-vs-sacred-spaces.html

European males who didn't want me to have a voice." Well. Given that it was dead white Europeans, granted, most of them male who articulated the concept that you should have a voice, perhaps it will help to have a few markers for how they came up with this concept in the first place.

THE SETTING

The first thing everyone needs know is that it didn't start with the American Revolution. I know, I know, we all point to the First Amendment as the place in which this idea is enshrined:

> Congress shall make no law respecting an establishment of religion, or prohibiting the free exercise thereof; or abridging the freedom of speech, or of the press; or the right of the people peaceably to assemble, and to petition the Government for a redress of grievances.

We tend to talk about the first two clauses of this amendment as if they are two separate concepts: "freedom of religion" and "freedom of speech," but—and this is vital to appreciate—in their origins, they were one. Freedom of religion was freedom of speech, more particularly, freedom of the press, because what concerned the English in the middle of the seventeenth century, when these ideas were first taking off (see graph), was not people's freedom (as Milo so dangerously puts it) to "read what you want, watch what you want, play what you want, think what you, say what you want," but rather their freedom to worship God in the way that they thought most likely to lead to salvation.

If you think the stakes are high today (which, to be fair, I agree with Milo, I think they are), they were even higher in the seventeenth century when you could still be sent quite literally to the stake for reading, thinking, and saying what you wanted about God. Well, okay, perhaps not in the mid-seventeenth century to the stake (I'm a medievalist, these modern centuries tend to blur), but you probably had ancestors in the sixteenth century who could have been, and then, thanks to the efforts of King Charles I[26] to get everyone, including the Scots, to worship from a common prayer book[27], if you hadn't already left England in disgust and settled in the Massachusetts Bay Colony[28], you would have found yourself forced to take sides in the Civil War[29]. No, not that one, the original one, the one fought between the Roundheads and the Cavaliers.

You haven't heard of this war? If you are a redneck, you should have[30]; it's the reason there are rednecks, a.k.a. Covenanters[31], Scots Presbyterians who banded together in 1638 to resist the king's imposition of the prayer book. It's complicated, but basically, it was the Covenanters who started the war, or series of wars, which led eventually to Charles's having his head cut off in 1649 (I told you the stakes were high). In the meantime, the Puritans (those who hadn't left for Massachusetts) and the Presbyterians gained the upper hand in Parliament and started trying to clamp down on their opponents, most particularly those riotous Royalists (like "Deplorables," "Cavaliers" was originally meant to be an insult) who supported Charles and his efforts at enforcing religious conformity under Archbishop William Laud[32]. (Laud got his head cut off even before the king. Like I said, the stakes were high.)

As if things were not already tense enough, in June 1643, the by-then Roundhead Parliament promulgated an Order for the Regulation of the Press, specifically intended to clamp down on the kinds of

---

[26] https://en.wikipedia.org/wiki/Charles_I_of_England

[27] https://en.wikipedia.org/wiki/Book_of_Common_Prayer

[28] https://en.wikipedia.org/wiki/Massachusetts_Bay_Colony

[29] https://en.wikipedia.org/wiki/English_Civil_War

[30] http://fencingbearatprayer.blogspot.com/2016/01/conservative-is-new-redneck.html

[31] https://en.wikipedia.org/wiki/Covenanter

[32] https://en.wikipedia.org/wiki/William_Laud

speech that they themselves had engaged in (I know, the irony). This was not the first such order "for suppressing the great late abuses and frequent disorders in Printing many, false forged, scandalous, seditious, libelous, and unlicensed Papers, Pamphlets, and Books to the great defamation of Religion and government" that Parliament had promulgated but, as the Long Parliament lamented, these previous orders ("notwithstanding the diligence of the Company of Stationers to put them in full execution") had had "little or no effect."

Printers were still printing and selling all kinds of troublesome stuff (gasp!) without license of the government-approved Stationers. Accordingly, the Roundheads wanted to make sure that the Stationers did their job, so they authorized regular searches for "unlicensed Printing Presses," which, if found, were to be seized and destroyed, along with all unlicensed books, papers, and pamphlets. "And all Justices of the Peace, Captaines, Constables and other officers, are hereby ordered and required to be aiding, to the foresaid persons in the due execution of all, and singular and assisting the premisses and in the apprehension of all Offenders against the same. And in case of opposition to break open the Doores and Locks."

The Parliamentarian John Milton[33], not yet the author of *Paradise Lost*, was not amused and published a pamphlet[34] (today it would be a blog post) lambasting Parliament for the Order and championing "the Liberty of Unlicensed Printing."[35] (*My comments in italics.*)

AREOPAGITICA: THE ARGUMENT

"I deny not," Milton acknowledged,

---

[33] https://en.wikipedia.org/wiki/John_Milton

[34] https://play.google.com/store/books/details?id=OREJAAAAQAAJ&rdid=book-OREJAAAAQAAJ&rdot=1

[35] http://www.gutenberg.org/ebooks/608

but that it is of greatest concernment in the church and commonwealth, to have vigilant eye how books demean themselves as well as men; and thereafter to confine, imprison, and do sharpest justice on them as malefactors: for books are not absolutely dead things, but do contain a potency of life in them to be as active as that soul whose progeny they are; nay they do preserve as in a vial the purest efficacy and extraction of that living intellect that bred them. (*Whew! It makes one at once proud and humble to be an author! Such power! Such life! Such efficacy!*)

I know they are as lively, and as vigorously productive, as those fabulous dragons teeth; and being sown up and down, may chance to spring up armed men. (*So, okay, books can be dangerous, they can lead to armed conflict.*)

And yet on the other hand unless wariness be used, as good almost kill a man as kill a good book; who kills a man kills a reasonable creature, God's image; but he who destroys a good book, kills reason itself, kills the image of God, as it were in the eye. (*Stakes high enough now?*)

Many a man lives a burden to the earth; but a good book is the precious life-blood of a master spirit, embalmed and treasured up on purpose to a life beyond life. It is true, no age can restore a life, whereof perhaps there is no great loss; and revolutions of ages do not oft recover the loss of a rejected truth, for the want of which whole nations fare the worse. We should be wary therefore what persecution we raise against the living labors of public men, how we spill that seasoned life of man preserved and stored up in books; since we see a kind of homicide may be thus committed, sometimes a martyrdom, and if it extend to the whole impression, a kind of massacre, whereof the execution ends not in the slaying of an elemental life, but strikes at that ethereal and fifth essence, the breath of reason itself, slays an immortality rather than a life. (*Oh, my! Killing a book a kind of homicide? Wiping out a whole print-run a massacre? Destroying books as an attack on the quintessence, reason? And you thought our current use of metaphor was overwrought! But what if the book raises up armed men? What if its ideas deserve to be killed? Ah, there's the rub: who decides?*)

Milton goes on to narrate a long line of previous attempts to murder books in this way, from the ancient Greeks and Romans down to the contemporary popes, albeit pausing, commendably, to note how in the Middle Ages under the Christian emperors books at least had the chance to be examined in council before they were prohibited and burned. Under the popes of Milton's day, however, the restrictions of the Imprimatur and the Index of Forbidden Books were fully in force, such that "no book, pamphlet, or paper" might be printed "unless it were approved and licensed under the hands of two or three glutton friars." (Anti-Catholicism, like the suppression of the press, has a venerable lineage.) "Are we," Milton is here challenging his fellow Protestants, "to be as bad as the popes? Well," he continues, "what exactly is it that we want to achieve?" Here is where the argument gets really interesting.

> How great a virtue is temperance, how much of moment through the whole life of man? Yet God commits the managing so great a trust, without particular law or prescription, wholly to the demeanor of every grown man.... (*Here Milton has been talking about how even the Scriptures contain quotations by heathen writers, and Christians have long depended on the learning of the Greeks. If even God does not step in, by way of the Scriptures, to prevent grown men from reading bad books, who is Parliament to make this decision for them?*)

> If we think to regulate printing, thereby to rectify manners, we must regulate all recreations and pastimes, all that is delightful to such matters as these, when all licensing will be easily eluded. Impunity and remissness, for certain are the bane of a Commonwealth, but here the great art lies to discern in what the law is to bid restraint and punishment, and in what things persuasion only is to work. If every action which is good, or evil in man at ripe years, were to be put under pittance, and prescription, and compulsion, what were virtue but a name, what praise could be then due to well-doing, what grammercy to be sober, just, or continent? Many there be that complain of divine providence for suffering Adam to transgress, foolish tongues! (*Milton would have more to say about this in his great epic.*) When God gave him reason, he gave him freedom to choose, for reason is but choosing; he had been else a mere artificial Adam, such an Adam as he is in

the motions. (*I.e. an automaton or robot.*) We ourselves esteem not of that obedience, or love, or gift, which is of force; God therefore left him free, set before him a provoking object, ever almost in his eyes herein consisted his merit, herein the right of his reward, the praise of his abstinence. Wherefore did he create passions within us, pleasures round about us, but that these rightly tempered are the very ingredients of virtue? They are not skillful considerers of human things, who imagine to remove sin by removing the matter of sin... (*Got all that? We'll come back to this in a moment.*)

The argument goes on: how, exactly, does Parliament think the licensers are going to be able to judge whether the works of authors more learned than they merit publication? How does Parliament propose to create a monopoly on truth and understanding? More to the point, is it not worse to in effect force men to believe even the truth without understanding, as must happen if men are no longer required to test their religion in argument? And what is Truth?

> Truth is compared in Scripture to a streaming fountain; if her waters flow not in perpetual progression, they sicken into a muddy pool of conformity and tradition. A man may be a heretic in the truth; and if he believes things only because his pastor says so, or the Assembly so determines, without knowing other reason, though his belief be true, yet the very truth he holds, becomes his heresy. There is not any burden that some would gladder post off to another, than the charge and care of their religion....

> Truth indeed came once into the world with her divine master, and was a perfect shape most glorious to look on (*i.e. Jesus*): but when he ascended, and his apostles after him were laid asleep, then straight arose a wicked race of deceivers, who as that story goes of the Egyptian Typhon with his conspirators, how they dealt with the god Osiris, took the virgin Truth, hewed her lovely form into a thousand pieces, and scattered them to the four winds. From that time ever since, the sad friends of Truth, such as dare appear, imitating the careful search that Isis made for the mangled body of Osiris, went up and down gathering up limb by limb still as they could find them. We have not yet found them all, Lords and Commons, nor ever shall do, till her Master's

second coming; he shall bring together every joint and member, and shall mold them into an immortal feature of loveliness and perfection. Suffer not these licensing prohibitions to stand at every place of opportunity forbidding and disturbing them that continue seeking, that continue to do our obsequies to the torn body of our martyred saint. We boast our light; but if we look not wisely on the sun itself, it smites us into darkness.... There be who perpetually complain of schisms and sects, and make it such a calamity that any man dissents from their maxims. 'Tis their own pride and ignorance which causes the disturbing, who neither will hear with meekness, nor can convince, yet all must be suppressed which is not found in their Syntagma. They are the troublers, they are the dividers of unity, who neglect and permit not others to unite those dissevered pieces which are yet wanting to the body of Truth. To be still searching what we know not, by what we know, still closing up truth to truth as we find it (for all her body is homogeneal, and proportional) this is the golden rule in theology as well as in arithmetic, and makes up the best harmony in a church; not the forced and outward union of cold, and neutral, and inwardly divided minds... (*Not as fun as thinking free speech means you can play whatever video games you like, chant whatever political slogans you like, listen to whatever dangerous speakers you like, however fabulous they may be? Are you sure?*)

THE STAKES

There's more, but that's enough to chew on for the moment. Suffice it to say, Parliament was not immediately impressed and went on with its licensing ways. According to Wikipedia (I told you: I'm a medievalist, I'm learning some of this for the first time now myself!), it took until 1695[36] to achieve true freedom of the press, by which time England had changed kings several times and was under the rule of a Dutchman[37]. (The Dutch are really important in this story; they're the reason New York, née New Amsterdam, became a bastion

---

[36] https://en.wikipedia.org/wiki/Areopagitica#Critical_response

[37] https://en.wikipedia.org/wiki/William_III_of_England

of tolerance, cosmopolitanism, and free trade[38].) But doesn't Milton's argument take your breath away? Okay, I get it, maybe not. He writes in even longer sentences than I do. But let's give it a go. This is the survival of civilization we're talking about here.

Why, according to Milton, was it wrong for Parliament to try to suppress the publication of "scandalous, seditious, libelous, and unlicensed Papers, Pamphlets, and Books"? To judge from the way in which we talk about freedom of the press and freedom of speech today, we would expect Milton's argument to be primarily political. Which, in a fashion, it was: he was writing to Parliament. But not about government, per se. Not about whether Parliament should restrict the publication of papers, pamphlets, and books calling for the overthrow of the government (they had already done that in going to war with the king) or for the reorganization of the economy (although Milton does warn them about restrictions on trade).

Rather, Milton's arguments are all, as Milo might put it, following Andrew Breitbart, at the level of culture. What matters is what people think, not just how they vote. (Of course, very few Englishmen could vote in those days, although the Levelers[39] were doing their best to try to change things.) Milton is worried not about sedition and treason, but about recreations and pastimes and the search for Truth. Even more to the point, Milton is worried about virtue. Think about it. Wouldn't it be better if the government could force everyone to be good? There would be no theft, no rape, no adultery, no murder. Nobody would ever say anything hurtful or mean.

Nobody would do or say anything that might cause anybody harm, everybody would be kind and thoughtful and generous. Like robots, programmed never to offend. Oh, wait. Isn't that what God

---

[38] http://www.russellshorto.com/bookbook/the-island-at-the-center-of-the-world/
[39] https://en.wikipedia.org/wiki/Levellers

is supposed to do? Make sure that nothing bad ever happens? And yet, as Milton would remind us, for some reason God made human beings with free will: "When God gave Adam reason, he gave him freedom to choose, for reason is but choosing: he had been else a mere artificial Adam, such an Adam as he is in the motions." Why on earth would God do that, knowing as he did (because, after all, God is omniscient) that human beings would fall into sin, do, say, and make things that would hurt each other or, at the very least, make each other feel uncomfortable day after day after day?

Milton's response: "We ourselves esteem not of that obedience, or love, or gift, which is of force; God therefore left him free, set before him a provoking object [the apple or Eve, depending on your mood], ever almost in his eyes herein considered his merit, herein the right of his reward, the praise of his abstinence. Wherefore did he create passions within us, pleasures round about us, but that these rightly tempered are the very ingredients of virtue?" There is no such thing as virtue if it is coerced. If, as Milton puts it, Parliament imagines that it can obliterate vice (for such was their ambition, particularly among the Puritans), they are deluding themselves. All they would be doing is regulating behavior, not making human beings more virtuous. But so what? Wouldn't everybody be better off if they could? For some reason, God didn't think so, and neither did Milton.

Nor did Milton think it a good idea to coerce people's thoughts. "A man may be a heretic in the truth": that is, all of his thoughts might be doctrinally (or politically) entirely correct, and yet, according to Milton, if he believes these things only because his pastor (or professor) or the Assembly (or political party) says he should, "without knowing other reason, though his belief be true, yet the very truth he holds, becomes his heresy."

It was not enough for Milton that people believe the right things about God or creation; they should put them to the test so that they know why they are right. Nor should they be so presumptuous as to believe that they had full access to the truth, dismembered as she had been since the ascension of Christ. It is not those engaged in the search for Truth that are "the troublers...[and] dividers of unity," but rather those who "neither will hear with meekness, nor can convince" and yet who would suppress everything "which is not found in their Syntagma," that is, their summary of their doctrine. (Ring any bells yet?)

"To be still searching what we know not, by what we know, still closing up truth to truth as we find it...this is the golden rule in theology as well as in arithmetic, and makes up the best harmony in a church; not the forced and outward union of cold, and neutral, and inwardly divided minds." (Maybe now? What if this were likewise the golden rule in academia? Or politics? I'll let you think about it a bit more. Back to Milton.) As Milton would have it, the whole point of publishing anything is to make the "living intellect" of their authors, the very image and likeness of God, and the exercise of their reason available to others. It was the height of presumption on the part of Parliament to imagine that its licensers would be equipped to pass judgment on the merits of the arguments they were ordered to declare worthy (or not) of publication.

Did they truly believe that Truth was so feeble that she could not defend herself in the open? "Let her and falsehood grapple; who ever knew things. Yet if all can not be of one mind, as who looks they should be? This doubtless is more wholesome, more prudent, and more Christian that they may be tolerated, rather than all compelled."

This was as difficult a concept in Milton's day as it is in our own[40]: tolerate people saying things that we know not just in our minds, but in our hearts are dangerous and wrong? (According to Milton, there was popery, which should not be tolerated, nor open superstition; even the greats find it hard to champion absolute freedom of speech.)

Horror of horrors! What if the weak stumbled upon such arguments to the very damnation of their souls? Not a sufficiently serious concern? What about arguments about their national history? Or the relationship between the sexes? Or the importance of social pressure in changing self-destructive behaviors? Or even about the reliability of revelation as opposed to prophecy? Oho! Now I have your attention. Certainly, to judge from the media response to his talks, Milo does.

Perhaps the greatest hubris that the living always have is the conviction that the pressures and anxieties of the present outweigh in magnitude those of the past. Never in human history have people faced the dangers that we do! Never in human history has there been such a threat to the very existence of our species! Never has society been more oppressive, people more vicious and hateful, the world more poised on the brink of destruction! Milton, at least, would beg to disagree. The fall has been with us since Lucifer seduced Eve (in Milton's version, she was the harder sell, which is why Lucifer went after her first) and Adam took a bite of the apple out of love for his wife. Truth has been hewed into a thousand pieces, "and we have not yet found them all...nor ever shall do, till her Master's second coming."

And yet, even with the Fall, Adam and Eve retained the power of choice; their reason impaired, God nevertheless left them free to make more mistakes, fall yet again into sin. Not because God enjoys his creatures' sinning, but because he loves freedom more. God could

---

[40] http://fencingbearatprayer.blogspot.com/2016/01/on-anger-righteous-or-otherwise.html

have shouted Eve down; forced her not to eat the apple; compelled her to be virtuous. And yet, for some reason, he didn't. Nor, even more to the point, did Milton think he should, dead, white, European, and male as he might be.

FREE SPEECH FUNDAMENTALS: BILL OF RIGHTS

November 2, 2016

Welcome, Milo fans! One of you over on the Facebook thread had a good question about my previous post: "Lots of people died for freedom of speech before USA existed. Then [an]...argumentum ad Adam and Eve..?" I agree, I needed to give you more links between Milton and the First Amendment. That was the original plan for the post, but then Milton took over, and as often happens when you actually read the primary sources, I found myself in places I had not intended to go but discovered (much to my delight) were far more compelling than the argument I had thought I wanted to make. (Seriously, the tension between freedom and compulsory virtue goes back to our first parents and their relationship with God? How's that for the importance of culture?!)

This happens—a lot—when you take the time to settle in with the texts, which is what makes being an historian so much fun, even better than being in a Dan Brown thriller, because the clues you are following are really out there, but there is no mastermind behind them, only your own ability to piece them together and make sense of them based on your own inevitably imperfect knowledge about the bigger picture that they supposedly fit into but which itself may change based on new evidence. This is very much where I am now, needing to piece together the bits of the story about freedom of speech that I know—basically, it goes from John Milton to J.S. Mill—with the hints that I have from the scholarship about where to look further, specifically in the history of the relations between the English and the Dutch.

There are a few highlights which I already knew to be important, a few more that I learned from Wikipedia as I was doing the linknotes on Milton: something something English Bill of Rights of 1689 something something the Virginia Declaration of Rights of 1776 something something the Bill of Rights appended to the U.S. Constitution in 1789 something something the French Declaration of the Rights of Man and of the Citizen of 1789. (The Declaration of Independence of 1776 does not, in fact, mention freedom of speech.) If I were a lawyer or legal historian, I would at this point most likely gesture towards the tradition of precedent underlying the development of the English common law on which the legal culture of the United States is ultimately based.

As Tocqueville brilliantly shows, this culture is one of the things that makes the United States radically different from France: in the English tradition, lawyers and judges argue from precedent, while in the French tradition they argue from principle.[41] In Tocqueville's words: "The English and American lawyers investigate what has been done; the French advocate inquires what should have been done; the former produces precedents, the latter reasons." The takeaway for our purposes is that the authors of the American Bill of Rights knew the

---

[41] http://www.gutenberg.org/files/815/815-h/815-h.htm

Virginia Declaration of Rights, whose authors knew the English Bill of Rights of 1689 (probably by heart), while the French most certainly were paying attention to what the Americans did, but thought about things in rather different terms.

My colleagues in seventeenth-century English history can tell you more about how the English came up with their Bill. Abridged version: they were reading Milton as well as lots of stuff published by the Dutch, including John Locke. So, basically, yes, it matters what Milton and Locke said, but for the moment let's look at freedom of speech as it was actually invoked in the various Bills and Declarations.

> *An Act Declaring the Rights and Liberties of the Subject and Settling the Succession of the Crown*, 1689: "That the freedom of speech and debates or proceedings in Parliament ought not to be impeached or questioned in any court or place out of Parliament."[42]

I have no idea what exactly this means. It is not a general right to freedom of speech, but rather a freedom for Parliament to hold debates without being questioned outside of Parliament. It is not at all what Milton was talking about in his Letter to Parliament "for the Liberty of Unlicensed Printing" (1644). It says nothing about freedom of the press or freedom of religion. In fact, at the time, Parliament was much more concerned about preventing the king from limiting their practice of religion: the whole reason they were in a position to present the king—William the Stadtholder, who had married the previous king's daughter Mary—with a Bill of Rights was that they had managed to oust Mary's father James, whom they disliked because he was set on making England Catholic again (or so they feared), and they had brought in William, a Dutch Protestant, in his stead.

This was the context in which Locke wrote his famous *Letter on Toleration* (1689, originally published in Latin).[43] He had been in exile

---

[42] https://avalon.law.yale.edu/17th_century/england.asp

[43] http://www.constitution.org/jl/tolerati.htm

in Amsterdam since 1683 hiding from the Catholics (it's complicated), and he wanted to make sure if and when he came back home he would be able to worship as he felt right, not as some magistrate (a.k.a. king) told him to. Which is why, among the groups that Locke discusses who should *not* be tolerated in their manner of worship, he includes Muslims ("It is ridiculous for any one to profess himself to be a Mahometan only in his religion, but in everything else a faithful subject to a Christian magistrate, whilst at the same time he acknowledges himself bound to yield blind obedience to the Mufti of Constantinople, who himself is entirely obedient to the Ottoman Emperor and frames the feigned oracles of that religion according to his pleasure.") and atheists ("Lastly, those are not at all to be tolerated who deny the being of a God. Promises, covenants, and oaths, which are the bonds of human society, can have no hold upon an atheist. The taking away of God, though but even in thought, dissolves all; besides also, those that by their atheism undermine and destroy all religion, can have no pretense of religion whereupon to challenge the privilege of a toleration.") Whether Protestant Parliament should tolerate Catholics was still an open question. (Catholics were not allowed to hold seats in Parliament until 1829.)

> A *Declaration of Rights made by the Representatives of the good people of Virginia, assembled in full and free Convention; which rights do pertain to them and their posterity, as the basis and foundation of Government*, 1776. "Article 12: That the freedom of the press is one of the greatest bulwarks of liberty and can never be restrained but by despotic governments."

As a medievalist, my grip on American history is somewhat shaky (albeit, I would venture, somewhat less so than that of many of my modernist colleagues on medieval history; seriously, nobody in medieval Europe believed the world was flat, just ask Dante). Here I am almost wholly dependent on what I have learned reading David

Hackett Fischer's *Albion's Seed: Four British Folkways in America*.[44] As Fischer shows, the Virginians had a distinct understanding of freedom, different from that of the three other major British colonies. While the Puritans of New England saw freedom in terms of community, the Quakers of the Midlands in terms of reciprocity, and the Borders of Great Appalachia in terms of absence of interference from the government, the Anglican gentry of Virginia saw freedom in terms of hierarchy: "the power to rule, and not to be overruled by others."

As Edmund Burke put it (cited by Fischer), explaining how the Virginians and Carolinians could hold slaves while championing liberty: "Freedom is to them not only an enjoyment, but a kind of rank and privilege. Not seeing there that freedom, as in countries where it is a common blessing and as broad and general as the air, may be united with much abject toil, with great misery, with all the exterior of servitude, liberty looks amongst them like something that is more noble and liberal." That is, among the Virginians, it was inconceivable that someone could be free and poor; to be free meant to be noble, at the top of the hierarchy.

Accordingly, my guess is that, in this Article, what the Virginians mean by "liberty" is not quite what the Puritans (now Progressives), Quakers (the source of most Americans' sense of what it means to be tolerant—Quakers hate fighting), or Borderers (now Rednecks) meant by "liberty," nor, therefore, "freedom of the press."[45],[46] But I would need to read more Fischer to be sure. What the Article itself seems to be most concerned about is protecting those with liberty from those that would try to rule over them.

---

[44] https://fencingbearatprayer.blogspot.com/2016/02/founding-freedoms-four-square.html

[45] https://fencingbearatprayer.blogspot.com/2016/01/progressive-is-new-puritan.html

[46] https://fencingbearatprayer.blogspot.com/2016/01/conservative-is-new-redneck.html

Joint Resolution of Congress Proposing 12 Amendments to the U.S. Constitution, 1789. "Amendment I: Congress shall make no law respecting an establishment of religion, or prohibiting the free exercise thereof; or abridging the freedom of speech, or of the press; or the right of the people peaceably to assemble, and to petition the Government for a redress of grievances."[47]

This is the ideal that we all know, or think we know, on which our country was founded. But what does it mean? Well, what I learn from the Wikipedia entry (seriously, folks, it's the greatest open source of information since Diderot and d'Alembert invented the *Encyclopédie*,[48] although the *Encyclopedia Britannica* was for a long time the greater; none, of course, is without bias, but that's what makes them interesting) is that the Bill of Rights "had little judicial impact for the first 150 years of its existence; in the words of Gordon S. Wood, 'After ratification, most Americans promptly forgot about the first ten amendments to the Constitution.' The Court made no important decisions protecting free speech rights, for example, until 1931."

As my own dean of College has shown, arguments about what kind of freedom professors employed by the university should have to express opinions concerning "controverted questions of public" go back a little further, to the last decades of the nineteenth century. It was at this time that American universities like the newly (re)founded University of Chicago adopted the ideal which the UofC at least professes to this day: that universities should be places of inquiry free from the constraints of contemporary political, theological, or monetary pressures, with the corollary, as President William Harper put it, that the professors employed by the university should not abuse this privilege through partisanship.

---

[47] https://www.archives.gov/founding-docs/bill-of-rights-transcript
[48] http://encyclopedie.uchicago.edu

In Harper's words: "The university is no place for partisanship. From the teacher's desk should emanate the discussion of principles, the judicial statements of arguments from various points of view, and not the one-sided representations of partisan character." This is clearly a rather different idea of freedom from that called for in the First Amendment, although we tend to conflate the two in contemporary discussions.

Perhaps the most interesting thing that I know about the Bill of Rights itself comes from Russell Shorto's *The Island at the Center of the World* (2005), a history of the Dutch colony of New Amsterdam and its importance for American history. According to Shorto, it was the New York delegates to the Constitutional Convention of 1787 that were among the most insistent on appending "a bill of specific individual rights" to a Constitution which they feared would give the federal government too much power. They were inspired, argues Shorto, by the Charter that New York City had been granted in 1686 by King James II, itself modeled on the Articles of Capitulation of 1664 by which New Amsterdam had surrendered to James, then Duke of York.[49] (This, for those keeping score, was the same James who was run out of England by Parliament in the Glorious Revolution of 1688 that brought William and Mary to the throne.)

As Shorto puts it: "The end result of the negotiations...is a remarkable document. Packaged into it—and extended later by the New York City Charter—was a guarantee of rights unparalleled by any English colony." Most notably for our purposes, according to article 8: "The Dutch here shall enjoy the liberty of their consciences in Divine Worship and church discipline." The soon-to-be Catholic

---

[49] https://www.thirteen.org/dutchny/interactives/document-dutch-articles-of-surrender/

James was more willing to allow the people of his new city liberty of worship than, it seems, the English were latterly willing to allow him.

Déclaration des Droits de l'Homme et du Citoyen, 1789. "Article 11: La libre communication des pensées et des opinions est un des droits les plus précieux de l'Homme: tout Citoyen peut donc parler, écrire, imprimer librement, sauf à répondre de l'abus de cette liberté dans les cas déterminés par la Loi."[50]

When I am teaching the History of European Civilization, I tend to talk about this *Déclaration* in terms of the readings that we have done from Rousseau's *The Social Contract* (1762), which the authors of the *Déclaration* most certainly read. Abridged version: The huge problem in *The Social Contract* is the idea of the general will, which somehow should govern the state but which cannot, according to Rousseau, be determined by any of the normal mechanisms of politics. It emerges, as it were, from the whole, but typically only some are able to discern it, making it simultaneously populist and elitist as an expression of the polity.

Likewise lurking behind all of the articles in the *Déclaration* is the fondness, as Tocqueville discerned, of the French for thinking in abstract principles rather than, like the English, more mundane precedents. For example, the U.S. Bill of Rights gets immediately down to business: "Congress shall make no law..." The first article of the *Déclaration* is much more lofty: "Men are born and remain free and equal in rights. Social distinctions may be based only on consideration of the common good."[51] Immediately, we are in a totally different world, concerned not with the limitations of the lawmakers, but with the essential nature of man.

---

[50] https://www.legifrance.gouv.fr/Droit-francais/Constitution/Declaration-des-Droits-de-l-Homme-et-du-Citoyen-de-1789

[51] https://www.conseil-constitutionnel.fr/sites/default/files/as/root/bank_mm/anglais/cst2.pdf

There is law, but it comes not from mere human deliberation. Rather, according to article 6: "The Law is the expression of the general will. All citizens have the right to take part, personally or through their representatives, in its making. It must be the same for all, whether it protects or punishes..." Remember what I said above about the concept of the general will. What does it mean to say that "all citizens" may take part in the making of Law both "personally or through their representatives"? Does that mean one person might be able to make the Law without going through the representative bodies? How, exactly, would that work?

Now notice the language in article 11. On the one hand, an opening statement of abstract principle: "The free communication of ideas and of opinions is one of the most precious rights of man." Followed, on the other, by what should strike Anglophone ears as an extraordinary limitation of this same right: "Any citizen may therefore speak, write and publish freely, *except what is tantamount to the abuse of this liberty in the cases determined by Law.*"

Now, if like me, you tend to think in English, what you will likely read in this last clause is something like precedents—that's what "cases determined by Law" are, right? So, no problem, any restrictions on the right to "the free communication of ideas and opinions" will be determined on a case by case basis. Except this is France, so they won't. They will be determined, as Tocqueville showed, by principle expressed abstractly, which principles may be adjudicated by judges without reference to any precedents whatsoever. Remember also what we just said about how the French think about Law: "The Law is the expression of the general will." Which is determined how exactly? From the perspective of the English-speaking peoples, to coin a phrase:

"Nobody knows, it's a mystery."[52] And you thought Robert Langdon got to have all the fun.

---

[52] https://youtu.be/jTQurAEmt64

HOLY SATIRE, BREITBART!

November 20, 2016

Last Thursday, our hero Milo did an interview with Cathy Newman on British television's Channel 4 News.[53] In the course of the interview, Ms. Newman challenged Mr. Yiannopoulos on some of the headlines that have appeared over his articles published on *Breitbart*.com, including this one: "The Solution to Online 'Harassment' is Simple: Women Should Log Off."[54] "You said," Ms. Newman read from her notes, barely able to suppress the contempt that she clearly felt at having to give voice to his prose, "'yes, we will certainly let women onto the men's internet a few times a year, as long as you follow a few basic rules.'"

At which our hero tried to suppress a smile, rejoining, "You can't hear the humor in that?" But Ms. Newman continued to speak over him, clearly finding nothing funny—or ironic—in the claim that, if women find it hard to understand men's "natural tendency to be boisterous, confrontational and delightfully autistic" when they encounter it on the internet, they might be better off leaving the

---

[53] https://youtu.be/eJiNeCBpCHQ
[54] https://www.breitbart.com/social-justice/2016/07/05/solution-online-harassment-simple-women-log-off/

internet to the boys. "No," she insisted, when Milo tried to explain that pieces like these were intended as satire, to get people to think, "I know you want women to log off the internet, but we are here in the Channel 4 news studio; you have to allow me to speak."

Which was rich, given that she barely let him speak or answer her questions, leading as they were, but never mind. The real question is, *why couldn't she hear the joke?* Milo was sitting there, willing to be interviewed by her, more accurately, allowing himself to be baited by a hostile interviewer, and she was accusing him (and, by association, his employer) of being divisive. And there she was, reading with a straight face lines out of context that in context were meant to acknowledge the very distress that she herself was expressing. Almost as if it were her purpose to prove Milo's central point: "The fact is, women are more easily rattled by nastiness than men.... Women are upset at men being rude to them, and feel 'oppressed,' we are told, whenever they are treated on equal terms as men in the maelstrom that is social media."

(As, to be fair, was I, when I attracted my very own troll;[55] I like to think I got over it, although you will have noticed that I have not turned the comments on my blog back on—which is to say, I think Milo is right, at least in my case.[56] I do have a hard time with the rough-and-tumble of the boys.)

But, of course, it is not only women like Ms. Newman who have found Milo's headlines hard to read. For the last week or so, ever since President-elect Trump appointed Milo's former boss Steve Bannon to his incoming White House staff, Milo's headlines about birth control making women "unattractive and crazy" and women in the tech industry sucking at interviews have been making the internet rounds as proof of Bannon's—and, by association, Trump's—sexism,

---

[55] https://fencingbearatprayer.blogspot.com/2013/04/a-demon-of-my-very-own.html
[56] https://fencingbearatprayer.blogspot.com/2013/04/no-complaints-please-were-privileged.html

always closely followed by the usual crowd of deplorable -isms.[57],[58] (I'm not sure I need to link for these; I suspect you can find them yourselves fairly easily.)

My own friends on Facebook have scolded me roundly for refusing to take the headlines literally, not to mention seriously. One friend shared a whole string of them, more or less demanding that I denounce them as sexist... or else: "Planned Parenthood's Body Count Under Cecile Richards is Up to Half a Holocaust" (an article against abortion, which as a Catholic, Milo is)[59]; "How Donald Trump Made It Cool to be Gay Again" (an article giving examples of Trump's support for gay conservatives)[60]; and "Teenage Boys with Tits: Here's My Problem with *Ghostbusters*" (an article explaining why the film was a flop—which it was).[61]

"I just don't understand," my friend who posted the headlines argued, "how you can sit there and say there's no cause for alarm or that these are okay messages to be broadcasting." Well, in a word: because I'm a medievalist—and can hear the echo in her words. "Verba vana aut risui apta non loqui," the *Rule of St. Benedict* intoned. "[Monks ought] not to speak useless words or words that move to laughter.... The tenth degree of humility is that the monk be not ready and quick to laugh, for it is written, 'The fool lifts up his voice in laughter' (Ecclesiastes 21:23)."

---

[57] https://www.breitbart.com/tech/2015/12/08/birth-control-makes-women-unattractive-and-crazy/

[58] https://www.breitbart.com/social-justice/2016/07/01/not-sexism-women-just-suck-interviews/

[59] https://www.breitbart.com/politics/2015/08/22/godwins-law-planned-parenthoods-body-count-is-up-to-half-a-holocaust/

[60] https://www.breitbart.com/social-justice/2016/08/11/trump-brought-subversion-decadence-back-gay-culture/

[61] https://www.breitbart.com/tech/2016/07/18/milo-reviews-ghostbusters/

Because, of course, as every schoolchild knows, monks, more particularly, medieval monks, were utterly joyless, not to mention the whole of the Middle Ages in which they lived. The great Italian medievalist Umberto Eco wrote a whole book about it, more accurately, a novel (*The Name of the Rose* [1983]), in which (spoiler alert!) the blind librarian of a (fictional) Benedictine monastery was willing to kill so as to assure that the monks never even laughed, never mind spent their days ornamenting the margins of their books with the marvelous creatures for which medieval manuscripts are still sometimes famous but which he himself could not see.

"Shame!" the Venerable Jorge of Burgos chastises the monks of the scriptorium as they laugh over the lyre-playing asses, owls ploughing with shields, seas catching fire, and wolves turning hermit that they have painted out of delight. "For the desire of your eyes and for your smiles!" Such images, Jorge would have it, are not just ridiculous, but dangerous: "Little by little the man who depicts monsters and portents of nature to reveal the things of God *per speculum et in aenigmate*, comes to enjoy the very nature of the monstrosities he creates and to delight in them, and as a result he no longer sees except through them."

And yet, his dialectical opponent and Sherlockian nemesis Friar William of Baskerville (played, inevitably, by Sir Sean Connery) suggests: "Marginal images often provoke smiles, but to edifying ends.... Monkeys do not laugh; laughter is proper to man, it is a sign of his rationality." (Here William, a Franciscan, is quoting Notker Labeo, an eleventh-century monk of St. Gall.) The Venerable Jorge will have none of Friar William's argument in favor of laughter. (Note that in Hollywood, the only good monks are Franciscans; Benedictines are always crazy or fat.) More to the point, once Jorge's plot is discovered, he is willing to kill himself for it by eating the pages of the book he has poisoned so as to keep its poisonous teachings lost to the world;

it is the Second Book of Aristotle's *Poetics*, on comedy, which Jorge fears will give its arguments greater authority. "But what frightened you in this discussion of laughter?" William asks Jorge when he finds him deep in the labyrinth of the library preparing to destroy the book. "You cannot eliminate laughter by eliminating the book."

"No," Jorge replies,

> to be sure. But laughter is weakness, corruption, the foolishness of our flesh. It is the peasant's entertainment, the drunkard's license...a defense for the simple, a mystery desecrated for the plebeians.... Laughter frees the villein from fear of the Devil, because in the feast of fools the Devil also appears poor and foolish, and therefore controllable. But this book could teach that freeing oneself of the fear of the Devil is wisdom.... That laughter is proper to man is a sign of our limitation, sinners that we are. But from this book many corrupt minds like yours would draw the extreme syllogism, whereby laughter is man's end! Laughter, for a few moments, distracts the villein from fear. But law is imposed by fear, whose true name is fear of God. This book could strike the Luciferine spark that would set a new fire to the whole world, and laughter would be defined as the new art, unknown even to Prometheus, for canceling fear.

Worst of all, Jorge insists, is the effect that laughter would have on belief in God, for

> if one day—and no longer as plebeian exception, but as ascesis of the learned, devoted to the indestructible testimony of Scripture—the art of mockery were to be made acceptable, and to seem noble and liberal and no longer mechanical; if one day someone could say (and be heard), "I laugh at the Incarnation," then we would have no weapons to combat that blasphemy, because it would summon the dark powers of corporeal matter, those that are affirmed in the fart and the belch, and the fart and the belch would claim the right that is only of the spirit, to breathe where they list.

"You are the Devil," William says in response. "I?" Jorge asks. "Yes," William replies.

They lied to you. The Devil is not the Prince of Matter; the Devil is the arrogance of the spirit, faith without smile, truth that is never seized by doubt. The Devil is grim because he knows where he is going, and, in moving, he always returns whence he came. You are the Devil, and like the Devil you live in darkness. I hate you, Jorge, and if I could, I would lead you downstairs, across the ground, naked, with fowl's feathers stuck in your asshole and your face painted like a juggler and a buffoon, so the whole monastery would laugh at you and be afraid no longer. I would like to smear honey all over you and then roll you in feathers, and take you on a leash to fairs, to say to all: He was announcing the truth to you and telling you that the truth has the taste of death, and you believed, not in his words, but in his grimness. And now I say to you that, in the infinite whirl of possible things, God allows you also to imagine a world where the presumed interpreter of the truth is nothing but a clumsy raven, who repeats words learned long ago.

We hear often these days how so-and-so wants to take us back to the Middle Ages, as pundits and academics point ominously to the fact that our media are awash with lies and accusations of lies, superstitions and half-truths, the scourges of misogyny and racism, ignorance and fear of science—almost as if all of the calamities that Jorge predicted have come to pass. The world is about to go up in flames, Lucifer has gained the upper hand, reason has fled, and half of humanity or, at the very least, of our nation's voters have become monsters, more akin to wild beasts ravening for their prey than the human beings whose form they wear. How, under such circumstances, we might ask Friar William, are we to tell the difference between the Devil's lies and God's truth?

Easily: The Devil hates laughter, would like nothing more than a world without laughter, without joy, without satire and jokes and monsters and marginalia, without Dangerous Faggots and their mischievous talks, without headlines that poke fun at the pieties of the present day. Jorge in his blindness would banish laughter from the lives not only of the monks, but ideally of all Christians, out of fear that mockery might lead to blasphemy and blasphemy to loss of faith in God. But Christians worship not a God afraid of jokes, but rather a God who made himself the butt of jokes, entering into the world with all its farts and belching so as to fart and belch along with his creatures. (Seriously, Jesus spent most of his time at drinking parties. You think he never farted or belched?)

It is the Devil who cannot hear the humor in the kinds of headlines that *Breitbart* has published under Milo's by-line, the Devil who finds the prospect of laughter unbearable, precisely because it frees those whom others would oppress from fear. What is the Devil? Friar William describes him: "The Devil is the arrogance of the spirit, faith without smile, truth that is never seized by doubt." The Devil is the grimness with which the self-righteous like Jorge profess to protect the world from its messiness and sin, to prevent the plebeians from enjoying their jokes at the expense of the powerful and elite.

The Devil is the humorlessness of taking offense at jokes pointing out uncomfortable facts or for using words otherwise banished from polite society. The Devil is believing oneself above criticism because one holds the right opinions, and the Devil is the fear of becoming oneself the butt of jokes. The Devil is every impulse that we have to protect ourselves from ridicule and embarrassment, the horror of being in the wrong. The Devil is refusing to laugh at ourselves for taking offense when none was intended or for feeling awkward when we realize that we have made fools of ourselves. I don't know whether Ms. Newman was able to hear herself as she read out Milo's headlines last Thursday or to appreciate the humorlessness in her voice as she chastised him for describing her own offense-taking so aptly. Certainly, few of my women friends seem to find Milo's jokes funny, even as they react in exactly the ways he says women often do to the name-calling and ribbing men seem to enjoy. Perhaps tellingly,

Eco's great joke—or the great joke on Eco—is that the Middle Ages were the exact opposite of joyless: Jorge is a caricature of a monk, a Hollywood freak of a monk, refusing to laugh at the whimsy and monstrousness of the absurdity of fallen and redeemed man.

Perhaps this is the reason that we, as medievalists, have struggled for so many decades to make sense of the marginal nonsense we find in the most holy books of the period—the psalters and books of Hours with which medieval Christians praised God. Our modern god of diversity and identity politics is a singularly joyless god compared with the God of medieval Christianity who delighted in monkeys riding goats and asses playing the lyre. As William tells the young novice Adso as they ride away from the library, now up in flames,

> Jorge did a diabolical thing because he loved truth so lewdly that he dared anything in order to destroy falsehood. Jorge feared the second book of Aristotle because it perhaps really did teach how to distort the face of every truth, so that we would not become slaves of our ghosts. Perhaps the mission of those who love mankind is to make people laugh at the truth, *to make truth laugh*, because the only truth lies in learning to free ourselves from insane passion for the truth.

Truth that denies our ability to laugh is no longer truth, but insanity. In the words of the medieval monks: "Laughter is proper to man; it is a sign of his rationality." Which means that Milo is quite possibly right when he says, as he often does, that he is doing the work of God.

KUNG FU MILO

November 25, 2016

You all know the story.[62] Kai, the Musk-Ox Warrior, has returned from the Spirit Realm intending to steal their chi from the other animal warriors and turn them into jade ornaments that he can wear on his belt. His original motive would seem to be envy that the pandas taught the Tortoise Warrior Oogway the secret of chi, but his overwhelming desire is to dominate and control. So all-consuming has his envy become that his very eyes glow green. His primary weapons are two glowing green blades, and when he captures the other animal warriors, they turn into small green stones, rendered lifeless by Kai's greed to possess their golden chi.

Meanwhile, our hero, the Dragon Warrior Po (a giant panda), has been named Teacher by the Red Panda Master Shifu, but quickly loses heart when his students are injured thanks to his training. Even worse, when Kai shows up in the valley with his army of jade zombies, Po is unable to protect his friends. Po follows his panda father Li Shan (whom he has only just met) back to the panda village where Li promises Po he will learn the secret of chi. But when Po gets to the

---

[62] *Kung Fu Panda 3* (2016)

village, he learns that the only things the pandas know how to do is eat, roll, and sigh; they are not warriors, and none knows the secret of chi. The village, it would seem, is most certainly doomed.

But of course it isn't. Because Po learns more than just how to be a panda in his brief time in the village. Even though he doesn't realize it until the moment he confronts Kai with his army of roly-poly relatives, he already knows the secret of chi and thus how to defeat Kai: not by hoarding chi, but by giving it away. Kai had been able to defeat all the other animal warriors precisely because they tried to protect themselves from him, but Po welcomes his attack. Transformed into the true Dragon Warrior, Po defeats Kai by surrendering to him. "You want my chi so bad?" he cries. "Then take it."

Filled with the golden light of the love of all the pandas, Master Tigress, and Po's adoptive father and noodle chef Mr. Ping (a goose), Kai explodes like a supernova and all of the animal warriors whom he has tried to possess are freed. The village is saved, the warriors restored to the land of the living, and Po takes his proper place as Teacher, while Mr. Ping makes noodles for everyone. It's so touching, you just know there's a moral to this story, don't you? Can you guess?

Some of my friends on Facebook have spent the better part of the past week trying to convince me that I am wrong about Milo, that he is not a merry trickster, but a dangerous fraud. Or, as one put it, "an opportunist provocateur and huckster." Others have been less polite. To my insistence that his articles were satire, one friend (himself gay) has responded: "*Breitbart* is Der Stürmer and you seem to be willing to support the current emulant of Julius Streicher." (I had to look this up.) He continued: "While I expect you will still be giggling when your friends are fired and attacked by the Trumpist state, I expect you know that in the long run there will probably be lists made in the future of academics who supported the alt-right who will have to be removed in an American denazification program. Too Much?"

Another friend (also a fellow academic) tells me: "Rachel, your willful blindness knows no bounds. Turning Point USA, which has compiled the Professor Watch List, REGULARLY SPONSORS your vile buddy Milo's lectures." (As everyone following the Dangerous Faggot tour knows, Milo does not charge the student groups like the College Republicans and Young Americans for Liberty who invite him to campus, so I am not clear what my friend means here.) This same friend also insists that Milo is a supporter of white supremacist [Richard] Spencer, on the basis of a single sentence in Milo and Allum Bokhari's now infamous article on the alt-right, in which they list Spencer among "The Intellectuals" responsible for one strand of the movement.[63]

A third friend (also gay) tells me, more succinctly: "Sorry, Rachel, your boyfriend MILO is loathsome." (Boyfriend?! Be still my heart!) A fourth friend, who has made it his mission to turn my own Facebook feed into the Milo Channel by sharing posts he thinks will prove the point, quotes extensively from an article by "author, journalist, social justice bard" Laurie Penny, entitled "I'm with the Banned."[64] (Note pun on "band" and "damned.") To judge from the article, Ms. Penny has a much better chance of being described as Milo's girlfriend than I do. One "hot, weird night in Cleveland" this past summer during the Republican National Convention, he took her riding in his "swank black trollmobile to the gayest neo-fascist rally at the RNC," introduced her to his whole staff, and refused yet again

---

[63] https://www.breitbart.com/tech/2016/03/29/an-establishment-conservatives-guide-to-the-alt-right/

[64] https://medium.com/welcome-to-the-scream-room/im-with-the-banned-8d1b6e0b2932

to accept that he and she are Not Friends despite (as she tells it) her best efforts to convince him otherwise.

"The more famous he gets off the back of extravagantly abusing women and minorities [*she must be thinking of different talks from the ones I've heard, and I'm pretty sure I've watched the full DF tour by now*], the more I tell him I hate him and everything he stands for, the more he laughs and asks when we're drinking. I'm a radical queer feminist leftist writer burdened with actual principles [*her conviction: he has none*]. He thinks that's funny and invites me to his parties." My friend quoted Ms. Penny's conclusion: "It doesn't matter that he doesn't mean it. It doesn't matter that he's secretly quite a sweet, vulnerable person who is gracious to those he considers friends [*thus the ride in the trollmobile*]. It doesn't matter that somewhere in the rhinestone-rimmed hamster wheel of his mind is a conscience. It doesn't matter because the harm he does is real."

Those who follow Milo on Facebook know that the first thing he does with articles like Ms. Penny's is share them on his Facebook page. I wasn't following him this summer, so I don't know what he did with this one; he couldn't share it on Twitter as he was suspended that very night. As the article is clever and vividly written—the rally to which Milo takes our heroine is a "den of goblins," Donald Trump is a "howling psychopath," Milo's followers are a "yammering army of trolls"—I am more than certain that he enjoyed it, just as Ms. Penny probably expected him to do.

She seems to understand his pleasure in the spectacle, even as she is convinced that he is all spectacle, no heart. "That's why I've always refused to debate Milo in public," she explains. "Not because I'm frightened I'll lose, but because I *know* I'll lose, because I care and he doesn't—and that means he's already won. Help and forgive me, but I actually believe human beings can be better than this." Like Ms.

Penny, my Facebook friends are convinced that I cannot see what she clearly does: that Milo is playing with energies he does not understand, risking the very existence of our country for the sake of a few jokes. "America is a nation eaten by its own myth," she prophesies. "The entire idea of America is about believing impossible things. Nobody said those things had to be benign."

She's right about one thing: Americans love myths. Arguably, America more than any country ever in the history of humanity thrives on myths. Just look at Ms. Penny's own prose: goblins and trolls and howling monsters galore! The majority of America's myths are somewhat more mundane: The myth "that all Men are created equal," "that they are endowed by their Creator with certain unalienable Rights," "that among these are Life, Liberty, and the Pursuit of Happiness," and that it is to secure these Rights that "Governments are instituted among Men."

The myth that it is "We the People of the United States...who ordain and establish" that Government through the Constitution according to which it is elected and structured so as "to form a more perfect Union, establish Justice, insure domestic Tranquility, provide for the common defense, promote the general Welfare, and secure the blessings of Liberty to ourselves and our Posterity." (I can't even type these resonant clauses without singing them in my head.)

The myth that the Rights with which we as Americans are endowed include free exercise of religion, freedom of speech and of the press (the ones Milo says he is particularly concerned about), the right to assemble peaceably and "to petition the Government for redress of grievances"; the right "to keep and bear Arms" (he mentions this one a lot, too); the right "to be secure in their persons, houses, papers, and effects against unreasonable searches and seizures"; the right not to have to bear witness against oneself "nor be deprived of life, liberty, or property, without due process of law"; the right to a "speedy and public trial, by an impartial jury of the State and district wherein the crime shall have been committed"; the right to trial by jury in suits of common law "where the value in controversy shall exceed twenty dollars"; and the right not to be subject to "cruel and unusual punishments."

Powerful as these myths are, they are not, however, the stuff of heroic narrative. No, I take that back: the narrative of the Courtroom is arguably the Great Set-piece of American Cinema, followed closely by the narratives of the Resistance to Tyranny and the Settlement of the Frontier. But the greatest American myth of all is one nowhere explicitly mentioned in any of our founding documents, and yet everywhere present in the stories that we tell about ourselves as a People (panda people included), however much my secular humanist colleagues in American history would argue to the contrary.

You all know the story. A young man of obscure birth and questionable parentage comes out of the countryside to the big city. He collects a following of other young men and even some women, who see him as a good person despite his reputation as a libertine. He speaks plainly and gathers large crowds of simple people who look to him for help and credit him with freeing them from ailments that they have suffered under for years.

He causes a disruption in the city, shames the members of the establishment for their hypocrisy and greed, and bests even the most learned teachers in argument. He violates the most sacred taboos and is accused of blasphemy and corrupting the youth. He is accused by the leaders of his community of fomenting rebellion and of sympathies with the most dangerous elements of the society. Eventually, he is betrayed by one of his own followers, handed over to the authorities for questioning, tortured, mocked, and subjected to a cruel and unusual punishment without proper trial. And yet, even as he hangs dying on the cross, he forgives his persecutors, taking all of the hate and anger and envy and fear that they can throw at him and giving it back as love.

No, I am not saying that Milo is literally the Messiah, any more than Po the Dragon Warrior is meant to be Christ (an alter Aslan, as it were), although you have to admit the parallels are riveting. What I am saying is that I believe Milo when he says he is a Christian and that, as a Christian, he strives to model himself on Christ by standing up for the weak and those who are otherwise afraid, given our current intellectual, social, and political climate, to speak the things that they actually believe for fear of losing their friends, their jobs, and their personal safety, if not, as in the case of some of our police officers of late, their lives: The women of all ages who would rather not shout their abortions because they see abortion as murder.

The young men who have retreated into video games rather than risk being hounded off campus as rapists by women whom they have more or less awkwardly kissed. The working-class people, black or white, who see a $15/hour minimum wage not as a guaranteed income but as an insult to the skilled work they do. (As one of my black neighbors once forcefully put it: "You think punching the pictures on a fast-food check out screen is worth $15/hour?!") The professional women who willingly accept lower earnings over their lifetime in order to stay home with their children. The women, lesbian or straight, who want to be able arm themselves against potential attackers. The men, heterosexual or gay, who want to be able to arm themselves so as to protect their families and homes. The Christians who worry what it means for their national culture no longer to be grounded in the story of sacrifice and love on which they have modeled their lives.

Like the pandas, none of these people are warriors, at least not in the way the Left likes to style itself. They are Americans who want to live out the myths that have made our country great, including the myth that Po learns, that our real strength is in what makes us uniquely ourselves and in our love for each other as family, pandas, tigers, and geese, out of many, one. They have responded to Milo not because, as Ms. Penny sees them, they are goblins and trolls and howling psychopaths, but because, like Po, he is willing to fight for them, to take all of the insults and ridicule and shame that the scribes of the day would throw against them, to absorb it in laughter and send it back out as love, perhaps even invitations to parties and rides in swank black trollmobiles.

In the movie, Po originally plans to take out Kai with a secret finger hold, only to discover that it only works on mortals and Kai, like Satan, is not mortal. So Po sacrifices himself, distracting Kai so that he can jump on his back and then perform the finger hold on himself, tricking Kai just as Christ tricked the Devil through his death on the cross so as to take the battle into the Spirit Realm. Once there, Po-Christ assumes his real form as an angel of light, a.k.a. Dragon Warrior, and overcomes Kai as we have seen by filling him with his chi, thus liberating the animal warriors whose chi-souls Kai has stolen and bringing them back to life.

Kai, to put it mildly, was not expecting such a gift, driven as he was by envy and hate. Like the Devil, he could not conceive of Po's sacrificing himself out of love for his family and friends, and so like the Devil, Kai was trapped, overcome by the outpouring of Po's chi. This, as I see it, is what our media and establishment elites—the scribes and Pharisees of our day—find so infuriating and perplexing about Milo. He really is as Ms. Penny describes him: generous, flighty, given to making jokes in poor taste. But he is also, like Our Lord whom he professes to follow, willing to take on the world for the sake of the meek. If in doing so he infuriates the rule-makers, those who would insist that it is wrong to pluck corn to eat or to reach out in compassion to heal on the sabbath (Matthew 12:1-14), all the better.

Like Kai, they can rage against him in fury, but he will return their envy with good humor and love. As Milo said at the conclusion to his talk at Rutgers University last February, the first in his Dangerous Faggot tour at which a group of young women famously covered themselves in "blood" to protest his "hate speech," this as he sees it is the only real way for the animal warriors of America to win against those who would steal their chi:

> Nobody can resist the truth wrapped in a good joke. The best way to win an argument is to tell the truth and to be funny.... When you graduate I think the smart thing to do is to start to, gently and with good humor and intellectual humility, to gently resist things when you hear them in life that are quite obviously not true and said to save somebody's feeling.... I prefer to disarm people with self-deprecating humor, I prefer to laugh at myself before I laugh at others, and I prefer then to just drill down and stick to the basic set of facts that tell me a little more about the world around me. The way to combat progressivism, and the way to make the Left [retreat] is to gently and persistently with politeness and firmness and with good humor remind them that the world they describe doesn't exist.

AN ESTABLISHMENT CONSERVATIVE'S GUIDE TO MILO'S METHOD FOR WINNING THE CULTURE WARS

November 30, 2016

It's the season of Advent, so you all know what that means: the Dangerous Faggot is back on tour. While our brothers and sisters on the Left repair to their fainting couches and get their smelling salts ready, those of us who think of ourselves as conservatives, more particularly American conservatives, need to start taking notes. The election may be over (please, God, let it be over!), but the culture wars are still going strong. As the bard once put it, "Faint heart never won fair lady." Lady Liberty needs us now more than ever to come to her defense! It behooves us to be ready. Here's the way Milo does it, for those who have ears to hear:

1. BE FABULOUS

Humility may have been the preferred topos in days of yore, but in these days of celebrity, all it gets you is a modest blog audience (I love you all!). Beauty may be skin deep and in the eye of the beholder, but it is also a source of real pleasure for those who are watching.

Milo gets this, which is why (as he explained to his boss Alex Marlow over the summer on one of his podcasts) the first thing he did when he was making plans to continue his tour of our college campuses this academic year was hire a personal trainer and go on a diet. Plus, giving talks three days a week is a grueling business—just ask your favorite professor! It takes real stamina to carry your students' interest long enough to get through an hour and a half lecture. Frankly, I am in awe at how well Milo carries himself in this context: you get no help from the camera, there are no commercial breaks, no fancy graphics other than your own slides. All you have is your voice and your physical presence. Which had better be fabulous or you will put your audience to sleep.

2. BE HUMBLE

Yes, you read that right. I know, I know, Milo spends as much time as he possibly can talking about how fabulous he is, but—trust me on this—it is supposed to be funny. There you are, standing up in front of a student audience, dressed nicely, as fit as age and your other responsibilities as an adult allow, and they are all staring at you. Okay, Milo can't see them staring at him because he doesn't wear his contacts while he is speaking, but they're there, expecting... something... and you know that the worst thing you can be is boring.

So you talk about how fabulous you are to make them laugh, put them at their ease, because of course you don't mean it... or maybe you do... how can they tell? What they know is that they are nervous (students are always nervous) and trying to disguise it as cool. It is up to you to give them confidence. On the one hand, they need your authority as a teacher—your fabulousness—but on the other, they need you to invite them into the conversation, make them feel comfortable with speaking out. It is a delicate balance between playing high-status and low-status, taking charge and giving them courage to speak.

3. PUNCH UP

Milo has a reputation in the mainstream media for "hating" women and minorities, but in fact, he has never said anything of the sort. He does not hate women—he loves them! And he loves black men even more, perhaps more than he should, but he does love them. What he hates are the celebrities and other thought-leaders who use their status to hurt women and minorities by lying to them about the real difficulties that they face as women and minorities, particularly young college-aged women who have been convinced that they are in more danger of being raped on their college campuses than women in the Congo where rape is used as a weapon of war, and American blacks who have been lied to for decades by Democrats about why their lives have not improved. When Milo attacks, he attacks specific women, like Lena Dunham and Amy Schumer, or specific organizations like Black Lives Matter, whose policies and pronouncements he perceives as harmful, often life-threateningly so, as in the case of our current presidential administration's unwillingness to confront the dangers associated with radical Islam. The Left, as usual, takes specifics as generalizations, failing as always to distinguish between the individual and the collective.

4. PROTECT THE WEAK

This is also known as being chivalrous.[65] To judge from the videos, most of the students who come to Milo's talks are men, many of whom when it comes to the Q&A thank him for his role in covering GamerGate. They see him as a champion for standing up for them—

[65] https://fencingbearatprayer.blogspot.com/2016/01/chivalry-american-style-ca-1840.html

the basement-dwellers with no sex life, as they are usually cast. But if you watch carefully, you will also see that there are women in the audience, often the young men's mothers and sisters, and Milo is always unfailingly polite to them. And then you realize that the rude jokes and constant references to gay sex are a part of the act to help put these young men at their ease, not to attack women or suggest that the young men should attack women, quite the reverse, as Milo likewise makes clear whenever he is speaking with Christina Hoff Sommers and students try to shout her down. And he always defends the students who protest his talks by insisting that it is not they, but their professors who are to blame for the incoherent ideas that they hold.

5. REPEAT, REPEAT, REPEAT

When I first started watching Milo's talks, I took this as a weakness on his part: he says a lot of the same things over and over again, making sure to bring certain standard talking points into almost every talk. Now, however, I realize it is genius and the only way we are ever going to win the culture wars. People do not think in lengthy arguments—well, most people; I seem to—they think in phrases and lists. "Would you rather your child have feminism or cancer?" and "Fuck your feelings" may not be the most sophisticated formulations of the arguments that Milo would like to make, but they stick and they energize and they help focus people's attention on the problems much more than lengthier pronouncements would. It is also only through repetition that we can hope to change people's minds enough to get them to listen to our arguments in favor of free speech and liberty in the first place, never mind getting them to acknowledge the merits of these ideals.

6. DO YOUR RESEARCH

This is standard fare for conservatives: we always have to know *everything* so as to be able to answer our opponents' emotionally-laden accusations with facts. It is harder to prove that you know everything when giving talks—this is what footnotes are for! But having done the reading will make you calmer and able to answer your opponents' questions and accusations with appropriate examples and references. Based on my own blog stats, I am getting a better idea how rarely people actually click through on the references, but at least if the text is highlighted in different colors, people get the idea that there are references to read. Milo's headlines may be trolly, but the references he gives in his articles are based on proper research, as I know from the pieces that I have read, for example, about the non-existence of the wage gap to which he regularly draws attention.

7. USE FACTS, NOT FEELINGS, TO MAKE YOUR POINT

This sounds straight-forward, but is actually somewhat complicated. Milo, of course, is using feelings—feelings of pleasure and delight and joy—to capture his audience's attention and help draw them into the arguments he would make. What he means by "facts not feelings" is feelings as arguments of themselves, particularly expressions of offense intended not to open up conversation, but to shut it down. As in: "I find that really offensive!" More particularly, he means the feelings that many have when presented with facts that go against everything they have been taught; even more to the point, taught typically by way of invoking the very feelings that they have when confronted with those facts, namely, anxiety and fear.

Is there a campus rape culture? Do Black Lives Matter? Is Islamophobia real? Who knows? Simply mentioning the possibility of rape, racism, or religious intolerance provokes almost instantaneous reactions of revulsion in most well-meaning Americans, leaving them incapable of hearing anything you say about the actual incidence of rape on college campuses, the real effects of the BLM movement on black communities, or the actual differences between religions on which the different cultures of the world are based. The first step that we have to make before changing people's minds about what they have heard is to get them to listen at all, to put aside the fear and anxiety overwhelming them whenever they hear the words "rape" or "racism" or "religious difference." This is the primary function of Milo's talks: simply to say the words in the context of facts that the students might not otherwise hear.

8. CHAMPION WESTERN VALUES

Oddly, to judge from the media coverage that Milo helpfully shares on his Facebook feed, this seems to be the thing that Milo's opponents find most offensive about his talks: he believes in America, its values and ideals. This is the reason that the young men at his talks are so often inspired to chant: "USA! USA! USA!" Milo says dangerous things like: "Free speech matters! Property rights matter! Democracy matters! Freedom of religion matters! America is the best country in the world because we believe things like women and men should be equal and people of all races should be able to succeed!" And then he is accused of hate speech. The only reason that our opponents can make the accusations that they do against America is because they believe in these ideals, too. At least some of them do. At least I hope some of them do. And if they don't, there is no point whatsoever in not championing these values or apologizing that America hasn't lived up to them as perfectly as we would like.

9. LOVE YOUR AUDIENCE

Milo always takes questions and, although those of us watching from home don't get to see it, he always takes selfies with all of his fans who want the chance to meet him in person after his talks. This more than anything is what won me over when I started watching his talks back in September: the way in which he responds to his audience as they make jokes and join in. Like the best teachers, he uses their feedback to help craft his speech; although he works from prepared remarks, he almost never delivers them strictly verbatim.

But he is truly at his best when taking questions, letting the students shape the conversation with the concerns that they bring. Nor are all of the questions necessarily from fans: sometimes the audience members are quite critical, but if they ask real questions, not just stand up to make tendentious speeches, he answers them honestly and with facts. And he always thanks everyone most graciously for coming and listening to him speak.

10. HAVE FUN

Conservatives are supposed to be Happy Warriors, let's be happy![66] Oddly, this seems to be the thing that our fellow conservatives have found most offensive about Milo: his jokes, even when they are at his own expense, as, for example, the patently ridiculous rider that he put out at the beginning of this semester's tour listing all of the things that he expected the students (whom he doesn't even charge speaking fees) to provide.[67] (I wonder if he got the 3 Siberian Husky puppies per talk? He must have quite the team by now! Maybe they are pulling the tour bus.)

---

[66] https://fencingbearatprayer.blogspot.com/2016/01/how-to-be-happy-warrior.html

[67] https://www.breitbart.com/entertainment/2016/08/30/milo-tour-rider-50-white-doves-released-upon-entrance-no-adele-two-dozen-mcribs-vegan-watch-eat/

Yes, the fight in which we are engaged is serious, but it is a fight for liberty, joy, creativity, freedom, and fun! If the fight is long and hard, so be it, but we should be joyous as we battle. Milo himself put it beautifully in the conclusion to the remarks that he made on receiving the Annie Taylor Award last month,[68] even more beautifully in the remarks that he had originally prepared:

> So let us fight, but let our motto be Risus et bellum, Laughter and war. Because nothing stings our foes, foreign and domestic, more than our hearty laughter at their lies and nonsense. And also because nothing will better remind us what we're fighting for than the laughter of Chesterton, of Chaucer and of Shakespeare, and of course the God who inspired them all.[69]

---

[68] https://www.breitbart.com/social-justice/2016/11/12/milo-david-horowitz-restoration-weekend-motto-laughter-war/

[69] https://www.breitbart.com/social-justice/2016/11/12/full-text-milos-annie-taylor-award-acceptance-speech-david-horowitzs-restoration-weekend/

SOCIAL JUSTICE SOPHISTRIES

December 22, 2016

The tenor is smug self-righteousness, the absolute certainty of being on the Right Side of History. Even some liberals are starting to find it a bit hard to take, the way in which their family and friends talk about Those People. The Deplorables. The Racists. The Misogynists. The Xenophobes. The People With the Wrong Opinions about Immigration, the Relation Between the Sexes, the Welfare State, and Islam. *You know.* The ones who read *Breitbart*, vote for Donald Trump, and listen to Milo.

It can get a bit wearing, even at a distance. It takes real stamina to be able to meet it head on, as Milo has done this past semester over the course of his Dangerous Faggot Tour. Quite frankly, I don't know how he does it. I get weary just watching the protests.[70],[71] The name-

---

70 https://www.breitbart.com/social-justice/2016/12/13/milo-cameraman-assaulted-communist-student-protesters/

71 https://www.breitbart.com/social-justice/2016/12/07/watch-milo-protesters-msu-arrested/

calling.[72] The unwillingness to listen to what he actually says.[73] On the other hand, the tactics rarely change, which makes them possible to list. And if we can list them, we can prepare for them. These are the weapons that our opponents will try to use against us if we are conservatives. As the Boy Scouts say: "Be prepared!" Here based on my observations of their responses to Milo's talks are the primary tactics the Social Justice Warriors (SJWs) use:

1. TAKE JOKES LITERALLY

I have already written extensively about this tactic. Cathy Newman used it to withering effect in her Channel 4 interview with Milo. It is the weapon of first resort for SJWs: to see everything through the lens of offense and grievance, such that nothing can be funny any more.

Counterattack: Laughter. As the SJWs come for you, stay cheerful at all times. Remember what Milo likes to say: "Nobody can resist the truth wrapped in a good joke." The thing the Devil hates most is laughter, and the thing that the Grievance Brigade cannot stand is not to be taken seriously.

2. WEAPONIZE COMPASSION

"I find that really offensive." "Don't you know how hurtful that sounds?" "You can only say that because you don't recognize your own privilege." If the accusation itself is not enough, there will be tears. A voice choked with emotion. Threats of self-harm and suicide for which you, the conservative, will be blamed. Every instinct that you have to care for the wounded and weak will be triggered. You will want, like Professor Nicholas Christakis, to apologize for having

---

[72] https://www.breitbart.com/social-justice/2016/12/07/left-wing-extremist-group-claims-milo-promotes-rape-violence-distributes-flyers/

[73] https://www.breitbart.com/social-justice/2016/12/13/milo-destroys-protester-university-wisconsin-milwaukee/

given offense.[74] You didn't realize how hurtful others would find your words. You did not mean to cause anyone pain.

Counterattack: Do *not* apologize. Stay calm. Listen patiently. This will be hard, but any effort you make to defend yourself against the accusation *or* to apologize for your unintended offense will only add fuel to the fire. At this point Milo would most likely tell his opponents: "Fuck your feelings!" But not all of us can be Dangerous Faggots, nor do we all need to use the same counterattacks. The attack is intended (consciously or not) to make you feel as anxious as the speaker, much as a toddler having a temper tantrum is trying to get the adults to react. Remember: feelings are not arguments. The speaker almost certainly is feeling the feelings she or he is using to lash out at you, but you are not responsible for her or his feelings. You are responsible for staying calm and steering the argument back onto the facts.

3. SHIFT THE MEANING OF TERMS IN THE COURSE OF THE ARGUMENT

For example, "feminism." If, like Jessica Valenti, you are a SJW who happily claims to bathe in male tears, when someone like Milo comes along and calls this kind of language misandrist, you will insist that feminism is not about hating men, but equality. (Cathy Newman used this move in her interview to try to get Milo to admit he is a feminist. Which he is, insofar as he believes in equality of opportunity for women and men, like any normal person in the West.) Conversely, "nationalism." Perhaps, innocently enough, you, the conservative, believe that "making America great again" means living up to the ideals on which this country was founded: equality of all persons before the law, property rights, free markets, respect for citizenship, representative

---

[74] https://www.theatlantic.com/politics/archive/2015/11/the-new-intolerance-of-student-activism-at-yale/414810/

democracy as described in the Constitution. Champion "nationalism," however, and a SJW will substitute "national socialism," and, *viola!*, you're a Nazi.

Counterattack: Define your terms. Repeat as necessary. Do not waver in your definitions. Repeat as necessary. Even if they do not know it, your opponents are using classic sophistical techniques. They are trying to trip you up by catching you in a contradiction by means of equivocation, using the same term to mean radically different things, and then forcing you to accept the changed definition. Do *not* accept their redefinitions. Define your terms. Repeat as necessary. Do not waver in your definitions. Repeat as necessary. Call them out when they try to substitute their definition. Repeat as necessary.

4. INSULT THE SPEAKER

Here is where things get really nasty, but even more predictable. We all know where the insults go: more or less instantly, if you confront a SJW with facts and are firm in your definitions, the next move he or she makes is to call you a racist. Or a sexist. Or a homophobe. Or an Islamophobe. Or a Nazi. Or a *Breitbart*-reader, which is even worse. For those familiar with the classical fallacies, this is called an *ad hominem* attack. It is an attack on the character of the speaker, rather than on the structure or evidence of his or her argument.

This fallacy may be extended to include guilt by association, as for example when the student at Miami University attempted to make Milo out to be a white supremacist solely on the basis that Milo supported Trump; the student couldn't quote anything actually racist or white supremacist that Milo has ever said, but it was enough, he tried to suggest, that Milo supported Trump.[75] Cathy Newman and

---

[75] https://www.breitbart.com/social-justice/2016/12/05/milo-obliterates-student-called-white-supremacist/

other reporters did the same thing with Milo and Steve Bannon, more often than not on the basis of Milo's satirical headlines (see Tactic #1, above).

Counterattack: "Prove it"—as Milo challenged the student at Miami—is a good first move. The chances are that your attackers have no idea what you have ever actually written or said. If they have resorted to insult, they have nothing on you but their sense of your reputation as a conservative, which in their minds is sufficient. When they can't prove their accusation, you have a number of options. Milo's response to James Cook in an interview for the BBC was particularly good. Cook asked him, apparently innocently, "Are you a white nationalist?" And Milo called him on it: "I'm talking about culture, not race, and it's typical of somewhere like the BBC to try to conflate the two."[76] If they persist, well, there is only one response, which Milo finds easier to say than I do, but it is the only one that is actually appropriate: "Fuck you."

5. PROJECT YOUR FEELINGS ONTO YOUR OPPONENT

By this point, you, the conservative (or libertarian) have stepped Through the Looking Glass into Wonderland. It doesn't matter what you say because your opponents will twist it to conform to their distorted vision of you. But—and this is important—the only reflection they can see in the Looking Glass is their own. They call you hateful—because they are. They worry about you putting their names on a list—because they want to put you on one. They claim that you will make students uncomfortable in your classes—because they do. They call you divisive—because they are. They are afraid of you—because they are certain that you will behave towards them

---

[76] https://www.breitbart.com/social-justice/2016/10/30/bbc-tries-ambush-milo/

exactly as they behave towards you. It is inconceivable to them that you might have motives different from their own.

Counterattack: Nothing. At this point, they cannot hear you. Even Jonathan Haidt, the great champion of heterodoxy, falls into this trap.[77] He cannot see that his description of conservatives as endorsing "the group-focused moral concerns of ingroup loyalty, respect for authorities and traditions, and physical/spiritual purity more than liberals do," with liberals focusing more on "compassion and fairness" is already a Looking Glass projection.[78] Liberals, that is, academic liberals are all about "ingroup loyalty," "respect for authorities," and "physical/spiritual purity." Just try being a tenured professor at a prestigious university and going against the group. You will learn very quickly how much your colleagues value compassion and fairness.[79]

6. SHIFT THE GROUNDS OF THE ARGUMENT

Once it is clear that you are not going to budge and cannot be shamed into apologizing for things you have never thought or said, do not expect your opponent to admit that maybe you have a point or that they have misunderstood your opinion. If you have been talking about the relationship between the sexes (and been called sexist), suddenly you will be accused of racism. If you have been talking about the rise in the murder rate in Chicago (and been called racist), suddenly you will be accused of intolerance. If you have been talking about the cultural differences between Christianity and Islam (and been called Islamophobic), suddenly you will be accused of mischaracterizing the conversation entirely, that it was never about sexism or racism or

---

[77] https://heterodoxacademy.org

[78] https://journals.plos.org/plosone/article?id=10.1371/journal.pone.0050092

[79] https://fencingbearatprayer.blogspot.com/2016/01/blogging-with-tenure.html

religious tolerance, but in fact about social justice and the minimum wage.

Counterattack: Do not take the bait. Call attention to the change of topic. Refuse the conflation of different forms of social interaction under the rubric "oppression" or "rights." Insist calmly but firmly on the original terms of the argument. Laugh.

2017

FREE SPEECH FUNDAMENTALS: THE MOST DANGEROUS GAME

January 4, 2017

The verdict is in. Simon & Schuster are wrong—courting danger!—to have offered Milo a book deal, even under their conservative Threshold Editions imprint.[80] "YUCK AND BOO AND GROSS," tweeted comedienne Sarah Silverman on the day the book was announced. "This guy has freedom of speech but to fund him & give him a platform tells me a LOT about @simonschuster."

"Simon & Schuster should be ashamed of giving vile *Breitbart* provocateur Milo Yiannopoulos $250K to publish book," echoed Jeff Stein. "Problem with just shrugging at Milo book as free speech is that not everyone has the same level of access to platforms for speech," tweeted Murtaza Hussain—who, like Silverman and Stein has a blue verification checkmark, which I think means he has a higher level of access on Twitter than say, I do, but never mind. Twitter is free.

Kyle Bella (no blue checkmark) commented: "Editors @ simonschuster could have said, 'No, Milo [*sic* missing comma] we

---

[80] https://www.hollywoodreporter.com/news/milo-yiannopoulos-strikes-250k-book-deal-959745

refuse to publish your book because you're racist and transphobic.' But they didn't." And this was just the opening Tweets![81] (All citations courtesy of Milo's Facebook feed—yes, he knows what they're saying about him.)

That same day, *The Chicago Review of Books* vowed, again through a Tweet: "In response to this disgusting validation of hate, we will not cover a single @simonschuster book in 2017."[82] Perez Hilton opined: "Unfortunately, Simon & Schuster decided they'd rather take a chance on sizable profits opposed to human decency by providing Milo with a mainstream platform to spew his hate."[83] Meanwhile, pre-orders on Amazon shot the book to #1 the day after its announcement. Since then, things have gotten really interesting.[84]

Simon & Schuster tweeted out a defense: "We do not and never have condoned discrimination or hate speech in any form. At Simon & Schuster we have always published books by a wide range of authors with greatly varying, and frequently controversial opinions, and appealing to many different audiences of readers. While we are cognizant that many may disagree vehemently with the books we publish we note that the opinions expressed therein belong to our authors, and do not reflect either a corporate viewpoint or the views of our employees."[85] To little avail—but continued sales.

Ruth Ben-Ghiat, professor of history and Italian studies at New York University, argues that Milo himself "is a barometer for the

---

[81] https://www.breitbart.com/tech/2016/12/29/twitter-leftists-up-in-arms-after-milo-book-dangerous-announced/

[82] https://www.breitbart.com/social-justice/2016/12/29/war-speech-chicago-review-books-boycotts-simon-schuster/

[83] https://perezhilton.com/milo-yiannopoulos-simon-schuster-book-deal-boycott-outrage/.WG1c-hTAYWl

[84] https://www.dailytelegraph.com.au/rendezview/the-left-has-absolutely-lost-the-plot/news-story/894b92831bf4734e7e2b11597e7e279a

[85] https://twitter.com/SimonBooks/status/814931631526072320

far rightward shift and expansion of the conservative movement in America to elevate figures that traffic in violent speech"[86]—despite the fact that Milo has never called for violence against anybody; quite the reverse, it is he who has been regularly threatened, including by self-defined members of the Alt-Right.[87] Constance Grady, writing for *Vox*, sees a similarly dire future for publishing:

> Milo Yiannopoulos is a hateful person who has built a career on bigotry, but it is not hard to see why an editor at a right-wing publishing imprint might think it would be a good idea to sign him. He is loud, he has a loyal army of followers, and he knows how to get people's attention. He has that all-important built-in platform. All of that equals press attention—such as the flurry of articles the book deal prompted, including this one—and press attention usually means increased book sales.

> In Yiannopoulos's case, it seems to have worked. *Dangerous* is currently a best-seller on Amazon... Having brought in one Milo Yiannopoulos, it will be increasingly easy to bring in another, and then another, until all of the hatred and all of the rage of the white supremacists and misogynists and bigots on the alt-right is considered a valid part of cultural discourse, and just another strain of thought, as legitimate as any other. It will become normal.[88]

Sady Doyle, writing for *Elle*, concurs: "Milo Yiannopoulos has an army of trolls who will do whatever he asks, and presumably, 'buy this book' is not a hard command to obey. Then again, neither is 'dox this movie star.' The very thing that makes Yiannopoulos marketable makes it irresponsible to publish him. If there were ever a man whose book should to be treated as a weapon, it's Milo Yiannopoulos. The book will presumably name another target—or, more likely, several—and

---

[86] https://www.cnn.com/2017/01/02/opinions/milo-yiannopoulos-and-trump-profitable-hate-ben-ghiat-opinion/

[87] https://dailystormer.name/lol-milo-now-being-smeared-as-alt-right/

[88] https://www.vox.com/culture/2017/1/3/14119080/milo-yiannopoulos-book-deal-simon-schuster-dangerous-boycott

people's lives will go up in flames as the result. The harassment that follows a brush with Milo isn't light teasing; it's violent assault."[89]

And Adam Morgan, as editor of *The Chicago Review of Books*, has reiterated his decision not to review any Simon & Schuster books thanks to their decision to publish Milo's: "I remain convinced that to protect the victims of discrimination from its traumatic and sometimes deadly consequences, the literary community must stand against anyone—author or publisher—who peddles hate speech for profit."[90]

Who knew publishing a book could be so dangerous? Especially a book that, thus far, *no one has read*. What, exactly, is it that makes this book so dangerous before it is even in print? To judge from the outrage: because it promises to make Simon & Schuster, the publishers, and most likely Milo himself, a profit. Think about it. Milo is already famous, much more famous than he would have been simply by publishing a book. (Trust me on this.[91])

And how did he become so famous? For starters, although I wasn't paying attention then, it would seem through his Tweets—which he published *for free*. Then, when he was banned from Twitter for chivvying Leslie Jones about playing the victim over *Ghostbusters'* bad reviews, through his Facebook page, which at the time I joined in September 2016 had about 200,000 followers, but which now counts

---

[89] https://www.elle.com/culture/news/a41798/milo-yiannopoulos-book-deal/

[90] https://www.theguardian.com/commentisfree/2017/jan/04/simon-schuster-alt-right-hate-breitbart-milo-yiannopoulos

[91] https://fencingbearatprayer.blogspot.com/2009/07/fame-indirectly.html

over 1,000,000—which, again, he publishes *for free*.[92],[93],[94],[95] But most of all through his writing for *Breitbart*.com, which, again, readers can access *for free*. (Try the link, I'll wait.[96])

And, of course, through his Dangerous Faggot Tour of college campuses, videos of which...wait for it...he posts on YouTube...*for free*. Nor does he charge the student audiences to whom he is speaking fees; the only fees they incur are those set by their schools for security, lest the protestors to Milo's talks get out of hand. And now we are supposed to believe that a book deal with Simon & Schuster is going to make him more accessible to the audiences he already has? How, exactly? They can already get Milo 24/7 (with repeats) as long as they have an Internet connection.

If Milo is dangerous—as his critics insist that he is—he is dangerous not because he has written a book—which, again, *nobody has yet read*—but because he knows how to use the Internet, through which, stop me if you'd heard this already, his fans can access all of his previous content for free. It is true: many of his fans were more than willing last Thursday as soon as he posted the announcement for his book to go buy it. But the reason they were so willing was because they have been reading his columns and watching his talks—do I need to say it again?—*for free*.

This book, this book that Simon & Schuster has signed with him for, is quite literally the first thing he has ever asked them to pay for, other than the t-shirts and mugs that he sells through his store

[92] https://www.breitbart.com/social-justice/2016/07/19/breaking-milo-suspended-twitter-20-minutes-party/

[93] https://www.breitbart.com/social-justice/2016/07/18/ghostbuster-leslie-jones-reports-milo/

[94] https://www.breitbart.com/entertainment/2016/07/20/leslie-jones-twitter-trolls-milo-yiannopoulos/

[95] https://www.breitbart.com/tech/2016/07/18/milo-reviews-ghostbusters/

[96] [I will let you guess which of these links still work as of July 2019.]

to help raise money for his college scholarship fund (now accepting applications). If Milo wanted to, he could publish his book on his website *for free*, and it would more than likely get just as many readers as it will through Simon & Schuster's edition. He could even publish it through his store and charge money for it. This is the age of the Internet, after all. And, as even his critics concede, Milo is a master at trolling the Internet for attention.

It is true, as Murtaza Hussain noted in his Tweet, "not everyone has the same level of access to platforms for speech." But—here's the irony—*neither would Milo if he hadn't built them himself.* Twitter and Facebook and YouTube and, yes, Blogger are just as accessible as platforms to me or you or Hussain as they are to Milo. With a camera and better make-up, I could be making videos. Sure, Milo is employed by *Breitbart*.com, but *Breitbart*.com started exactly the same way: through Andrew Breitbart's own ingenuity in harnessing the Internet. (Breitbart wrote his own book about it, if you want the full story.[97]) And *Breitbart*.com has millions upon millions of readers, far more than Milo has fans.[98]

If the fear, as Grady puts it, is that publishing Milo's book will normalize the kinds of things he says, I have news for her: they are already normal to a large portion of our population. Even if Simon & Schuster never publishes another book, the things that Milo says are already "considered a valid part of cultural discourse, and just another strain of thought, as legitimate as any other." Newsflash: That's why so many people voted for Trump. (Whether Grady has characterized Milo's speech accurately is another matter. In my view, she hasn't.)

Which leaves only the money. We all want to get paid for our writing. I would love to get paid for my writing, although, of course,

[97] *Righteous Indignation: Excuse Me While I Save the World* (2012)

[98] https://www.breitbart.com/the-media/2016/11/19/breitbart-news-hits-300-million-pageviews-45-million-uniques-last-31-days/

indirectly as a professor I do. But I don't make money as such off my writing, certainly not $250,000, although I have made enough over the years to buy a few foils. But I would—and I know this is the case—if I knew how to build an audience as well as Milo has. So, in fact, it isn't really the money. It's the attention. And nobody gives their attention for free.

WHY SHAMING WORKS

January 5, 2017

You've felt it, I know you have. Okay, maybe not if you're a sociopath like Milo or Sherlock claims to be. (I have my doubts, on both counts.) But if you are a normal person who cares about what other people think of you. You've felt it. The dry mouth. The skin on your forehead tightening. The clenching of your whole body as if in anticipation of a blow. The blood rushing to your limbs as you prepare for flight. Your pulse quickening. Your thoughts racing. The urge to apologize, make yourself small, promise you will never do it again. The *SHAME*.

"Shame on you, Rachel," my friends on Facebook are wont to say when I post yet another of my reflections on Milo and his talks. "Don't you know what a monster he is? He's a racist. A sexist. A misogynist. A homophobe. A white nationalist. An anti-Semite. A member of the alt-right! How can you defend him? Don't you know what he did to Leslie Jones?" It doesn't matter that I *know* he is none of these things and that it is Leslie Jones who has benefited most from his Twitter ban.[99] I still feel the panic rising as the devil makes his move. "They <u>will think less</u> of you. You are risking everything standing up for this

[99] https://www.breitbart.com/social-justice/2017/01/04/fake-news-usa-today-issues-correction-after-falsely-branding-milo-as-white-nationalist-alt-right/

man. What if the neighbors found out? What if your colleagues on campus found out? What if your students found out? *How would you face them?*" And the final threat: "You would be cast out."

"So what?," you try to reassure yourself. "I don't need their approval." But you know you do. You want them to like you, to smile at you, to make jokes with you, not about you. You want their respect. You want them to listen to you, look up to you, greet you warmly. You want them to approve of you not just because they like you, but because you are in the right. In short, you want, as Adam Smith would put it, to be lovely. In Smith's words (III.I.8)[100]:

> Man naturally desires, not only to be loved, but to be lovely; or to be that thing which is the natural and proper object of love. He naturally dreads, not only to be hated, but to be hateful; or to be that thing which is the natural and proper object of hatred. He desires, not only praise, but praiseworthiness; or to be that thing which, though it should be praised by nobody, is, however, the natural and proper object of praise. He dreads, not only blame, but blame-worthiness; or to be that thing which, though it should be blamed by nobody, is, however, the natural and proper object of blame.

It is not enough, Smith goes on, to find oneself the object of praise; one wants to be actually worthy of praise. Worse than being hated, in Smith's account, is to know oneself a proper object of hatred. *This* is shame, the feeling of being less than one knows in one's heart one ought to be, not only because one is not loved, but because he or she is not worthy of love. As Smith puts it (III.I.13-14):

> Nature, when she formed man for society, endowed him with an original desire to please, and an original aversion to offend his brethren. She taught him to feel pleasure in their favourable, and pain in their unfavorable regard. She rendered their approbation most flattering and most agreeable to him for its own sake; and their disapprobation most mortifying and most offensive.

---

[100] https://www.econlib.org/library/Smith/smMS.html?chapter_num=4#book-reader

But this desire of the approbation, and this aversion to the disapprobation of his brethren, would not alone have rendered him fit for that society for which he was made. Nature, accordingly, has endowed him, not only with a desire of being approved of, but with a desire of being what ought to be approved of; or of being what he himself approves in other men.

We want, Smith says, not just to be loved, but to have the confidence that we are worthy of love; that we are the thing that should be loved and so are loved for our own sake, not just for what we appear. Accordingly, we take no pleasure (if we are not sociopaths) in being loved for being something that we are not; for being able to fake loveliness, as it were, rather than ourselves being lovely. In Smith's view (which is a fairly sunny one, if you think about it), we do not like feeling ourselves hypocrites. This, then, if we follow Smith's reasoning, is the source of the pain that one feels on losing one's friends' approval: the horrible suspicion that *they may be right*. That maybe one has done the thing that they say, stood up for a person or cause or idea that itself is shameful, thus losing one's own sense of being in the right.

Shame, in other words, is a species of doubt. Which is why Sherlock and Milo (purportedly) never feel it. Not (only) because they do not care what other people think, but because they know (or think they know) themselves to be in the right, whatever other people think of them. Children and dogs feel much the same way, as do fools. And saints.

FREE SPEECH FUNDAMENTALS: FAME

January 6, 2017

I get it: lots of people don't like Milo. But here's the really fascinating thing: lots of people do. All you have to do is visit his Facebook page (go on, I'll wait) to see how many people love him. And if you don't believe the five-star Facebook reviews, there are also the videos of the students and other fans who have spoken up at his campus talks to tell him how much he has encouraged them.

The young black woman who stood up against the Black Lives Matter protestors in Chicago and said to her peers who were trying to shout Milo down, "I know who I am. I am Kati Danforth. I am a math major and a junior at DePaul University and I'm working my ass off to become something!" The army sergeant in Houston who gave Milo his dog tags for speaking on behalf of the military against political correctness. The young woman from Kuwait who thanked Milo for standing up for her experience as a woman fleeing from an arranged Muslim marriage. The young woman who talked about how Milo helped her become more truthful in her political views, when formerly she had thought of herself as feminist.

The young men who thanked Milo for his fat-shaming because it inspired them to lose weight. The young woman who talked about how it was easier coming out as bi-sexual than as conservative. The older woman who declared herself a two-time cancer survivor and insisted, to the cheers of the audience: "I'd rather have cancer than feminism." The young gay man who championed Milo's stance on Islam and its treatment of gays. The young man from China who thanked Milo for standing up against cultural Marxism.

The young woman from France who declared Milo right about everything that is happening in Europe. The young woman from Mexico who talked about how Milo's being gay and Catholic gave her courage as a minority not to give into the identity politics expected of her. The young woman from Singapore who talked about how she sees Milo defending the right of students to have an actual conversation about different issues, not just follow the liberal line.

The young woman who talked about how Milo gives conservatives courage to speak up in class. Not to mention Tom Ciccotta and Ariana Rowlands who, in their introduction to his speech for the Annie Taylor Award for Courage in Journalism, talked about how much he had inspired them in their own fights to sustain their Republican student organizations on campus.

These are the people who have been pre-ordering Milo's book and who have made him a star. These are the people whom Ruth Ben-Ghiat writing for CNN accuses of "making hate profitable."[101] These are the people whom Constance Grady writing for *Vox* accuses of helping to mainstream "all the rage of the white supremacists and misogynists and bigots on the alt-right."[102] These are the people whom

[101] https://www.cnn.com/2017/01/02/opinions/milo-yiannopoulos-and-trump-profitable-hate-ben-ghiat-opinion/index.html

[102] https://www.vox.com/culture/2017/1/3/14119080/milo-yiannopoulos-book-deal-simon-schuster-dangerous-boycott

Sady Doyle writing for *Elle* anticipates will send people's lives up in flames at Milo's command.[103] These are the people whom Adam Morgan writing for *The Guardian* accuses Milo of encouraging "to think of entire groups of people as less than human."[104]

Even worse, these are the people whom Ian Tuttle, writing for *National Review* and ostensibly fellow conservative, accuses of being duped. In Tuttle's words:

> Milo Yiannopoulos is the sort of interloper by whom Americans have long been enamored: Part P.T. Barnum, wrangling the latest circus of novelties; part Sebastian Flyte, flaunting his heathenism in the face of bourgeois mores; and part Frank Abagnale, dashing from con to con... Yiannopoulos is one of that new, unfortunate species: the right-wing Internet celebrity. It used to be a requirement that those who aspired to weigh in on matters of public concern experienced the occasional advent of a thought in their heads. But after years of conflating sobriety and informed judgment with "elitism," such barriers to entry have disappeared, replaced by a system in which success is based on one's ability to—as Yiannopoulos himself has put it—get "LOLs." The same impulse that turned the patriarch of a family of duck hunters into a political sage needs news to be entertainment, too.[105]

Jealous much? Milo, of course, responded on his Facebook page with his usual tact, correcting Tuttle's use of "LOLs" ("The preferred formulation for anyone under 35 is 'lulz.' You're welcome") and his claims that Milo stiffed contributors to *The Kernel* or left the UK ignominiously; he didn't, much as the media loves to suggest that he did ("Working for *National Review* in 2016 you will be familiar with magazines falling on hard times"; Milo paid all the late invoices out

[103] https://www.elle.com/culture/news/a41798/milo-yiannopoulos-book-deal/

[104] https://www.theguardian.com/commentisfree/2017/jan/04/simon-schuster-alt-right-hate-breitbart-milo-yiannopoulos

[105] https://www.nationalreview.com/2017/01/milo-yiannopoulos-critics-feed-troll-attention/

of his own pocket). Most damning of all, however, as Milo himself pointed out, is what Tuttle said about Milo's fans:

> Your analysis, Ian, of how left-wing anguish rules my popularity has merit, but the conclusion I draw from your snobbery is simply that you don't much like how fame or celebrity works, and therefore perhaps don't like ordinary people very much either. Perhaps that is why no one has heard of you. As clownish and unsophisticated as you find me, I find your smug fogeyishness just as dull—as, apparently, do readers, who continue to wisely abandon your magazine in the thousands.

Young fogey that he is, Tuttle (whose writing I have actually long enjoyed) should be reading more of that great conservative go-to, Alexis de Tocqueville, if he wants to understand his fellow Americans better.[106] Milo certainly does. The problem, as Tocqueville would put it, is that Tuttle wants conservatives to write for aristocrats, while Milo writes—and speaks—for the people. The question for conservatives in America is which better serves democracy—and freedom of speech.

"In an aristocratic people," Tocqueville observes (2.XIII),

> among whom letters are cultivated...intellectual occupations, as well as the affairs of government, are concentrated in a ruling class.... When a small number of the same men are engaged at the same time upon the same objects, they easily concert with one another and agree upon certain leading rules that are to govern them each and all. If the object that attracts the attention of these men is literature, the productions of the mind will soon be subjected by them to precise canons, from which it will no longer be allowable to depart.

Such aristocratic circles produce literature and art of a high quality, carefully crafted according to certain canons of style, refined, elegant, delicate, always in exquisite taste.

> The slightest work will be carefully wrought in its least details; art and labor will be conspicuous in everything; each kind of writing will have rules of its own, from which it will not be allowed to swerve and which distinguish it from all others. Style will be thought of almost as much

[106] http://www.gutenberg.org/ebooks/816?msg=welcome_stranger#link2HCH0013

importance as thought, and the form will be no less considered than the matter; the diction will be polished, measured, and uniform. The tone of the mind will be always dignified, seldom very animated, and writers will care more to perfect what they produce than to multiply their productions. It will sometimes happen that the members of the literary class, always living among themselves and writing for themselves alone, will entirely lose sight of the rest of the work, which will infect them with a false sense and labored style... By dint of striving after a mode of parlance different from the popular, they will arrive at a sort of aristocratic jargon which is hardly less remote from pure language a than is the coarse dialect of the people. Such are the natural perils of literature among aristocracies.

It is quite the reverse, Tocqueville goes on, among people living in a democracy like that in America. There, there are almost as many writers as readers, every man (or woman) encouraged to participate in the production of the arts. Nor is it to be expected that "all who cultivate literature have received a literary education; and most of those who have some tinge of belles-lettres are engaged either in politics or in a profession that only allows them to taste occasionally and by stealth the pleasures of the mind." Accordingly,

they prefer books which may be easily procured, quickly read, and which require no learned researches to be understood. They ask for beauties self-proferred and easily enjoyed; above all, they must have what is unexpected and new. Accustomed to the struggle, the crosses, the monotony of practical life, they require strong and rapid emotions, startling passages, truths or errors brilliant enough to rouse them up and to plunge them at once, as if by violence, into the midst of the subject.

Under such circumstances, authors will seek to achieve not perfection of detail and style, but a "rapidity of execution" marked by "rude vigor of thought.... The object of authors will be to astonish rather than to please, and to stir the passions more than to charm the taste." Even more importantly, they will have the opportunity as well as the compulsion actually to sell their books, not having a captive and leisured audience upon whom they can depend for fame, if not money.

Let's face it, Milo can at times be downright vulgar (L: *vulgus*, the crowd, mob, rabble, populace). He does not cultivate a particularly refined speaking style—quite the reverse. He gleefully encourages his audiences to be roused to emotions of patriotism and laughter. He likes startling them with provocative images and performing in costume. And he is a master at plunging them, by way of jokes and memes, into the midst of the difficult subjects on which he chooses to speak. Tuttle might prefer for Milo to be more refined in his speech, less flamboyant in his presentations, more aristocratic in his diction. But the audiences to which Milo is speaking are American—and Americans, being democratic, love a good show.

This does not mean, as Tuttle implies with his snobbishness about *Duck Dynasty*, that they are not also interested in refined thought. (Milo was much more gentlemanly in his interview with Robertson.[107]) What it does mean is that they like their literature to be practical, to speak to them directly, to address their everyday concerns. They don't want theories and abstractions, but real solutions to actual problems. Such as "Fuck your feelings" in answer to those who seek to silence them by being offended if they voice the wrong opinions about abortion or the minimum wage.

Such as "America is the greatest country in the history of human civilization" in answer to those who would spend more time complaining about its imperfections than celebrating the liberties they enjoy. Such as "Feminism is cancer" in answer to those who would try to convince middle-class women and girls in America that they are somehow oppressed by the desire to have children and thus

---

[107] https://www.breitbart.com/social-justice/2016/05/19/phil-robertson-milo-yiannopoulos-show-weve-tried-sanders-socialism-doesnt-work/

make their own choices about the balance between homelife and their careers. Such as "Build the wall" in answer to those who would insist that our nation should have no borders and no enforced legal restrictions on who gets to live here.

Tuttle, no great master of style himself, predicts that Milo's book will appeal to this lowest common denominator of literary production: "[It] will be forgettable by any reasonable standard of literary merit. It will not feature any passage of sparkling prose... It will not contain any particularly interesting ideas... It will be a between-two-covers repackaging of his on-going performance-art piece, which felt tired even on its opening night." You can almost hear him yawning with boredom at the thought of yet another refined evening at the opera. Meanwhile, Milo's fans will be cheering for him as lustily as the French at a cabaret.

HOW TO ANSWER
THE OFFENSE

January 16, 2017

There you are, giving a lecture. Perhaps you are talking about the difference between wages and earnings so as to explain why there is no such thing as a "wage gap" affecting women in the United States. Or perhaps you are talking about the Christian West as the source of ideals such as freedom of religion and freedom of speech. Or perhaps you are talking about the legal situation of gays in countries that are governed by strict adherence to sharia. And then it happens. Someone starts screaming: "I find that really offensive!" "This is hate speech!"

Your mind boggles. (Okay, it boggles if you aren't Milo. He's used to this kind of response.[108]) You thought you were stating facts. How is it hateful, you think to yourself, to say that women in the freest countries in the world, when given the choice, choose certain kinds of careers over others and sometimes even prefer to stay home with their children when they are growing up? How can it be offensive to suggest that the ideals of our American culture have particular

---

[108] https://www.breitbart.com/social-justice/2017/01/15/milo-media-meltdown-breitbart-editors-uc-davis-event-dominates-headlines/

historical and religious roots? Why is it hurtful to note that, according to Islamic law, homosexuality is punishable by death, and in many Islamic countries, is?

"Lies, lies, lies!" you hear someone in the audience scream when you try to point these things out. "Take your hate speech off this campus! Take your hate speech off this campus!" Your pulse racing, you try to think how best to respond. What should you do?

1. FUCK YOUR FEELINGS

More precisely, watch your feelings carefully, as the first thing you are likely to feel is alarmed, followed by a desire to go on the offensive. Breathe. Relax. You are not in danger from someone else's speech. They can yell and scream all they want, and it will not hurt you. More to the point, their yelling and screaming is not, in fact, about you. It is about them, their feelings, their emotions.

This is the most important rule in learning how to listen empathetically: paying attention to the way in which your own feelings interfere with your ability to hear what the other person is saying.[109] Your first impulse will be to try to defend yourself against what you are feeling: that you have been unjustly attacked (which you have), that the other person is trying to shame you (which he or she is). It is critical at this point that you do not take the bait. The person who is yelling at you is already in distress, for reasons that almost certainly have nothing to do with you. If you are giving a public lecture and the person is yelling at you, this is above all a failure of manners, which means the screamer is behaving like a child who wants attention. The whole reason for screaming is to get your attention, which for some reason or other, the screamer feels he or she must have.

---

[109] https://fencingbearatprayer.blogspot.com/2011/08/how-to-be-bad-listener.html

This rule applies in less public conversations as well, when someone challenges you on something you have said and his or her voice (or written affect) takes on an aggrieved or hurt tone. He or she is hurting *and wants you to hurt, too*. The whole point of the attack is to make you respond, to go on the offensive yourself, so as to make the feelings of hurt seem justified. Again, you did not cause these feelings, they were already there. It is not your job to take them away. *Pro tip*: It helps to keep yourself on a relatively low-carb diet. Attacks like these trigger our "fight or flight" response, which relies greatly on the availability of glucose. There is a reason the Desert Fathers fasted in order to be better able to control their emotions: it works. Plus, it keeps you fabulous and beautiful.

2. BE LIKE WATER

As Bruce Lee put it: "Empty your mind, be formless, shapeless—like water." Keep yourself fluid, not rigid, and don't get stuck in knee-jerk responses. First, *do not apologize*. You are under an emotional attack, not a logical one. You have been talking about facts, but the person screaming at you does not care about facts, only emotions—the emotions he or she is feeling on hearing things that do not accord with his or her previous understanding of the world. Do not apologize, do not let them make it about you.

Second, *be gentle, stay cheerful*. The whole purpose of the attack is to justify the screamer's feelings of anxiety and hurt. He or she may have the body of an adult, but the child inside is terrified and wants to lash out at the world for being so hateful and cruel. "Darling!" you might say. "Pumpkin! You need to settle down."

Third, *find something in what has been said that you can agree with, ideally something you can make a joke about*. My favorite: "Milo sucks!" which the protestors at West Virginia wrote on one of their signs. As

Milo said, "I do!" Alternately, give them a gift, a selfie, some form of attention. Their whole narrative for why they are hurting depends on believing that you are the source of their feelings of being hated. The more you resist, the more they are confirmed in their need to attack. The more you can be like water, giving way just enough, the less they have a reaction to build off of.

Fourth, *be firm.* You might make a joke about yourself or acknowledge in some other way that you have heard them, but *do not apologize* for what you have been saying or allow them to change the terms of the argument. If they persist in their accusations, simply say, gently but firmly, "No." Repeat as necessary without further elaboration. Remember Arlo Guthrie, sitting there on the Group W bench, not proud...or tired, just singing his song.

> "You hate women!" "No, I hate people who lie to them about things like the wage gap and campus rape culture."

> "You hate minorities!" "No, I hate people who lie to them about the problems that they face in American society."

> "You hate Islam!" "As an ideology that oppresses women and gays, yes."

Special case: The screamer refuses to stop screaming, claiming that his or her free speech is being violated. At this point, you give a lesson in manners: "Wait your turn." If he or she does not understand this concept, it is time for the adults to intervene and take him or her for a time out.

3. 'THAT'S NOT A QUESTION'

You think, in giving a lecture or sharing an article on Facebook, that you are giving information or suggesting an argument, but this is not necessarily what you will get in return. "I find that offensive!" is not an argument. Nor is: "That's really shameful of you, Rachel. I can't believe you would say that." Nor is: "I suppose you support killing everyone who disagrees with you." Nor is: "I'll bet you are happy when people are discriminated against." (I am sure you can give other examples from your own experience.)

Here's the thing: *none of these accusations deserves or requires your response.* They are not requests for more information; they are emotional attacks designed to put you on the defensive and elicit a counterattack. You cannot counter them with facts because at this stage facts are irrelevant. You need to shift ground. How you do so depends in large part on the relationship that you have with the person who claims to have been offended. If you are speaking, like Milo, before a public audience and someone comes to the Q&A with such an accusation, simply be firm (as above), and reiterate: "That's not a question," until your accuser formulates an actual question or it becomes clear that he or she has none, at which point you say, "Next question."

If you are speaking with one of your friends, there is likely something somewhat different, albeit related, at stake: your accuser's sense of self in relation to you. Bluntly, at some level, your friend needs or wants your approval for his or her perspective on the issue—and you are refusing to give it. In either case, at some point, you may find it works to ask your accuser: "Why is it so important to *you* what *I* think?" Turn their personalization of the issue back on them, not as an accusation (which is what they expect), but as a reflection of their own interest in shaming or silencing you.

In a more intimate context, this tactic may enable you to get them to talk about what is actually troubling them, which will help clarify the emotions that they are feeling and projecting onto you (see above, on feelings). In public, it will tend to reinforce your authority, which they themselves are acknowledging through their need to fight you: they are afraid of you because they fear you may be right, which challenges their sense of their own righteousness. If they respond, "I'm not afraid of you," then you win as long as they continue to attack you—now, by their own account—for no reason.

4. KEEP A RECORD

The whole point of such attacks is to silence you as a speaker, preferably by making you censor yourself, thus in your accusers' minds acknowledging the righteousness of their original initial attack. Do the opposite: make everything that they say as public as possible, either by posting videos of the interaction or, if the exchange has been less public, for example on your own Facebook feed, by writing about it on your blog.

Here it is important to take the high ground: name only those who have gone public with their accusations themselves. Otherwise, leave your interlocutors anonymous, generically defined as "friends" or "people at my talk." Expose yourself fully, but protect those who have not named themselves. They will howl and scream and vow to come after you. (Trust me on this; it is not just Milo who has attracted their attention.) They will insist that you should be denied a platform from which to speak. To which the only appropriate response is, speak louder. Talk more. If you do not have a platform of your own, for example, a news site, create your own, like, for example, this blog.

The only reason Milo has the platform that he does is that he built it by way of hard work and persistence. He thought of the idea of doing a campus tour; he wrote newspaper columns; he wrote a book. It is nonsense to claim that he has taken away someone else's freedom of speech through his speaking. Likewise, it is nonsense for them to claim that your speaking prevents theirs. They are simply jealous that you have attracted an audience—and they haven't.

5. SUPPORT OTHERS

You know what it is like to be standing alone before the crowd, how frightening it can be even when you know that their only real weapon (as long as they stick with speech) is their ability to turn others against you through their accusations. There are many reasons that people choose not to get involved when they witness this kind of attack: fear of the crowd turning against them, fear that they will not be able to withstand the attack, sometimes even fear of losing their loved ones or livelihoods.

But you have taken the podium, published that blog post, shared that article on Facebook. You are out there now, taking the heat. Do not let others take it alone. Be there for them, whether by writing blog posts in their defense or commenting on their Facebook shares. Refuse to be silenced by the fear of what others might think. Morale, as Vox Day has argued, is here key: "Be quick to come running when your allies call... Pay closer attention to them than usual if you know they're under attack and provide them with tactical advice if you've got any and moral support if you don't." (Milo, this blogpost's for you!)

Bear witness. In other words, accept your role as a martyr (Gk: *witness*). It is your responsibility to stand up for freedom of speech and support others because if you don't, *no one else will either*. This is especially true, the dean of my college reminded me this past week, for those of us who are faculty in academia. If the faculty do not stand up for academic freedom, the culture of academic freedom dies. And if academic freedom and freedom of speech die, we all suffer. Men, women, whites, blacks, straights, gays, Christians, Muslims, atheists, and Jews alike. No offense, but it's true.

FREE SPEECH FUNDAMENTALS: BUILDING A PLATFORM

January 18, 2017

It is without a doubt one of the sillier complaints that protestors at Milo's talks have regularly made when they are trying to shut him up for having conservative political opinions about freedom of speech. For example, at UC Davis, where the protestors effectively shut down Milo's event the night before with their violence,[110] after which the next day one of them demanded of Milo as he was talking to the crowd gathered outside to hear him speak: "Where's my platform? Where is everyone else's platform?" Milo admonished him: "You had it last night, brother," but of course the young man was not satisfied. He thought that it was Milo's fault that nobody wanted to listen to him.

Trigglypuff at UMass Amherst had the same complaint, if imperfectly expressed: "But this is free speech! If you're so concerned about free speech..."—meaning presumably hers, as she clearly wanted to continue shouting, "Fuck you!" in the middle of Christina Hoff Sommers's remarks rather than sit quietly and wait for the Q&A. Somebody needs

---

[110] https://www.breitbart.com/social-justice/2017/01/13/reports-leftists-pull-hammers-milo-uc-davis-event-smash-windows/

to get these kids a conch. (Does anyone still read *Lord of the Flies* in high school, or does it cut too close to the bone?) Not only do they seem to have no understanding of taking turns while speaking, they don't seem to have a clue about what it means to have a platform from which to speak. Maybe they think all they need is a megaphone—like the one Milo used at UC Davis when he was speaking outside—or a podium, like the one from which Sommers was attempting to speak.

Well, I have news for them. Nobody cares what they think. If they don't have a platform, it is not because someone has taken it away from them. It is because they have not built one in the first place. Much as they would like to think that they are striking a blow for freedom of speech, their response to popular, invited speakers like Milo and Sommers is pure envy. In effect, they are saying: "Why are all these people listening to him or her and not me? Shut him or her up, I want to speak!"

It is they who want to steal somebody else's platform and make it their own, but as Milo has proven over and over again with his campus talks, that doesn't work. They can shout him down and make him change the venue for his talks, but they cannot steal his platform because his platform isn't a thing like a megaphone or a podium. It is the audience that he has built through his writing and speaking. And that is something that they cannot steal, only enhance by drawing attention to his speaking through their protests.

I have a message for all of Milo's protestors, as well as some words of advice that I hope will be helpful to his fans. If you don't want people giving their attention to particular speakers or writers, censorship and shouting is not the answer. What you need to do is build your own platform and offer something better. Vox Day put it perhaps most powerfully: "Give a man a platform and he will speak his mind. Deny him a platform, and he will build his own...and you will never silence him again." Here's how to build your own, starting with what not to do:

1. IT'S NOT ABOUT YOU

Nobody except possibly your mother is ever going to care as much about you as they do about themselves. Less bluntly, if you want to capture people's attention, start with something that will be of benefit to their own lives. This, in a nutshell, is why identity politics are so seductive: they provide a ready-made platform for capturing people's attention. Everyone likes hearing about themselves, so if you give them something to identify with—being a woman or man, being white or black, being straight or gay, being American or Christian—you've already got them partially hooked.

Even Milo does this. If you aren't paying proper attention, you might think he talks only about himself, but in fact he almost never does. Sure, he talks in general terms about his black boyfriends and his hair, but what his audiences hear him talking about is themselves and the kinds of things that they are worried about. It is much harder to get people to pay attention when they cannot see how what you are saying has any relevance to them. It is next to impossible when you have not earned their trust by offering them something of real value in exchange for paying attention to you.

2. CONTENT MATTERS

This should go without saying, but if you want people to listen to you, you have to have something to say beyond, "Fuck you!" You may get As on all your papers for school, but your teachers are paid to read them for you. (Your mother will read them for free.) Out in the marketplace of ideas, if you want someone to pay attention to you and perhaps even pay you for your words, you have to have something to sell. Ideas do not come cheap. It may not take precisely 10,000 hours to become expert in your field, but it is going to take a long time and a lot of hard work.[111] The reason that people invite Milo and Sommers to come speak to them on campus is because both have put in the years of work that it takes to become skilled and knowledgeable in a particular field. (I know, Milo is ridiculously young, but Brits mature early. It has something to do with their schools, although even there, they are doing their best to change it.[112])

Nor is it enough simply to know a lot of things. You need to be able to express your ideas clearly, which means practicing writing and speaking. All those papers you have written in school are just the beginning. Most writers have drawers and drawers full of journals, drafts, unpublished papers, notes from college and graduate school, exams, more unpublished papers, blog posts nobody will ever read. Nobody becomes a writer or a speaker overnight, even if the vicissitudes of fame sometimes make it seem that way. If you start now, it will most likely take a minimum of ten years before you develop sufficient expertise and skill to impress anybody other than your dissertation committee. It will take even longer to impress your colleagues at your tenure review. Or to get a literary agent to read your work.

3. SELL YOURSELF

You have ideas, you want to share them. And still nobody will listen. This is because you have forgotten lesson number one: it is not about you. Attention is humanity's single most valuable resource. Nobody is going to give it to you unless you can persuade them to make the exchange. Sure, you could tie them to a chair and force them to listen

---

[111] https://fencingbearatprayer.blogspot.com/2008/11/10000-hours.html

[112] https://www.breitbart.com/social-justice/2016/11/25/british-teachers-union-drafting-new-speech-guidelines-stop-milo/

to you (you can untie your mother now), but ideally you use words to capture their interest. Images can work, too, such as the photo of Milo looking gorgeous that I used to capture your attention for this blog post.

Aristocrats like Tocqueville could expect their readers to put up with almost anything—the more dignified and recherché the better—but those of us living in rough-and-tumble democracies have to build our audiences from the ground up. (Seriously, are you surprised that Trump was good at sales?) Which is a good thing. It means we have to dig deep down into ourselves and figure out WHY what we are doing matters and then communicate that WHY to others.[113] It means we have to learn how to make a pitch.

Pitches come in lots of sizes.[114] They may be a single word: "Prayer." A question: "Would you like to learn how to pray like a medieval Christian?" They may rhyme: "Fencing Bear at Prayer." Or come in a subject line of an email or as the title to a blog post. Unless you're Milo or Martin Shkreli, they might even come in a Tweet.[115]

If you're Pixar, they will come in the form of a story: "*Once upon a time* people prayed to the Virgin Mary. *Every day* they would say her Hours. *One day* a famous Frenchman named Voltaire made fun of this practice. *Because of that* everybody got embarrassed. *Because of that* nobody says her Hours anymore. *Until finally* Fencing Bear wrote a book explaining how important these prayers were for the history of Western civilization."

As Daniel Pink has shown, for a pitch to be successful, it needs to do one of two things: arouse curiosity or offer something useful.[116]

---

[113] https://fencingbearatprayer.blogspot.com/2016/01/my-why-how-what.html

[114] https://www.danpink.com/wp-content/uploads/2013/01/sixpitches.pdf

[115] https://www.breitbart.com/social-justice/2017/01/11/martin-shkreli-guest-star-milos-uc-davis-talk/

[116] https://www.danpink.com/books/to-sell-is-human/

Promise to explain "how to" or get someone to wonder "why," and it is much more likely they will read your blog post or come to your talk. If you do it really well, they might even buy your book. *Pro tip*: It also helps if you frighten them or make them think about sex. As in: "The Dangerous Faggot Tour."

4. SERVE OTHERS

Are you sensing a theme here? Again, it is not about you. If you have gotten their attention, you now have a responsibility to come through with your promise to teach or entertain. This is why capitalism, contrary to everything you have most likely ever heard, is not just effective, but ethical. It depends, as George Gilder has shown, on thinking first about others and what they need. In Gilder's words:

> Capitalism begins with giving. Not from greed, avarice, or even self-love can one expect the rewards of commerce, but from a spirit closely akin to altruism, a regard for the needs of others, a benevolent, outgoing, and courageous temper of mind... Not taking and consuming, but giving, risking, and creating are the characteristic roles of the capitalist, the key producer of the wealth of nations, from the least developed to the most advanced.[117]

Academics have a hard time with this truth. We think everyone should want to read our work because it is finely crafted and well-thought. But, again, we're not aristocrats; we have no captive audience, not even our students (who pay *us* to teach *them*). If we want them to listen to us, we need to think first about what they need. We need to learn to say what every shop assistant learns to say on the first day on the job: "How can I help you?" Trump won because he promised to help Americans: "Make America great again." Clinton lost because she was worried more about herself: "Ready for Hillary."

---

[117] *Wealth and Poverty: A New Edition for the Twenty-First Century* (2012)

5. BUILD RELATIONSHIPS

Start long before you have something to say. Attend obsessively to the media in which you hope to build a platform. If you want to write, read books, journals, magazines, blogs, even the news. If you want to make videos, spend hours of your day watching YouTube. (You already do that? Good!) If you want to make music, listen to music. Pay careful attention to the writers, video and film makers, musicians, and other artists whom you admire. Follow their work, notice how it changes over time. Think about what they are doing to sell themselves and why you are attracted to their content. And then find ways to get in touch with them.

This is essential advice for those thinking of going to graduate school. Professors are people, too. (I know, we seem like robotic monsters sometimes, but trust me on this!) If you want to learn how to become a professor, you need to talk with a few of us. (*Pro tip*: That's why we have office hours.) And if you want to apply to the institutions where we teach to study with us, you need to convince us that you know something about our work that would make us a good fit to teach you.

Other professions have similar cultures of building contacts and relationships, but all have this feature in common: the people in them care more about themselves than they do about you. (They are not your mother.) Take an interest in them, their work. Find out what they are interested in, study it if it interests you. This way you will have something upon which actually to build a relationship, other than your desire to participate in their status, which, see above, is more about your wanting to steal their platform than serve them. *Pro tip:* They will know in an instant if your interest in their interest is faked.

Begin by listening to what others have to say. Encourage them to talk about themselves and take a genuine interest in their interests.

You will win more friends if you make them feel important than you will by trying to make yourself seem important to them. Be sincere in your interest and your attention. Smile. Know their name.

6. WATCH FOR ENVY

You know the saying, I'm sure. "Academic politics are so bitter because the stakes are so low." But, in fact, the stakes are incredibly high, they just don't always involve money. They involve something even more precious: attention. And nothing is more bitter than seeing somebody else get the attention that you feel like you deserve. Well, you don't. Nobody deserves attention (except from his or her mother, and not even always then).

Here's the other thing about attention: you can never get enough. With the corollary: there will always be others who get more than you do. Suck it up, and don't be greedy. This, as Bob Sorge has brilliantly shown, is the real lesson of the parable of the talents that Jesus told.[118] Not, as those of us who grew up Presbyterian usually think about it: "Don't let your talents go to waste!" (Good Protestant work ethic there.) But rather: "Acknowledge the importance of having even one talent, rather than feeling envious of the ones who have two or five."

Every writer at some time or another obsesses about how many hits she is getting on her blog or how many copies of his book have sold. In academia, we get to practice this discipline every time we do a job search and have to eat our guts out over how much more our colleagues have managed to publish or how many invitations to lecture they have received. It is the green-eyed demon who is goading you on to scream at other speakers so as to shut them down. Don't listen to it. Get on with your own work.

---

[118] https://fencingbearatprayer.blogspot.com/2012/05/one-talent-wonder.html

7. GIVE YOURSELF A MEDAL

Because no one else will. No, it is still not about you. But it is you who is trying to build a platform from which to speak. And this will take courage because nobody but you (and your mother) will want you to. Your family will most likely mock you. Your friends will be nervous, lest you say something embarrassing about them. Or worse, say nothing about them at all. Others will be afraid of you, especially when it becomes clear that, thanks to the hard work you have put into developing your expertise, you know something that they don't.

And if you say something that conflicts with what they have believed about themselves or their place in the world, they will come howling for your blood. At which point, even your friends who encouraged you in your earlier efforts will desert you, and you will be on your own. And this is if you are lucky: it means someone will have noticed what you have said. It may take years for you to capture enough people's attention to be considered a threat. It may never happen.

But if and when it does, cherish the few who do not desert you. Like Wisdom, they are more precious than rubies. You think it is easy to stand up in front of an audience, even one that is not trying to shout you down? Thrilling, yes. Easy, no. Not even when you are as popular as Milo. It is even worse having no audience at all, other than your mother. But in the end, she is the only one who really matters.[119] All other rewards for speaking are but dust in the wind.

---

[119] https://fencingbearatprayer.blogspot.com/2016/11/in-press.html

LIES OF THE LEFT: 'WHITE NATIONALISM'

January 21, 2017

I don't know if you've noticed, but the professional Left[120] loves thinking in terms of binaries: black and white, male and female, rich and poor, Left and Right. For the media, it means easy headlines: find the Black Hats, and you've got your story. Likewise for Hollywood: drama depends on conflict, and what better conflict is there than that between the forces of Good and the forces of Evil? Academics tend to take a little more prodding before they will admit to thinking in such reductive terms, but get them talking about power and oppression and the categories will become clear.

"We" (the speakers) are necessarily the Good Guys. "They" (those who think wrongly about sex, race, and gender) are the Bad Guys. All the Good Guys are on the side of the Oppressed (blacks, women, the poor); all the Bad Guys are on the side of the Powerful (whites, males, rich). It does not matter that the categories make no historical sense, whether because they are recent inventions ("race" as something

[120] The mainstream media, most of my colleagues in academia, the paid protestors at Trump's rallies and presidential inauguration, most Hollywood actors and actresses, the Beltway elite, you know.

determined by evolution rather than culture or language), or because they are a fact of being mammals who reproduce sexually, or because there has never been a human society in which there were not some who commanded more resources than others. To refuse to think in the terms of these binaries is of itself to declare yourself a Black Hat.[121]

From the perspective of the professional Left (trust me on this, Jane Fonda said it just the other day[122]), there are no viable categories of human community that exist outside these binaries. Every other category—nation, church, commerce, friendship, family—must be collapsed into them. Conversely, because the Left themselves think always in these binaries, they assume that everyone else does, too. Have you ever wondered why "the Right" seems to have such a hard time defining itself? This is why. There is no such thing as "the Right" *except as a projection of the Left.* The Left needs a "Right" to oppose itself to, which is why the Left talks all the time about "fascism" as the enemy when both Leftists and fascists are, in fact, totalitarian. Actual conservatism cannot exist as far as the Left is concerned. Which is how we get "white nationalism."

---

[121] David Horowitz puts it somewhat more apocalyptically in *Big Agenda: President Trump's Plan to Save America* (2017): "Why do progressives have hatred in their hearts for conservatives? Why do they sound like hellfire-and-damnation preachers when they are on the attack? Because they are zealots of what can only be described as a crypto-religion modeled on the Christian narrative of the Fall and Redemption—the difference being that they seem themselves as the redeemers instead of the divinity. To progressives, the world is a fallen place—beset by racism, sexism, homophobia, and the rest—that must be transformed and made right. This redemption was once called communism and is now called socialism, or 'social justice.' Theirs is a vision of a world that has become a 'safe place'—where there are no deplorables, or where such irredeemables are outlawed and suppressed."

[122] https://www.breitbart.com/clips/2017/01/20/jane-fonda-include-race-class-everything/

DEFINING NATIONALISM

Nationalism, properly speaking, has nothing to do with race as biologically defined, never mind with something so literally superficial as skin color. As Roger Scruton has limpidly argued in *How to Be a Conservative* (2014), it is a way of answering the questions "to what do we belong, and what defines our loyalties and commitments" *without* adverting to "a shared religious obedience, still less in bonds of tribe and kinship." Nationalism defines "us" through "the things that we share with our fellow citizens, and in particular in those things that serve to sustain the rule of law and the consensual forms of politics."

What are these things that "we" share? To start with, Scruton says: territory. "We believe ourselves to inhabit a shared territory, defined by law, and we believe that territory to be *ours*, the place where we are, and where our children will be in turn. Even if we came here from somewhere else, that does not alter the fact that we are committed to this territory, and define our identity—at least in part—in terms of it."

From this perspective, it is as nonsensical to talk about "global citizenship" as it is to claim that democracy can or should exist without national borders. In Scruton's words: "Democracy needs boundaries, and boundaries need the nation state. All the ways in which people come to define their identity in terms of the *place where they belong* have a part to play in cementing the sense of nationhood."

Second, albeit closely tied to territory, are the history and customs according to which a particular territory has been settled. These customs may include, but do not need to include, religious ceremonies; secular rituals observed in common are equally potent, as are stories about how the territory was settled. These stories, as Scruton notes, tend to be of three kinds: tales of glory, tales of sacrifice, and tales of emancipation. But they change according to who thinks of themselves as *we*: we English, we Scots, we Americans, we Mexicans, we Chinese, we Russians, we French. For the English and those nations derived from England (like America), one of the most important of their national myths is that of the common law. Again, in Scruton's words: "We who have been brought up in the English-speaking world have internalized the idea that law exists to do justice between individual parties, rather than impose a uniform regime of command."

(In contrast: "To someone raised on the doctrine that legitimate law comes from God, and that obedience is owed to Him above all others, the claims of the secular jurisdiction are regarded as at best an irrelevance, at worse a usurpation"—for example, among those raised in dar al-Islam. This, as Scruton points out, is one of the most important reasons for many Islamists' resentment of the West and its representative, the United *Nations*: the imposition of the idea of the nation with its ideals of secular law and citizenship on Muslim communities founded rather on "divine law, brotherhood, and submission to a universal faith." Perhaps paradoxically for many modern secularists, the secular nation is a peculiarly Christian construct, grounded in the idea of the separation of Church and State.)

Showing once again his English roots, Scruton insists: "The essential thing about nations is that they grow from below, through habits of free association among neighbours, and result in loyalties that are attached to a place and its history, rather than to a religion, a dynasty, or, as in Europe, to a self-perpetuating political class." From this perspective, America would seem to embody the ideal nation.

DEFINING AMERICA AS A NATION

Still in Scruton's words:

> Under the American settlement, people were to treat each other, first and foremost, as *neighbours*: not as fellow members of a race, a class, an ethnic group or religion, but as fellow settlers in the land that they shared. Their loyalty to the political order grew from the obligations

of neighbourliness; and disputes between them were to be settled by the *law of the land*. The law was to operate within territorial boundaries defined by the prior attachments of the people, and not by some trans-national bureaucracy open to capture by people for whom those boundaries meant nothing.

My colleagues in the History department gathered again yesterday to talk about the implications for America of a Trump presidency. While they seemed to believe that it was important that America continue to exist—the one American historian talked explicitly about whether the Republic was in danger—it was difficult for me to understand *why* they thought it should. Except for the one Americanist, all the others work on other parts of the world: China, Eastern Europe, medieval Germany, Mexico, Marxist theory in the original German.

As a group, those who work on the modern world seemed willing to champion the idea that other nations should exist in their own territories with their own histories and customs, but whether America has a place in that constellation seemed somewhat unclear. Our Mexican historian spoke forcefully (and correctly) about the degree to which America is already and always has been Mexico. I get this intuitively, having grown up in New Mexico and spent my childhood wondering why all American history seemed to begin on the East Coast. (I'm old; I know this is not the version of our national history kids these days are learning.)

"But what," I asked him in the Q&A, "do Mexicans think about us? Do they agree with you when you say that Mexico is already and has always been America?" "Oh, no, they think I am crazy for siding with the *gringos*." Likewise, our Chinese historian spoke eloquently about the way in which China looks at the rest of the world through the lens of its own national history, particularly the imperial system of competitive examination. The current ruling elite in China, he told us, value expertise above all. To them it is nonsensical that we as

America seem so willing to undermine ourselves competitively, while at the same time they are unsurprised.

China, after all, is the Middle Kingdom, the place where heaven and earth meet. (I paraphrase somewhat, adding my own understanding of imperial China from my undergraduate days—I got to play Empress in our recreation of Qing politics.[123]) But what President Trump said yesterday in his inaugural address?[124] Dangerous. Unless, of course, you have been reading Scruton.

"We, the citizens of America, are now joined in a great national effort to rebuild our country and to restore its promise for all of our people." That is, we are neighbors who live and work together, fellow settlers in the land we share, obliged to each other through neighborliness.

"Together we will determine the course of America and the world... We will face challenges. We will confront hardships. But we will get the job done." Here Trump invokes all three tales of the nation at once: glory, sacrifice, and emancipation.

"This is your day. This is your celebration. And this, the United States of America, is your country. What truly matters is not which party controls our government, but whether our government is controlled by the people." The nation is defined, again, as a shared territory, the we of those of us who live here as citizens under the same law.

"At the center of this movement is a crucial conviction: that a nation exists to serve its citizens. Americans want great schools for their children, safe neighborhoods for their families, and good jobs for themselves." Note the explicit emphasis on neighborliness and the implicit appeal to the understanding that the nation grew up from the free associations between neighbors.

"We are one nation...We share one heart, one home, and one glorious destiny." America is a shared home with a story, a territory with a history and a future as the place where our children will live.

---

[123] https://scholarship.rice.edu/handle/1911/88961

[124] https://www.whitehouse.gov/briefings-statements/the-inaugural-address/

"We must protect our borders..." Trump's signature promise: America exists as a territory, not just an idea or a people, but a region in which particular laws are enforced to do justice to the individual parties involved.

"We do not seek to impose our way of life on anyone..." We recognize that our customs are not others' customs.

"...but rather to let it shine as an example for everyone to follow." But our customs are real and can serve as an example to others for how to imagine their nations.

"At the bedrock of our politics will be a total allegiance to the United States of America, and through our loyalty to our country, we will rediscover our loyalty to each other." Our nation depends on feelings of neighborliness and belonging to the territory and customs that we share.

"When you open your heart to patriotism, there is no room for prejudice." We are the ones who live here in America together. Our sense of nation depends on this shared neighborliness, not on a shared religious obedience or on bonds of tribe and kinship, but on our shared history (which is why it is so important that we have one) and our national narrative of living under a common law.

Those, like my colleagues who have spent their lives building communities of scholarship with likewise elite intellectuals around the world, have a hard time with such territorial claims to allegiance and belonging. They (as I know from long experience living here in Chicago) do not tend to think of themselves as Chicagoans or even know that much about our city where they live. They participate only in a limited fashion in the life of the community around us, whether through church or other hobbies. (Most of them aren't here that much, if they can help it; I take my sabbaticals on my couch.) When I pushed them at another point in the conversation about the long-term effects of automation on the American workforce and how important it is for human dignity to feel oneself skilled at making things, they had a hard time imagining actual hobbies in which one might engage if he or she did not read books.

"Looking at screens" was the only thing they seemed to think most Americans not in academia do with their leisure time. (To be fair, one suggested raising heritage chickens.) In their imaginations, I am sad to report, except for my fellow medievalist and I (you gotta wonder), America did not exist. Which is most likely why they, like most of the mainstream media, could not hear President Trump when he said: "It is time to remember that old wisdom our soldiers will never forget: that whether we are black or brown or white, we all bleed the same red blood of patriots, we all enjoy the same glorious freedoms, and we all salute the same great American flag." In other words, our nation qua nation is not about race—and never was.[125]

WHY THE LEFT NEEDS 'WHITE NATIONALISM'

The Left depends for its very existence on the narrative that nations exist only as expressions of something other than territory inhabited by those with shared customs and history. As Scruton shows elsewhere, it came into being explicitly as a rejection of history (that of France), and has depended ever since on the imposition (often by violence, as in the Terror) of universalizing ideals at the expense of local custom and practice.

From the beginning, it has likewise depended on identifying all those who stand against its narrative of rupture and cleansing as enemies, counterrevolutionaries who would turn back the clock on the redefinition of society according to the Left's own uncompromising standards of virtue (as, for example, in the Vendée). Like its founding

---

[125] And, no, of course, we have not always lived up to our own ideals as Americans in this respect. I am talking about the way in which we imagine ourselves as a nation.

father, Maximilien Robespierre, the Left thinks in terms of absolutes, of virtue guaranteed through terror. The nation built up through custom and the habit of free association between neighbors is anathema to such a top-down, idealizing vision. It, therefore, cannot be allowed to exist.

"White nationalism," like the patriarchy, is a myth.[126] To be sure, there were Scots in the late nineteenth century, most famously among them Rudyard Kipling, who talked in terms of "the white man's burden," but as Arthur Herman has shown in his history of the Scots and their influence on the development of the West, this "burden" was never, at least in the English-speaking world, what later post-colonial theorists have imagined it to mean.[127] (Perhaps it was for the French, which would explain Foucault.)

The Left, however, given its own founding mythology, cannot admit that it is working with a radically different understanding of nation. Nor, it seems, will those of us who are forced by definition to call ourselves conservatives be able to get them to see why we are conservative not in the sense of wanting to preserve all customs unchanging or the control of this or that biologically-determined race over our country, but simply in the sense of being neighbors living and working together under a common law. It is rather like the Sphere in Edwin Abbott's *Flatland* (1884) trying to explain itself to the Square. The Square only knows how to see in two dimensions, but the Sphere exists in three.

---

[126] https://www.breitbart.com/social-justice/2016/12/02/milo-explains-patriarchy-ohio-university/

[127] https://fencingbearatprayer.blogspot.com/2016/01/the-unbearable-whiteness-of-west.html

LIES OF THE LEFT: 'GENDER FLUIDITY'

January 24, 2017

I have to confess that I tend to have a hard time staying awake when colleagues in academia start talking about *gender*. There you are in a seminar talking about, I don't know, nationalism or the Ark of the Covenant or Milo's hair, and as sure as eggs is eggs, someone, not necessarily a woman, will clear her throat and intone: "I think what we really need to consider here is *gender*." At which point I fall asleep. It is just so *boring*.

Gender (you have to say it with that special emphasis, as if pronouncing the Name of the Deity) has been *the* hot topic of analysis since I was in college thirty years ago. To give credit where credit is due, I might not have taken up the work that I have done on devotion to the Virgin Mary without the interest in *gender* of many of my teachers at the time. My dissertation advisor, Caroline Walker Bynum, is famous for making *gender* a category of analysis in the study of medieval Christianity. (It says so on her faculty page at the Institute for Advanced Study.) But even she stopped writing about gender after publishing *Holy Feast and Holy Fast* in 1987 (where she was actually talking about women and men and their relationship with God, not *gender* per se). Somehow the rest of the field never got the memo.

Sure, they have since added other identities to the mix. The field as a whole might better be defined now as "Christian-Jewish-Muslim relations in the Middle Ages," with the emphasis decidedly on the latter two groups for which the Christians provide the normative (i.e. boring) background. (You can tell by how breathless people get when talking about Judaism and Islam in comparison.) But *gender* remains the primary analytical category for those of us studying the history of medieval Christianity, so much so that I regularly have prospective graduate students tell me about how much they want to work with me on *gender* despite the fact that I never use that term to describe my work. (Presumably because I'm a woman who works on Mary?) Sex, sure; I'll talk about sex. But *gender*? I am putting myself to sleep just talking about it here. (Which is why I have a picture of Milo on the side, to keep both you and me awake.)

Gender, you see, unlike sex, does not exist, except in the head. People have ideas about *gender*, but *gender* as such, being a construct of the imagination, has no existence in physical reality. Unlike sex, as it says in the Bible: "Male and female he created them." (As one of my gay professors in graduate school liked to put it: "Sex is what is between your legs, *gender* is between your ears.") You say *gender* exists? Show me. Where? In your clothes? Your hair? Your use of make-up? Your voice? Your ability to hold reasoned argument? Your emotional self-discipline?

But what if you change these? Does that mean your *gender* changes or just your ability to stay calm in an argument? What if you can't change your hair or your voice without changing yourself hormonally or anatomically? Does that mean your *gender* is in fact tied to your physical sex? Or is it all just in your and other people's heads? John

Milbank put it perhaps most succinctly: "Without bodily sexual difference, there would of course be no prompting to the social imagination of gender."[128]

Are you old enough to remember the character Klinger in *M*A*S*H*? Do you remember what he did in order to try to get a Section 8 so that he could be discharged from the army and sent home? Wear heels and a dress. Because, of course, a man wearing heels and a dress would have to be crazy, dressing as if he were a woman (and out of uniform, but somehow that never featured in Klinger's gambit). It never worked, again, of course, because wearing heels and a dress has nothing to do with being crazy (or a woman); it is just a choice of fashion.

Look at Louis XIV, famous for his red heels and long skirts. Neither Klinger nor King Louis (ask his many mistresses) ever looked like anything other than a man, despite wearing clothing that would now (arguably) gender him feminine. And yet, who—woman or man—does not find Dr. Frank N. Furter sexy? Or, for that matter, Milo? Do you care what gender they are, or just want to have sex with them? (Stop lying!) Which, if you think about it, is really what *gender* is all about: sex, whom you get to have it with, and why you want to fuck at all. Take Origen, for example.

Origen of Alexandria (d. 254) was so in love with God that, according to tradition, he cut his dick off in order to be worthy of the kingdom. (Or maybe just his testicles, reports vary. Which according to our contemporary parlance might make him a woman—I'm not entirely sure about this; but according to the New Testament lexicon made him a eunuch.[129]) Famously, he wrote about his love for God in his commentary on King Solomon's love song, the Song of Songs,

---

[128] https://catholicherald.co.uk/commentandblogs/2017/01/13/long-read-what-liberal-intellectuals-get-wrong-about-transgenderism/

[129] https://www.truthrevolt.org/news/transgender-activist-womens-march-too-many-white-cis-women

casting himself (or the Soul) in the guise of the Bride and God in the role of the Bridegroom. In Origen's words:[130]

> This little book is an epithalamium, that is a wedding song, which it seems to me that Solomon wrote in dramatic form, and sang burning with heavenly love, like a bride to her bridegroom, who is the Word of God. For whether she is the soul, made in his image, or the Church, she loved him greatly.

This was the reading of the Song of Songs that inspired medieval commentators like the Cistercian monk Bernard of Clairvaux (d. 1153) to exclaim:[131]

> Only the touch of the Spirit can inspire a song like this, and only personal experience can unfold its meaning. Let those who are versed in the mystery revel in it; let all others burn with desire rather to attain to this experience than merely to learn about it. For it is not a melody that resounds abroad by the very music of the heart, not a trilling on the lips but an inward pulsing of delight, a harmony not of voices but of wills. It is a tune you will not hear in the streets, these notes do not sound where crowds assemble; only the singer hears it and the one to whom he sings—the lover and the beloved.

Although Bernard, unlike Origen (or for that matter Bernard's great rival, Heloise's husband Abelard), still had (and kept) his dick when he became a monk, you might be excused for thinking he didn't. Here he is, preaching on the Song of Songs to his fellow monks:

> "Let him kiss me with the kiss of his mouth," she said. Now who is this "she"? The bride. Why bride? Because she is the soul thirsting for God.... No sweeter names can be found to embody that sweet interflow of affections between the Word and the soul, than bridegroom and bride.... They share the same inheritance, the same table, the same home, the same marriage-bed, they are flesh of each other's flesh.... "I cannot rest," she says, "unless he kisses me with the kiss of his mouth.... It is desire that drives me on, not reason.... My shame indeed rebukes me, but love is stronger than all.... Headlong love does not wait for

---

[130] *The Song of Songs*, trans. R. P. Lawson (1957)

[131] *On the Song of Songs* I, trans. Kilian J. Walsh and Irene M. Edmonds (1981)

judgment, is not chastened by advice, not shackled by shame nor subdued by reason. I ask, I crave, I implore; let him kiss me with the kiss of his mouth."

Who is speaking here: the bride of the Song or Bernard? Bernard constantly insists that he has not enjoyed the experience he is describing himself, apologizing lest his exposition not measure up "to the dignity of the subject." And yet, how could he talk about it at all if he had not experienced at the very least a taste of the divine kiss for which he, like the bride of the Song, yearned? Bernard's older contemporary, the Benedictine Rupert of Deutz (d. 1129) was less shy. You've heard Rupert's name, I'm sure.

Milo mentioned him in one of his talks, as being entered into by God, much like the Virgin Mary.[132] Milo was being coy. It is more accurate to say that Rupert, like Mary, was ravished by an all-consuming fire, filled with the living light, and transformed. "Behold," Rupert recounted in his commentary on the Gospel of Matthew, where he was attempting to explain to his friend Cuno, the abbot of St. Michael's at Siegburg, how it happened that he came to write—*and write, and write, and write, and write*:[133]

> I was lying on my bed at the close of the day, and I had scarcely closed my eyes in sleep, when a figure in the likeness of a man prone and uniformly extended came down from above, with only his face hidden. Sinking down on me, he filled the whole substance of my soul, impressing me in a way that I can in nowise describe in words, more swiftly and deeply than the softest wax is able to receive the strongly impressed seal. Immediately I was shaken out of the dream which had just come over me, and now wakeful I sensed a sweet weight, wakeful I was delighted, and what shall I say? "My soul melted" (Song of Songs 5:6); my soul, Lord, almost broke loose, almost poured out of my body.... Indeed, it is true to say that, if that sudden overflowing of

[132] https://www.breitbart.com/social-justice/2016/09/27/10-things-milo-hates-islam/
[133] On Rupert and Mary, see Rachel Fulton [Brown], *From Judgment to Passion: Devotion to Christ and the Virgin Mary, 800-1200* (2002)

holy pleasure had continued much longer, it would have by its very strength drawn the soul swiftly from the body like a torrent and carried it away.... But as I said, that overflowing force of love soon stopped, and went away little by little. From that time on, however, "I have opened my mouth" (Psalm 118:131), and I have not been able to stop writing. Up to now, even if I wanted to, I could not be silent.

A few years later, in his commentary on the Song of Songs, Rupert attributed this same experience to a certain "young woman" lying on her couch, who saw the crucifix on which she was gazing in vision come alive "with a regal visage, radiant eyes, and an aspect utterly to revered." As she looked on,

> the beloved one condescended to pull his right hand from the cross-beam and to make the sign of the cross over her....[and] the power of the sign bore her upwards...so that it seemed her whole body was brought to his, her hands stretched out to his hands fixed on the cross, and her mouth likewise pressed to his; and when she awoke from sleep...she trembled delightfully for some time with that divine tremor.

Now do you see what I mean by Milo's being coy? In the Song commentary, Rupert leaves it highly ambiguous who, exactly, this "young woman" (*adulescentula*) who shared her vision with her maidservants is. (One medieval reader got it and wrote in the margin to the manuscript: "Here he is speaking about himself.") According to Rupert, he told the story so as to give a hint of the kind of experience the Virgin Mary must have had when, in the words of the Song, "My beloved put his hand through the lattice, and my belly trembled at his touch" (Song of Songs 5:4).

"This," Rupert says casually at the end of the story before returning to the Scriptural text, "is what has been said by some concerning the experience of the hand or the touch, and of the divine tremor," in comparison with which Mary's experience of the touch of the Lord's hand must have been all the greater, "far exceeding our understanding." And yet, somehow, Rupert knew.

"Let him kiss me with the kiss of his mouth," Mary says at the beginning of the Song in Rupert's reading. "What is this exclamation so great, so unlooked for?" Rupert asks her. "O blessed Mary, the inundation of joy, the force of love, the torrent of delight, covered you entirely, possessed you totally, intoxicated you inwardly, and you sensed what eye has not seen and ear has not heard and what has not entered into the heart of man." Bernard may not have had this experience—but Rupert had.

It was the night of Ash Wednesday around the year of Our Lord 1108. "Lightly sleeping," Rupert found himself in a dream talking to a friend about what he believed to be his impending death when, suddenly, it seemed he saw heaven opening just to the right over the head of his friend, from which opening a luminous talent of an ineffable substance descended and flowed into his breast, waking him immediately with its magnitude and weight. It was, Rupert remembered ever after, "heavier than gold, sweeter than honey."

By this point, Rupert was fully awake and lying quietly, waiting to see what might happen next. At first, the heavy sweetness lay where it had fallen, in his breast, but soon, however, "it began to move, and to circle round the womb of the interior man, the womb of the interior soul." Continuing its circuit "in a wonderful and ineffable way," "this living thing and true life" at last filled Rupert's whole heart and soul "so that it could hold no more." The movement stilled and Rupert waited, longing to see what this living substance might be. After a while, it began moving again and poured like a river from Rupert's left side so that he could now see (with his interior eyes) that it was an exquisitely beautiful liquid gold. A liquid gold with which, like a crucible, he found himself filled.

Have you had such an experience? Would it make a difference what sex you were? Rupert describes himself being filled, almost as if he were pregnant, with a "living thing and true life," a heavy sweetness that he could see with his interior eyes as a liquid gold as it poured from his side. Does it matter that he was not a woman, but a man when he experienced, in a later vision, the image of the Lord crucified opening the altar to him, receiving him inside, and kissing him eagerly with open mouth? Although he disguises his experience in the commentary on the Song as that of a "young woman," in the commentary on Matthew written about the same time, he is clear that it was he who experienced these ecstasies of being kissed, pressed down, and filled with God.

Bottoms know what this experience is like. Just ask Milo. (Okay, don't, you'll probably embarrass him.) Here are what long-time lovers, S/M players and co-authors Dossie Easton and Janet Hardy advise wannabe bottoms to expect:

> A crucible is the pot a metalworker uses to melt together ores—a receptacle for strong metals and high heat, transforming two lesser things into a greater thing, the alchemist's cauldron where lead becomes gold. You, as a bottom, are a crucible. You take the top's energy into you. Within you, liquified with the heat of spirit and sex, that energy swirls together with your own energy, and turns into something stronger, sharper, brighter than either of you could generate alone. When your top believes you are beautiful, you become beautiful. When you believe your top is powerful, he becomes powerful. Your body and spirit are the locus for the creation of a newly minted reality...a reality with all the power and wisdom that you and your top can together bring to it.[134]

The Virgin Mary herself could not have said it better. What greater ecstasy could there be than to be "the locus for the the creation of a newly minted reality," the incarnation of the Knowledge and Wisdom

---

[134] *The New Bottoming Book* (2001)

of God? It is every masochist's dream. Who would not give him or herself over to being topped and made beautiful by the power of the divine Word?

"I sleep," the bride of the Song of Songs says, "and my heart keeps watch. The voice of my beloved knocking: 'Open to me, my sister, my love, my dove, my spotless one, for my head is full of dew and my hair of the drops of the nights.'.. I rose to open to my beloved, my hands dripped myrrh, my fingers full of the finest myrrh... I opened the bolt of the door to my love... My soul melted as he spoke." "I rose up," Mary says in Rupert's commentary. "For how could I sleep any longer or fall back asleep after this?... 'I opened the bolt of the door to my love'...that is, I opened my mouth in teaching, so as to make known the beloved to those listening."

From what I understand about the scene-space of contemporary S/M, topping or bottoming has very little to do with gender traditionally conceived, nor is topping, the more typically "masculine" role, the preferred experience. According to Patrick Califia, bottoms (by no means exclusively women) are proverbially said to outnumber tops (of whom the most prominent stereotype, the dominatrix, is of course a woman) by a ratio of 10 to 1.[135] Given the opportunity, how many bottoms, one wonders, would imagine themselves as Mary? I would.

What, after all, could be more exquisite than to be topped by God, ravished in the knowledge that one was loved by Love, beheld as beautiful by Beauty, infused with wisdom by Wisdom, thereby enabling Love/Beauty/Wisdom to see itself reflected as such? Neither, I am convinced, is what we are dealing with here primarily or even necessarily a question of gender. Severin von Kusiemski, the prototypical masochist, was, after all, a man.

---

[135] *Sensuous Magic: A Guide to S/M for Adventurous Couples*, 2nd ed. (2001)

Bottoming God—and for those who still have doubts, I highly recommend Rupert's commentary on the Song—Rupert and Mary, contrary to most feminists' expectations, were not silenced, but empowered. If, at the Annunciation, Mary declares herself God's handmaiden, and submits to his will: "Let it be to me according to your word," she is not humiliated, but exalted, filled with the living light of the glory of God and blessed above all other women to become the Mother of the Most High.

Likewise, Rupert, as he lay on his bed and felt himself pressed down by "the likeness of a man," was so filled with holy pleasure that it seemed his very soul might be carried away—after which he was filled with the wisdom to write. Far from dying or even wilting away, having submitted to God, Rupert found himself compelled to become the single most prolific Scriptural commentator of his day. And Mary, as Rupert tells it, humbling herself before the Lord as his Mother became the great teacher of the Word, feeding all the souls of the world with milk from her breasts. (Do you still wonder where Milo gets his courage to speak and to write?).

"Male and female he created them." There would be nothing transgressive in a man dressing like a woman if there were nothing in our gendered expectations about biological sex to transgress. This, it seems to me, is the real problem with almost every discussion of *gender* during which I have managed to stay awake: the more people talk about transgressing something that they are trying to convince themselves doesn't matter (sex as a source of wisdom, beauty, and fertility), the more boring they are obliged to become lest they become conscious of the lies.

And by far the greatest lie that we are told is that we are not creatures, but accidents, animals for whom sex is nothing more than an instinct and a physical pleasure (if that), with the corollary that the sense we have of our sexuality is all in our heads and thus wholly up to ourselves to construct.

If all we want is to fuck each other so as to feel physical pleasure or validate our sense of self, we can imagine ourselves in relation to each other however we like. But how much the more transgressive—and exciting—is it to imagine oneself as a creature surrendering to the Creator of heaven and earth so as to be filled, body and soul, with liquid, living, empowering, transforming, beatific light? I'm sorry, did you say something? I must have dozed off.

FREE SPEECH FUNDAMENTALS: LOCKE

January 30, 2017

Strap in. I am about to tell you something that may make you uncomfortable. "Toleration" as a political virtue is *not* about being nice. It is a *not* a shorthand for the Golden Rule: "Do unto others as you would have them do unto you" (Matthew 7:12). It is *not* about not judging others lest you be judged, or about giving good things to others when they ask you for help. It is *not* about multiculturalism or "diversity" or being open to other's perspectives. Above all, it is *not* about refusing to defend your own religious and political traditions against those who would seek to replace them with theirs. What it *is* is a uniquely Christian virtue predicated on specific pronouncements of the Lord Jesus Christ.

1. *"My kingdom is not of the world"* (John 18:36), meaning that there is no State of which Christ claims to be ruler.

2. *"Render unto Caesar the things which are Caesar's, and unto God the things that are God's"* (Matthew 22:21), meaning that there are things over which the State has jurisdiction, but that these things do not include what is owed to God, specifically worship.

3. *"And whosoever shall not receive you, nor hear your words, when ye depart out of that house of city, shake off the dust of your feet"* (Matthew 10:14), meaning that worshipping God should not be coerced. Here Jesus was instructing his disciples on how to preach the kingdom of heaven to the lost sheep of Israel: not with swords, but with words.

Politically, it is about the separation of Church and State, which thanks to the evangelicals of the sixteenth century (we call them Protestants) became an explosive and deadly issue in Europe for almost two hundred years. (There were issues about the relationship between the Church and State in the Middle Ages, but they were different. Henry VIII took care of all that by having Parliament declare him "Supreme Head in Earth of the Church of England," only to open another can of worms.) This is the history we in America need to be studying because this is the history that gave birth to the political institutions of our country, more specifically, to the North American colonies founded by the English and Scots-Irish over the course of the seventeenth and eighteenth centuries.[136]

Not that the colonists themselves spoke in terms of the separation of Church and State. Many of them, particularly the Puritans (think "Progressives"), came to the New World with the express intent of establishing more pure (thus their nickname) communities in which to worship God as they believed they should.[137] But as refugees from the religious wars that wracked England and Scotland for the better part of two centuries, they knew what it was like for the government to try to tell them how they should pray—and they didn't like it. The English Civil War of the 1640s began over a prayer book, which the

---

[136] https://fencingbearatprayer.blogspot.com/2016/02/founding-freedoms-four-square.html

[137] https://fencingbearatprayer.blogspot.com/2016/01/progressive-is-new-puritan.html

King of England tried to impose on the Scots. (It's complicated, just ask a Redneck.[138])

This was the context in which John Locke (1632-1704) wrote his famous *Letter on Toleration*, the ultimate source for the arguments that many make nowadays for why we should worry more about being tolerant than about preserving the public institutions and laws the colonists (we call them Founders) put in place.[139] Locke would beg to disagree. Locke wrote the letter while living in exile in Amsterdam. It was first printed in Latin, then in Dutch and French. William Popple translated it into English and published it anonymously in London in 1689.

Its publication was directed specifically against an act of Parliament of May of that same year, which denied freedom of worship not only to Catholics, but also to Protestants like Locke and Popple who dissented against the doctrine of the Trinity, with the exception of those who took an oath of allegiance (which not all would do). Neither dissenters, even those who took the oath, nor Catholics were allowed to hold public office. This Toleration Act of 1689 remained in force well into the nineteenth century, with Unitarians being barred from meeting for worship until 1813 and Catholics from public office until 1829.

You might think, therefore, that Locke, as a dissenter, would call for the dissolution of King and Parliament and the institution of a whole new political system more amenable to such diversity of opinion. It was, after all, what the Roundheads had tried to do, and what Oliver Cromwell succeeded in doing for a decade. Okay, not quite: Cromwell was as close as the English have come to a religious dictator (second only to Henry VIII and his daughter "Bloody" Mary, as the Protestants called her), and it was in response to his intolerance

---

[138] https://fencingbearatprayer.blogspot.com/2016/01/conservative-is-new-redneck.html
[139] http://www.constitution.org/jl/tolerati.htm

and the fears that James II would bring back Catholicism and Mary's enthusiasm for the stake that prompted the Glorious Revolution of 1688. (I paraphrase what I have learned from my early modernist colleagues; it is far more complicated than I am making it here.)

My point is: the English had spent decades reorganizing their political structures and did not want to have another war. But those like Locke did want to be able to worship in a way that accorded with their consciences without being persecuted or killed. Accordingly, Locke started with a theological argument. "Honoured Sir," he wrote to his friend Philip von Limborch, a Dutch dissenter. "Since you are pleased to inquire what are my Thoughts about the mutual Toleration of Christians in their different Professions of Religion, I must needs answer you freely, That I esteem that Toleration to be the chief Characteristical Mark of the True Church." Note that Locke claims at the outset that toleration is something Christian: the mark of the true Church.

The problem was that Christians could not agree on what method of worship—what Locke means by "Religion"—to practice and had been killing each other over disagreements in how to praise God. What they had tried—forcing everyone to live under the same canon of worship by rule of law and threat of death—had manifestly not worked. People stubbornly persisted in dissenting against the King, Parliament, and anyone else who would try to make them pray in a particular way, all the while calling themselves Christians for trying to preserve the True Church.

Locke had another suggestion. On the one hand, he opined, there was *the Commonwealth*, which "seems to me to be a Society of Men constituted only for the procuring, preserving, and advancing of their own Civil Interests." These interests, Locke explained, "I call Life, Liberty, Health, and Indolency of Body; and the Possession of outward things, such as Money, Lands, Houses, Furniture, and the like." "It is the Duty of the Civil Magistrate, by the impartial Execution of equal Laws, to secure unto all the People in general, and to every one of his Subjects in particular, the just Possession of these things belonging to this Life." It is these things, Locke is saying, and these alone that are of Caesar's concern. What is not Caesar's concern, *pace* Henry VIII, is the Salvation of Souls: "For no Man can, if he would, conform his Faith to the Dictates of another. All the Life and Power of true Religion consists in the inward and full perswasion of the mind; and Faith is not Faith without believing."

According to Locke, the only thing that the Civil Magistrate could command were those things that could be compelled by outward force. But Faith, being inward, is not susceptible to such coercion as the Civil Magistrate might exercise: "Confiscation of Estate, Imprisonment, Torments, nothing of that nature can have any such Efficacy as to make Men change the inward Judgment they have framed of things." More to the point, what if the Civil Magistrate were wrong?

"There being but one Truth, one way to Heaven, what Hopes is there that more Men would be led to it, if they had no Rule but the Religion of the Court, and were put under a necessity to quit the Light of their own Reason, and oppose the Dictates of their own Consciences, and blindly to resign up themselves to the Will of their Governors, and to the Religion, which either Ignorance, Ambition, or Superstition had chanced to establish in the Countries where they were born?" People might be damned simply by virtue of where they were born.

On the other hand, Locke went on, there was *the Church,* which "I take to be a voluntary Society of men, joining themselves together of their own accord, in order to the publick worshipping of God, in such a manner as they judge acceptable to him, and effectual to the

Salvation of their souls." NB what Locke is *not* saying here. He is not arguing for the idea of "spiritual but not religious" which many Americans now take to be the essence of "real" religion: not bound to anybody else's ideas of what spirituality should be.

The whole point of a Church, as Locke sees it, is to gather together in public to worship God. It is a voluntary society, not something one is born into, but it is a society for worship which can make laws for itself and the regulation of its membership. It is not obliged to allow just anybody to be a member, but neither can its punishments go beyond exclusion from membership in the society for its purpose of worship: "For Churches have neither any Jurisdiction in Worldly matters, nor are Fire and Sword any proper Instruments wherewith to convince men's minds of Error, and inform them of the Truth." Just as the Civil Magistrate cannot force people to believe things about the way in which they should worship, nor can the Church deprive anyone of his Civil Rights to Life, Liberty, Health, and the Possession of outward things.

Here Locke was categorical: "No man whatsoever ought to be deprived of his Terrestrial Enjoyments, upon account of his Religion. Not even *Americans* [by which he meant the indigenous peoples of the New World], subjected unto a Christian Prince, are to be punished either in Body or Goods, for not embracing our Faith and Worship. If they are perswaded that they please God in observing the Rites of their own Country, and that they shall obtain Happiness by that means, they are to be left unto God and themselves." (Here Locke had clearly been reading Las Casas or arguments derived from Las Casas's *In Defense of the Indians*.)

And yet, there were limits. *First*: "No Opinions contrary to human Society, or to those moral Rules which are necessary to the preservation of Civil Society, are to be tolerated by the Magistrate." Happily,

Locke believed, such opinions were rare: "For no Sect can easily arrive to such a degree of madness, as that it should think fit to teach, for Doctrines of Religion, such things as manifestly undermine the Foundations of Society, and are therefore condemned by the Judgment of all Mankind: because their own Interest, Peace, Reputation, every Thing, would be thereby endangered." (Locke had clearly never met a Marxist revolutionary.)

Second: The Civil Magistrate ought not to tolerate those who refuse to keep their promises or who argue that the prince ought to be dethroned or who claim Dominion over the Community as a whole.

Third: "That Church can have no right to be tolerated by the Magistrate, which is constituted upon such a bottom, that all those who enter into it, do thereby, *ipso facto*, deliver themselves up to the Protection and Service of another Prince." Most particularly, Locke insists, Muslims: "It is ridiculous for any one to profess himself to be a *Mahumetan* only in his Religion, but in every thing else a faithful Subject to a Christian Magistrate, whilst at the same time he acknowledges himself bound to yield blind obedience to the *Mufti* of *Constantinople*; who himself is intirely obedient to the *Ottoman* Emperor, and frames the feigned Oracles of that Religion according to his pleasure. But this Mahumetan living among Christians, would yet more apparently renounce their Government, if he acknowledged the same Person to be Head of his Church who is the Supreme Magistrate in the State."

Fourth: There were Atheists, upon whom "Promises, Covenants, and Oaths, which are the Bonds of Society," could have no hold: "The taking away of God, tho but even in thought, dissolves all. Besides also, those that by their Atheism undermine and destroy all Religion, can have no pretence of Religion whereupon to challenge the Privilege of Toleration. As for other Practical Opinions, tho not absolutely free from all Error, if they do not tend to establish Domination over others, of Civil Impunity to the Church in which they are taught, there can be no Reason why they should not be tolerated."

৪৯

Locke goes on to consider the question of schisms and heresies, but at no point does he say anything about being nice or doing unto others or trying to see things from another's point of view. At stake are not feelings, but Truth and the access to Truth, which Locke insists the State cannot deny. Nor does Locke claim that there are multiple Truths, all of which should be considered equally true. Quite the reverse.

In Locke's view, as in that of his contemporaries, there was one Truth, one Way, one Life to which human beings were called. The problem was discerning which way was the true one, what form of worship was correct. The danger, as Locke saw it, was in giving the Civil Magistrate the power to coerce any particular form of worship against the conscience of the people living under his jurisdiction, as the Magistrate, being Caesar, not God, might be in error, and thus coerce the whole Commonwealth to damnation.

This did *not* mean, however, that there should be no State. The whole concept of Civil Society depends, in Locke's view, on there being such a thing as a Civil Government under the authority of a Magistrate who is empowered by law and use of force to protect the Life, Liberty, Health, and Possessions of the people of the Commonwealth.

Toleration was a matter of civic order: the Church kept within its proper bounds, the State kept within its. Just as the Church was defined by its function (public worship), so the State was defined by its function (protecting the Life, Liberty, Health, and Possessions of those living under its jurisdiction). The problem, as Locke explained to his friend, came when these two jurisdictions became confused: the

State attempting to regulate worship, the Church claiming jurisdiction not only over people's souls, but also their bodies and property. Toleration, for Locke, meant not confusing these jurisdictions.

Which is why, as a political concept, it has its limits. Christianity may claim that God's kingdom is not of this world, but this is not, as Locke appreciated, the way in which Muslims conceive of the jurisdiction of their law. Certainly, if there were Muslims who were willing for the jurisdiction of *sharia* to apply only to their souls and not to their property and bodies, Locke's definition of toleration would apply.

Likewise, as Locke would have it, if there were atheists willing to swear oaths, that is, to bind themselves with their promises to abide by the rules of Civil Society, they might be tolerated, but for Locke, as for his contemporaries, it was inconceivable that people who did not believe in God might be so bound. Nor, according to Locke, ought the Civil Magistrate to tolerate those dedicated to the destruction of the Civil Society or to Morals. Toleration would not be a virtue if it led to the downfall of the State, which, in effect, Locke was reassuring his friend it would not. What mattered was the freedom to worship God according to the dictates of one's conscience while at the same time enjoying Liberty, earthly Possessions, and Life.

§

As we like to say at the University of Chicago, *so what?* Well, it all depends on what kind of society we want to live in. Thanks to Protestants like Locke, the Founders of our country were convinced that the way people worship God should not be a matter for the State, although their descendants in the nineteenth century had problems with accepting Catholics as fellow Christians, whom they feared were beholden to a foreign prince (the pope). (If you doubt me, see Mark Twain's *A Connecticut Yankee in King Arthur's Court.*) The real question is what to do with those who do not see the State in the same terms, as a protector of property rights and liberty (which Marxists reject) or as distinct from the Church (which, according to their own ideals, many Muslims do not).

Locke, being Christian, was able to conceive of a society in which the Church (what is God's) remained distinct from the State (what is Caesar's). Do we really want to live in a society in which there is only the State (Marxism) or in which the Church and the State are one (Islam)? If the answer to either of these options is no, as I suspect for most Americans it is, then how do we deal with those in our State who would choose the State alone, abolishing both property rights and liberty, or conversely who would identify the State with the Church, such that the law of the Church would be identical with the law of the land?

WHY I LOVE MILO

February 1, 2017

It's been quite the journey. Back in September, when the Dangerous Faggot Tour was just getting back on the road, Milo had about 200,000 followers on Facebook, but of course none of his previous 350,000 by that point on Twitter. At about the same time, the dean of students at the University of Chicago, where I teach, sent out a letter to our incoming freshmen reasserting our commitment to academic freedom. The dean's letter along with its accompanying booklet caused quite the storm both on our campus and throughout the academic world at large. It was nothing compared to what was to come over the next few months in reaction to Milo's tour.[140]

"We do not cancel speakers because their topics might prove controversial, and we do not condone the creation of intellectual 'safe spaces' where individuals can retreat from ideas and perspectives at odds with their own," Dean of Students John Ellison informed our students, their parents, my colleagues, and everyone else who cares about higher education in our country.

---

[140] https://www.breitbart.com/social-justice/2017/01/30/wsj-milo-stirring-things-campuses-speaker/

At the time, I had heard of Milo, that he was gay and saying things that seemed to upset my academic colleagues, and I was dimly aware that something had happened when he came to our city to speak at DePaul. I was fairly sure it was his talks (as well as Ben Shapiro's) that had been part of the stimulus behind the dean's letter. I had read some of Milo's articles on *Breitbart* and liked them, but I knew nothing of his history with GamerGate, and although I had read his review of *Ghostbusters*, I was blissfully unaware of the Twitterstorm over Leslie Jones.

Being curious, and like Milo, a natural contrarian, I wanted to know what all the fuss was about, particularly since I had been involved in my very own skirmish with the Social Justice Warriors at about the same time Milo was starting the first leg of his Tour the previous winter. (The blog post that sparked my personal feminist gaspfest was entitled "Talking Points: Three Cheers for White Men."[141] Yes, really!) That week in September, I spent three days back-to-back watching the videos of the talks that Milo had given the previous spring. And fell in love. A few Sundays ago, our catechumen class was discussing the passage in the gospel of Matthew (4:18-20) where Jesus, having been baptized, had begun to preach and gather followers.

> As he walked by the Sea of Galilee, he saw two brothers, Simon who is called Peter and Andrew his brother, casting a net into the sea; for they were fisherman. And he said to them: "Follow me, and I will make you fishers of men." Immediately, they left their nets and followed him.

"Have you ever had an experience like this?" our teacher asked. "Can you imagine simply dropping everything to follow someone in the way that Peter and Andrew did? What must it have been like for them, to give up their livelihood, everything they had known, in order to follow Jesus? What do you think they saw in him?" One of the

[141] https://fencingbearatprayer.blogspot.com/2015/06/talking-points-three-cheers-for-white.html

students replied: "It didn't come out of the blue. They had probably been praying for something like this to happen to them. They were most likely very spiritual men and had been longing for the Spirit to come into their lives."

Don't get me wrong. Milo, godlike though he may be, is not God. But he dropped into my life and, to judge from their testimonies, into the lives of his now 1.3 million Facebook followers like the answer to a prayer. In September, he told the incredulous ABC interviewer who was grilling him about being a troll in the *Ghostbusters* Twitter exchange: "I like to think of myself as being a virtuous troll... I'm doing God's work.... Trolls are the only people who tell the truth these days." My own friends on Facebook, people I went to high school and college with, people who like me have spent our careers in academia, have spent the last several months trying to shame me out of my admiration for Milo. One calls him my "vile boyfriend." Another makes rude comments on my threads and says he is just following Milo's example.

Another accuses me of not caring about truth because "it is part of the alt-right's strategy" now to "lie, lie, lie." Another, just yesterday, spent hours insisting I have "lost it": "Please explain how Milo is doing 'good,' helping poor disrespected white supremacists?.... You embarrass me.... You have indeed lost your mind.... Have you considered that you have a common obsessive compulsive disorder focused on media Milo?" (This latter was an interesting exchange: the more I posted what I thought of as evidence for Milo's positive appeal, the more my friend became convinced I was crazy.)

By far the most important thing that Milo has taught me is how to counter such attacks with laughter. As Milo always says, "Nobody can resist the truth wrapped in a good joke." And yet, as we have seen with the protests mounted with increasing fervor over the course of his Tour, they will try as hard as they can never to listen. And they will scream and scream and scream and scream lest somebody let the laughter in.

I love Milo because he tells the truth. He tells the truth about women (for which he is called a misogynist), that some of them quite like the thought of becoming mothers and are willing to make choices about their careers that mean they do not work the same kinds of hours or in the dangerous—and therefore higher-paying—jobs that men do. He tells the truth about Black Lives Matter (for which he is called a racist), that the movement does not focus on the real problems in the black community like bad schools and the high rate of abortion and the lack of fathers that make it so difficult for black Americans to get out of the cycles of gang-violence and poverty that afflict so many of them, particularly black young men.

He tells the truth about Islam (for which he is called Islamophobic), that in countries under Muslim-majority rule, women and gays do not enjoy the freedoms that they do in the Christian-majority countries of the West; indeed, in many such countries under *sharia*, women are denied what we consider in the West basic human rights, and gays are legally killed. He tells the truth about immigration (for which he is called a white nationalist), that America and the U.K. deserve to have borders that are legally enforced so that they can choose who comes into their countries, because preserving their culture and traditions matters.

He tells the truth about being fat (for which he is called hateful), that it is not healthy, that most people do not find it as attractive or pleasurable as being thin, and that encouraging young women to become fat is only to guarantee that they will be miserable and alone. He tells the truth about young men (for which, again, he called a misogynist, as well as a white supremacist), that they are not served well by our educational system's focus on women at the expense of the kinds of activities and discipline that would enable boys to become responsible and successful men.

He tells the truth about gays (for which he is called homophobic), that it is vindictive and mean to go after family-owned pizza restaurants simply for standing up for their religious convictions in not supporting gay marriage. He tells the truth about the gamers (for which he is called, again, a misogynist), that they were right to push back against the politically-correct journalism trying to tell them what games they were allowed to play.

He tells the truth about feminists (for which is he called...you know by now), that those who now call themselves feminists seem more intent on bashing men than in ensuring equality of opportunity for women and men. He tells the truth about the media (for which they will never forgive him), that they lie and lie and lie and lie *all the time* about conservative and libertarian values and ideals and the people who hold them. And he tells the truth about the Left (for which he is called a fascist), that it is they who turn to violence when they do not get their own way.[142]

He is also, of course, devastatingly handsome, to the despair of women and white men everywhere. (Don't tell me you haven't heard about his black boyfriends.) But he is likewise a talented speaker, riveting in his ability to draw his audience into his talks. Even more important, however, he has fun as he speaks—the costumes, the stunts, the slides, the jokes—all the while making serious points that those screaming outside refuse to hear. As Tom Ciccotta beautifully explained in his recent account of the Tour:[143]

---

[142] https://www.breitbart.com/social-justice/2017/02/01/protesters-gather-uc-berkeley-milo-show-police-helicopters-appear/

[143] https://www.breitbart.com/tech/2017/01/31/ciccotta-milos-provocation-catalyst-conversation-common-ground/

MILO's provocation forced progressive students to take their conservative and libertarian peers seriously. He reminded us of the necessity of intellectual diversity in academia. He taught us to hit back hard when we were treated unfairly. He taught conservatives how to loosen up and laugh at themselves. And he gave college campuses the wake-up call that they desperately needed.

I love Milo because rather than sitting wringing his hands over the lack of intellectual diversity on our college campuses, he brought the fight out into the open and exposed the lies of the Left for the lies that they are. He told the truth that the Left, along with all of my colleagues who think of themselves as progressive and liberal, has been unwilling to hear: that America is the greatest country in the history of human civilization, but that it is ours only so long as we are willing to fight. Milo himself put it best, back in November, when he received the Annie Taylor Award for Courage in Journalism:[144]

So let us fight, but let our motto be Risus et bellum, Laughter and war. Because nothing stings our foes, foreign and domestic, more than our hearty laughter at their lies and nonsense. And also because nothing will better remind us what we're fighting for than the laughter of Chesterton, of Chaucer and of Shakespeare, and of course the God who inspired them all.

And you wonder that I dropped everything to follow his Tour.

---

[144] https://www.breitbart.com/social-justice/2016/11/12/full-text-milos-annie-taylor-award-acceptance-speech-david-horowitzs-restoration-weekend/

HERESIES OF THE LEFT: UNHOLY TRINITY

February 13, 2017

Evil does not exist except as a corruption of the Good. Every falsehood or lie contains something of Truth. The same is true of heresies. Every heresy is a corruption of some aspect of orthodox doctrine, which is why heresies are so hard for the orthodox to answer.[145] The orthodox trip themselves up trying to negate the heresies directly, which they cannot do without denying the truth and goodness at their core. This is why conservatives have so much trouble answering the Left (other than the fact that, as Milo rightly says, we are too often spineless cunts). Everything that the Left believes is grounded in a central claim of Western civilization, more often than not a central claim of Christianity or the Judeo-Christian tradition.

The Left, of course, denies this hotly, pointing for support for their doctrines to the "scientific teachings" of the prophet Marx or the "Enlightened" ideals of the prophet Robespierre. But the Left defend their beliefs with the vehemence that they do—as every conservative

---

[145] https://fencingbearatprayer.blogspot.com/2017/01/how-to-spot-heretic.html

who has ever tried to engage them in debate instantly learns—because their beliefs are neither "scientific" nor "rational," but matters of faith.

For example, the claim that all men and women are created equal, to which both conservatives and Leftists in the West subscribe, albeit they differ on what it means for social policy. Or the claim that it is the responsibility of those who have, to care for those who have not, ditto on application. Or the claim that every human being has an inherent dignity and right to life, to which even the Left subscribes when the mother says so.[146] (I'm sorry, I am having real problems not being catty about abortion these days.)

Just as the above claims have their root in the belief that *all* human beings, male or female, are made in the image and likeness of God (Genesis 1:26-27), so the tenets of multiculturalism, identity politics, and the fear of hate speech—to name only some of the things that the Left is currently up in arms about, sometimes literally—have their roots in orthodox teachings of Christianity.[147] The problem, which is what makes these tenets heresies, is that they have become unmoored from their orthodox origins and allowed to drift.

If they seem to have no bottom and to be sinking Western civilization fast, this is why. Each of these three is a heresy against one of the Persons of the Trinity, a distortion of the proper relationship between the Idea (Father), Energy (Son), and Power (Spirit) of the Divine Artist's working in the world.[148]

THE HERESY OF THE SPIRIT: MULTICULTURALISM

Not every culture in the world is as welcoming of other cultures as is the West. Yes, the world is now aesthetically and technologically

[146] https://fencingbearatprayer.blogspot.com/2017/01/gods-vagina.html

[147] https://www.breitbart.com/social-justice/2017/02/01/rioters-beat/

[148] Dorothy Sayers, *The Mind of the Maker* (1987)

Westernized—everyone who is anyone wears jeans or business suits, drives cars, watches television and movies, talks on mobile phones, builds skyscrapers and highways—but this is not so much multiculturalism as, in Milo's words, the way art and technology work. Human beings are great imitators. If we see something we like, we try to make more things like it.

Multiculturalism is not just enjoying food or clothes or music from other parts of the world. It is the insistence that every human culture is equal to every other in dignity and value, much as is every human being. What those in the West who enjoy traveling to other countries and appreciating the differences in customs and mores do not typically appreciate, however, is that their admiration for other cultures and mores is not necessarily reciprocated.

Many Muslims have no interest whatsoever in becoming Westernized or appreciating the differences between Muslim and Christian culture. Likewise, many Chinese or Indians are quite happy being Chinese or Indian and not Westerners. What we Westerners admire as the rich diversity of human experience, others see as vice or disorder, the breakdown of proper custom, disrespect for tradition. They don't care if we come in and praise their culture: they know their culture is superior to ours.

So why are Westerners so keen on other cultures, sometimes even at the expense of their own? In a word: Pentecost, the moment when the Holy Spirit descended upon the apostles and they were empowered to speak so that everyone who had gathered in Jerusalem for the feast (Pentecost was originally a Jewish feast) heard them speaking in his or her own tongue:

> And [the people] were amazed and wondered, saying, "Are not all these who are speaking Galileans? And how is it that we hear, each of us in his own native language? Parthians and Medes and Elamites

and residents of Mesopotamia, Judea and Cappadocia, Pontus and Asia, Phrygia and Pamphylia, Egypt and the parts of Libya belonging to Cyrene, and visitors from Rome, both Jews and proselytes [Gentile converts], Cretans and Arabians, we hear them telling in our own tongues the mighty works of God" (Acts 2:7-11).

Christians took this moment of multilingualism as a guide: God meant to speak to humanity in all the languages of the world. There was no one language, for example, Arabic, in which the divine words needed to be preserved. Rather, the Scriptures were to be translated, made accessible to everyone in his or her native tongue. The Hebrew Bible had already been translated into Greek in the third century BC. In the first centuries of the Christian era, the Scriptures including the New Testament were translated into Latin, Gothic, Armenian, Syriac, Coptic, Old Nubian, Ethiopic, and Georgian. Even in the darkest of the Dark Ages, there were translations into Old English, Old Saxon, and Old Church Slavonic. By the high Middle Ages, there were also translations into Old French, Middle English, and Czech.

The Reformation brought a great landslide of new translations, but the ideal had long been in place. When the Spanish arrived in the New World, one of the first things the missionaries attempted was to translate the Scriptures into Nahuatl. According to Wikipedia, the Bible has now been translated in full into 636 languages and into 3,223 in part.[149] (Here's another Wikipedia list with different numbers.[150] Let's go with "lots.")

What to many modern Leftists looks like cultural appropriation or, worse, cultural imperialism on the part of the Christian missionaries of the nineteenth and early twentieth centuries was seen at the time (and still is by those who care about spreading God's word) as a way to fulfill the promise of Pentecost: that God's mighty works might be told

[149] https://en.wikipedia.org/wiki/Bible_translations
[150] https://en.wikipedia.org/wiki/List_of_Bible_translations_by_language

to everyone in his or her own language so that all might hear and be saved. This is likewise the source of the admiration in which Western Christians hold all the cultures which produced these languages. God, they believe, did not privilege any particular language or culture, but meant for his works to be made known to all.

This is the reason that the nineteenth- and twentieth-century missionaries made such great efforts to learn the languages of the peoples to whom they were sent and why the West to this day is convinced that everyone ought to be brought into the literate, developed world, regardless of culture or tradition. The irony, of course, is that without the belief in Pentecost, multiculturalism has no creed, no reason for all peoples to become one in their diversity. As a heresy of the Spirit, this means that rather than an expression of the Power of God's word acting for the salvation of all, it becomes simply an expression of power, the imposition of a single cultural ideal (diversity for the sake of diversity) on every culture in the world.

THE HERESY OF THE SON: HATE SPEECH

"What is hate speech?" Tucker Carlson asked Milo the night after the Berkeley riots.[151] "I don't know!" Milo replied.

> I'm probably going to get into terrible trouble with [Simon and Schuster], but I have no idea and I don't think anybody else knows either, I mean it seems to be speech that somebody doesn't like somewhere, a joke that's wrong, something that offends somebody's sensibilities or hurt feelings or politics or something, certainly the Supreme Court doesn't recognize it as a kind of speech that should be treated with any special reverence or whatever.
>
> Hate speech, it seems to me, has been defined by the political left as "anything we don't like," anything that violates social justice doctrine,

---

[151] https://www.breitbart.com/social-justice/2017/02/02/full-transcript-milo-tucker-carlson-tonight/

feminism, Black Lives Matter kind of ideology; it's not something that I have ever heard particularly effectively defined.

Milo is right to be confused. There is no such thing as hate speech in the sense of speech that by its content can be identified as such, and thus, for example, edited out of a book. Hate speech is not about the content of one's speech, but about speech conceptualized as a form of action. It is speech *as an act,* in the formulation made famous by J.L. Austin's *How to Do Things with Words* (1955/1962).

The most famous example of Austin's premise—that words are sometimes not just expressive of ideas, but themselves actions—is the wedding vow: "I do." Such utterances are not assertions of truth or falsehood, but performances, what Austin would call "speech-acts," speech that effects the thing that is said. Saying "I do," the bride and bridegroom effect their marriage. It is their speaking the words that makes their marriage real. Naming people or things, making a vow or a bequest in a will are other examples of such "speech-acts."

Judith Butler—who teaches at Berkeley and is, not incidentally, one of the most prominent gender theorists in the academy—took this idea of performative speech and ran with it in her *Excitable Speech: A Politics of the Performative* (1997). According to Butler, hate speech, given that it is a kind of performance rather than content (which is why Milo can't define it) exists only retrospectively (I am cribbing here from Wikipedia), making it a matter for the state to define—and silence—regardless, it would seem of the intent of the speaker. Here, therefore, Milo is right: hate speech is what those in power do not like.

Which in itself is pretty terrifying. What should be even more terrifying, however, is the reason that Butler gives for the state to become involved in censorship at all. Here I am dependent on my colleague Amy Hollywood, who has studied Butler's work in depth.

Bear with me, I think the answer to Tucker's question is buried somewhere in this passage from Hollywood's most recent book:

> To clarify the relationship between the force of the performative and the body, Butler points to the importance of body lying behind the threat of hate speech. The language of the body itself, in fact, is part of the speech act and determines its force and how its force is read (that is, as threat, joke, citation). When asked why speech and the body should be given precedence given the fact that anonymous hate mail is potentially as hurtful as spoken utterances, Butler suggests that even if "performatives cannot always be retethered to their moment of utterance...they carry the anemic trace of the body in the force that they exercise." In other words, hate mail threatens insofar as it carries the trace of the addresser's body and the body of the addressee is then marked by the force of the utterance. There seems to be a certain circularity to Butler's argument, however, for the force of the utterance on the body of the addressee points to the speaking body. Perhaps the materiality of hate mail and of language itself effects this movement from the body of the addressee to that of the speaker.[152]

With all due respect to my academic colleagues, again in Milo's words, this is bonkers. Speech cannot act on bodies, only on minds. (Unless perhaps you are yelling loudly enough to hurt someone's eardrums, in which case it is not what is said, but the volume that hurts.) Words cannot do anything except change people's minds or excite their emotions, and even then, as every good Stoic knows, it is up to the listener how to respond. Why, then, do so many people believe that there is such a thing as *hate speech*, speech that *as speech* can hurt?

Here's an even more famous example of words doing something: "And God said, 'Let there be light,' and there was light." (Genesis 1:3). (You can see where I am going with this, yes?) Here's another: "And the Word became flesh and dwelt among us, full of grace and

---

[152] *Acute Melancholia and Other Essays: Mysticism, History, and the Study of Religion* (2016)

truth; we have beheld his glory, glory as of the only Son from the Father" (John 1:14). If Butler insists that words can take on flesh, "carry the anemic trace of the body in the force that they exercise," this is why. Deny it though I am certain she would, she is thinking Incarnationally, within a tradition that asserts that the Word became Flesh. Speech became Body. Locution became Act.

As a heresy of the Son, the idea of hate speech has terrible energy to work on the world. It is a distortion of the mystery of the relationship between God and creation, of the outpouring of love by which God entered into the world he made in order to remake it through his own suffering. Yes, incarnation hurts, bodies feel pain. But that is not the fault of speech; it is the fault of our fallenness for believing a lie.[153]

THE HERESY OF THE FATHER: IDENTITY POLITICS

Identity politics defines people according to their physical and heritable attributes rather than their ideas or character. Women, blacks, gays, Muslims: all are essentialized by identity politics according to their biology (women), biology and heritage (American blacks), biology and behavior (gays), biology defined as religious belief (Muslims).

The idea behind identity politics is that you, regardless of what you think about God or the relations between the sexes or the morality of abortion or the benefits of restrictions on government authority, ought to participate in a consciousness of yourself as a member of your identity group. From this perspective, thinking differently from other members of your identity group is not just unthinkable, but evil.

---

[153] https://fencingbearatprayer.blogspot.com/2016/12/rhetoric-101-clickbait.html

Why should it matter so much that Milo thinks about homosexuality differently from other gays?[154] Or that I think about abortion or feminism differently from other women? Or that Stacey Dash thinks about the role of the State differently from other black Americans?[155] Why? Because thinking differently quite literally threatens the existence of the group.

All human groups depend to a certain extent on ideas, even families, certainly neighborhoods and nations. With most such groups, the big question is how individuals come to understand themselves as belonging, with such understanding recognized as a voluntary act. I may be born an American citizen, but growing up, I need to be educated in order to understand what acting as an American means. I may be baptized as a baby, but growing up, I need to be educated in order to understand what believing as a Christian means. Neither state of belonging is a given: I may choose to renounce my American citizenship or apostatize from the faith. I may even choose to distance myself from my family, for example, by following Christ.

With identity politics, there is literally no way out: I am born a woman, white, heterosexual, Christian (see why the category "Muslim" doesn't quite fit?). To think differently from other women, whites, heterosexuals, or Christians is to deny my very existence as a white, heterosexual, Christian woman. It is not voluntary, it is determined, much as my species is determined: I am human.

Can you think of any other categories for which it is typically claimed that there is only one proper way to think about what it means to be a member of that group? How about "bourgeoisie"? (Do you see where I am going with this argument yet?) Or conversely,

---

[154] https://www.out.com/out-exclusives/2016/9/21/send-clown-internet-supervillain-milo-doesnt-care-you-hate-him

[155] https://www.cnsnews.com/news/article/mark-judge/stacey-dash-im-being-persecuted-hollywood-ive-been-blacklisted

"proletariat"? What is the central claim of Marxist thinking about these two groups? *The ABC of Communism* (1919) is helpful here.[156] In Nicolai Ivanovich Bukharin and Yevgeni Preobrazhensky's words:

> In order that the proletariat may gain the victory in any country, it is essential that it should be compact and well organized; it is essential that it should have its own Communist Party which has clearly recognized the trend of capitalist development, which has understood the actual situation and the true interests of the working class, which has adequately interpreted that situation, which is competent to marshal the ranks and to conduct the battle.

And why do the proletariat need the Party to act for them?

> Nowhere and at no time has any party been able to enroll all the members of the class which it represents; never has any class attained the requisite degree of consciousness.

The proletariat exists as a class, but it is oppressed by the bourgeoisie because it is not conscious of itself as a class. The bourgeoisie, of course, are conscious of themselves as a class and work always to further their own interests, but the proletariat, in Marxist thinking, needs leaders to act for them, because otherwise they will be duped into acquiescing to bourgeois thinking about the nature of society and never come to consciousness of the struggle in which they are involved.

Sound familiar? I, as a woman, am not conscious of the degree to which I am oppressed by the patriarchy, so feminists need to speak for me. I, as a white person, am not conscious of my privilege, so I need Black Lives Matter to point it out for me. I, as a heterosexual, am not conscious of my normativity, so I need gender theorists like Butler to raise my consciousness. I, as a Christian...no, you can't get me there, as I hope I am making clear.

Marx focused mainly on class, but as feminists, Black Lives Matter, and gender theorists have made clear, this idea of group

---

[156] https://fencingbearatprayer.blogspot.com/2017/02/the-church-of-left.html

self-consciousness has broad applications. (If you want to understand the force of the accusations "male," "white," "heterosexual," just substitute "bourgeois." The sneers are all of a piece.) This is because the idea wasn't originally Marx's and wasn't, in fact, about class. It was about our consciousness of ourselves as a species, that is, as human.

Here is the argument as Marx discovered it in Ludwig Feuerbach.[157] (You may have heard Milo mention Feuerbach, here's why). According to Feuerbach, the essential nature of man, as opposed to that of animals, is to be conscious of himself as belonging to a species. While animals may think about themselves as individuals, human beings think not just about themselves, but about all human beings as if they are one: "Science is the cognizance of species. In practical life we have to do with individuals; in science, with species. But only a being to whom his own species, his own nature, is an object of thought, can make the essential nature of other things or beings an object of thought."

Feuerbach moves from this essential characteristic of human beings— that we think about ourselves *as human*—to posit how we think about God. "Man," he says, "—this is the mystery of religion—projects his being into objectivity, and then again makes himself an object to this projected image of himself thus converted into a subject... Man is an object to God... God is the highest subjectivity of man abstracted from himself." In Feuerbach's argument, what we think about as God "is nothing else than... the human nature purified, freed from the limits of the individual man, made objective—i.e. contemplated and revered as another, a distinct being."

To talk about God, according to Feuerbach, is in effect to talk about man: "To doubt of God is to doubt of myself... Hence he alone is the true atheist to whom the predicates of the Divine Being—for example, love, wisdom, justice—are nothing; not he to whom merely the subject

---

[157] *The Essence of Christianity*, trans. George Eliot (1854)

of these predicates is nothing.... The fact is not that a quality is divine because God has it, but that God has it because it is in itself divine."

Think for a moment about what Feuerbach is arguing here. Our highest being, our humanity, is defined by our consciousness of being human. Conversely, not to be so conscious of ourselves would be to descend to the level of the beasts (George Eliot used the word "brutes" in her translation of Feuerbach), to become subhuman, dehumanized. Arguably, therefore, only those who attain full consciousness of themselves as human are, by Feuerbach's definition, human, meaning that those who do not, are not. They are animals. Bourgeois. White. Heteronormative. Not-us.

This is the heresy against the Father, against the idea according to which all human beings were created in the image and likeness of God. Feuerbach thought he was being clever, making God a projection of human self-consciousness, an artifact of human making, but as with the heresies of multiculturalism and hate speech, his argument makes sense only from within a Judeo-Christian understanding of God. Feuerbach made of God the Great Artifact.

But, as Dorothy Sayers would put it, he was already primed by the Christian creed—"I believe in God the Father Almighty, Maker of heaven and earth"—to look for an Artist in whose image and likeness he had been made. Identity politics are evil because they insist that only some of us share in this image. That because only some of us are conscious of ourselves as certain kinds of creatures, only some of us are fully human beings.

JOKING MATTERS

February 18, 2017

Milo is dangerous, everyone agrees. Well, not quite everyone. (Me, for example.) Certainly journalist Jeremy Scahill thinks he is. Invited to appear with Milo on *Real Time with Bill Maher*, Scahill refused, insisting, along with almost everyone else who has written about Milo except Tom Ciccotta and me that Milo incites violence.[158],[159] (He doesn't; the only person Milo has ever called for violence against is Dylann Roof, in the form of the death penalty.[160]) In Scahill's words: "Yiannopoulos has shown he will use his appearances to publicly attack and shame specific ordinary people by name, a practice which could lead to violence or even death."[161]

---

[158] https://www.breitbart.com/tech/2017/01/31/ciccotta-milos-provocation-catalyst-conversation-common-ground/

[159] https://divinity.uchicago.edu/sightings/why-milo-scares-students-and-faculty-even-more

[160] https://www.breitbart.com/border/2017/01/05/convicted-killer-dylann-roof-faces-sentencing/

[161] https://www.breitbart.com/social-justice/2017/02/15/jeremy-scahill-accuses-milo-fomenting-violence-refuses-appear-bill-maher/

Bill Maher would beg to differ.[162] "You are so, let's say, helped, by the fact that liberals just always take the bait," he acknowledged in his interview with Milo last night. And then Maher cautioned his side: "Stop taking the bait, liberals! The fact that they all freaked out about this little, impish, British fag.... You f*cking schoolgirls. You schoolgirls!" Most people never hear what Milo actually talks about, they only hear about his jokes. Jokes about Lena Dunham, Amy Schumer, and Sarah Silverman. Jokes about Caitlyn Jenner. Above all, jokes about Leslie Jones.

These are the jokes for which Milo was banned from Twitter last summer and for which the media will never forgive him. It doesn't matter that nothing Milo said about Jones was anything remotely like what Scahill and others claim that he said. Milo, a gay man, makes jokes about celebrity (not ordinary) women, including one celebrity black woman, and it is his fault that others agree with him that Lena Dunham, Amy Schumer, and Sarah Silverman aren't funny (they aren't) or that Caitlyn Jenner is (this one is harder for me, but I take Milo's point about the need to talk about transgenderism as an issue; plus Jenner, like Milo, has been slammed for being conservative, go figure[163]).

Or, yes, that Leslie Jones looks like a man, more precisely, "black dude," which as Milo constantly points out, was as much a joke at his own expense as hers. (Milo likes black male lovers, if you haven't heard.) *Full transcript for those who missed the spat*[164]: Jones had been Tweeting about the bad reviews *Ghostbusters* was getting, one of

---

[162] https://www.breitbart.com/clips/2017/02/17/maher-to-lefties-angry-about-milo-stop-taking-the-bait-youre-freaked-out-over-a-little-impish-fg-you-schoolgirls/

[163] https://www.breitbart.com/entertainment/2016/02/18/bruce-jenner-trans-hollywood-easier-republican/

[164] https://www.breitbart.com/social-justice/2016/07/18/ghostbuster-leslie-jones-reports-milo/

which Milo wrote, "Teenage Boys with Tits: Here's My Problem with Ghostbusters."[165] Milo jumped into the Twitter fray with: "If at first you don't succeed (because your work is terrible), play the victim. EVERYONE GETS HATE MAIL FFS." Jones reported Milo to Twitter and called one of his fans a "racist b*tch" for saying "how sad that a comedian would want to limit free speech. Lenny Bruce is rolling over in his grave."

Milo responded to Jones: "Ghostbusters is doing so badly they've deployed @Lesdoggg to play the victim on Twitter. Very sad!" "Barely literate. America needs better schools." At which point, he was blocked from linking to her account. To which Milo replied: "Rejected by yet another black dude." And that was it.

To be fair, Milo also makes jokes about Muslims (because in many Muslim-majority countries they believe that it should be legal to kill gays for being gay), about gays (because they believe that all Muslims are their friends and that Christian pizza makers are their enemies), about lesbians (whom he says give bad advice to other women about how to relate to men), about professors (particularly those who penalize their students for holding conservative or libertarian political views), and about Black Lives Matter (because they seem not to care about all black lives, particularly those lives lost to other blacks as opposed to the police).

But he also makes jokes about conservatives (whom he has called "spineless cunts"), Republicans (ditto), and gamers (whom he now defends, but once described as "dorky weirdos in yellowing underpants"). Above all, however, he makes jokes about himself. As, for example, his choice of costume last night for his interview with Bill Maher. Milo is perfectly capable of dressing in a suit; look at the one he wore for his interview with Tucker Carlson the night

---

[165] https://www.breitbart.com/tech/2016/07/18/milo-reviews-ghostbusters/

after the Berkeley riot.[166] Okay, yes, there is the pink shirt, but Milo's tailoring is impeccable. Compare this look with what he chose for his interview with Maher. Full-on pearls, there must not be an oyster left with its dewdrop from heaven[167]; bomber jacket from ALLSAINTS (yes, he's Catholic, he's doing this on purpose), camouflage pants, and limited edition Black History Month Air Jordans (in homage to his boyfriends). Could he be any more gay? Okay, yes, which is my point![168] He is doing this on purpose.

Likewise, his trolling of his fellow panelists in the Overtime segment. Do you think it was an accident that he suggested in the midst of the give-and-take with comedian Larry Wilmore over Milo's opinions on transgenderism and gays that Maher should invite guests with higher IQs on his show?[169] To which Wilmore replied, right on cue: "First of all, you can go f*ck yourself alright... If your argument is that these people are stupid, you didn't hear a word that this man said earlier in this segment because he can talk circles around your pathetic, douchey little ass." The audience loved that! But so did Milo, as you can see from his grin.

Maher is right. Milo is an imp—and he relishes it. He is an imp, a clown, a fool.[170],[171] Or, as I prefer to call him, a holy fool. He is dangerous not because he incites violence (again, he *never* does, except

---

[166] https://www.breitbart.com/social-justice/2017/02/02/full-transcript-milo-tucker-carlson-tonight/

[167] https://fencingbearatprayer.blogspot.com/2009/01/pearl-of-great-price.html

[168] https://www.breitbart.com/social-justice/2016/09/21/full-photos-milo-appears-louisiana-state-drag-queen-ivana-wall/

[169] https://www.breitbart.com/social-justice/2017/02/17/larry-wilmore-melts-bill-maher-tells-milo-go-fuck/

[170] https://www.out.com/out-exclusives/2016/9/21/send-clown-internet-supervillain-milo-doesnt-care-you-hate-him

[171] https://psmag.com/news/how-much-longer-can-the-milo-yiannopolous-show-last#.6adp29k3h

against Dylann Roof), but because in being willing to make himself a fool, he forces others to recognize their own foolishness. Who really came off better in the exchange between Milo and Wilmore? Wilmore, who lost his cool and started cursing Milo? Or Milo, who thereafter happily egged all the other panelists on? Particularly after Wilmore responded to Milo's description of how everyone both on the far Left *and* on the far Right hates him (no offense, but it's true!): "I think you're leaving out a lot of people."

"You see," Milo said after everyone laughed, including himself, "this is the perfect example of how humor can bring people together." Contrary to what comedians like Wilmore and journalists like Scahill would contend, it is not the laughter Milo incites that is dangerous, but the lack of it. As Milo has often said, and said again last night, the thing that people should be really afraid of is not laughter, but the desire to police it.[172]

In his words: "The one thing authoritarians hate is the sound of laughter, because they can't control what people find funny." To which Maher responded: "And also because when people laugh, they know it's true.... Laughter is involuntary.... When you laugh, even if you don't really agree, in that part of your mind you're like..." "Exactly," Milo agreed. "Nothing annoys people or amuses people like the truth."

"If you can take a dick, you can take a joke," Milo likes to say. Which, since we are going for inclusivity here, potentially includes nearly everyone, women and men. Human beings are funny, it is amazing we can get through the day without dying of laughter at how ridiculous we are. Our anxieties about status, whether someone has treated us with the proper respect. Our fears of what others are thinking about us, how disappointed they are with our likes and

---

[172] https://www.breitbart.com/clips/2017/02/17/maher-joan-rivers-made-provocative-jokes-and-shes-considered-a-national-treasure-authoritarians-want-to-police-humor/

dislikes. Our desire to be perfect, when we know very well that we aren't. Every man who wishes that women (or other men) would find him more attractive, every woman that longs for a certain man to pay attention to her. We make ourselves ridiculous trying to get each other's attention—and then hate the objects of our affection because they do not respond in the way that we wish they would.

At which point, along comes a man whom both women and men find devastatingly attractive (trust me on this, his Facebook fans talk about it all the time) and who says the things that they themselves have been thinking but have been too afraid to admit to themselves. For example, that they hate when feminists like Lena Dunham say it would be better for everyone if white men were to go extinct.

Or that they hate when the media insist that it is Christians' fault when a Muslim man shoots up a gay bar in Orlando. Or that they hate when they are told that it is they who have a problem when they are worried about men who think that they ought to have been born women sharing dressing rooms with young girls. (If only they were medievalists, then they would know it is far more complicated than even Milo imagines.) Or that they hate being told that it is they who are the bigots for believing that nations should have legally enforced borders and criteria for citizenship.

These are the tensions that are driving our culture wars at the moment, the things that nobody says we are allowed to talk about or, if we talk about, to have differing opinions on. These are the things that the authoritarians on the Left want us to *shut up about already*. Accordingly, these are the things that Milo makes jokes about. Incessantly. Mischievously. Trollishly. And this—to the Left who hates jokes more than anything—is what makes Milo so dangerous. If he makes people laugh, the Left knows that it will lose, because in the laughter that Milo incites is truth.

Truth that young women rather like having boyfriends, contrary to what many feminists might say. Truth that Christian bakers and florists are not a danger to gays. Truth that black Americans deserve better treatment, but that voting Democrat has not been to their benefit, just look at cities like Chicago.[173] Truth that wanting Americans to think that their nation is great is not racist or xenophobic, but simply what it means to have a nation, particularly one founded on ideals such as freedom of speech.

Tragically, what the Left misses most is how making jokes can also help our culture to heal. Notice what happened in the Overtime segment when Milo was willing to laugh at himself. Even Wilmore joined in. Humor helps defuse even the tensest conversations, as every husband and wife who have ever shared a sexist joke at their own expense know. Again, in Milo's words: "Humor isn't how you drive people apart...When you make a joke that's how you connect with somebody... Humor is what brings people together."

What my colleagues in academia, like those in the media and, oddly, entertainment industry do not see, but Milo's phalanxes of sh*tlords and memesters do, is that laughing helps people bond precisely because it exposes how ridiculous they are *even to themselves*. If women cannot laugh at themselves for, I don't know, being weepy at times and desperate for attention, then we are in worse shape than if a man whistles at us. If men cannot laugh at themselves for, I don't know, finding it difficult to deal with intelligent, conservative women, then they are in worse shape than if an impish British fag calls them names.

If Christians cannot laugh at themselves for, I don't know, believing in something so ridiculous as the Trinity, never mind the Virgin Birth, then they are in worse shape than if someone calls them out for being

---

[173] http://heyjackass.com

hypocrites (which, being sinners, we almost certainly all are, as Milo himself would be the first to admit; human beings are messy). Above all, if human beings cannot laugh at themselves for being, yes, animals with a propensity to think that they are special for being conscious of themselves as animals, then we are all in far worse shape than if someone compares us to a gorilla—or a donkey.[174]

Milo is dangerous for the reason that all tricksters are dangerous. He punctures with laughter the pretension that any human being is above ridicule, however offensive he or she might find it to be the object of fun. In his defense, Milo is always careful in his jokes to take on only those who have already made themselves public with their opinions, even the transgender former student at UW Milwaukee whom Maher asked him about.[175],[176] Being a gentleman, he never punches down or calls out people who have not made themselves his adversaries first, for example, by shouting during his lectures rather than waiting for the Q&A. But what the Left cannot stand and the conservative establishment hates even more is that neither does he back down when he is challenged to a duel. Nor, in the midst of the duel, does he pull his punches when he strikes. Milo, as I do, believes we are in a fight for the very existence of our culture.

This is not a fight we, women, gays, minorities, all those who depend on America and the West for its ideals, can afford to lose. If on occasion he cracks a joke that makes some people uncomfortable, so be it. Jokes sting only our pride. If the joke hurts your feelings, it was something you were already anxious about yourself.

---

[174] https://fencingbearatprayer.blogspot.com/2017/02/heresies-of-left-unholy-trinity.html

[175] https://www.tmj4.com/news/local-news/uwm-student-says-shes-been-discriminated-against-at-the-klotsche-center

[176] https://mediamilwaukee.com/special-projects/uw-milwaukee-transgender-locker-room-policy-remains-under-wraps

MOTHER AND SON

February 20, 2017

"Already [her Son] was taken, already he was bound, already he was spat upon and struck, and it was said over him: 'He deserves death,' and it was shouted to the prefect: 'Crucify, crucify him.' These things were not hidden from the pious mother, who doubtless had come to Jerusalem at this time, whether for the festival of unleavened bread, or rather to see with pious eyes the agony of her Son, which had been specially revealed to her.

"And thereupon she heard from many: 'Don't you know, woman, what has happened to your son?' 'I knew,' she says, 'so be silent, and do not add to the pain of my wounds.' Thus however she was saying to herself: *I will go to the mountain of myrrh and to the hill of frankincense. I will go and I will see his agony, and maternally I will die with him,* because that prophecy which truth-telling Simeon said to me—*His sword will pierce through your own soul*—is to be fulfilled in this way.

"'I will go, and I will see his cross terrible with evil spirits, the price of the world, his blood, the death of death, his death, and the gates of life, his wounds. I will go, and I will say farewell to him about to depart for distant parts, namely about to descend into hell, although there to make no delay. I will go to the mountain of myrrh and to the hill of frankincense, to whom once the Magi, when he was being fed at my breasts, offered frankincense and myrrh, to which they added also gold to show forth his kingdom.'

"So she spoke, and so she proceeded with heavy step to the place of salvation-bringing passion. Indeed, her Son drew her strongly with chains of motherly love, not wanting her unsaved to go so far, that is, even unto hell, since from there he was about to return quickly in triumph. Therefore, she came to that place, which is called Calvary, and as it is written: *The mother of Jesus stood next to his cross*, gazing with motherly eyes on the harshness of his execution, as she herself was fixed to a cross inwardly with the nails of motherly pain, those nails that were more penetrating than any two-edged sword, reaching even to the division of the soul and the spirit, the joints and the marrow (cf. Hebrews 4:12).

"When therefore Jesus saw his mother, crucified with the nails of pity and standing by his cross with his disciple whom he loved, he said to her: *You are all beautiful, my love, and there is no spot in you.*"

—William of Newburgh, *Explanatio sacri epithalamii in matrem sponsi*, lib. IV (Song of Songs 4:6-7), my translation

BULLY CULTURE

February 21, 2017

Everybody hates a bully, or so we say. Yesterday, the national media bullied into silence a young man who had risen to fame speaking to audiences of young women and men about the lies that the grown-ups had told them for decades. Lies about the relationship between women and men. That women don't need men. That all men are potential rapists. That women should aspire to something other than motherhood or they are wasting their lives. That women should like casual sex with strangers, hooking up just for the sake of the orgasm. That the children will be fine if their parents divorce. That abortion is morally good.

Everyone knows these are lies. The young woman who wakes up in the morning having lost her virginity to a man who isn't there and will not marry her. The young man who is tempted into exciting and transgressive sex with an older man and finds himself trapped by his desire in a lifestyle he cannot leave. The young woman who spends her most fertile years working in a career that leaves her childless at forty because she can no longer conceive and has no husband. The young man who has no ambition to work because he has no wife to care for or children to feed.

But the grown-ups tell them to shut up, not to complain. Don't they know how awful it is that women don't earn as much over the course of their lifetime as men? Don't they know that men are still the ones with all the power, even though the number of men completing higher education has continued to drop? Don't they know that nobody should be able to force a woman to bear a child she does not want, even if she did enjoy the sex by which the child was conceived?

And then a young man comes along and tells them, they were right all along. The young women wanted to be pretty, not grotesquely overweight. The young men wanted to be strong and vigorous and manly. The young women wanted babies as well as careers, and were willing to make adjustments to their ambition in order to stay home with their children. The young men wanted to be challenged to be gentlemanly and chivalrous. "Gender roles work," the young man told them. "Feminism is cancer. Abortion is murder." And the young women and men cheered for him, because they loved him for telling the truth.

All their lives they had been wanting to push back against the grown-ups for taking away their sense of self as boys or girls. For telling the girls that they should want to play with trucks as much as dolls. For telling the boys they were evil for wanting to play with swords. But the grown-ups had bullied them into silence. Some bullies were worse than others. Some were their parents, forcing them to pretend to like their step-parents and step-siblings. Some were their teachers, forcing them to pretend that they liked talking crudely about sex while learning English or math. Some were actors and actresses, forcing them to pretend that they enjoyed watching ever more violent sex. Some were their peers, forcing them to pretend to like not being boys or girls. Some were adults who called themselves friends and promised to take care of them if they let the older person have sex with them.

The young man was an unexpected messenger. He talked all the time about having sex with other men. About wanting to be penetrated by black dicks. About how good he was at giving head. But he told the young women they were right to want babies and the young men they were right to want wives. He spoke often about how sad he was that he would never be able to make a child with the person he loved so long as the person he loved was another man. He joked about wishing that he might be cured, perhaps through prayer or electric shock. And he described how he had learned to be gay.

Sometimes people would ask him, "How can you call yourself Catholic when you are gay?" To which he would reply: "What else would I be?! I'm a sinner." At which the audience would laugh, as the young man died just a little more inside. Because he meant it. He never lied. Not like the priest who had taught him to suck dick when he was a teen-ager. Not like the many lovers he had had since. Not like the movement supporting his lifestyle, who had bullied and lied its way into the mainstream culture over the course of his life, so that even to suggest that he was hurting was cause for ridicule and shame.

So he made jokes about it. About Father Michael and how he, the young man, was the predator, not the priest. About the parties he had been to where boys or young teen-agers had sex with older men. About how exciting it was to be so transgressive and dangerous. About how gays had a special contribution to make because they were able to push against the boundaries by which normal people live. And he meant that, too, because he never lied. But he hated the bullies for lying, and said so.

He hated the bullies for telling young women that it was okay to be fat, despite the health risks and guarantee that it would be harder for them to find boyfriends if they were morbidly obese. He hated the bullies for telling young women that it was okay to murder their babies in the womb if they did not feel "ready" to have a child. He hated the bullies for forcing others to pretend that it was okay for men to use women's restrooms and changing rooms as long as the men felt themselves to be women. He hated the bullies for wanting to force Christians to participate through their craft in ceremonies which went against their faith.

And so the bullies came for him. They called him self-hating. Homophobic. Transphobic. Misogynist. Sexist. They mounted protests against his talks. They accused him of spreading hate. Endangering innocents. Inciting violence. They made him out to be the villain because he told the truth. And then they called him a pedophile. Because he had been abused as a young teen-ager and would not swallow the lies. *Shame on all of you. You spineless cunts.*[177] *The bullies are YOU.*

---

[177] The phrase "spineless cunts" was Milo's. He used it specifically as a description of conservatives in his speech at Albuquerque. I had quoted from that speech in an earlier post ("Heresies of the Left: Unholy Trinity"), and wrongly assumed that readers would be able to recognize the allusion. I am writing in Milo's defense when the whole world has turned on him. It was conservatives (whatever that means anymore) who decided to slander him with the "advocates pedophilia" label so as to prevent his speaking at CPAC. The insult was meant to express my anger at the bullying coming from both sides.

JESUS, MASTER TROLL

February 21, 2017

It's hard being a Christian. On the one hand, there is the image that everyone has from going to Sunday School, of Christians as goody-two-shoes. They dress nicely, eat bland cookies, don't swear, wait until marriage to have sex, always have a smile on their face, and are, basically, boring as Heaven. On the other hand, there's Jesus. Jesus drank with sinners (Matthew 11:19). Jesus ate with tax collectors (Matthew 9:10). Jesus made friends with women of ill repute (Matthew 21:32). Jesus wandered about the countryside gathering crowds and scaring the authorities. *Jesus was a troll.* Think about the day he announced himself to his village. He stood up and read the Scriptures for the day (Isaiah 61:1-2):

> "The Spirit of the Lord is upon me, because he has anointed me to preach good news to the poor. He has sent me to proclaim release to the captives, and recovering of sight to the blind, to set at liberty those who are oppressed, to proclaim the acceptable year of the Lord."

And then he gave the book to the attendant, sat down, and said:

> "Today this scripture has been fulfilled in your hearing."

And all wondered and said, how could it be, wasn't he Joseph's son? At which he replied,

> "Truly, I say to you, no prophet is acceptable in his own country."

And the people rose up against him, and drove him out of town (Luke 4:18-30).

This was only the beginning of his trolling. Constantly, Jesus would say things that enraged the learned authorities of his day, overturning the Law by which they strove to live (Matthew 5:43-48).

> "You have heard that it was said, 'You shall love your neighbor and hate your enemy.' But I say to you, Love your enemies and pray for those who persecute you, so that you may be sons of your Father who is in heaven; for he makes his sun rise on the evil and on the good, and sends rain on the just and the unjust. For if you love those who love you, what reward have you? Do not even the tax collectors do the same? And if you salute only your brethren, what more are you doing than others? Do not even the Gentiles do the same? You, therefore, must be perfect, as your heavenly Father is perfect."

As if—Jesus seems to be saying—it makes no difference whether you follow the Law, and yet following the Law is never enough? What do you think those like the Pharisees who spent their lives trying to live according to the Law would have to say about this? Or the scribes who kept the records in the Temple, and oversaw the sacrifices of the people to the Lord? And Jesus shows up and says, "None of this matters"?! They came after him, as you know. Setting traps for him in debate. As the former tax collector Matthew tells it (Matthew 22:15-22):

> Then the Pharisees went and took counsel how to entangle him in his talk. And they sent their disciples to him, along with the Herodians, saying, "Teacher, we know that you are true, and teach the way of God truthfully, and care for no man; for you do not regard the position of men. Tell us, then, what you think. Is it lawful to pay taxes to Caesar, or not?"

But Jesus, aware of their malice, said, "Why put me to the test, you hypocrites? Show me the money for the tax."

And they brought him a coin. And Jesus said to them, "Whose likeness and inscription is this?"

They said, "Caesar's."

Then he said to them, "Render therefore to Caesar the things that are Caesar's, and to God the things that are God's."

When they heard it, they marveled, and they left him and went away.

Methinks Matthew is overplaying his hand here in favor of his Lord. Most likely what they did was go away grinding their teeth, trying to think of some other way to snare him and have him declared an enemy of the state. Jesus knew they all hated him, both the Pharisees on the Right, who tried to live purely according to the Law, and the scribes on the Left, who were functionaries of the Jewish state. And he denounced them regularly in his preaching as hypocrites and fools (Matthew 23).

"Woe to you scribes and Pharisees, hypocrites! for you are like whitewashed tombs, which outwardly appear beautiful, but within they are full of dead men's bones and all uncleanness. So you also outwardly appear righteous to men, but within you are full of hypocrisy and iniquity."

And then he marched into Jerusalem, straight up to the most holy place in the city, and vandalized it (Matthew 21:12-13). "It is written," he said, "'My house shall be called a house of prayer'; but you have made it a den of thieves." Authorities on both the Right and the Left were not pleased. You know the rest of the story. Jesus so enraged the holders of power in his community that they trumped up charges against him, trying to get him to blaspheme so that they could invoke the death penalty against him. When Truth speaks to Power, Power bites back. Hard. But what Power does not know is that Truth will prevail. Because Jesus's kingdom is not of this world.

> And Jesus came and said to them, "All authority in heaven and on earth has been given to me. Go therefore and make disciples of all nations, baptizing them in the name of the Father and of the Son and of the Holy Spirit, teaching them to observe all that I have commanded you; and lo, I am with you always, to the close of the age." —Matthew 28:18-20

THE MILO EFFECT
February 22, 2017

Milo, like everything he talks about, is polarizing.[178] "Are you the real, true face of the alt-Right? Because I thought the Nazis were in there. How did they take you on board?," former intel analyst Malcolm Nance asked Milo during the Overtime segment on *Real Time with Bill Maher*.[179] "No, they hate me," Milo responded. "The worst people on the very far Left and the very far Right all hate me. They all hate me."

"I think you are leaving a lot of people out," comedian Larry Wilmore quipped. *Guess what? Wilmore was right!* If Milo talks about third-wave feminists as being misandrist and vindictive and hurtful to both women and men, the liberal Left says he is insulting all women. The conservative Right can't stand that he uses colorful language like "cunts" and "pussies." If Milo talks about Black Lives Matter as not attending to the real issues putting black lives at risk, the liberal Left says he is insulting all blacks. The conservative Right can't stand that he talks about "sucking black dick."

---

[178] https://www.breitbart.com/social-justice/2017/02/18/leftists-and-establishment-conservatives-freak-out-over-milo-cpac-speech/

[179] https://www.breitbart.com/social-justice/2017/02/18/malcolm-nance-bill-maher-stephen-miller-baby-goebbels/

If Milo talks about Islam and most Muslims' attitudes towards homosexuality or women as evidenced by opinion polls in the U.K. and the legal situation in many Muslim-majority countries, the liberal Left calls him Islamophobic. The conservative Right is shocked that he mentions that Mohammed had a wife who was only nine, making him a "kid fucker." (I'm making this up, I'm not sure what shocks the Right about what Milo says about Islam; they were certainly willing to be shocked about pedophilia this week, as they should be.)

If Milo talks about transgenderism and what it means for both women's safety and the mental health of the individuals affected, the liberal Left calls him transphobic. The conservative Right chides him for saying "faggot" and pretends it doesn't agree with him in the transgender debate. If Milo talks about GamerGate and praises the gamers for being willing to take on the politically-correct suppression of their hobby, the liberal Left calls him misogynist and mean.

The conservative Right can't see the value in playing video games and thinks gamers are losers. And if Milo talks about being abused as a young teen-ager by his priest, the liberal Left accuses him of self-hate for his homosexuality. The conservative Right claims he advocates pedophilia and tries to ruin his career. *Why do I see and hear such a different person from so many of my colleagues and friends?* I am quite honestly struggling to understand.

I never hear Milo speaking out of hate, although I do hear him speaking out of justice (which can sound harsh) and mercy, which he always is, even if he makes jokes at pretty much everyone's expense, including his own. But others, some very close to me, hear the exact opposite. They hear him speaking only out of hate, above all hatred of himself and of his homosexuality, which as we have learned this week, has complicated and uncomfortable roots.[180] (He has often said that he thinks being gay is about 50-50 nature-nurture. He is not persuaded that there is such a thing as "born gay," which he argues was a political invention of the LGBT lobby in the 1980s to take advantage of arguments on the basis of civil rights.)

I see a young man willing to take enormous professional, social, political, physical, and, yes, spiritual risks to say things that nobody else is willing to say, in venues that nobody else is willing to dare, in order to defend the people he sees as hurt by the way in which other people talk about them, above all, women and blacks, young men, child abuse victims, victims of illegal immigrants—in fact, everyone the Left says he should care about, except that he refuses to do so in terms of their identity politics.

My friends and colleagues beg to disagree with me. Milo is an attention seeker. A menace. A danger. He is doing it only to get a rise out of people, not because he cares. He cares only for himself. He is selfish, vindictive, unprincipled. He creates situations in which people get hurt regardless of the consequences. It is his fault the trolls went after Leslie Jones on Twitter. It is his fault transgender people, lesbians, and gays get beaten up. It is his fault that the gamers were encouraged to send death threats to Anita Sarkeesian and Zoe Quinn. It is his fault everybody is so angry with him. *Eius culpa, eius maxima culpa.*

Or is it? Christians are often chided by non-Christians for saying that they hate not the sinner, but the sin. "No, no, no," non-Christians reply. "If you hate the sin, it must mean you hate the sinner, too." Sin is a very hard concept to understand. Like Milo, it is also polarizing. The conservative Right wants people to be virtuous, principled, sober. As *National Review* argued in its editorial on CPAC's canceling Milo's

---

[180] https://www.breitbart.com/the-media/2017/02/21/full-remarks-milo-delivers-speech-press-conference-amid-video-scandal/

speech, this was a good thing, they didn't think he should have been asked in the first place because "whatever Yiannopoulos's politics they are not conservative in any meaningful sense."[181] Nor, they continue, is his demeanor. In the editors' words:

> It has become fashionable in conservative circles to cheer every apparently right-leaning gadfly. But "trolling" is not conservatism, and there is no virtue merely in upsetting campus Democrats. There are many conservatives who do regular battle with left-wing agitators—but who also are of high character, and advance conservative arguments and defend conservative principles with poise, wit, and good cheer.

The liberal Left likewise wants people to speak in particular ways so as to avoid saying anything that anybody might find troubling or offensive. It doesn't matter that they might agree with anything Milo says. If he is rude to anyone they perceive as belonging to particular identity groups (basically, everyone other than straight white men), he cannot be forgiven. I have news for both sides: speech codes are not about virtue. They are about social conformity, not sin. *Sin is much, much more dangerous than mean words that hurt people's feelings.* People have been writing to me all week, first in response to my article published in *Sightings*, then in response to the media storm launched against Milo.[182] Some people are angry with me.

> for all i know, you are a brilliant scholar in your chosen field. but when it comes to live in the 21st century, you are a pathetic joke... i notice in your self-description you believe that "ideas matter," so here's my idea: shut the fuck up about matters outside of your subject expertise.

> I actually think that you fail to understand the religiously-informed positions of those protesting against Milo's positions. It seems laughable to me that of all the contributing factors you believe this is

---

[181] https://www.nationalreview.com/2017/02/cpac-milo-yiannopoulos-invitation-disgraceful-mistake/

[182] https://divinity.uchicago.edu/sightings/why-milo-scares-students-and-faculty-even-more

what most represents a "deep crisis in religious thinking." We are most certainly religiously illiterate as a nation and uncomfortable with how religion enters into the public conversation in a religiously plural and secular society, and so on, but part of the resistance to Milo is that his positions are an abomination to the ideals and mores and deeply shared values across our many religious traditions.

You really are a fan-girl, aren't you?... James Kirchick did the best analysis of Yiannopoulos, and his peculiar mix of vacuity and incitement... [Milo's] a slimy piece of shit; the only positive thing he's doing is bringing out from under cover those people who share his point of view.

By far the majority, however, are grateful. Here are but a few:

I wanted to tell you how much I enjoyed your article about Milo. Thanks to those that sought to shut down actual free speech by burning their own buildings, we became aware of Milo for the first time. We are an older, conservative, white (horrors!) traditional couple. I agreed with just about every word in your article. I am so happy the snowflakes propelled Milo to such heights. I love his humor and your explanation of it. We have watched some of his interviews and speeches at colleges, and I've said many things you said after watching. The left has zero sense of humor and that cracks me up.... Thank you for such a thoughtful piece.

Thank you for your blog posts about Milo... I am horrified by the power of our political/cultural elites to shape the perceptions of otherwise decent and well-meaning people, especially conservative Christians. The effort to destroy Milo...is just one more sad example. I appreciate your articulate witness against it.

I just wanted to let you know that, like you seem to be, I am a conservative Christian (I was raised Reformed Baptist) with an obsession for Tolkien/Lewis/Williams/Sayers...as well as Chesterton and others. I have thoroughly enjoyed your blog since I discovered it (Thanks, Milo!). I haven't read this sort of detailed thought since I left college too long ago... Condolences on the whole Milo Thing. I firmly agree with your position.

You don't know me, but I have recently begun to follow you after seeing your name on Milo's FB. I want you to know how much I admire and respect your bravery. I wanted you to know that there are those of us out here who are unseen who have the greatest respect for you. I understand what you are doing (re Milo) and why. That we should all be so Christian to be brave enough to do what you are doing. I am especially happy that you are a Marian scholar, having been named after Mary when my mother almost died and she pledged that if she had another girl she would name her Mary. I have always felt a special connection and know that I beat cancer with my rosary. And I know she is with you now.

I apologize for emailing you (uninvited), but I had to thank you for the above blog entry[183]. I have been following the chaos that is Milo today, and I pray he reads your blog and finds comfort in your words. Whether or not you posted that reading from Hebrews with Milo in mind [*I did—FB*], I think I am not far off in my thoughts that you, also, are lifting him in prayers of protection and forgiveness. For your affection and honest words, in your previous blog entries, show an open heart to his strength and intelligence, while understanding that he, like us all, is a sinner whom God and His Son love with no restraint. My heart aches for that young man, for I think in spite of his sassy-ness and his penchant for pissing off people while making them laugh, he has a gentle heart and must feel much fear in the anger that surrounds him.

Most of the people who write me directly seem to be older. They mention children and grandchildren. Long struggles that they have lived through. Conversions and ecstasies. Suffering and joy. But some of them are young, many in graduate school in my field of medieval studies, and they say they are writing to thank me for giving them courage in the future, as up till now, as conservatives in academia, they have felt very much alone.

And all, almost to a person, mention something in Milo that they see in themselves. *Particularly his pain.* As I tried to argue in my *Sightings* piece, we are experiencing a terrible crisis in our national culture.

---

[183] http://fencingbearatprayer.blogspot.com/2017/02/mother-and-son.html

Even as people are struggling to hear each other over the screaming, their own anger at not being heard escalates into animal howling.[184] It seems that it is impossible for many even to listen to what Milo says without feeling he is personally attacking them. It is all well and good to make jokes about snowflakes and trigger warnings, they seem to be saying, but don't make jokes at *my* expense.

Everybody—Left, Right, liberal, conservative, progressive, Christian, atheist, Muslim, Jew—is on a hair trigger, ready to explode at the first instance of someone saying something with which they don't agree. What has happened to us? Why are we so incapable of hearing things with which we disagree? Words that we find off-color? Jokes that cut a little to close to the bone? Why are we all so *afraid* all the time about what others might say or what we might hear? Because we have no virtue. We have no discipline. We have lost our sense (if we ever had it) of what it means to train our souls.

Milo has said many, many off-color things. Yesterday in his press conference, he described his edgy style as a "blend of British sarcasm, provocation and gallows humor," which he is now horrified may have given the impression that he did not take seriously his concern for other victims of the kind of abuse he suffered in his early teens.[185] Perhaps it is because I have lived in England, I am more familiar than most Americans with his style. So I never heard him saying that he did not care about the things he was making jokes about. What I heard, and he said yesterday, was a wounded soul trying to find a way to cope with what he now realizes in retrospect were experiences too terrible to explain.

---

[184] https://www.breitbart.com/social-justice/2016/06/01/bizarre-milo-protester-throws-trashcan-screams-video/

[185] https://www.breitbart.com/the-media/2017/02/21/full-remarks-milo-delivers-speech-press-conference-amid-video-scandal/

"I still don't view myself as a victim," he said. "But I am one." Milo translated the pain that he could not otherwise deal with into the "black comedy, gallows humor and love of shock value" that has become his signature style. "My experiences as a victim led me to believe I could say anything I wanted to on this subject, no matter how outrageous." But, of course, it was actually the subject about which he talked the least.

He is on record, on camera and in his journalism, talking about feminism, Black Lives Matter, Islam, and GamerGate over and over and over again. But the only time he talked about being gay, it was in jokes: about his black boyfriends, gay porn, big dicks and bigger parties. He made jokes about being cured, but when he talked about wishing he could have a child with the person he loved, he always talked softly and sincerely.

You could feel—every mother who has written to me over the past week to thank me for standing up for him—could feel how much pain, how much soul-searing pain was in those words, which he, as a gay man, has been told over and over and over again by his own people *he is not allowed to say*. "When I came to America, I thought it would be a place where you could *do* anything, *be* anything, *say* anything." How awful it has been for him that he found this isn't the case. Instead, he found when he came here that he was still told he could not say what he most needed to say, but that all of us who have been watching his talks heard him say over and over and over again.

"I have sinned, I have sinned, I have sinned. Father, forgive me, I have sinned." The day before his public humiliation, Milo posted this status on his Facebook feed, but it was taken from something I had written to him describing what was happening to me over the *Sightings* article:

The progressive left hates me because they know they cannot win in an open fight. Because I have said nothing wrong. And they know it. All

I have done is help up to them a mirror—and they hate what they see, and blame me.

Milo has held a mirror up to us all. If we hate what we see in his jokes and his facts, his costumes and arguments, his willingness to make himself a fool in order to get people's attention long enough to get them to listen, it is our fault, our great fault. It is our sin that we see in him. We see ourselves in Milo, a fellow sinner, and want to destroy him, because when we look in the mirror it is not him, but Our Lord that we are supposed to be able to see. The Creator in whose image and likeness we were made.

There is a reason that Milo utterly refuses to play the victim when he was one. There is only one Victim who can take away our sins (Hebrews 7:26-27). And He already has, if only we can stop screaming long enough to listen to His Word: *"I love you"* (John 3:16).

GOD'S FOOLS

February 23, 2017

Like Jesus, Francis of Assisi did some pretty outrageous things. Everybody knows how he went and preached to the birds, but not everybody knows why he did it.[186] It wasn't, as certain 1970s movies would have it, because he was a nature-loving hippie (although I do love Donavan's soundtrack, especially the theme song). It was because the human beings he was preaching to wouldn't listen. He had wanted to preach the word of God in Rome, but when he arrived there, the people scorned him because he was dressed poorly, so they thought him an idiot. He tried for several days to gain their attention, but could not overcome their hardness of heart.

"I grieve deeply over your misfortune," he told them, "because you are not only spurning me as a servant of Christ, but you are also really despising Him in me, since I have been preaching to you the Gospel of the Redeemer of the world. And so I am now leaving Rome. And I call as witness of your desolation Him who is the faithful Witness in heaven. And for your confusion I am going to preach the Gospel of Christ to the brute animals and the birds of the sky, so that by

---

[186] Raphael Brown, *Fifty Animal Stories of Saint Francis as told by his companions* (1958)

hearing the soul-saving words of God they may obey and have peace."
At which, the people of Rome drove him from the city.

Preaching to the birds was far from the most outrageous thing
Francis did. Another time when he was in Rome to see the pope
to get approval for his Rule, the pope looked at Francis in his "ill-
fitting robe," with his "ugly face, long beard, disheveled hair, and
overhanging black eyebrows," and couldn't believe that Francis, an
unknown "nobody," could possibly be a servant of God—or even a
human being. "Brother," Pope Innocent rebuked him, "go find some
pigs—to which you should be compared rather than to men—and roll
in the mud with them. And take the Rule you have made to them—and
give them the benefit of your preaching!"

So, of course, Francis did. He bowed his head, went out into the
street, found some pigs, and rolled with them in the mud until he
was completely covered with it. Then he went back inside, presented
himself to the pope, and said, "Lord, I have done what you ordered.
Now please listen to my petition." As with Jesus, so with Francis,
we have a terrible tendency to bowdlerize what these young men
must have been like in person. In retrospect, we have made them as
clean-cut and boring as the most stereotypical 1950s suburbanite: no
swearing, no sex outside marriage and only decorous sex within, no
stepping outside society's norms.

In our imaginations, both Jesus and Francis look and behave
like wispy, gentle hippies (thanks, Zeffirelli!), a mix between Walter
Sallman's famous *Head of Christ* (1940) and Graham Faulkner's
folk-singing Francis. They speak softly, wandering wistfully about
the countryside picking flowers, and never, ever embarrass anyone
by doing anything outrageous. Except they did. In later life, Francis
may have been all pious and sweet (not exactly), but in his youth,
you will recall, he was a regular rapscallion. He dreamed of being a

knight, lived high on his father's wealth, and even went off to war to fight on behalf of his hometown Assisi.

And when the crucifix at San Damiano told him: "Go, and repair my house," what did he do?[187] Take a bunch of his father's best textiles to sell for funds. His father was *not* pleased. Francis hid for a month in a cave to escape his father's wrath, and on emerging made his most outrageous gesture yet. He marched into the center of Assisi, took off all his clothes, and stood naked before the bishop and people, saying to his father, "Hitherto I have called you my father on earth; henceforth I desire to say only, 'Our Father who art in Heaven.'"

How, exactly, do we know how Jesus behaved in his youth? Answer: we don't. We know nothing of his life before he began his preaching tour, except for the story in Luke 2:41-51 about how, one year at the age of twelve, he stayed in the Temple arguing with the priests when his family had gone up to Jerusalem for the feast of Passover. Sure Luke says that, after his frantic parents found him, afterwards Jesus was obedient to them, but that's it. Let me repeat: *we know NOTHING of what Jesus did between the age of twelve and his showing up at the Jordan for John to baptize him.* And then what did Jesus do? This is the way I phrased it back in November when I was first trying to give a sense of how extraordinary what Milo was doing seemed—and yet, how oddly familiar:

> You all know the story. A young man of obscure birth and questionable parentage comes out of the countryside to the big city. He collects a following of other young men and even some women, who see him as a good person despite his reputation as a libertine. He speaks plainly and gathers large crowds of simple people who look to him for help and credit him with freeing them from ailments that they have suffered under for years. He causes a disruption in the city, shames the members of the establishment for their hypocrisy and greed, and bests even the most learned teachers in argument. He violates the most

---

[187] http://www.newadvent.org/cathen/06221a.htm

sacred taboos and is accused of blasphemy and corrupting the youth. He is accused by the leaders of his community of fomenting rebellion and of sympathies with the most dangerous elements of the society. Eventually, he is betrayed by one of his own followers, handed over to the authorities for questioning, tortured, mocked, and subjected to a cruel and unusual punishment without proper trial. And yet, even as he hangs dying on the cross, he forgives his persecutors, taking all of the hate and anger and envy and fear that they can throw at him and giving it back as love.

I am getting some flak from my colleagues in academia for this particular comparison.[188],[189] Of course, I do not mean that Milo is the Second Coming of Christ. *Duh.* What I meant was—and said in the original post—was that Milo is sincere when he says he is a Catholic, and that as a Catholic he understands his ultimate model to be Christ. Whether he himself is conscious of the parallels I saw between his going on his campus tour and the way in which Jesus traveled round the country, I don't know. (He didn't share "Kung Fu Milo" on his Facebook page, which makes me think I embarrassed him a little bit, although as his fans know, Milo doesn't embarrass easily.) Certainly, however, Francis saw the parallels in what he was doing—quite purposefully.

Like Jesus, Francis went round the countryside gathering young men as followers. Like Jesus, Francis focused on preaching to the people. Like Jesus, Francis stood up to the established authorities of his day on behalf of the people whom he felt needed caring for. Like Jesus, Francis used extravagant gestures and stories to make his point. Like Jesus, Francis spoke simply and vividly. And like Jesus, Francis made jokes. For example, with his preaching to the birds or rolling in the mud with the pigs. His biographers recorded many more.

---

[188] http://www.thismess.net/2017/02/milo-and-university-of-chicago.html

[189] https://www.patheos.com/blogs/lovejoyfeminism/2017/02/university-of-chicago-professor-uses-c-word-in-defense-of-milo-yiannopoulos.html

One day, one of the brothers in Assisi asked Francis to allow him to have a psalter. To which Francis replied: "Once you have a psalter, you will insist on having a breviary. And when you get a breviary, you will sit on a professor's chair and give orders to your brother like some mighty prelate: 'Here, you, bring me my breviary.' Francis then strewed ashes on his head and cried from the depths of his soul: 'I am the breviary! I am the breviary!'" Another time, Francis made a brother who had picked up a coin off the altar in the church of St. Mary of the Portiuncula to take the coin up in his mouth and carry it outside to a pile of donkey dung. Milo, who was raised a Catholic, seems to use similar techniques as Jesus and Francis to help get his audiences' attention. As I told Oliver Bateman for his essay on Milo,[190]

> Milo is playing a particular kind of role: that of the holy fool. He is a clown—like St. Francis of Assisi—using jokes to shock us out of our established pieties. Like Francis, people find him outrageous and embarrassing: If Francis stripped off all his clothes in the piazza of Assisi to shock the wealthy elite of his hometown, Milo has dressed in drag, had himself 'hazed,' disguised himself as a protestor at one of his own talks, dressed in police fetish gear carrying a giant pink dildo water bottle, and had himself carried into the lecture hall on a golden throne [FB—*that was actually the students' idea*]. He wants to shock people out of their complacency and make them think, but like Francis, he does so by making himself a figure of fun.

Back in January, when I wrote the above, Milo was just getting back on the road with his Dangerous Faggot bus and staff of young men. As they traveled round the country for the last leg of his tour, it soon became clear that the reception they were getting in the West was somewhat different from that which the tour had received in the South and Southeast. Out West, the protestors got more and more aggressive. A shot was fired in Seattle. Fires were lit and windows

---

[190] https://psmag.com/news/how-much-longer-can-the-milo-yiannopolous-show-last#.20jmou6nj

broken in Berkeley. Some of the scheduled talks were canceled on the day. The shouts of "No Milo, no Nazis, no fascist KKK!" got louder and louder and louder.

And then came the night with Bill Maher and soon after the invitation to speak at CPAC. At which point the conservative establishment struck and brought Milo down. You will forgive me, I hope, for not pointing out the obvious parallels. The invitation to speak was rescinded, Milo lost his book contract with Simon & Schuster, and in the midst of the shame storm that fell upon him from all sides, including even conservatives like Stefan Molyneux who had previously been on his side,[191] he felt the only honorable thing to do was to resign his position at *Breitbart*. Not a crucifixion, I grant you. But hardly a basket of accolades. Mocked, shunned, humiliated, spat at by former colleagues. Betrayed by his friends. Socially speaking, it was pretty close.

And, therefore, quite frankly, uncanny. I have been writing for and about Milo since September. He has become a friend and an ally in the battle against the SJWs, the pearl-clutchers and nannies, who gasp at the use of the C-word and refuse to let anybody have any fun, lest somebody feel offended or the language not be "inclusive" enough.[192],[193] (I was upset, and besides it was Milo's phrase. If you had been paying better attention to my blog, you would have recognized it as an epithet for conservatives. Spineless cunts.) Many of my Facebook friends had been gleefully predicting Milo's downfall for months.

Commendably, most of them have held their tongues this past week, although I am wondering about how happy they feel having

---

[191] https://youtu.be/2wsZSE-iJAk

[192] https://newrepublic.com/minutes/140786/university-chicago-professor-gone-off-milo-yiannopouliss-opponents-calling-spineless-cnts

[193] https://chicagoist.com/2017/02/22/uchicago_milo_yiannopoulos_spineless.php

watched their prediction come true.[194] There he was, the young man in whom so many had placed so much hope, brought down by the media mob and crucified (metaphorically speaking) by the authorities. Two days later, he did a press conference, made his confession, announced his resignation and the end of his journalism career. And promised his followers that he was not giving up. He has plans to develop a new round of campus talks and to focus more on "entertaining and educating everyone, left, right and otherwise." And then he threw out his gauntlet:

> Don't think for a moment that this will stop me being as offensive, provocative and outrageously funny as I want on any subject I want. America has a colossal free speech problem. The land of the First Amendment has some of the most oppressive social restrictions on free expression anywhere in the western world. I'm proud to be a warrior for free speech and creative expression. I want everyone in America, the greatest country in the history of human civilization, to be able to be, do, read and say anything. I will never stop fighting for your right to do that.[195]

Could you have recovered from such a public humiliation that fast? Yeah, right. Let me say this again so everybody in the back can hear me: *I do not think Milo is Christ.* What I do think is that he, like Francis, is attempting to live out the imitation of Christ, as in fact every Christian should. (It's hard to get perfect, but then only Jesus was—is God.) Contrary to what you might think from Donavan's version of the song, Francis was not celebrating "nature" in his *Canticle of the Creatures*, he was celebrating the creation of God. As Thomas of Celano explained in his biography of Francis:

> Though he was eager to leave this world as a place of exile, this happy pilgrim took a great deal of joy in the things that are in the world. In

---

[194] https://psmag.com/news/on-the-milo-bus-with-the-lost-boys-of-americas-new-right
[195] https://www.breitbart.com/the-media/2017/02/21/full-remarks-milo-delivers-speech-press-conference-amid-video-scandal/

fighting the princes of darkness he used the world as a battleground, but in relation to God he used it as a very clear mirror of the Creator's goodness.

In order that all things might arouse the love of God in his heart, he would praise the Divine Craftsman for each thing which He had made, and whatever he found in things he would refer to their Maker. He rejoiced in all the works of the Lord's hands. And his insight penetrated beyond these pleasing appearances to their life-giving principle and cause.

In beautiful things he recognized Him who is beauty itself. Everywhere he followed his Beloved by means of the traces of Himself which God has imprinted on all things. He made all things a ladder by which he climbed up to the throne of God.

In his interview with Maher, Milo mentioned that he was not sure any more whether he would call himself a conservative. Given how things played out in the following three days, perhaps it was because he had an inkling of what was to come. No, Milo is not a conservative as the organizers of CPAC seem to think of conservatism, because at the end of the day, Milo doesn't care about politics.

What he cares about, and constantly explains, is culture. He is much more focused on beauty and joy, laughter and art, than he is on the machinations of politics. He never wanted to be press secretary; he wanted to have fun. Which, in the end, is far more important than politics. How was it Jesus put it? "My kingdom is not of this world."

MILO AND ME

February 25, 2017

Oh, for goodness' sake! I like Milo because he is Catholic, conservative, and trying to do good after spending his twenties living riotously and hurting more people than he should—or meant to. I stood up for him this week and all along during his campus tour because he was doing something that nobody else in academia, including myself, would: bring out into the open the things that, in academia as in our culture at large, nobody has been willing to say lest they get shamed, shouted down, and told to shut up.

He talks about the things I care about: the problems with gender studies, the importance of Christian virtues, the value of Western civilization, the greatness of America as a country founded on ideals. Yes, he made jokes at the expense of other people, particularly people whom the entire national media and all my liberal friends and colleagues say he shouldn't, but this is part of the point: unless you have been a conservative in academia for the past thirty years, you have no idea how hard it has been not making these jokes all along.

As one of my new friends on Facebook tried to explain to another of my friends this week, conservatives, especially Christian conservatives, are tired of being the butt of everyone's jokes and not being able to hit back (because, being Christians, we usually don't). Milo gives them permission to laugh. Being a Christian, he does not tell them to hit anybody, except with laughter.

What happened to Milo this week was a planned, targeted political take-down. The video clips that were used to make it seem like he supported something against which he fought his entire journalistic career were taken out of context, both out of the immediate context of the conversations in which Milo was engaged when he made these statements, and out of the life context that became clear in his press conference: he himself is a victim of underage sexual abuse and was incapable, until now, of letting himself think that.

Unlike those who use their own status as victims or the victimhood of others whom they make it their cause to protect, Milo never claimed to speak as a victim, only a champion of the weak. Because he hates those who use their own victimhood or the victimhood of others as a kind of shield, he never claimed that he should not be attacked. But he refused not to hit back.

Milo is saying we have the categories of victimhood wrong and that we, as a society, are hurting the very people liberal Leftist ideologies claim to protect. For this, the Left cannot forgive him, but neither, as we learned this week, can the Right. So, yes, I stood up for him against my colleagues, my family, and my friends. Because he has been standing up for me and conservative academic Christians like me when nobody else would.

TURNING THE OTHER CHEEK

March 2, 2017

Like Milo, I have been called quite a few names in the past two weeks, although I like to think that mine are special. Because, of course, we're talking academia here. Here are a few of my favorites: "Addled, awful, and plain stupid thinking." "Plain wrong." "Out of this world." "Racist, civilizationist, and theocratic opinions." "Abhorrent views." You can tell these are my fellow academics speaking. They go after my thoughts.

Others, commenting more publicly, have gone after my status as a tenured professor. Per *The Guardian*: "Rachel Fulton Brown is, believe it or not, an associate professor of medieval history at the University of Chicago...a woman with a graduate degree and academic publications.... Clearly, we can't put [what she says about Milo] down to stupidity"[196]—although they would clearly like to! Per *Patheos*: "I

---

[196] https://www.theguardian.com/us-news/2017/feb/23/milo-yiannopulos-conservative-articles-to-read

sincerely hope her grasp on scholarship in [medieval history] is not as shallow has (sic) her writing [in 'Bully Culture'] suggests."[197]

"It's very smart of her," one of the more courageous graduate students in my own department wrote in an op-ed for *The Maroon*, our campus newspaper, "to come out after she had tenure."[198] Nevertheless, he continues, what I have said about the crisis of faith I see afflicting our academic culture at large is "selective historicist bullshit," while my own views about the importance of faith are "morally bankrupt." To be fair (we are talking a Chicago graduate student here), he credits me with expertise in my own field, but this expertise has "warped" my understanding of history "outside [my] imaginary niche of medieval Europe." Which means I am exactly the kind of "spineless" coward I have accused Milo's critics of being. (I used a far more colorful term.)

Colleagues in Medieval Studies across the country, including Jeffrey Cohen of George Washington University, David M. Perry of Dominican University, and Julie Orlemanski of the University of Chicago (yes, my own colleague), have piled on to make sure that everyone understands I am in the minority in the field. Or the tip of a dangerous iceberg, I'm not sure which. According to Josephine Livingstone, writing for the *New Republic*,

> strong veins of conservatism run through the field. Despite the efforts of scholars like Suzanne Conklin Akbari and Geraldine Heng, contemporary white supremacists and gender traditionalists sometimes look to an imagined version of the Middle Ages for a 'purer' time, when (they imagine) sexual, racial, and theological identities were simpler.[199]

---

[197] https://www.patheos.com/blogs/lovejoyfeminism/2017/02/university-of-chicago-professor-uses-c-word-in-defense-of-milo-yiannopoulos.html

[198] https://www.chicagomaroon.com/article/2017/2/24/professor-brown-love/

[199] https://newrepublic.com/minutes/140786/university-chicago-professor-gone-off-milo-yiannopouliss-opponents-calling-spineless-cnts

They're wrong—the white supremacists and gender traditionalists, of course—but my saying so is another of the things that has angered my colleagues. (Things were much, more complicated. Just ask Rupert of Deutz.) Apparently, my language was too blunt. Not ladylike, you might say.

Professor Perry is "troubled…to see someone using their (*sic*) academic status to craft a nonsensical defense of Milo as a Christian visionary."[200] (Jordan Peterson of the University of Toronto seems rather to agree with me, that Milo is a kind of trickster or jester.[201] So there's that. Eric Mader at *Clay Testament* would also seem to agree with Peterson and me.[202] My take is that Milo is a holy fool, like Francis, another great imitator of Christ.) Professor Orlemanski is upset that the *Sightings* piece did not come with a trigger warning (in her words, a proper frame):

> Instead, as a junior faculty member who works in medieval studies at this university, I have spent more than a dozen hours since the article's publication three days ago responding to appalled graduate students, faculty at other institutions, and faculty here. Speaking personally, I feel angry and disappointed that "Sightings" did not take up any of this intellectual, institutional, and affective labor in advance and instead left it to me and others.[203]

Plus, of course, in her view I am a bad scholar. All the more reason that *Sightings* should have given a trigger warning:

> The logic and historical basis for her claims regarding Christianity and the university are…poor. Given the straightforwardly inflammatory content of the article, "Sightings" might have insisted on a high standard of argumentation and evidentiary support, and I am disappointed [*that word again!—FB*] that they did not. Instead, my colleagues and I are

---

[200] http://www.thismess.net/2017/02/milo-and-university-of-chicago.html

[201] https://youtu.be/tiaGBbdIA-8

[202] https://claytestament.blogspot.com/2017/02/defending-milo.html

[203] http://www.thismess.net/2017/02/milo-and-university-of-chicago.html

compelled to spend our time producing "more free speech" pointing out basic failures of journalistic and intellectual discourse.

To reiterate: I am writing with a sense of profound disappointment [*noun variant—FB*] and frustration regarding how Professor Rachel Fulton Brown's piece was published.

Okay, then. I don't have quite Milo's thick skin, so it has taken me a bit of time to get around to reading these take-downs. *Ahem.* Measured and thoughtful critiques. Plus, I have been busy defending him against the next great smear that the national media has tried to use against him, after exhausting "white nationalist." Working through my colleagues' comments to give you something of a taste of what I am up against in continuing to stand up for him—which, never fear, I will—has helped. A bit. But the lesson here, at least for the moment, is not "fuck your feelings." It is, as Milo always reminds me, "remember to laugh."

This can be hard. I am going to have to sit next to Julie in our Medieval Studies Workshop—or maybe not. I wonder if my mere presence will cause her to leave. I will likely encounter David and Jeffrey and Josephine and Suzanne and Geraldine at conferences. I am more sanguine about Usama Rafi, the graduate student in our department who wrote the op-ed. He wrote back to me after I left a comment on *The Maroon* site, and we have since realized that we play similar roles among our colleagues. Namely, to piss them off. You gotta laugh. In his words:

> Thankfully, both of us have the same attitude towards feelings, so no hard feelings. For what it is worth, I find virtue in what I feel are vices too. The fact that so many are shocked about your views is evidence that you must have been a hell of a teacher in class. I will continue to respect your for that and encourage others to appreciate that.

Which is pretty good going, if you ask me, considering he and I have never met and we have now exchanged only a handful of emails.

It took three for us to get to this point. "You have heard," Jesus told his disciples, "that it was said, 'An eye for an eye and a tooth for a tooth.' But I say to you, Do not resist one who is evil. But if any one strikes you on the right cheek, turn to him the other also" (Matthew 5:38-39). Until this past week, I had always thought of this teaching in terms of letting others attack me, which seemed hard and impossible. I want to hit back. Now, however, I think it has a different meaning. Turning the other cheek does not mean you don't parry. It means you take the attack and transform it, as somehow, miraculously, I did with Usama.

I realize I have been practicing this turning all year as a Happy Warrior.[204] Trying to find a way to turn the attacks coming at me from my colleagues, family, and friends, into opportunities for further conversation. It takes training. I could not have survived this past week without having practiced these kinds of conversations, online and in person, *a lot*. But it also takes joy. Milo is right about this as he is about everything (well, okay, not quite everything, as he has now humbled himself to confess): we must never lose our ability to laugh. The question is, how do we help others to share our joy?

---

[204] https://fencingbearatprayer.blogspot.com/2016/01/how-to-be-happy-warrior.html

BEAR'S TWO BODIES

March 5, 2017

The chair of my department wanted to talk with me last week. No, I am not going to lose my job. I do have tenure, and at the University of Chicago, we take academic freedom very seriously.[205] Likewise, as a member of the faculty, I am free to express my opinions publicly, even on a blog, as the statement that my chair sent out to the department on our various listservs sought to make clear. In the chair's words:

> Individual faculty members are entitled to express and publish their opinions on any public issues of concern to them, and when they do so they speak only for themselves. As a faculty body, the Department of History does not endorse or defend the political or personal views expressed by any of its members. Nor as a collectivity does it take critical positions on matters of individual faculty opinion, be they personal or political. Other faculty members are, of course, also free to express their own countering points of view, to criticize or repudiate publicly whatever they disagree with or find offensive, and when they do so they likewise speak only for themselves.

> More broadly, the Department of History is committed both to fostering an inclusive environment for teaching, learning, and reasoned intellectual debate and to furthering the exercise of free speech.

[205] https://www.wsj.com/articles/why-the-university-of-chicago-opposes-trigger-warnings-1487646602

No, the problem that my chair wanted to talk with me about was not my speech *per se. It was how I labeled it in the public sphere.* On the one hand, there was my personal homepage.[206] Although it is hosted on one of the University of Chicago servers, I curate this page myself (yay! I know how to tag in baby-html). It includes a list of my academic publications, a list of the courses I have taught at the University of Chicago with links to the syllabi for these courses, and a list of my best results as a fencer. Plus images of Ankerstein buildings for fun and my WHY, HOW, and WHAT for studying the Middle Ages. There is a link to this page from my faculty page on the departmental website, but my personal homepage is my own, not the department's.[207] I include links to my blogs from this homepage. There are three blogs, but *Fencing Bear at Prayer* is the main one.

On the other hand, there was my blog (you're here already!). I describe myself in the banner for the blog as a "medievalist," but I do not say where I teach or make any assertions about my professional status other than that I am a "medievalist." Nor do I say anything at the top of the blog about my sex. (As I know from comments on Milo's Facebook page, some of his readers have assumed I am a man, which I take as a compliment. They can't tell my sex from my words.)

There is a tab under my banner image for a link to my "Who am I?" page.[208] In this page, I describe myself as "by day...a not-so-mild mannered associate professor of medieval European history," with a link to my personal homepage. But, again, I do not assert that this is the voice in which I write on the blog. Rather, the blog is where I express myself "by night," when I become the "ursine swordswoman" (get it?) in whose persona I write as "Fencing Bear."

---

[206] https://home.uchicago.edu/~rfulton/index.html

[207] https://history.uchicago.edu/directory/rachel-fulton-brown

[208] https://fencingbearatprayer.blogspot.com/p/about.html

Now, it is true that if you scroll *all the way down* to the bottom of the blog, you will find out more about me from my profile, where for starters you can learn I am a right-handed female (human being implied) with white hair and green eyes. There I note under Occupation that I am a "professor of medieval European history." You may also notice from the profile that I live in Chicago. And you may find the badge for a link to my Facebook page under "My Other Self," where, again, you will see that I live in Chicago. Nowhere on the blog itself do I make it a point to claim any particular institutional affiliation as my authority for the blog. I do not as such hide my affiliation—it is there in the links—but I do not assert it as warrant for my voice as a blogger.

But, of course, you all know now that I teach at the University of Chicago. Which, my chair told me, *is* a problem. Again, not because I am a faculty member or because I have expressed my political, cultural, and religious opinions publicly. But because I had not (he said) made it clear on my personal homepage and blog which persona I was using when I spoke as Fencing Bear. (I have since, I hope, fixed my personal homepage to distinguish my two persons; this blog post is an effort to make the distinction clearer here.) Which makes my head spin.

I told you on Thursday about the way in which the outside world has read my blog posts about Milo. Many are incredulous that I could be a tenured scholar to have written the things that I have in the lexicon and style that I have, complete with dirty words, analogies between Milo and Jesus, and incomplete sentence structures. (I think that is what one of the commentators on *The Maroon* article meant by how badly written my "Bully Culture" post was.[209] I don't think they meant the *Sightings* piece; that one was edited for me and had only

---

[209] https://www.chicagomaroon.com/article/2017/2/24/professor-comments-yiannopoulos-spur-controversy/

complete sentences and no expletives.) They seem to be saying that, as a scholar, I should write one way and one way only: politely with full academic-style references. Not provocatively, engagingly, wittily. So that, you know, somebody other than my academic colleagues might like to read what I write.

It gets worse. I have told you how my colleague Julie Orlemanski here at Chicago has insisted that *Sightings* should have provided a trigger warning on my piece, "How Milo Scares Students, and Faculty Even More."[210] She also insisted that, even as an opinion piece, it should have come with fuller references, which is not the style that *Sightings* follows, being an online newsletter, but never mind. In her view, I should have given proper academic-style citations for my outrageous claims about what Milo said. I gave the primary sources—Milo's own talks and interviews—but apparently those don't count. According to Professor Orlemanski, I should have related all the hearsay about what he has said, like almost every other journalist who has written about him.

And then, according to others in my field, there is my use of medieval examples, analogies, and manuscript images. Oy, vey! How dare I, a trained medievalist, make light of the difficulties of our academic field by using manuscript images as illustrations for my blog posts—without giving you the full context for what the images *really* mean?!²¹¹ How dare I be so provocative as to suggest that a modern trickster like Milo might have similarities to other, more revered trickster figures like Francis—or Jesus?! How dare I speak slightingly of interpretive methodologies ::cough cough *gender studies* cough cough *feminism*:: which I personally dislike and find not just less than useful,

---

[210] https://divinity.uchicago.edu/sightings/why-milo-scares-students-and-faculty-even-more

[211] https://fencingbearatprayer.blogspot.com/2017/03/turning-other-cheek.html

but sinful?! How dare I—and here's the real issue—assert my political views so forcefully *so that even my students will know what I think?!*

Professor Orlemanski insists that, in publishing my piece, *Sightings* directly contributed to the "racist and sexist climate" already a feature of our university culture as evidenced in the Spring 2016 Campus Climate Survey, which rather suggests that the problem a) is not of my making, since the report predates my blogging for Milo and b) is not the fault of the very few conservatives on campus.[212] (Only two fellow faculty members have declared themselves to me in the past couple weeks, so I am guessing there aren't many. I would love to be proved wrong! *Write me!*) *But, to be fair, that was not what the chair of my department was worried about.*

My chair was worried that I not give the impression that I have *only one self* by linking the blog to the personal website and the personal website to the blog so as not to confuse my Professional Self with my Public Self, my scholarly self with my public role as Fencing Bear. Which raises a number of interesting questions about what it means to have a self, never mind a public identity.

On the one hand, it *does* matter for Fencing Bear's blogging on behalf of Milo that I teach at the University of Chicago. That was the whole reason I started writing for him in the first place. My institution has come out more forcefully in support of freedom of speech than any other in the country this past year. If he was going to be taking this fight to campuses across the country, I wanted to be there with him, standing up for our students' right to hear opinions and arguments that they would not otherwise hear, so oppressive has the response from one of our two political poles become. (Do you doubt me?

---

[212] https://cpb-us-w2.wpmucdn.com/voices.uchicago.edu/dist/6/294/files/2016/09/
UCM300717.ClimateSurveyReport.v4.111716-zl5tj8.pdf

Ask Professor Allison Stanger how her neck feels.[213]) So it would be disingenuous to insist that my Professional Self was not a feature of the reason that I took up the role that I did in my Public Self.

On the other hand, that my former students have expressed shock—nay, worse, *disappointment*—to learn that I hold the political, cultural, and religious views that I do suggests that I never talk about them in class, otherwise why would they be so surprised? They are shocked—*shocked*—because, of course, I have not talked about my views in the manner which my chair cautioned me I ought not and which colleagues across the country in my own field of medieval studies have somewhat gleefully—and maliciously—assumed I must, that is, so as to promote all of the -isms that they also assume Milo promotes on the basis of never having listened to him speak.

Which rather suggests that I am fully capable of keeping my Public Self distinct from my Professional Self when I am speaking in my Professional Self as, well, Professor. *But why, after all, should it matter so much that I make it clear that I have these two Selves?* Because Kant, of course. Okay, more precisely, what Immanuel Kant said in September 1784 about Enlightenment and what it means to be Enlightened.[214]

You'd think that all of these confusions between Public Self and Professional Self were new, to hear my colleagues gasp at my temerity in writing my blog in a style and a voice distinct from the voice that I use in the classroom or my scholarship, but they aren't. They were just as alive and as fraught in Kant's day, when university professors (like Kant) were expected to maintain a particular confessional stance in the classroom, whatever they might believe about the Church or the State in their private lives. Except that, according to Kant, it was their private lives that were public and their professional role as

[213] https://www.sevendaysvt.com/OffMessage/archives/2017/03/03/mob-attacks-middlebury-prof-and-controversial-speaker-charles-murray

[214] http://www.columbia.edu/acis/ets/CCREAD/etscc/kant.html

teachers that was private, if you see what I mean. No? Okay, let's try it in Kant's words (my emphasis).

> Enlightenment is man's emergence from his self-imposed nonage. Nonage is the inability to use one's own understanding without another's guidance. This nonage is self-imposed if its cause lies not in lack of understanding but in indecision and lack of courage to use one's own mind without another's guidance. *Dare to know!* (*Sapere aude.*) *"Have the courage to use your own understanding," is therefore the motto of the enlightenment....*

> This enlightenment requires nothing but *freedom*—and the most innocent of all that may be called "freedom": *freedom to make public use of one's reason in all matters.* Now I hear the cry from all sides: "Do not argue!" The officer says: "Do not argue—drill!" The tax collector: "Do not argue—pay!" The pastor: "Do not argue—believe!" Only one ruler in the world says: "Argue as much as you please, but obey!" We find restrictions on freedom everywhere. But which restriction is harmful to enlightenment? *Which restriction is innocent, and which advances enlightenment? I reply: the public use of one's reason must be free at all times, and this alone can bring enlightenment to mankind.*

> On the other hand, the private use of reason may frequently be narrowly restricted without especially hindering the progress of enlightenment. *By "public use of one's reason" I mean that use which a man, as scholar, makes of it before the reading public. I call "private use" that use which a man makes of his reason in a civic post that has been entrusted to him.*

> In some affairs affecting the interest of the community a certain [governmental] mechanism is necessary in which some members of the community remain passive. This creates an artificial unanimity which will serve the fulfillment of public objectives, or at least keep these objectives from being destroyed. Here arguing is not permitted: one must obey. Insofar as a part of this machine considers himself at the same time a member of a universal community—a world society of citizens—(let us say that he thinks of himself as a scholar rationally addressing his public through his writings) he may indeed argue, and the affairs with which he is associated in part as a passive member will not suffer. Thus it would be very unfortunate if an officer on duty and under orders from his superiors should want to criticize the

appropriateness or utility of his orders. He must obey. *But as a scholar he could not rightfully be prevented from taking notice of the mistakes in the military service and from submitting his views to his public for its judgment.* The citizen cannot refuse to pay the taxes levied upon him; indeed, impertinent censure of such taxes could be punished as a scandal that might cause general disobedience. *Nevertheless, this man does not violate the duties of a citizen if, as a scholar, he publicly expresses his objections to the impropriety or possible injustice of such levies.*

A pastor, too, is bound to preach to his congregation in accord with the doctrines of the church which he serves, for he was ordained on that condition. *But as a scholar he has full freedom, indeed the obligation, to communicate to his public all his carefully examined and constructive thoughts concerning errors in that doctrine and his proposals concerning improvement of religious dogma and church institutions.* This is nothing that could burden his conscience. For what he teaches in pursuance of his office as representative of the church, he represents as something which he is not free to teach as he sees it. He speaks as one who is employed to speak in the name and under the orders of another. He will say: "Our church teaches this or that; these are the proofs which it employs." Thus he will benefit his congregation as much as possible by presenting doctrines to which he may not subscribe with full conviction. He can commit himself to teach them because it is not completely impossible that they may contain hidden truth. In any event, he has found nothing in the doctrines that contradicts the heart of religion. For if he believed that such contradictions existed he would not be able to administer his office with a clear conscience. He would have to resign it. Therefore the use which a scholar makes of his reason before the congregation that employs him is only a private use, for no matter how sizable, this is only a domestic audience. In view of this he, as preacher, is not free and ought not to be free, since he is carrying out the orders of others. *On the other hand, as the scholar who speaks to his own public (the world) through his writings, the minister in the public use of his reason enjoys unlimited freedom to use his own reason and to speak for himself.* That the spiritual guardians of the people should themselves be treated as minors is an absurdity which would result in perpetuating absurdities.

We like to talk about academic freedom as if we, as scholars, are freest in the work that we do in our profession. But, as Kant suggests, the work that we do as professors—like the work that military officers or pastors or citizens do—is not, in fact, free insofar as we are bound to the requirements of our various offices. "But, wait!" I can hear you say. "Kant was not free as a professor because he was a functionary of the State. As Professor at the University of Königsberg, he was employed by the State to teach particular subjects. We, however, as American academics are not state employees, but free scholars."

Except, of course, many of "us" aren't. Technically, I am because I teach at the University of Chicago, which is a private institution. But all of us are employed one way or another in service of the State, whether we teach at public or private institutions, because all of us, as my colleagues will be quick to remind you whenever the government changes hands, are dependent directly or indirectly on money taken from our fellow citizens to support our work.

Nor are we free—as my colleagues like Julie have been determined to remind me these past several weeks—to teach from within our status as members of our profession as if the things we teach are something we actually believe, if, that is, our belief, for example as Christians, goes against the orthodoxy of "objectivity" by which we, through peer review, enforce belief. It is only in our Public Selves, as Kant would put it, that we are in fact free to criticize what we see our colleagues doing. It is only in our Public Selves, in Kant's formulation, that we are fully free to exercise our own understanding. *And, therefore, according to Kant, it is only in our Public Selves that we are able to speak the truth.*

I have said over and over again, much to the ridicule of many of my academic colleagues and the journalists who have gotten wind of my blog, that the reason I love (yes, love, in the Christian sense of profound charity) Milo is because he tells the truth. What I saw when

I started watching his talks back in September was someone who was willing to step out of the private role of journalist—his professional self—and into the public role of scholar and truth-teller.

He did so, as we have all seen, at considerable personal risk, both professionally—he has resigned his job at *Breitbart*—and physically. (You don't employ Navy Seals as body guards unless the death threats you are getting are to be taken fairly seriously.) For this, as I tried to explain in the *Sightings* article, we in academia owe him a profound debt. Yes, there are conservative speakers out there (here's looking at you, Ben Shapiro) who may be better at debate (I say *may*—we are still waiting on the great Milo-Ben debate), but who of you who is not already conservative has heard of them?

I am still meeting people to this day who have barely heard of Milo (*I know*, amazing, isn't it?), except for the rumors about what the mainstream media insists he has said. We are, as, again, I said in the *Sightings* article, experiencing a profound spiritual crisis in which all our most deeply held beliefs are being put to the test. But most of us seem content to live in what Kant called mankind's "self-imposed nonage," giving over to the guardians of our culture the governance of our understanding.

Who at this point will have the courage to use his or her own understanding? Who will stand up against the crowd and say, "*Dare to know!*"? Milo did. Inspired by Milo, Fencing Bear has tried to. A fool and a teddy bear take on the world. You gotta laugh.

TWO MASTERS BAD

March 8, 2017

Jesus, like Milo, is right about everything. Okay, so Milo has made some mistakes. Okay, a few pretty big ones. But not Jesus. Jesus is right about everything. Especially what it means to serve a master. "No one can serve two masters," he told his disciples (Matthew 6:24). "For either he will hate the one and love the other, or he will be devoted to the one and despise the other. You cannot serve God and mammon."

Mammon, of course, is a fancy Aramaic word for "money or riches," so we usually take this passage to mean: "You have to choose between serving God or making money." Which is true, but banal. Of course holy people aren't in it for the money; they have higher, more spiritual things on their mind than filthy lucre.

Which would seem to let the rest of us off the hook, as it were. As long as we aren't, I don't know, billionaire real-estate developers, we aren't really serving mammon, right? We want just enough money to live comfortably, we want everyone else to have enough money to live comfortably, but as long as we aren't *in it for the money*, we're safe. Yeah, right. Don't kid yourself, you're serving the money.

Okay, maybe you don't think of it as the money. Maybe you say: "I need this job to be able to take care of my family." Or you say: "I don't care about the money, but I do need this status to be able to do the work that I want to do." Or you say: "I worked hard for this position, I deserve other people's respect." Or you say: "It isn't about me, it is about serving social justice." To coin a phrase, spineless cunts! (Jesus would say, "Hypocrites!" Milo is blunter.) You are still serving the money as long as you are not serving God.

I have, of course, been thinking about this passage a lot, ever since we read it two Sundays ago in RCIA class. "What does it mean to serve mammon?," our discussion leader asked. We came up with a long list of things. You might serve status or ambition or security or fear, particularly fear of losing your livelihood. Which, again, don't necessarily seem to be bad things. Surely God doesn't want us to starve? Ah. Do you remember what Jesus said next? "Therefore, I tell you, do not be anxious about your life, what you shall eat or what you shall drink, nor about your body, what you shall put on. Is not life more than food, and the body more than clothing?" (Matthew 6:25)

Colleagues and friends, former students and readers of my blog have been writing to me in the hundreds these past two weeks. (For which, don't get me wrong, I am more grateful than words can express. As Milo has told his followers, you've kept me sane. But you guys and dolls are strong, I know you can take some tough love.) Their letters have certain themes. "Thank you," they say, "for saying what I have been wanting to say about the crisis in our culture, but have been too afraid to express." "Thank you," they say, "for standing up for Milo, I have been praying for him, I don't know how he has the courage to do what he does." "Thank you," they say, "I wish I could say the things that you and Milo are saying but I am afraid that I would lose my job and/or all my friends." This is what it means to serve mammon. It is serving the fear.

How do you know when you are serving the fear? You lie. You lie to yourself about what really matters to you. You lie to others about what you believe. You lie so as to protect yourself from what others might think about you if you spoke what you believe. You lie because it feels easier than speaking up. Which, let me tell you, in a way it is. It is much easier to sit in the department meeting as your colleagues are talking about changing the requirements for your degree program and not say anything when you realize that they are all in agreement and you disagree.

It is much easier to nod and smile when they start talking about theories of gender or politics or religion and not say anything when you realize they are all in agreement and you disagree. It is much easier to nod and smile when they make jokes about President Trump or Christians and not say anything when you realize they are all in agreement and you disagree.

But, as Jordan Peterson has so eloquently put it, it really isn't. "You don't get to choose not to pay a price" if you decide not to speak.[215] Speaking or not speaking, there is a price. And the price of not speaking is death. "You get to choose which poison you are going to take. That's it. If you are going to stand up for something, stand up for your truth.... And you don't get to wait." Particularly if, like me, you are a professor already. In Professor Peterson's words:

> If you're a professor already, you're like the most protected person in the history of the planet... It is almost impossible to provide people with enough protection so that they feel safe to speak.... It is not safe to speak. It never will be....
>
> But the thing you have to keep in mind is that it is even less safe not to speak! It's a balance of risks. Do you want to pay the price for being

---

[215] https://youtu.be/tiaGBbdIA-8

who you are and stating your mode of being in the world, or do you want to pay the price for being a bloody serf? One that has enslaved him or herself?

Well, that's a major price...that thing unfolds over decades, and you'll just be a miserable worm at the end of about twenty years of that. No self-respect. No power. No ability to voice your opinions. Nothing left but resentment because everyone's against you. Because of course you never stood up for yourself....

[Speaking the truth is] the price you want to pay if you believe truth is the cornerstone of society.... If you're willing to take that leap, then tell the truth and see what happens. Nothing better could possibly happen to you... There will be push back...but it doesn't matter. The truth is what redeems the world from hell. And that's the truth.... Wake up, tell the truth! Tell the truth! Or at least don't lie.

The Devil, as we all know, is the Father of Lies (John 8:44). It is the Devil who tells us not to speak for fear of losing our jobs or our colleagues' respect. It is the Devil who tempts us with power over others if we tell his lies and not God's truth. It is the Devil who offers us ease and riches and powerful friends if only we keep our mouths shut. But, as Professor Peterson says, as high as the price may be for speaking the truth, the price for not speaking is higher.

What price would you pay to enter into God's kingdom? Milo knows, it's why he wears all those pearls. As the Master put it, in one of his many parables to his disciples (Matthew 13:45-46): "Again, the kingdom of heaven is like a merchant in search of fine pearls, who, on finding one pearl of great value, went and sold all that he had and bought it." There will never be a safe time to speak. Not when you have tenure (as I do), not when you are a full professor (as I still hope to become, but it will depend on what my colleagues say about my new book). Not when you have been established as a leader in your field for decades. If you speak, and you speak the truth, they will come for you.

They will tell lies about you that even your closest friends will believe. They will tell you how *disappointed* they are that you have spoken up. They will write letters to your administrators to try to censor you. They will predict that you will lose all your students, or at least many of them. They will tell you about how everyone is talking about *what you said*. They will threaten you with the greatest weapon at their disposal: *shame*. And they will hold out the promise of the Devil's temptations if only you will *shut up*.

You cannot serve both God and mammon. As Jesus told the Devil when the Devil tempted him with all the kingdoms in the world if only Jesus would fall down and worship him (Matthew 4:8-10): "Begone, Satan! for it is written, 'You shall worship the Lord your God, and him only shall you serve.'" It is a great temptation to serve the Devil and to go along with the lies.

The Devil promises us ease: "If you are the Son of God, command these stones to become loaves of bread." The Devil promises us followers: "If you are the Son of God, throw yourself down [from the pinnacle of the temple]; for it is written, 'He will give his angels charge of you.'" The Devil promises us power. But the Devil lies.

It is Jesus who tells us the truth (Matthew 16:24-26): "If any man would come after me, let him deny himself and take up his cross and follow me. For whoever would save his life will lose it, and whoever loses his life for my sake will find it. For what will it profit a man, if he gains the whole world and forfeits his life? Or what shall a man give in return for his life?"

We who live in America live in the freest country ever in the history of human civilization. As citizens and even as visitors, we have the right enshrined in the founding document of our country to speak without fear that the government will seek to censor us. And yet, as a society, we are busy attempting to censor ourselves for fear that others will find what we say offensive. How much more offensive will it be, if in fearing to speak for the sake of mammon, we lose not just our Lives, Fortune, and our sacred Honor, but the world?

TWISTING THE DEVIL'S TAIL

March 10, 2017

"Barely literate." "Lesbianic man-hating harpies." "Professor Stuff-Your-Face-With-Froot-Loops." "Hamplanets." "Kid fuckers." "Beta orbiting cucks" (said of male feminists). "Black dude" (said of a woman). "Man in a dress" (said of a transwoman before surgery). "Spineless cunts" (said of older conservatives). "Illiterate fucks" (said of his own staff). "Race-mixing kike faggot" (said of himself). My colleagues at the University of Chicago want you to know that these words are dangerous, particularly when spoken by my Vile Boyfriend, Mr. Milo Yiannopoulos.

So dangerous, in fact, that simply *writing* about how I think his Dangerous Faggot tour of American college campuses has exposed significant tensions in our university culture is—they would insist—cause for serious concern, whether I mention the jokes that he makes or not. Particularly, it would seem, when I do not. "It is a statement of fact," my colleague in English Languages and Literatures Julie Orlemanski has asserted,

> that Mr. Yiannopoulos expresses xenophobic, racist, and transphobic ideas and carries out discursive violence by doxing (intimidating

individuals by dumping personal information into the public domain [*which Milo never does, but my colleagues wouldn't know this because they assume they know him without doing the proper research—FB*]) his critics as well as persons he identifies as undocumented immigrants [*this is slander—FB*] or trans [*ditto—the one trans student he has talked about was already on public record* for filing a complaint against the university where Milo was speaking—FB[216],[217]]. The Anti-Defamation League refers to him as "a misogynistic, racist, xenophobic, transphobic troll."[218]

Just yesterday, twenty-seven of my colleagues in the Divinity School followed suit:

In accordance with the University's commitment to promote free expression, we do not dispute Professor Brown's right to voice her opinions... However, we want to be clear that the publication of her column in *Sightings* does not imply that we condone these opinions, especially as her column supports an individual whose views are widely regarded as promoting racism, sexism, transphobia, and Islamophobia.[219]

Which is pretty good going for an article that was about how we in the academy need to talk more about religion, precisely in order to prevent the kinds of "hate crimes" that my colleagues insist are on the rise thanks to the jokes Milo tells.[220] (Milo keeps a list of these kinds of crimes, the vast majority of which appear to have been hoaxes.[221],[222]) They sound a little like Jorge of Burgos, don't you think? "The spirit is serene only when it contemplates the truth and takes delight in

---

[216] https://www.dailywire.com/news/5419/man-angry-university-not-letting-him-show-his-junk-amanda-prestigiacomo

[217] https://www.breitbart.com/social-justice/2016/12/15/milo-uwm-trans-locker-room/

[218] http://www.thismess.net/2017/02/milo-and-university-of-chicago.html

[219] https://divinity.uchicago.edu/sightings/statement-concerned-faculty-divinity-school

[220] https://www.thecollegefix.com/u-chicago-divinity-school-support-free-speech-unless-offensive/

[221] https://www.breitbart.com/social-justice/2016/05/02/hate-crime-hoaxes-growing-epidemic/

[222] http://www.fakehatecrimes.org

good achieved, and truth and good are not to be laughed at. This is why Christ did not laugh. Laughter foments doubt."

I asked my friends in my Facebook salon yesterday what they think about Milo's jokes.

— Milo tackles topics that are too un-PC for mainstream comedians to touch, and it's hilarious.

— I personally love Milo's jokes. It's very much like an amusement park ride—you never know what he might say but they are crazy funny. I don't get offended at all because I know he is just joking. I know he is NOT a hateful person by observing how he interacts with his opponents—he always tells his fans to be polite to his challengers no matter how silly or rude the questions can be. He always tried to answer them in a very respectful way with some street "French" at times. He has said on many occasions that "if we don't hold ourselves [to] the same standards as we do...our opponents, we are no better than them."

— Nothing he says makes me uncomfortable, but that's because I'm not an oversensitive snowflake, whose labia get chafed over mean words. Plus, he's certainly more amusing than these swine "comedians," whose idea of funny and original is copious use of the F-bomb and making stupid faces (see the graphic comparison of Amy Schumer to a potato).

— I see it as no worse than listening to the 80's "alternative comedians" who appeared to make a living via the words "fu*k Thatcher." Yes, some of the things he says are a little near the knuckle for my personal taste, but if Milo wasn't outrageous, I doubt he would have the platform he has. Some of the things he says are genuinely extremely funny, and yes, some might be hurtful. But he is not commanding that people listen to him, I see no reason why someone should be lynched for irreverent humour.

— Milo's humor serves two purposes, it is both an irritant and a catharsis. He irritates by tearing down conventions, and like a grain of sand in an oyster it promotes the response—a pearl of wisdom if you will. [*See, I told you Milo wears pearls on purpose!*—FB] It is also a catharsis, wherein he irreverently exposes and critiques the inequalities and inconsistencies that bother the rational mind.

— Milo is incredibly crude with his jokes, but if a Leftist were making the very same jokes no one would even raise an eyebrow or clutch a single pearl. [*More pearls!—FB*] That's how I know his sense of humor is a non-issue.

— IMHO, humor is funny because it brings us face to face with an incongruity that we otherwise wouldn't be very (or at all) aware of.... [Humor] is always at least a little uncomfortable... Now in my fifty-almost-two years on the planet, I've figured out that life is messy. If you're searching for perfect ideological consistency you're going to be disappointed. We're all hypocrites to one degree or another.... I think it's extremely valuable for one to keep an eye on where one's own inconsistencies lie. Doing that usually requires that someone else point them out. Someone like Milo.

— I enjoy [Milo] because the left owns entertainment right now— from sitcoms to SNL. We have nothing. And it doesn't make you a bad person to laugh at the stereotypical jokes [Milo] makes. Jokes like that have a degree of truth to them, that's where the stereotype comes from.

— He's hilarious as are his followers. I just was reading the comments on a post he put up today featuring a pic of a young Steve Bannon and I laughed so hard I nearly peed myself (OK I did, but it was only a little... Incontinence comes with old age). It's a rarity to laugh like that. Akin to something like joy.

— I think Milo's a brilliant young man, and I enjoy the bulk of his speeches. I do think a lot of his jokes are unnecessarily cruel, and pretty much irrelevant to the points he's trying to make. And I honestly don't appreciate most of his humor. That being said, I understand Milo literally grew up in a different world than I did (different generation, different country, different social circle, different culture), so I try to keep that in mind, and make allowances. I also realize I'm not his target audience. It's obvious from his following that his humor IS hitting the mark with his generation and his demographic, so I wouldn't want him to change in any way except as he sees fit to further his own career and purposes. That's the beauty of an open, free-speech society. I can list to Milo...and appreciate what he has to say without approving of his humor.

— His jokes are funny. Sounds simple, but it's actually profound. Humor cuts down to the truth in a way nothing else can. His jokes make us uncomfortable on purpose, to try and push us outside our little personal idea bubbles.

— I find him hilarious, and I know he intends his words to provoke and tease and I hear it as such. He is like a matador that dances around the enraged bull. But rather than stabbing and blooding with spears, the mighty Milo Matador tickles it with feathers, pulls its tail, and fixes giant pompoms onto the tips of its horns.

— I love his jokes. Either everything is OK to joke about or nothing is.

— Milo's jokes are as layered and nuanced as everything else about him. Milo says that no one can resist the truth wrapped in a good joke, and he described his Dangerous Faggot Tour to Tucker Carlson as half lecture, half standup. As such, his jokes become the mechanism of delivery for his more salient points.... [His] jokes also serve to remind everyone to not take themselves too seriously, and to bring fun back into a notoriously boring realm. One of the things I love about Milo is that he can laugh at himself. When the other panelists on Bill Maher's show roasted him, he was the one who laughed the hardest, and then turned it into an even bigger joke.

— Most of his jokes make me howl with laughter like a hyena, especially the jokes about gay sex. I'm generally not offended by anything he says; I got the satire in things like the modest proposal that women be kicked off the internet. There's only one thing he does that I have a big issue with: advocating fat shaming. I think I get what's going on: Milo is always looking for ways to put his awesome trolling powers to use for good and not for evil, and he thinks this is one such area because it will improve public health. Also the fat acceptance movement is imprudently pushing the other way. But I believe Milo doesn't yet see the whole picture about fat shaming.

— I think what he is doing is so important. He is showing people that there is no definition of what it means to be a Christian conservative. He is freeing us from the stereotype. And by joking about these ideals that the progressives have held onto for so long as Bible he is allowing us, as conservatives, to finally expose how absolutely unsubstantiated some of these claims (so-called facts) really are.

— At a time when classrooms have turned into prison cells (in the manner of disciplining thoughts) and the same goes for the family...and the MSM, Milo has been doing a service to us all. By provoking jokes, he is cajoling us to think differently about things that we had taken for granted.

— For the most part I love his sense of humor. I never find any of his jokes about women, for example, to be offensive, mostly because I think he delivers the best one-liners with such warmth and joviality that you can't be offended unless you are trying. Through sheer volume, however, he occasionally misses the mark. He's not on every single time, and I notice that he generally slips where his patience is at its lowest. He bears the scrutiny and brow-beating remarkably well, but it's enough to get to anyone eventually. Where he wavers, whether from speaking exhaustion or irritation, his humor slips into a kind of "mean girls" bitchy high school bully vibe. Never violent, but kind of cringe and cliquey. I am thinking in particular when he singled out the hijabi women in the crowd at one of his talks [*who had been heckling him—FB*], joked at their personal expense instead of at their ideas or the culture generally, and then dismissively mocked them as they left. He's at his best when he's like "come to Jesus; we love you even though you have cancer" [*i.e. feminism—FB*].

— So when I hear his jokes I think of the satirist who holds up a mirror to show us our real selves, our real behavior, our real hypocrisy even. It's very helpful for society to have that. When he "jokes" about feminism and feminists or Muslims and Islam, I hear the truth. The only jokes I don't like are the ones he makes about himself—or even when he "acts" excessively gay because I know how deep his pain is and how he wishes he wasn't gay or hurting... I wish he wasn't an icon.

— One important thing to note is that about half his jokes are aimed at himself. He doesn't consider himself beyond reproach. He's self-deprecating. This lends credibility to his humorous critiques.

— Some of his jokes have made me uncomfortable. And some may just save my life. I have his "Fat Shaming Works" talk cued up on my iPad at all times. Because sometimes I need to hear it again when I want to give in.... No ridiculous "body positivity" crap will be able to get me where I need to be. Only the hard work I was too lazy to do when I was younger is going to help. So thank you, Milo, for this horribly uncomfortable joke/message. Wish I had heard it sooner.

— Milo turns a mirror toward us. Just because we do not like what we see does not make it false. Now, the mirror may at times have blemishes and cracks which may obscure, but when we look into even such a mirror we know enough to fill in the cracks. Most often I find Milo to be a riot. When times are most dark, we need humor. We need to laugh, even at ourselves (especially at ourselves). I vape. Milo makes fun of vapers all the time. I find it funny. Milo may go beyond the pale at times, but it is necessary.

— His jokes are always about a concept...if someone aggressively and publicly represents that concept, then he uses their words/ actions as an example, e.g. 3rd wave sjw feminism—Lena Dunham. He never picks on the private or the respectful persons...only the garishly totalitarian public abusers of intellectual and cultural concepts and freedoms.

— Milo's sense of humor is actually pretty common in the United Kingdom and Ireland... Factories, offices, pubs, clubs: most places where people gather, there'll be somebody on the receiving end of some cutting humour. Some of the chants and songs you hear at British football grounds all around the country are far worse than anything you'll hear from Milo. There's no doubt that people who profess to be offended by jokes and opinions are themselves guilty of telling "offensive" jokes and expressing "offensive" opinions. And if Milo was on the Liberal Left, he'd have a regular column in the Guardian, be invited onto a wide variety of BBC shows and would still be on Twitter.

— Being from Australia, I have a somewhat biased view. We were brought up on British humour. John Cleese says that the point of humour is that it's going to offend someone, but often in humour, we can see who we are and what we really think. It holds a mirror up to our eyes and we see our foibles but instead of condemning them, we can smile. People who are offended by dark humour may find that they have few opportunities to love and accept the darkness within. Yet that is what brings healing to the soul!

— I am fine with Milo's jokes although I cringe about the "fat lesbian" jokes regarding feminism. I have some very level-headed lesbian friends who need to hear what he is saying; however, they might not be able to "hear" past these kinds of jokes. In the gay male community, there has been a long-standing anti-woman vibe with many jokes pointed in lesbians' directions. I don't feel like Milo needs to continue this "tradition." Where are the conservative "fat lesbians" supposed to go, after all? They have no one to champion their cause.

— Black political scientist Shelby Steele suggests that Americans have replaced their sexual Puritanism of the 1950s with racial and gender Puritanism. They react to edgy political jokes with the same fury that their parents and grandparents would have focused on sexual jokes by, e.g., Lenny Bruce or George Carlin. Come to think of it, one of Carlin's great bits was "the seven words you can't say on television." We probably still have seven words you can't say, but they're different words.

— Humor, or rather (incredibly) the absence of an emphasis on Milo's commentary as humor, has been the "elephant in the room" throughout the Milo controversies. I've been amazed that however off-the-cuff or with whatever comic intent his words may have been (ill) chosen, his remarks have been treated as though they came from Joseph Ratzinger as Prefect of the Congregation for the Doctrine of the Faith or perhaps by the Surgeon General of the United States. Milo's lack of self-seriousness as he talks about what could be serious issues has been the hallmark of his comedy and provided a great deal of necessary oxygen in these otherwise suffocating stifling Maoist tribunals about what constitutes acceptable public speech.

— Pardon me if this has already been mentioned, but Milo's jokes aren't any worse than any of Joan Rivers's ever were, and she is worshipped as a comedic icon.

— Milo uses humor to force us to examine our deeply held beliefs—often erroneous beliefs. If you actually listen to him, that is. Those who don't listen cannot possibly understand either what he's saying or what he's doing. Yes, he's a troll, but he's a self-aware troll. And he's funny. It's unfortunate that progressives have no sense of humor, no sense of fun, no notion of the absurd. They miss so much—in life and art.

I have the best friends. All my friends are the best. Including Milo.

This is what he said as the introduction to his most "Islamophobic" talk, given in Orlando, Florida, in October 2016, four months after a Muslim gunman killed forty-nine people in a gay nightclub [ad lib from his talk as delivered in brackets]:[223]

One of the first things to disappear in the wake of a terrorist attack is humour. That's one of the things they want. They want to make us afraid. When we're afraid, we don't dare laugh in case it's the wrong thing to do. But laughing is one of the ways we show we're okay, and that there can be a future beyond what has happened.

We aren't going to beat Islamic terror only with tanks and bombs. We're going to beat it with ideology. We're going to beat it with laughter—by showing the people who live in countries ruled by dictators and thugs that they will not make us afraid. By showing them that the West is best.

That's how the Berlin Wall fell. People in East Germany knew that West Germany was better. [And one of the ways they knew was that they could hear the sound of laughter over the Wall.]

[Laughter is one of the first things to leave us when the authoritarians take hold. The thing that tyrants hate the most is the sound of laughter because it means somebody somewhere has gone off script. Someone has gone off message.]

---

[223] https://www.breitbart.com/social-justice/2016/09/27/10-things-milo-hates-islam/

The freedoms enjoyed in this country, the best country [in the world], are, or should be the envy of the world. [They are best exemplified by the ability to laugh, to enjoy jokes with one another.] It's often said that in order to find out who [has power, who has control in a society], you have to find out who you're not allowed to laugh about.

Today that's feminists, Black Lives Matter and Islam. Those are the groups that will get you into trouble if you crack jokes about [them]. You'll have your newspaper column taken away. You'll be banned from Twitter. Of all these groups, Islam is the most inherently hilarious....

It's easy to bleat about Christianity. It's low-hanging fruit. It's more difficult, and it takes more bravery, to criticise Islam with sincerity and seriousness. And with jokes.

The past three weeks, ever since my *Sightings* article posted, I have been constantly reminding myself of what Milo said when I showed him what my colleagues were saying about me: "Remember to laugh." Remember to laugh as you walk into the party where you are about to meet your potential new students and have to face the colleagues with whom you work in your field. Remember to laugh as you walk into the department meeting room where you are about to meet the students who wrote about you in the campus newspaper and who have been talking about you for weeks.

Remember to laugh when you attend the seminar with the senior colleagues who have been your mentors and friends for over twenty years and who have been hearing what all your colleagues in the field are saying about you. Remember to laugh—because it is only in laughter that we are able to be free of the fear. The Devil hates laughter because laughter is to a certain extent involuntary. We laugh in spite of ourselves when we are forced to confront the absurdity of our existence, our hypocrisy, self-importance, anxieties, and fears. As one of my Facebook friends put it:

At root, the human condition is absurd. Think about it, we've got this magnificent intellect, with all of its pretensions of dignity that sits atop a body that...well, provides fodder for fart jokes. Anyone who is still human who can't laugh at themselves is seriously deluded about his place in the universe. Alas, we are beset with deluded people.

Jorge was right. Laughter foments doubt. But it also frees in order to heal. What I said in my *Sightings* piece was that Milo is important because he exposes the fear. He scares students and faculty because he makes clear how high the stakes in our current debate over freedom of speech really are, while at the same time drawing attention to the things that students and faculty insist they themselves are no longer allowed to talk about—or question.

I labelled these things "theological" because I believe that, at root, this is what they are: claims about what we hold sacred, our deepest convictions about the meaning and purpose of life. In joking about these things, Milo, in effect, is guilty of blasphemy: ridiculing the sacred, making that-which-should-not-be-named a figure of fun. Except according to Christian teaching, God has already made himself ridiculous so as to save his ridiculous human creatures from their sins.

What's white, sticky and moves across the sky at a thousand miles per hour? The coming of the Lord.

How does Jesus masturbate? Like this... (place your hand flat on your groin, palm side down and mimic jerking off using the hole in your hand).

What's the difference between Jesus and a picture of Jesus? You only need one nail to hang up a picture of Jesus.

I dare you. Tell me again why I am not supposed to laugh.

❧

My colleagues also want you to know that my views on religion are outside the pale: The "Packet for Rachel Fulton Brown," published in *Sightings* on March 2, makes clear that Professor Brown promulgates a view of religion and theology that is not widely represented among the Divinity School community's diverse views.[224] I am, as it were, *too* diverse for the Divinity School. As Milo would say, "Stop it! *Stop it!*" Whimsical head tilt. *"Behave!"*

---

[224] https://divinity.uchicago.edu/sightings/packet-rachel-fulton-brown

SEVEN WITH ONE BLOW

March 17, 2017

I can hear my father: "Now, Rachel, don't be nasty." Four weeks, a day, and a lifetime ago, *Sightings* published my article "Why Milo Scares Students, and Faculty Even More."[225] Two weeks and a day before that, Milo had planned to give the last of his talks on his Dangerous Faggot Tour, but had had to be evacuated by his security team when the protests on the campus of the University of California, Berkeley, became too violent for the campus police to contain.

By the beginning of February, I, of course, had been writing on this blog in support of Milo, his method, his message, and his fans for over four months, ever since the College deans at the University of Chicago sent out their now infamous "no safe spaces" letter to our incoming freshmen. As I know now, my blog had already been exciting comment on my own campus, so when the barricades hit the windows at Berkeley, the Editor of *Sightings* contacted me and asked me to write something about Milo.

More particularly, as he explains in the Editor's Introduction to the Packet of responses that my *Sightings* piece provoked, he came to

[225] https://divinity.uchicago.edu/sightings/why-milo-scares-students-and-faculty-even-more

me because he had heard that there was a professor on our campus "who not only supported Milo Yiannopoulos but also understood her support of him as concomitant with her work as a medieval historian and scholar of religion."[226] Sensing—rightly!—a prime journalistic opportunity to spark productive debate, the Editor invited me "to argue for the significance of Yiannopoulos's activities, specifically in relation to the academic study of religion." Which, being a good Fencing Bear, I did. Little did I know what a *furor* I was to spark. (Okay, rhetorical feint; I kinda knew.)

First there was the weekend that my colleagues spent on the listserv to which I subscribe talking about how to deal with what I had said—and not said.[227] Then there was the bombshell dropped on Milo for his comments about the sexual abuse that he suffered as a minor. Then there were the articles written about my blogging for him, complete with a whole new range of insults to add to the usual "racist, sexist, homophobic, Islamophobic, white supremacist" cloud that has plagued Milo's own speaking over the past year. Then there was the letter signed by twenty-seven of my colleagues in the Divinity School, assuring the world that my opinions do not represent the diversity of our conversation at Chicago.[228]

In the midst of all this, seven of my colleagues, some from on campus, some from elsewhere, including one of my own former students, wrote more substantive responses to what they thought I had said, which *Sightings* published two weeks ago yesterday. Milo has spent the past week in Hawaii, away from the fray, which has given me a chance to catch up on some of my more professorial duties and to reflect on the arguments that my colleagues have made. They will be sad to hear, I suspect, that I still think that I, like Milo, am right.

[226] https://divinity.uchicago.edu/sightings/packet-rachel-fulton-brown

[227] https://fencingbearatprayer.blogspot.com/2017/02/you-schoolgirls.html

[228] https://divinity.uchicago.edu/sightings/statement-concerned-faculty-divinity-school

But they are honorable opponents—they have openly entered into the lists—and they deserve some response here.

On some points, as I hope to show, we agree. On others, I believe they have willfully misunderstood me. On yet others, I acknowledge that even in a short online article intended to provoke discussion I might have been clearer. I refuse, however, to say that I was in any way wrong to defend Milo in the terms that I did, whether in my blogging or in *Sightings,* my proof being the very volume and volubility of my colleagues' response. As I said in my *Sightings* article, Milo is important because, unique in my experience in academia, he has brought the very questions that my colleagues say they care about back into play in a way that they have not been for the whole of my career.

I say that, as a Christian, I have found it difficult to speak as such in the academy; they say that religion has been a constant feature in our conversations. Yes, I say, from the outside, but not, I would insist, from within, which, I maintain, is why our students across the country, particularly at elite institutions like the University of Chicago (or Middlebury), find them so threatening.[229],[230],[231],[232] They do not know how to deal with direct challenges to their beliefs. To quote myself: "If students cannot practice these difficult conversations in school, there is nothing to stop them from spilling into the streets." So let's practice. *Ladies and gentilhommes, report to the lists!* These are the colleagues who offered formal challenges.

- Emily D. Crews, Ph.D. candidate in the History of Religions, University of Chicago Divinity School

---

[229] https://theamericanscholar.org/on-political-correctness/

[230] http://nymag.com/intelligencer/2017/03/is-intersectionality-a-religion.html

[231] https://www.nationalreview.com/2017/03/herbert-marcuse-discriminatory-tolerance-expansive-tolerance-middlebury-college-riot/

[232] https://www.nationalreview.com/2017/03/berkeley-middlebury-riots-liberal-mob-suppressing-free-speech/

- Maggie Fritz-Morkin, Ph.D. (2013) in Romance Languages and Literature, University of Chicago; Assistant Professor of Italian, University of North Carolina at Chapel Hill
- William Schweiker, Edward L. Ryerson Distinguished Service Professor of Theological Ethics, University of Chicago Divinity School
- Miles S. Hopgood, B.A. (2010), M.Div. (2013) University of Chicago, Ph.D. candidate, Princeton Theological Seminary
- David Hollinger, Preston Hotchkis Professor of History Emeritus, University of California, Berkeley
- Amy Dru Stanley, Associate Professor of History and the Law School, University of Chicago
- Nancy Frankenberry, John Phillips Professor in Religion Emeritus at Dartmouth College, fellow at the Marty Martin Center, University of Chicago Divinity School 2015-2016

&•

There are, if I have read my colleagues' arguments correctly, seven points on which they would challenge me, with a few points at which they would seek to distract from the issues at hand. First, the feints. None of them seems to have done what I hoped by giving the references that I did to the *Sightings* piece. I assumed, rightly, I suspect, that almost none of them (or any of my other colleagues) would have been following Milo's tour this past year with anything like the attention I—or his now two million Facebook fans—have. My goal in the *Sightings* article was to make them curious. "Oh, look," I imagined them thinking. "Rachel, our colleague, sees something in Milo that I have not heard before, perhaps I should take a look." (Stop it! I'm an optimist!)

Sightings typically publishes pieces of no more than 1,000 words or so in length. My original draft ran to more like 2,000 words, which (to my mind) the Editor did a fine job of trimming down to a mere—but still lengthy for *Sightings*—1,300. With only so much space, I needed to make some choices. What I did was try to show Milo in his own words talking about the issues that even my colleagues acknowledge are important. In the Editor's words: "the commitment to free expression, and its limits; the relationship between 'religion' and 'culture' ('Western,' 'Christian,' or otherwise); the place of religious studies within the modern academy, and of theology within religious studies; the intellectual, social, and ethical responsibilities of scholars, educators...and editors."

I knew that my colleagues would doubtless have heard the insults thrown at (and by) Milo. What I wanted to do was make them wonder on the basis of the words that I quoted—from his interviews with Tucker Carlson and Stefan Molyneux and his talk at Minnesota State University—whether maybe there was more to the hysteria over his speaking than the standard media reports allowed. My sense from their responses on *Sightings* is that I failed. None of them seems to know any more about Milo than he or she did before I published my piece; none of them mentions anything that Milo said in any of the links that I gave.

Perhaps most tellingly, my longtime colleague from my own department Amy Dru Stanley reiterates simply that Milo espouses "hateful beliefs" and that my own opinion on "race, sex, gender, and faith is both so specious and so odious as not to be worth debating." She assumes on this basis that I want to use my classroom "as a place for conversion of students to Christian religious faith"—which I never said. And she concludes, without evidence, that I want "the minds of students...[to] be 'filled' with Christian religion to counter dangerous secular ideas. That false proposition hardly counts as opinion based on scholarly research."

She is right: I do believe that Christian religious faith is worth teaching for its own sake, but I do not and never have taken my classroom as a place for indoctrinating students. Quite the reverse. As I said in the *Sightings* article, they have already been indoctrinated. What I want to do is challenge them, as I say Milo—through his own championing of Christian values—has. What they, and my colleagues, do with that challenge is up to them. There are seven worthier blows that my colleagues have attempted to make.

1. ON THE IMPORTANCE OF ENTERING THE FRAY

Here Emily Crews shows herself a true Chicago graduate student. She recounts how many members of the University of Chicago community insisted that the best response to my *Sightings* article was to ignore it. Her response: not at all!

> The time for saying, "Let's not dignify this with a response," has passed. That method has been painfully unsuccessful. The reality facing us now is that the things we have thought would disappear if we looked the other way have not only remained, but put down roots. They've set up camp. They've been elected president. And so it seems to me that Fulton Brown's piece, as objectionable as many find it, provides scholars of religion with an ideal opportunity to do something we have, by and large, failed to do in recent years, and particularly in the months since the election of Donald Trump: step into the fray.

So, basically, I was right. Scholars of religion have, in Crews's own words, "been largely silent," despite the fact, as I said, that we as a country are involved in a major religious crisis. Crews and I may (okay, almost certainly do) disagree on the contours and content of that crisis, but she, like I, sees that we as scholars of religion have a responsibility to engage. *Simultaneous attacks, no touch.*

2. ON BEING WARY OF 'FAKE NEWS'

Medievalists know all about "fake news." Just ask anybody about the historical King Arthur.[233] Maggie Fritz-Morkin gives another apt example, drawing on a story in Boccaccio's *Decameron*, where Ciappelletto, "the worst man ever to live (including his impressive catalogue of vice)...spins his final confession into a rhetorical masterpiece narrating his own superlative virtue." By way of his confession, Ciappelletto manages to cast himself posthumously as a saint, but "there is no question but that the tomb [at which the Burgundians make their devotions to him] is an idol, an empty fetish." In Fritz-Morkin's words: "It is a testament to the frisson of blind and impulsive mass piety stirred up by a lone friar who, seduced by a dazzling autobiography, neglects to 'fact-check' Ciappelletto's story before publicizing it with all the tacit institutional approval inherent in his pulpit. Score an epic trolling victory for Ciappelletto."

Fritz-Morkin does not say, but I'm guessing we are meant to take Ciappelletto here as a stand-in for Milo. Her (implied) critique would be more salient if I had not, in fact, taken the time to listen to *all* of Milo's campus talks, *all* of his podcasts, and *all* of the interviews that he has done since coming to America and several of those that he did in England,[234] as well as reading deeply in his archive for *Breitbart* and back into his reporting for *The Catholic Herald.*

As noted above in answer to Amy Stanley's feint attack, it was precisely in order to counter the "fake news" circulating about Milo that I wrote the *Sightings* piece with the focus I did. Milo's fans love him because he is honest with them about who and what he is, unlike those who would seek to cast him as "the worst man ever to live" because they disagree with him on his politics, sexuality, or religion.

---

[233] https://fencingbearatprayer.blogspot.com/2016/12/fake-news.html

[234] https://www.youtube.com/user/yiannopoulosm/featured

I have written extensively in this blog about how I believe Milo's critics misread both his satire and his confession. Unlike Ciappelletto, Milo has never described himself as anything other than a sinner. When asked how he can be both Catholic and gay, his invariable response has been: "What else would I be, as a sinner?" It is I, not he, who has compared him to a saint, which blog posts he has persistently refused to share on his Facebook feed, almost as if he disagrees with me. *Attack, parry, riposte, my touch.*

3. ON THE ROLE OF UNIVERSITIES AS PLACES FOR ARGUING RELIGION

Having acknowledged the importance of arguing religion, Crews refines her critique with an attack on my purported "nostalgia for the medieval European university." What I said in the *Sightings* piece, just to be clear, was that "the medieval university on which American colleges were modeled was founded as a place to wrestle with theology; all the other arts and sciences were intended to stand in service to this task"—a statement which not so many decades ago would have been simply textbook boilerplate. It was during the Middle Ages, after all, that the Church had a monopoly on education. It didn't? Sorry, I must have dozed off while we were rewriting that narrative.

Crews further chides me for not acknowledging that the medieval universities "did not welcome...the presence of women [true, although Christianity has been the greatest force for women's education ever; even women wanted to learn to pray, for which they needed to be able to read], or Jews [technically true, although Christian scholars of the twelfth and thirteenth centuries spent a great deal of time consulting with learned Jews], or homosexuals [John Boswell would doubtless have something to say *on this point*],"[235] while suggesting that I do not appreciate the privilege that I or Milo have in being able to participate in university culture in the way that we do today. (I most certainly do.[236])

David Hollinger suggests that I do not appreciate the importance of science in the history of education, while, as noted above, Amy Stanley assumes that I mean to use the classroom as a pulpit. And Nancy Frankenberry would insist that students should be able to come away from university "without endorsing any particular faith or sectarian creed"—with which assertion I would agree, if that includes rejecting what I called the "bad theology" of unexamined secularism in favor of, say, Judaism, Islam, Hinduism, Buddhism, African religions, Chinese and Japanese religions or even, heaven forfend, Christianity. (I think she has been reading Stephen Prothero's *God is Not One: The Eight Rival Religions That Run the World—and Why Their Differences Matter* [2010], which I likewise recommend.[237])

Medieval universities were a model for exactly the kinds of arguments I say our students should be practicing, women, Jews, and homosexuals included. Not because I want students to be indoctrinated in Christian theology (or any other theology) without questioning, but precisely because I don't. I want them to learn to argue as the scholastics argued, by raising objections and marshaling their evidence. I want them to wrestle as the scholastics did throughout the thirteenth century with the introduction of Aristotle's natural philosophy and the Arabic commentators on his thought, with ideas that challenge the orthodoxies with which they have grown up, not simply reinforce them.

---

[235] *Christianity, Social Tolerance, and Homosexuality: Gay People in Western Europe from the Beginning of the Christian Era to the Fourteenth Century* (1981)

[236] https://fencingbearatprayer.blogspot.com/2016/11/white-privilege.html

[237] https://fencingbearatprayer.blogspot.com/2016/03/all-cultures-are-not-one.html

I want them to know what it takes to counter real objections to their arguments, not simply tilt at straw men. I want, as Milo constantly says, for their opponents to bring their best arguments to the table so that they have to argue their best. And, yes, I want them to argue not just science and politics, but also religion, because religion matters. *Attack, parry, riposte, my touch.*

4. ON THE DEFINITION OF RELIGION

But to argue religion, we need to know what we are talking about, which involves another good medieval discipline: defining our terms. Here I acknowledge that I should perhaps have marked more clearly that, when I said students (and my colleagues) need practice arguing about religion, I did not mean only Christian theology. I did try to mark what I meant by listing the things that I say Milo challenges his audiences to think about: "the proper relations between women and men, the definition of community, the role of beauty, access to truth."

It is true that Milo speaks more openly as a Catholic than I tend to in places other than my blog, but I specifically did not invoke the tenets of the Christian faith as elements of what I think "religion" means. "Religion," as I understand it, goes deeper than any particular confessional claims. William Schweiker would insist that what Milo and I say about religion is "too simple." There is no such thing as "Christianity," but rather only "Christianities." There is no such thing as "religion," but rather only "religions."

> It is not the case that "Christianity" is the root of "Western civilization," or that the defense of liberty was the concern of the medieval Church (recall the Inquisition!), or that the freedom to question "Christian" values is a mainstay of most "theologies" or even obviously Christian. The roots of the freedom of speech and conscience, as well as human equality, are more complex. Let's not replace one simple reading of history—the bland secularization theory that still holds the liberal

academy in thrall—with an equally trite myth of decline where we supposedly race into decadence with the waning of the moral muscle of the (Catholic) Church. *Scholarship* and *teaching* demand that we articulate, analyze, interpret, and assess the full complexity of our lived reality.

I could not agree more. What puzzles me in this response is that it is attacking something I never said. I never said there is only one answer to the questions that Milo raises, only that the answer is religious, having to do with our deepest convictions about what it means to be human. That the answers are multiple—and contested—should go without saying. Of course they are—that is the reason we need to practice talking about them! Crews insists that I am wrong to suggest that "religion is the 'wellspring' of culture." Religion, she says, "is culture naturalized as supernatural." It is "the structures, biases, prerogatives, and asymmetries of culture projected into and justified by a realm beyond the human." To which I say: Feuerbach. *Attack, parry, riposte, my touch.*

5. ON OUR ABILITY TO QUESTION FROM WITHIN OUR FAITH

Continuing with Schweiker's critique, I most certainly did *not* say, as Schweiker implies, that "people of faith are better armed to wrestle with ultimate questions" because they are "less manacled by ideology." *Everyone* is manacled by ideology, we could not function otherwise. This is what makes arguing such fundamental convictions so frightening, and the challenge, I say, that Milo brings to college campuses. While other conservative speakers argue generally about freedom of speech and the articles of the Constitution, Milo raises questions that cut to the very core of who we are as individuals in society.

That he does so through jokes and satire as well as through reasoned argument is one of the things that makes him all the more dangerous—and impossible to ignore. Of course he does it to get attention! That's the first rule of rhetoric: capture your audience's attention. And of course he is offensive. He is talking about things that are more or less guaranteed to offend. Plus, he's not the only one to make the arguments that he has, and with which I have agreed. If you don't like Milo or Fulton Brown, how about a bit of Camille Paglia to add to the mix?[238] Milo says: "Feminism is cancer." Paglia says: "Women's studies is institutionalized sexism."

Milo says: "The campus rape culture is a myth." Paglia says: "Rape is an outrage that cannot be tolerated in civilized society. Yet feminism, which has waged a crusade for rape to be taken more seriously, has put women in danger by hiding the truth about sex from them.... The date-rape controversy shows feminism hitting the wall of its own broken promises.... The only solution to date rape is female self-awareness and self-control." Young women have been made to feel afraid of the very men who would protect them, while refusing to take responsibility for the bad choices that they make. These are not words that are easy to hear, when they go against everything that the adults have been telling you for years. More Paglia:

> The idea that feminism is the first group that ever denounced rape is a gross libel to men. Throughout history, rape has been condemned by honorable men. Honorable men do not murder; honorable men do not steal; honorable men do not rape... Men have also protected women. Men have given women sustenance. Men have provided for women. Men have died to defend the country for women.

Which is pretty much what I was trying to say last winter in my blog posts about chivalry. For which, as longtime readers of my blog will

---

[238] *Free Women, Free Men: Sex, Gender, Feminism* (2017), conveniently released just this week.

know, I was likewise roundly condemned.[239] This is what I meant in the *Sightings* article when I said students' minds were being filled with bad theology. Where I was wrong was in suggesting that universities are institutionally structured so as to encourage such debate. They aren't. They are places where we come to learn how to defend the prevailing orthodoxy, whether we label it "religious" or not. *Attack lands, touch against me.*

6. ON BEING NICE

My former student Miles Hopgood is not pleased with me. "We seem," he says, "still to share much in common," but otherwise he can no longer see in my admiration for Milo "the professor I knew and respected." I seem, he says, to be suggesting that simply because Milo offends, "he is right, and that because he upsets, his claims are true." Further, Hopgood insists, I am wrong to suggest that Christians are not welcome in the academy.

"In my seven years at the University of Chicago," he recounts, "never was I attacked, maligned, shunned, sneered at, or in any way maltreated for my faith.... To suggest that there is within American academia anything approaching a systematic animus toward Christianity or religious conviction in general is not to tell the truth. Rather, it is to repeat a shameful lie that serves the only agenda Yiannopoulos knows: to anger and divide. I cannot," he concludes, with some pain, "fathom why you repeat it." But Hopgood is not finished. I must be further chastised for misrepresenting our shared faith:

> In your piece you regard Yiannopoulos as a proponent of Christian values and a defender of the many contributions our faith has made to the world. You have even gone so far as to compare him to Christ.... Ask yourself: does Yiannopoulos speak or act like one who has tasted

---

[239] https://fencingbearatprayer.blogspot.com/2015/06/talking-points-three-cheers-for-white.html [See also *Middle Rages*.]

the living water which quenches all thirst (John 4:14)? Does he live a life marked by gentleness and bound by the love of Christ (Ephesians 4)? Certainly he does not, and this should be for us the sign that his attachment to our faith is not a love for the way of our Christ but merely a lust for a jeweled raiment to clothe the fictitious Western identity he peddles. What he offers the world is not a knowledge of Christ, for he does nothing to knit us together in love (Colossians 2:2).

More quotations from Scripture follow, but you get the gist: Milo cannot be doing what he does out of love or knowledge of Christ because Milo is *not nice*. I am reminded of C.S. Lewis's essay *The Abolition of Man* (1943), where he talks about the way in which modern education is producing "men without chests," men without hearts or the willingness to fight. Paglia observed a similar loss of function some fifty years later, with the generation of those who by most conservative accounts ought to have been the most radical. Here I stand corrected for my optimism about the university as a place where we might have the difficult conversations, as well as my previous conviction that I am surrounded by activist radicals. I'm not. I'm surrounded by *niceness*.

> There is [Paglia commented in the *Times Literary Supplement* in 1992] a widespread notion that [the current inhabitants of academia] are dangerous leftists, "tenured radicals" in Roger Kimball's phrase, who have invaded the American establishment with subversive ideas. In fact, they are not radicals at all. Authentic leftism is nowhere to be seen in our major universities. The multiculturalists and the politically correct on the subjects of race, class, and gender actually represent a continuation of the genteel tradition of respectability and conformity. They have institutionalized American *niceness,* which seeks, above all, not to offend and must therefore pretend not to notice any differences or distinctions among people or cultures.

To paraphrase Lewis, Milo, like Aslan, is not a *tame* lion. Nor am I a tame Bear. We follow Our Lord, who, contrary to popular children's Bible representations, was himself something of a troll. *Attack no, counterattack lands, my touch.*

7. ON CHRISTIANITY IN THE ACADEMY

I am of course happy to hear that Hopgood has never felt ostracized in quite the way I have for having faith in Christ. Other colleagues over the course of the past several weeks have tried to convince me that they, too, have had no difficulties talking about or teaching religion. Except, when I press them, it is clear that they do not mean quite what I mean when I talk about modeling what it means to have faith. Yes, they *talk* about religion and ethics and difficult questions in their classrooms. But what they model is secular humanist objectivity. In Crews's words: "Fulton Brown's major critique of American higher education is that it 'lacks any clearly articulated and tested faith.' She is wrong. Our faith is in the fundamental commitment to the rights of any person, regardless of perspective, to enter into principled, disciplined debate, and advance an argument supported by credible evidence."

Schweiker would concur: "[If] one wants free and critical discourse among people treated with equal respect, where students engage fundamental convictions, then the model of the classroom must be Socratic debate, not Sophistic advocacy.... The power differential in classrooms means that too often students will follow the leader. That is what enslaves minds. Here, too, religious studies and modern theology can help lead. Those in my guild have worked exceedingly hard to differentiate confessions of faith from the work of pedagogy." Again, I think of something C.S. Lewis said, about how helpful it would be to have a real, live Christian at one's elbow while reading Milton's *Paradise Lost*.[240]

> We must...turn a deaf ear to Professor Saurat when he invites us "to study what there is of lasting originality in Milton's thought and especially to disentangle from theological rubbish the permanent and human interest." This is like asking us to study Hamlet after the

---

[240] https://fencingbearatprayer.blogspot.com/2009/02/in-praise-of-particular.html

"rubbish" of the revenge code has been removed, or centipedes when free of their irrelevant legs, or Gothic arches without the pointed arches. Milton's thought, when purged of its theology, does not exist. Our plan must be very different—to plunge right into the "rubbish," to see the world as if we believed it, and then, while we still hold that position in our imagination, to see what sort of a poem results.

In order to take no unfair advantage I should warn the reader I myself am a Christian, and that some (by no means all) of the things which the atheist reader must "try to feel as if he believed" I actually, in cold prose, do believe. But for the student of Milton my Christianity is an advantage. What would you not give to have a real, live Epicurean at your elbow while reading Lucretius?

This is what I try to offer my students when the texts we are reading or the themes we are discussing depend on Christian faith. Not to indoctrinate them, but to stimulate their imagination to wonder what it would be like to read *Beowulf* or Milton's *Areopagitica* or Tolkien's *The Lord of the Rings* as if they were, like Lewis or myself, believing Christians. How would that change what they were able to see? I would do the same if we were reading texts from other traditions which make different assumptions about what it means to worship or pray or make objects of beauty for the purpose of praise. What would it be like to read as a Buddhist or a Hindu? A Muslim or a Jew? An Orthodox Christian or a Protestant? The exercise of imagination is necessary in every case, including when one returns to the perspective from which one began. What is it like reading as a third-wave feminist or a secular humanist after trying to read as a medieval Christian?

This exercise can be challenging—and not a little dangerous. It is what I meant when I said in the *Sightings* piece that Milo's speaking carries with it "the possibility of conversion, of changing hearts and minds." Not because he speaks, as my academic colleagues wish he would, as they do, with properly referenced sources (he does give references in his published writings) or without emotional appeal.

But because he speaks *as a believing Christian* in a context in which it is rare to hear this kind of speech.

He offends precisely because he does not place the brackets around his claims that academics require ourselves to use. He offends because he speaks his opinions on matters of faith. He offends because, for the sake of the Truth, he refuses to be *nice. Attack, parry, riposte, my touch. Final score: 5-1, my bout.*

MIRROR, MIRROR

March 19, 2017

Of the responses to my blogging for Milo that I have gotten from colleagues over the past few weeks, this exchange is perhaps the most interesting. It comes from a Facebook conversation screen-captured for me by a friend in academia. The three speakers are women. To judge from the photos that I have been able to find, they are all younger than I. I believe they are all in my own discipline of medieval studies. Certainly, they identify as feminists. And they have clearly seen photos of me, whence their conversation.

> I realize that it's untoward and unkind, but when I looked at the photos of herself she had posted on her wide open "look at me!" Facebook page, I almost recoiled because I felt she looked so...ugly. I say this not to body shame in any way. It is rather that when someone's behavior is so repugnant, their face can sort of morph into horror for me.

> I think it's her expression, which can only be described as a shit-eating grin.

> Snide. She aspires to be a nasty, snarky troll like the imaginary boyfriend she deifies.[241]

[241] The photograph they are talking about was published in the campus newspaper: https://www.chicagomaroon.com/article/2017/2/24/professor-comments-yiannopoulos-spur-controversy/

I shared this conversation with Milo. His response? "This is what winning looks like." Which is to say: They're jealous. I have the handsomest boyfriend on campus, and the other girls can't stand it. Well, maybe not on my campus, since he has not yet brought his tour to the University of Chicago. But on college campuses across the country and, if the Glasgow students vote the right way tomorrow, even back in the U.K.[242] Except, of course, many of my fellow academics, particularly these three women, do not see him this way. They see him more or less as they see me, as hideous, not beautiful. Horrifying, shit-eating, nasty, and snarky. Nor does it matter which image of him—or me—they see, as the first speaker acknowledges. My behavior (by which I think she means my writing) is "so repugnant" there is no way she can see me as anything other than ugly, regardless of what I look like in the photo.

Try it yourself. Perhaps not on an image of me (you're my readers, of course I'm beautiful!). Or of Milo (I'm guessing more of you are fans than not). But on somebody else you have cause to have strong feelings about. Barack Obama, say. Or Hillary Clinton. Or Donald Trump. How did you do? Were you able to look at each image dispassionately? Do you think I chose fairly? I tried to find images that were happy, situationally similar—all three standing in front of an American flag—with each looking friendly and confident. And yet, I'm guessing at least one of the three images strikes you as somewhat sinister, while at least one of them makes you feel happy, even elated.

What's going on? In a word: bigotry. If you cannot look at all three of these photos and see simply a person smiling, yes, you're a bigot. Which is to say: you are judging the person not by what he or she has said or done—in the photos, all they are doing is smiling—but by what you already believe about him or her. Philosopher Edward

---

[242] https://www.gla.ac.uk/news/archiveofnews/2017/march/headline_516975_en.html

Feser has some fascinating things to say about bigotry and how it works.[243] In Feser's words:

> The bigot is someone whose attachment to his beliefs is fundamentally emotional rather than rational. He evaluates the evidence in light of his beliefs rather than evaluating his beliefs in light of the evidence. He is reluctant or unwilling to give a fair hearing to opinions other than his own or to arguments against his own. He tends to be hostile to those who hold those different opinions, prefers to avoid them altogether rather than engaging them and their views, and resorts to invective instead of reasoned debate.

As, for example, talking about me behind my back on a Facebook thread rather than contacting me directly to ask me about what I had written. (I know from the same friend that the above conversation went on for some time, getting progressively nastier.) The opposite of bigotry is the ability to engage in reasoned argument, to listen to the evidence a speaker or writer is presenting without letting preconceptions about the person or his or her ideas override one's ability to hear what is being said. Which does not mean one will necessarily agree with what is said—disagreement as such is not bigotry—only that one will be *able* to hear or to see what the other person is trying to say or show without prejudice, quite literally, pre-judging.

Wouldn't it be better if we could all listen not out of bigotry, but out of reason? Or even better, out of love? "Love," as the apostle Paul famously put it, "is patient and kind; love is not jealous or boastful; it is not arrogant or rude. Love does not insist on its own way; it is not irritable or resentful; it does not rejoice at wrong, but rejoices in the right. Love bears all things, believes all things, hopes all things, endures all things" (1 Corinthians 13:4-7).

Except that love, like hate, is a form of bigotry, insofar as it too is grounded in affect as much as intellect, emotion as much as reason.

---

[243] http://edwardfeser.blogspot.com/2017/03/meta-bigotry.html

I have said I love Milo, which has many of my friends, even friends who like Milo, worried. Can I not see how the things that he has said make many people uncomfortable? Well, yes, I can, but not with the same emotion they feel. It is a purely intellectual exercise for me, trying to imagine myself feeling threatened by his jokes when I am not. He does not mean them to be threatening, only startling, of this I am sure. But then I do not view him with the prejudice that my colleagues do, so how can I know what they see or hear?

Here's the catch, which I am sure you have all already realized. We're all bigots at one time or another. All of us make judgments about other people based on our emotions rather than reason. But here's the rub: we cannot make judgments any other way. The whole point of judging is to make an evaluation about someone's behavior or ideas, and evaluations, however much we might try to reason about them, necessarily come down to our emotional response.

Notice what Paul does *not* say. He does not say that love is blind. Love may be patient and kind, but it also does not rejoice at wrong, but only in the right. Love is a kind of judgment just as much as hate is. It is a judgment about the good and the true and the beautiful. But so is hate. We hate the evil and the false and the ugly just as we love the good, the true, and the beautiful—or, as the English say, the lovely.

Last week I had to watch a training video required by my employer about our campus policies on sexual abuse and harassment. It was a curious experience, having to work through the various multiple choice scenarios, but by far the most curious moment came towards the end, when I was being schooled in the phenomenon of "unconscious bias."

Everyone has unconscious biases that affect their decisions. For example, someone may form an opinion about a co-worker because of unconscious preferences and generalizations. Awareness of these biases is not enough. It is also important to take concrete steps to reduce or prevent how unconscious bias influences our daily interactions with co-workers. "Still trying to wrap my head around how you can be conscious of an unconscious bias," I quipped on my own Facebook page.

But the thing is, I know that it is not that hard. To know your biases, all you have to do is check your emotional response. "Mirror, mirror, on the wall," the Wicked Stepmother asked. "Who's the fairest of them all?" The mistake is to believe that there is some absolutely objective standard. There isn't—unless you believe (as Milo and I do) in God.

THE JESUS STORY

March 26, 2017

Sixteen hundred years ago, a man asked a friend for advice.[244] The man was anxious because he had gained a reputation as a teacher for speaking well, but when students were brought to him for instruction, he became tongue-tied. He was particularly upset because at times in the course of a long narration he found his speaking profitless and distasteful even to himself, and he was worried that his teaching was doing more harm than good. "Help me!" he begged his friend. "Tell me what to say!"

His friend replied: "First and foremost, you need to enjoy what you are talking about." Actually, that is not quite what his friend said. It was somewhat more formal. But the gist was the same. "In reality," the man's friend replied, "we are listened to with much greater satisfaction...when we ourselves also have pleasure in the same work; for the thread of our address is affected by the very joy of which we ourselves are sensible, and it proceeds from us with greater ease and more acceptance."

---

[244] Augustine to Deogratias, *On the Catechising of the Uninstructed* (ca. A.D. 400), trans. S.D.F. Salmond, http://www.newadvent.org/fathers/1303.htm

"More to the point," his friend insisted, "you need to lighten up." Again, I paraphrase. This is what his friend actually wrote:

> Now if the cause of our sadness lies in the circumstance that our hearer does not apprehend what we mean, so that we have to come down in a certain fashion from the elevation of our own conceptions, and are under the necessity of dwelling long in the tedious process of syllables which come far beneath the standard of our ideas, and have anxiously to consider how that which we ourselves take in with a most rapid draught of mental apprehension is to be given forth by the mouth of flesh in the long and perplexed intricacies of its method of enunciation; and if the great dissimilarity thus felt (between our utterance and our thought) makes it distasteful to us to speak, and a pleasure to us to keep silence, then let us ponder what has been set before us by Him who has "showed us an example that we should follow in His steps" (1 Peter 2:21).

I know just how Jesus felt. Augustine—for it is Augustine, the great teacher of rhetoric, who is speaking—continues:

> For however much our articulate speech may differ from the vivacity of our intelligence, much greater is the difference of the flesh of mortality from the equality of God. And, nevertheless, "although He was in the same form, He emptied Himself, taking the form of a servant [being born in the likeness of men. And being found in human form he humbled himself and became obedient unto death, even] death on a cross" (Philippians 2:7-8).

Sometimes of late, I just want to give up. My colleagues are baying for my blood...okay, not quite...but they aren't happy with me. Friends try to correct my speech, telling me if only I would stop using naughty words, I would find more receptive listeners. Former students tell me that they are dismayed at my description of what it has been like for me being a Christian in the academy. And nobody it seems...okay, I exaggerate, my Facebook friends have been rocks...but nobody outside my Facebook salon seems to want to listen long enough for me to explain what it means to be Christian.[245] They just assume that they know what I think—and condemn me.

It's my own fault, I suppose. I haven't really tried to explain, not lately, at least.[246],[247] It is so hard to know where to begin when everything I think and see is infused with the understanding of what it means to be part of this story, the story of God's descending into the world through the womb of a virgin to take on flesh. Like Deogratias, Augustine's friend, I flounder, worried lest I bore my listeners or drive them away.

Maybe I should say something about how Christianity isn't about believing a set of propositions, but about God's loving relationship with his creation. Or maybe I could make the historical argument that I draw on in my forthcoming book, about how Christianity developed from the ancient temple tradition, not at odds with, but in fulfillment of what the ancient Hebrews believed about the LORD they celebrated in the psalms. Or maybe...but no, my colleagues could still accuse me of teaching lies.

And, in a way, they would be right. Not that I am lying about being Christian or what Christianity means, but because to them, nothing I can say will sound like anything other than a fairy story. Because it is. The greatest fairy story ever told. J.R.R. Tolkien said it even better than Augustine:

> The Gospels contain a fairy-story, or a story of a larger kind which embraces all the essence of fairy-stories. They contain many marvels—peculiarly artistic, beautiful, and moving: "mythical" in their perfect, self-contained significance; and among the marvels is the greatest and most complete conceivable eucatastrophe. But this story has entered History and the primary world; the desire and aspiration of sub-

---

[245] https://fencingbearatprayer.blogspot.com/2017/03/the-fear-of-lord.html

[246] https://fencingbearatprayer.blogspot.com/2008/06/shield-of-faith_29.html

[247] https://fencingbearatprayer.blogspot.com/2009/06/bears-proof-for-existence-of-god.html

creation has been raised to the fulfillment of Creation. The Birth of Christ is the eucatastrophe of Man's history. The Resurrection is the eucatastrophe of the story of the Incarnation.... There is no tale ever told that men would rather find was true, and none which so many sceptical men have accepted as true on its own merits. For the Art of it has the supremely convincing tone of Primary Art, that is, of Creation.... [This] story is supreme; and it is true. Art has been verified. God is the Lord, of angels, and of men—and of elves. Legend and History have met and fused.[248]

Conversion, if you will, is an exercise in telling oneself a different story, an exercise in seeing through a different lens, a different account of *what it all means.* How can I help you see the story that I live through unless you yourself can find yourself inside it? This is what Deogratias asked Augustine: not for instruction in how to lay out the tenets of the faith as a list of propositions, but for advice on what to say in his *narratio,* the story that he was trying to tell.

The difficulty he was having was a storyteller's difficulty, how to help his listeners realize that the story was *about them.* Deogratias knew the story, but it came to him in a flash (what Augustine calls a "rapid draught of mental apprehension"): how God loved his creation so much that He entered into it so that He, as Maker, might remake it from within, so that He, as Artist, might repair his own work, which He loved.

It was a story that began many ages ago, when God first made the world and human beings turned away from him. It is a story of great sadness and many defeats, as over and over again God attempted to turn his creatures back to him, only to watch his prophets be shunned and his creatures stray. And yet, He loved his children and wanted them back. So He did an even mightier work, He became a creature himself. Imagine if Tolkien could enter into his own story, be there with Merry and Pippin as they waited at the gate of Isengard for their

[248] "On Fairy Stories," in *The Tolkien Reader* (1966)

friends to arrive or with Frodo and Sam as they struggled to find a way down the cliffs of the Emyn Muil. Not just as the author whom we, as readers, know crafted the work, but as a character himself. And then imagine that the characters realized that they themselves were in a story. A story that went back to the beginning of time, and that somehow was all leading up to the moment in which they found themselves, as it were, stranded and losing hope.

"...I wonder what sort of tale we've fallen into?" [asked Sam].

"I wonder," said Frodo. "But I don't know. And that's the way of a real tale. Take any one that you're fond of. You may know, or guess, what kind of a tale it is, happy-ending or sad-ending, but the people in it don't know. And you don't want them to."

"No, sir, of course not. Beren now, he never thought he was going to get that Silmaril from the Iron Crown in Thangorodrim, and yet he did, and that was a worse place and a blacker danger than ours. But that's a long tale, of course, and goes on past the happiness and into grief and beyond it—and the Silmaril went on and came to Eärendil. And why, sir, I never thought of that before! We've got—you've got some of the light of it in that star-glass that the Lady gave you! Why, to think of it, we're in the same tale still! It's going on. Don't the great tales never end?"

"No, they never end as tales," said Frodo. "But the people in them come, and go when their part's ended. Our part will end later—or sooner."[249]

"*No, they never end as tales.*" One of the things that less sympathetic readers have chided me for over the past few months is my propensity for drawing parallels between Milo and Jesus. (They seem not to have noticed my propensity for comparing myself to the Virgin Mary.) But what other story would Milo, as a Christian, find himself in? The story doesn't care, it just wants to be told. Or, rather, the Story-teller *wants*

---

[249] J.R.R. Tolkien, *The Lord of the Rings* (1955), bk. 4, chap. 8

us to find ourselves inside this Story, the supreme story of which all other stories are merely counterfeits.

Because stories are important.

People think that stories are shaped by people. In fact, it's the other way around.

Stories exist independently of their players. If you know that, the knowledge is power.

Stories, great flapping ribbons of shaped space-time, have been blowing and uncoiling around the universe since the beginning of time. And they have evolved. The weakest have died and the strongest have survived and they have grown fat on the retelling...stories, twisting and blowing through the darkness.

And their very existence overlays a faint but insistent pattern on the chaos that is history. Stories etch grooves deep enough for people to follow in the same way that water follows certain paths down a mountainside. And every time fresh actors tread the path of the story, the groove runs deeper.

This is called the theory of narrative causality and it means that a story, once started, *takes a shape*. It picks up all the vibrations of all the other workings of that story that have ever been.

This is why history keeps on repeating all the time....[250]

Except, of course, it doesn't. We only think it does because we are so sensitive to stories. It makes sense to me that it is my colleagues in history and medieval studies who have felt most angered by my writing about Milo. I challenged them to see him through a different lens, read him as part of a story other than that by which they have tended to order their understanding as scholars. Like the scribes and Pharisees whom Jesus challenged, they *know* the way we are supposed to read the evidence of history. They *know* what patterns to look for and how to read the signs. They *know* that there is no such thing as a Story-teller, only human tellers of stories. They *know* that the Story

[250] Terry Pratchett, *Witches Abroad* (1991)

behind it all is one of struggle and survival of the fittest. They *know* that truth lies only in the way in which they interpret the evidence at hand.

Which puts them at terrible risk. *What if the story they have been telling is wrong?* They don't see it that way, almost no one in academia does. It is why it is so hard to describe the experience of faith to those habituated to a different story-line. It is not about having access to more or better *facts,* but about ordering those facts according to a different narrative, a narrative in which the very same facts take on radically different meanings.

What does it mean to have faith? For my own part, faith is a habit of thinking analogically, through stories. Rather, through a particular Story that carries the truth of all stories. It is not about proving something scientifically, as it were, but about seeing the patterns by which we, as creatures, live out our lives as artists made in the image and likeness of a Maker, who loves us and desires nothing except our love in return.

Within this Story, our actions take on certain meanings that they would not, could not otherwise. But it is also a Story in which we, as creatures, are called upon ourselves to create, whether biologically, as parents, or aesthetically, as artists, thus the great mysteries (as Tolkien constantly emphasized in his stories) of marriage and art. The one thing that this Story forbids—the great sin of this Story—is the desire to dominate other people's will, to force them either to believe or to act in any particular way. Such is Evil, and thus, again in Tolkien's story, the power of the One Ring: to dominate and rule.

"My kingdom is not of this world," Jesus told Pilate (John 18:36). *I did not come to rule.* "[But] taking the form of a servant...he humbled himself and became obedient unto death, even death on a cross." Christ is the lens through which Christians read history; Christ is the model in whom Christians are called to recognize themselves. To be Christian means to find oneself in the same story as Christ. The Story in which God so loved the world that he entered into it in order to give his children eternal life (John 3:16). *Do you really expect me tell this Story with anything other than the utmost joy?*

FREE SPEECH
FUNDAMENTALS FAIL:
J. S. MILL

March 28, 2017

I have a love-hate relationship with J.S. Mill's *On Liberty*.[251] I love that Mill describes the Middle Ages as a time when it was possible for an individual to be a "power in himself...if he had either great talents or a high social position." Not so, according to Mill, in the present age:

> At present individuals are lost in the crowd.

Mill was writing in 1859, but it could almost be now, don't you think? Does any of this sound familiar?

> In politics it is almost a triviality to say that public opinion now rules the world. The only power deserving the name is that of masses, and of governments while they make themselves the organ of the tendencies and instincts of masses.

Mill blamed the "whole white population" in America for this state of affairs, while "in England" it was "chiefly the middle class."

---

[251] https://www.econlib.org/library/Mill/mlLbty.html?chapter_num=1#book-reader

Their thinking is done for them by men much like themselves, addressing them or speaking in their name, on the spur of the moment, through the newspapers.

Can you imagine what he would say about the media nowadays? "I do not," Mill asserted,

...assert that anything better is compatible as a general rule, with the present low state of the human mind. But that does not hinder the government of mediocrity from being mediocre government.

Mill contrasted this present-day mediocrity with the excellence that may be attained when the many let themselves be guided "by the counsels and influence of a more highly gifted an instructed *one* or *few*":

The initiation of all wise or noble things comes and must come from individuals; generally at first from some one individual. The honor and glory of the average man is that he is capable of following that initiative; that he can respond internally to wise and noble things, and be led to them with his eyes open.

Not that the many should be compelled to bend even to the will of such excellent individuals! Quite the reverse.

The power of compelling others into [a particular way] is not only inconsistent with the freedom and development of all the rest [of a people], but corrupting to the strong man himself.

No, what is wanted is not the tyranny of the individual to supersede the tyranny of the masses, but rather eccentricity:

In this age [of mediocrity], the mere example of nonconformity, the mere refusal to bend the knee to custom, is itself a service. Precisely because the tyranny of opinion is such as to make eccentricity a reproach, it is desirable, in order to break through that tyranny, that people should be eccentric. Eccentricity has always abounded when and where strength of character has abounded; and the amount of eccentricity in a society has generally been proportional to the amount of genius, mental vigor, and moral courage which it contained. That so few now dare to be eccentric marks the chief danger of the time.

You can see where Milo and I get our reputation for being dangerous, can't you? Oh, wait...we're the eccentric ones.

৬৶

I hate Mill because he makes it all sound so straightforward. I have taught this essay every other year for the better part of the twenty-first century, and the struggle that I always have is making Mill seem at all remarkable. Everything he says seems to fit the prevailing orthodoxy not just of academia, but of our society as a whole. For example, he says such unremarkable things as this:

> If all mankind minus one were of one opinion, and only one person were of the contrary opinion, mankind would be no more justified in silencing that one person than he, if he had power, would be justified in silencing mankind.

Or this:

> The whole strength and value...of human judgment depending on the one property, that it can be set right when it is wrong, reliance can be placed on it only when the means of setting it right are kept constantly at hand. In the case of any person whose judgment is really deserving of confidence, how has it become so? Because he has kept his mind open to criticism of his opinions and conduct.

Or this:

> It is a bitter thought how different a thing the Christianity of the world might have been if the Christian faith had been adopted as the religion of the empire under the auspices of Marcus Aurelius instead of those of Constantine.

Or this:

> [The] dictum that truth always triumphs over persecution is one of those pleasant falsehoods which men repeat after one another till they pass into commonplaces, but which all experience refutes. History teems with instances of truth put down by persecution.

My colleagues in academia know these truths to be self-evident. They *know* that knowledge grows only insofar as we are able to weigh different opinions against reason and experience. They *know* that it is all too easy for those in power in a society—whether individual tyrants or the tyranny of the majority—to silence differences in opinions. They *know* that persecuting people simply for their ideas is a bad thing. They *know* that

> [a] state of things in which a large portion of the most active and inquiring intellects find it advisable to keep the general principles and grounds of their convictions within their own breasts, and attempt, in what they address to the public, to fit as much as they can of their own conclusions to premises which they have internally renounced, cannot send forth the open, fearless characters and logical, consistent intellects who once adorned the thinking world. The sort of men who can be looked for under it are either mere conformers to commonplace, or timeservers for truth, whose arguments on all great subjects are meant for their hearers, and are not those which have convinced themselves.

Have I told you what I think about anthropogenic climatic change? Right. And yet,

> [who] can compute what the world loses in the multitude of promising intellects combined with timid characters, who dare not follow out any bold, vigorous, independent train of thought, lest it should land them in something which would admit of being considered irreligious or immoral?

What was it my departmental colleague Amy Stanley said about my opinions on race, sex, gender, and faith? Oh, yes. They are not only "hateful," but "so specious and so odious as not to be worth debating." Further, my desire to give students an opportunity to consider religious beliefs "from within" as a contrast to the ideas which they may already hold (including "dangerous secular" ones) is a "false proposition [that] hardly counts as opinion based on scholarly research."

☙

It's our fault, really. By which I mean Christians. Mill has something to say about this as well. Back in the day when Christianity was young, Christians struggled mightily to define and defend their faith. They understood that it is only those ideas that are subjected to the most rigorous criticism that we can ever fully claim to know. Indeed,

> [so] essential is this discipline to a real understanding of moral and human subjects that, if opponents of all-important truths do not exist, it is indispensable to imagine them and supply them with the strongest arguments which the most skillful devil's advocate can conjure up.

Once a faith reaches the status of orthodoxy and doctrine takes its place, it dies, even if people profess to believe its tenets. Mill was scathing:

> From this time may usually be dated the decline in the living power of the doctrine.... And to this cause, probably, it is chiefly owing that Christianity now makes so little progress in extending its domain, and after eighteen centuries is still nearly confined to Europeans and the descendants of Europeans.... The sayings of Christ coexist passively in their minds, producing hardly any effect beyond what is caused by mere listening to words so amiable and bland.... Both teachers and learners go to sleep at their post as soon as there is no enemy in the field.

The problem, as Mill saw it, was that so much progress has already been made. (He's not really talking about Christianity anymore, it is just his example of a faith that once knew how to defend itself.) Indeed, the "gradual narrowing of the bounds of diversity of opinion" seemed to him "at once inevitable and indispensable."

> As mankind improve, the number of doctrines which are no longer disputed or doubted will be constantly on the increase; and the well-being of mankind may almost be measured by the number and gravity of the truths which have reached the point of being uncontested.

Which, according to my colleagues, would seem to be where we are today. As Nancy Frankenberry scolded me, the ideas that are prevalent in the academy now about multiculturalism, race, class, and gender, are not opinions, but simply truths: my and her students' "'milieu,' not their 'religion'... their analytic categories, not their politically correct avoidance of critical thinking." *Nothing to see here, ladies and gentlemen, move along. Move along.* I blame Mill. On the one hand, he claims to be defending the liberty of the individual against the despotism of society.

But on the other, he, like my liberal academic colleagues, believes contradictory things. Not that believing contradictory things makes him a bad person, just a person, but that he said these contradictory things with such authority (a.k.a. long-winded sentences more or less designed to convince you he is smarter than you are) that it is all too easy ending up agreeing with him—and never putting his arguments to the test.

Remember those remarkable ancient and medieval individuals who had power in their own right? Power from talent and high status, by which they were able to achieve social and intellectual greatness? You know very well who those people are today. The ones who pride themselves on knowing more than the masses because they *think for themselves.* Those are the people—the liberals—whom Mill imagined saving society from its mediocrity. *Quis custodiet ipsos custodes?*, as Mill might put it, thanks to the classical education his father made sure he received.

It is all well and good looking down on the masses when you are confident that you do not participate in their mediocrity. When you, as a member of the institution founded on the proposition that understanding depends on constant Socratic debate, pride yourself on having put your ideas to the test. When you are confident that the only reason people could disagree with you is that they, unlike you, have not tested their opinions properly, through reasoned debate. It becomes a kind of—dare I say it?—religious belief to be defended at all odds against heresy. Mill had his own orthodoxy:

> The only freedom which deserves the name is that of pursuing our own good in our own way, so long as we do not attempt to deprive others of theirs or impede their efforts to obtain it. Each is the proper guardian of his own health, whether bodily *or* mental and spiritual.

The problem is that this freedom was all Mill cared about—and thus all he hypothesized ought to be put to the test. He gives a number of examples in the fourth and fifth parts of his essay, where he describes a variety of "experiments in living." What ought society to do about the question of free trade, the sale of poisons, drunkenness, fornication, and gambling? To what extent ought society be involved in the education of children?

How far ought society restrict the adherents of one religion, say Christianity, from offending those of another, say Islam? What about those instances in which the Puritans attempted to put down both public and private amusements? Should there be sumptuary laws that prevent the rich from spending their income in a way that offends the less rich? What about the Mormons and their practice of polygamy?

It is almost as if Mill were giving a blueprint for the debates which we are having now. Which, in a way, he did. Mill, like the majority of my liberal colleagues in academia, was an atheist or, at the very least, not a theist. He credits Christianity with a moral code not thanks to its theology, but rather, tellingly, as a "protest against paganism." In his view, Christianity is essentially a negative doctrine:

> It holds out the hope of heaven and the threat of hell as the appointed and appropriate motives to a virtuous life: in this falling far below the best of the ancients, and doing what lies in it to give to human morality an essentially selfish character, by disconnecting each man's feelings of duty from the interest of his fellow creatures, except so far as a self-interested inducement is offered to him for consulting them.

In a word, Christians are selfish. All they care about is themselves. The pagans were much more virtuous.

> If Christians would teach infidels to be just to Christianity, they should themselves be just to infidelity. It can do truth no service to blink the fact, known to all who have the most ordinary acquaintance with literary history, that a large portion of the noblest and most valuable moral teaching has been the work, not only of men who did not know, but of men who knew and rejected, the Christian faith.

&❧

Even Mill was not optimistic. Europe, he opined, was on the way out if Europeans could not overcome their stifling mediocrity.

> In our times, from the highest class of society down to the lowest, everyone lives under the eye of a hostile and dreaded censorship.

Custom had triumphed over eccentricity. Real freedom was almost non-existent. Europe was on the verge of losing its capacity for history, for the spirit of improvement and progress. Only its diversity of character and culture had hitherto prevented Europe from going the way of the custom-bound East.

> But it already begins to possess this benefit in a considerably less degree. It is decidedly advancing toward the Chinese ideal of making all people alike.

Indeed, it was arguably already too late. But if so, according to Mill, good riddance. If a civilization is no longer able to defend itself from the barbarians, too bad.

> If this be so, the sooner such a civilization receives notice to quit, the better.

Time to send in the barbarians to stir things up. Look, after all, what they did for Europe the first time around. Of course, those barbarians also converted to Christianity—a fact Mill seems purposefully to overlook.

THE CHICAGO WAY

April 8, 2017

There was a reception on campus yesterday afternoon in honor of John Boyer, our newly reappointed Dean of College. I have been back in the classroom for two weeks, but since coming out for Milo this was the first function I have attended where I expected to see a fair number of my Chicago colleagues. I was nervous, to say the least. Would they talk with me? Would they shun me? Would I find myself standing awkwardly in a corner, the cynosure of all eyes?

Yeah, right. Are you kidding me? This is Chicago. We eat Nobel prize winners for lunch. Mere provocateurs barely raise eyebrows. Or maybe I am just really, really good at being a Happy Warrior.[252] After all, I've been training with the Master these past six months. See? I'm stuck now, not sure how to explain. It was all so... *normal.* For Chicago, that is. One colleague admitted to seeing Milo's interview with Bill Maher, but smiled and waved me off when I tried to explain how Milo chose his outfit for the occasion. (It was highly significant!) But, no, my colleague was far more interested in my opinion on the faculty searches upcoming for our department.

---

[252] https://fencingbearatprayer.blogspot.com/2016/01/how-to-be-happy-warrior.html

Another told me bluntly that he disagreed with my position (unspecified) but that he did not like engaging in arguments by email (as had some of our colleagues when my *Sightings* piece came out) and thought that I had not been given a fair hearing. I agreed. We then talked for a bit about how important it is to be able to listen to arguments like Charles Murray's without having them shut down. I asked my colleague whether he had read Murray's recent book. "No," he admitted, "but I know what he says from the reviews that I have read. He has replaced poor black people with poor white people as the bad guys." (I paraphrase.)

When I explained what Murray actually says in *Coming Apart: The State of White America, 1960-2010* (2012)—that poor whites are suffering from the breakdown in their communities as a consequence of losing their professional elites to the coastal bubbles—he acknowledged with some surprise, "That's not what I had heard. That sounds worth thinking about." And then he smiled at me and said, "You enjoy being a provocateur!"

A third admitted to me that he used to read *National Review* when he was a teen-ager and even wrote a fan letter to William F. Buckley, so he appreciated where I was coming from. There was one awkward moment better unmooted, but most of my colleagues seemed to have no idea that they were supposed to shun me. (Full disclosure: those who have written most strongly against me weren't there.)

After Dean Boyer gave his usual uplifting speech, I beetled over to our president Robert Zimmer and told him: "I have to thank you for making my life here so *boring!* Think how different it would be for me if I were at Berkeley or Middlebury or UCLA."[253],[254],[255] He agreed: "It is even worse out there than many people realize." In his own words, from a talk he gave last week at Colgate:

> Cultural reinforcement or cultural change is a long process that needs long term commitment and long term focus as a high priority. How many institutions are willing and able to undertake this? We shall see.
>
> Am I optimistic that the trend we see now can be reversed? There are some hopeful signs. Until recently, it was frankly difficult on many campuses to even discuss these issues. Areas where many would not tread are now being openly discussed. There are many more statements coming out in favor of free expression. But there is a long way to go and the outcome, frankly, is not certain. As always, this will come down not simply to what institutions say is good, but to what trade-offs they are willing to make and what they are prepared to do.
>
> To stifle free expression and open discourse and suppress speech that you don't like is just an invitation for others to do the same. Accepting this behavior sets universities on a path that is antithetical to fulfilling our highest aspirations. For the sake of our students and their future success, our faculty and their capacity to develop original and impactful research, and our country remaining a magnet for the most talented from around the world, all this suppression needs to be resisted.[256]

As I explained back in September, I started following Milo's Dangerous Faggot tour after Dean Boyer and Dean Ellison wrote to our incoming freshman about what to expect at Chicago. No intellectual "safe spaces," no trigger warnings, no controversial speakers being banned. "You will find that we expect members of our community to be engaged in rigorous debate, discussion, and even disagreement. At times this may challenge you and even cause discomfort."

[253] https://www.cnn.com/2017/02/01/us/milo-yiannopoulos-berkeley/

[254] https://www.bostonglobe.com/metro/2017/03/04/middlebury/hAfpA1Hquh7DIS1doiKbhJ/story.html

[255] https://www.thecollegefix.com/war-cops-author-heather-mac-donald-shouted-ucla-hysterical-black-lives-matter-protest/

[256] https://president.uchicago.edu/page/address-colgate-university/

Throughout his tour, Milo held up our institution as the shining example of what it means to be a university dedicated to open discussion, free speech, and academic inquiry. Institutions would have to choose, he cautioned. Would they be like the University of Chicago and stand up for academic freedom? Or like Mizzou and watch their enrollments plummet?

It was dismaying, to say the least, when my article for *Sightings*—intended for my colleagues in academia at large—excited the responses from my colleagues on campus that it did. What would happen if I brought Milo to campus? Would Chicago live up to its professed ideals? After yesterday, my guess is yes, if in fact the only colleagues upset with me are the ones who have already made their opinions known. Let us hope I am right—for all our sakes. Elsewhere, as President Zimmer has warned us, the lights are going out. Without Chicago, shall we see them lit again in our lifetime?

LORD OF THE SNAKES

May 7, 2017

Our primate ancestors lived in trees. For primates living everywhere other than Madagascar, there were snakes at the bottom of those trees. Snakes who, if they had been able to speak, would have called our ancestors "lunch." Lots of fascinating things happened in those trees. Our male ancestors competed with one another for dominance, just like lobsters, with whom they (like us) shared ancient serotonergic systems. (That means our brains have lobster-like elements for detecting social hierarchies, *pace* the social constructionists.)

The better our male ancestors competed with each other, the more likely the females were to look kindly on them and choose them as mates. They might even offer them fruit. (Which put a premium on competing well long before Wall Street was a twinkle in our great-great-great-grandfather's eye, *pace* those convinced that capitalism invented competition.)

Sometimes, however, things got even more exciting. Maybe the snakes started climbing the trees. Maybe our ancestors got thirsty and climbed down the trees to go to the river. One way or another, our ancestors had to deal with the snakes. Professor Jordan Peterson talks all the time about snakes.[257] They are at the root of all human mythologies, the dragons lurking in the chaos at the bottom of the trees. They are the monsters that the hero goes out to fight to bring back treasure and knowledge, the source of terror and wisdom. They are the reason that we developed such keen eyesight. Snakes taught us to see.[258]

Most people have some fear of snakes. Me, for example. Certain members of my family discovered this by the age of three. All they had to do was wave something vaguely snakelike just below my line of vision, and I would be screaming before I was even aware that I had seen the toy. And I would keep screaming long after I could tell it was fake.

See something out of the corner of your eye that you can't quite identify, some problem that you aren't able to solve, and your primate ancestors all scream, "Snake!" The neural circuits are that ancient. It is the reason Medusa had snakes for hair and Hercules had to fight the Hydra. Snakes are synonymous with anxiety. All that clutter in your life is like a nest of snakes, waiting to strike. No wonder you procrastinate. Who wants to fight snakes?

Heroes do. Heroes are the ones who fight off the snakes. They are the ones who grow teeth themselves and face the terror, rather than cowering in the trees. They are the ones who save us from the dragon of chaos and death. You think you can fight monsters without being yourself a bit of a monster? This, as Professor Peterson tells it, is what Adam and Eve learned when they listened to the snake. They learned they were naked. They learned they were vulnerable. Which means they learned how to hurt. And became human, knowing good—and evil. In Professor Peterson's words:

---

[257] https://www.jordanbpeterson.com

[258] https://www.sciencedirect.com/science/article/pii/S0047248406000182

You might say that someone who is incapable of cruelty is a higher moral being than someone who is capable of cruelty. And I would say… that that's incorrect. Dangerously incorrect. Because if you are not capable of cruelty you are absolutely a victim to anyone who is. Part of the reason people go watch anti-heroes and villains is because there is a part of them crying out for the incorporation of the monster within them which is what gives them strength of character and self-respect, and because it's impossible to respect yourself until you grow teeth.

And if you grow teeth then you realize that you are somewhat dangerous. Or maybe somewhat seriously dangerous. And then you might be more willing to demand that you treat yourself with respect and other people do the same thing. And so that doesn't mean that being cruel is better than not being cruel. What it means is that being able to be cruel and then not being cruel is better than not being able to be cruel. Because in the first case you're nothing but weak and naive. And in the second case you're dangerous but you have it under control.

A lot of martial arts concentrate on exactly that in their philosophy of training. [They say,] We're not training you to fight. We're training you to be peaceful and awake and avoid fights. But if you happen to have to get in one…and you're competent at fighting, that actually decreases the probability that you're going to have to fight because when someone pushes you, you'll be able to respond with confidence, and with any luck—and this is certainly the case with bullies—with any luck a reasonable show of confidence, which is equivalent to a show of dominance, is going to be enough to make the bully back off.

And so the strength that you develop in your monstrousness is actually the best guarantee of peace.[259]

Back in February at the beginning of time, the bullies tried to take out Milo. But on Friday he came back…wearing a snake.[260] And vowed never to let the bullies silence him or any other conservative or libertarian again.

---

[259] https://youtu.be/wLc_MC7NQek
[260] https://fencingbearatprayer.blogspot.com/2017/05/here-be-dragons.html

'JUST CALL ME MEDUSA'

May 17, 2017

The graduate students in the Divinity School are not happy with me.[261] Mind you, the burden of the letter that they published in the campus newspaper last Friday was to make various demands of my colleagues in the Divinity School: to include students on the Diversity Committee at the Divinity School, to have more programming at orientation "to proactively combat current climate issues," and to conduct annual surveys of the members of the Divinity School "to maintain transparency as we continue to define our institution in the future."

But mainly, of course, they are upset with me. So much so that sixty of them—four anonymously—signed the letter. I guess they won't be taking any classes with me. (Not that I have any slated for next year that they could take for their Divinity School requirements. My faculty appointment is in the Department of History; I only cross-list some of my courses with the Divinity School.) But neither does it seem that any of them knows anything about what I teach, never mind what I have actually said. Certainly, they do not quote me in their letter.

[261] https://www.chicagomaroon.com/article/2017/5/12/divinity-school-students-call-inclusive-environmen/

Rather, they make inferences from what I (purportedly) said to point to its effect in the "current political climate" at large. To wit:

> ...we are compelled to contextualize Fulton Brown's argument in our current political climate.... No institution can thrive while significant portions of its population are at risk of being marked, targeted, threatened, or silenced. The publication of Fulton Brown's article [*they mean my* Sightings *piece*] must be understood in its proper context: the escalation of bigotry and its violent effects, both locally and nationally. In fact, the central ideas Fulton Brown relates in her essay resonate with and act as means of harassment and recruitment common to the informal coalition of the self-identified alt-right.... One need not establish whether or not Fulton Brown supports or collaborates with these groups [*I don't, nor has anyone approached me on campus or through other avenues expecting I would*], given the bare ideological similitude. What remains essential is the welcome offered to such individuals and organizations by national politics, University policy, and *Sightings* editorial standards. Unwittingly or otherwise, the publication of Fulton Brown's article has provided a platform for the proliferation and mobilization of white supremacy, nativism, and patriarchal chauvinism.

In other words, they don't need to quote me, because it doesn't matter what I have said. All that matters is the climate that I wrote in. If there are bad people out there who might agree with me, I should shut up. I am, in their minds, a snake. (You saw that coming, right?[262]) I'm cribbing now from Professor Peterson, but what strikes me most about the students' letter is how it proves once again that I was right. What I said in the *Sightings* article was that Milo "scares students, and faculty even more" because he is a fool. Peterson says harlequin, jester, comedian. In Jungian terms, Milo is a trickster, a sacred clown. Think Loki. Coyote. St. Francis. Or Jesus. In Peterson's words:

> Trickster figures emerge in times of crisis. And they point out what no one wants to see. And they say things that no one will say.

[262] https://fencingbearatprayer.blogspot.com/2017/05/lady-wisdoms-school-for-snake-lords.html

In mine:

> It is much easier to call Milo names than to accept the challenge he presents. Milo's tour has made clear how high the stakes are. If you drive out explicit theology from public education, you get not *no* theology, but only *bad* theology, theology never properly examined as such.

Which apparently is about the scariest thing you can say. According to my colleague Amy Dru Stanley, also in the History department, suggesting that religion should be taught *as religion* (that is, as something worth studying as a source of knowledge and understanding in its own right, not just a cipher for studying society or culture or some other secular mechanism) is worse than wrong. It is "both so specious and odious as not to be worth debating." To be fair, Amy also included my "opinion on race, sex, [and] gender" in this anathema of my opinion on faith. My beliefs, as Amy reads them, are "hateful" and, just to be clear, "not the values of the History Department—but solely her own."

> "Do not come near," the LORD said to Moses from the burning bush. "Put off your shoes from your feet, for the place on which you are standing is holy ground" (Exodus 3:5 RSV).

There are only certain species of opinions which are too "odious" or "hateful" to discuss. What might they be? Statements slandering the reputation of particular individuals by, for example, attributing to them things they never said? Calls for ostracism from a community for holding opinions different from the majority? The insistence that intentionally or not something that someone has said is threatening to others because it might be taken out of context and misused? Blaming someone for the actions of others or, worse, the likely actions of others on the basis of no evidence, never mind the total absence of intent?

I understand why Amy and the Divinity School students are upset with me. They are upset because, just as I said in the *Sightings* article, Milo—and I—have threatened their faith. I am the snake in the garden, the predator who opens the eyes. I am the one saying the things that should *not* be said lest the values of the community be called into question. I am the one breaking the frame of the myth that gives their life meaning. Worse, I am the one exposing the myth *as a frame*, calling into question the very reality they perceive. The students are categorical:

> We reject any characterization of students that assume we are incapable of discerning the critical quality of arguments [*okay, to be fair, I kinda did, but I meant to exonerate them and lay the blame on their teachers, my colleagues in academia at large for the last thirty or forty years*].... We discern and describe our terrain with analytical categories of race, class, and gender that require capacious critical thinking as well as serious engagement with so-called "politically incorrect" speech, not its avoidance.

Excellent! Let's be politically incorrect! I like the way Professor Peterson puts it, explaining the importance of the fool:

> Carl Jung regarded the Trickster as the precursor to the Savior.... It's a very complicated idea. What it basically means is that in order to find your genuine voice or even to move the truth forward, you have to be willing to be a fool. Because you don't know enough really to speak on behalf of the truth. By even attempting to do so you're going to put yourself in an awkward position and make mistakes.... And so you have to be willing to do that. And so that's really Milo's position. He's a provocateur...a comedian.... And comedians say what everyone is thinking but won't say. And that's why people laugh.[263]

You remember what I told you back in November about the importance of laughter and why people like the librarian in Umberto Eco's *The Name of the Rose* hate it, yes? Laughter is dangerous—or so

---

[263] https://youtu.be/sv17a0uIX2Y

Jorge of Burgos would insist—because it threatens to drive out the fear of the Devil, which means that people will not fear God anymore. Without fear, Jorge insists, there would be no way to enforce belief in the Incarnation. There would be no way to enforce the faith. Why are people so afraid in the "current political climate"? The Divinity School students insist there is cause.

> Freedom of expression cannot exist without freedom of subjects... Freedom of subjects requires a prior commitment to protecting the physical, emotional, and intellectual security of all people, especially those most concretely and historically threatened: people of color, LGBTQ+, trans, gender non-conforming people, immigrants, undocumented people, women, religious minorities, and people with disabilities.

They are writing on behalf of those threatened, urging the University to concern itself first with their "physical, emotional, and intellectual security," and only thereafter with freedom of speech. Their primary value is the safety of the group, above and beyond the exploration of new ideas. They want to scare me—and the University—because they are scared. They see the Devil in Milo (and me) because they see us as blaspheming against the truth, the truth that says all of the subjects that they name are oppressed—and, therefore, in danger.

One of the most fascinating things I have learned listening to Professor Peterson's lectures on personality and the way in which we experience meaning is how important motivation and values are for how we perceive *anything at all*. Speaking neurologically, we perceive the world only insofar as we are motivated to act in it. Our perceptual structures are, as Peterson puts it, determined by our goals. Without goals—reasons to act—there is nothing to perceive. Our goals—our projections of our desires into the future—enable us to see. (He talks about this perceptual condition frequently; see his complete series of lectures on personality.[264])

Where do these motivations come from? Simple: the stories that we tell about the way in which we ought to or want to behave. Our perceptions are, quite literally, governed by myth, the stories told over and over again for generations about what it means to be human, to encounter the unknown. At least some of them are. Some are governed by more recent stories that we have told, about how capitalism is evil because it creates inequality as well as wealth. About how patriarchy (a.k.a. Western civilization) is responsible for all the evils in the world, up to and including the impending destruction of the planet thanks to climate change. About how white heterosexual men have historically been the oppressors of everyone else.

For the Divinity School students, as well as many of my colleagues, these stories are not myths, but matters of fact, to deny which is to be not only willfully blind, but evil. These are the frames through which they orient themselves in the world, the stories that motivate them and give their lives meaning. The stories that, at the deepest level, they *need* to believe in order to be able to act. My frame story, like Professor Peterson's, is rather different. (This is what I meant by "religion" in the *Sightings* piece: the deep stories by which we see the world.) Again, in his words:

> The idea that the West is founded on is that the human soul confronts the potential of Chaos and generates habitable order out of it. And that's why the individual has divine status in the West. That's why in our oldest books the human being was made in the image of God. Because God is also the thing that takes potential and transforms it into order.

---

[264] https://www.youtube.com/
playlist?list=PL22J3VaeABQApSdW8X71Ihe34eKN6XhCi

This is a profound idea. It's something that the postmodernists, they hate that idea. They absolutely hate it. And that's why they won't do things like engage in dialogue.

Dialogue is the shared Logos, that's the root of the word. They won't engage in dialogue because in their world your identity is either oppressor or oppressed. And that's all you are. Whatever your ethnicity or your racial group or your sexual identity or whatever identity group they want to come up with, because they can be infinitely fractionated. And you're either an oppressor or an oppressed. And that's all there is to you. You're just a member of a group.

And if you're oppressed, then you're good. And if you're an oppressor, then you're bad. But the problem with that, even though there's some truth in it. Because, like, I could pick out an identity dimension for any of you that you're an oppressor along, and another dimension along which you're oppressed. No problem. But the problem with that is, it doesn't actually tell you what to do.

This is also the problem with postmodern identity. Identity isn't just who you think you are. And it's certainly not your bloody ethnicity or sexual preference or anything so stupid. And the reason for that is your identity is what you use to operate in the world. It's what makes you a functional person. And not only as far as other people are concerned, but as far as you're concerned. And also so far as nature itself is concerned.

An identity is more like the toolkit you use to operate in the world. Being black or being white or being gay, that's not a toolkit to operate in the world. At best it's a shallow description of one dimension of your being. An identity is something you have to negotiate with other people because they need to trade with you. If you have something to offer and I have something to offer, then we can communicate. And hopefully it's good for you, and it's also good for me. We both benefit from that. And that's identity.

These ideas that identity is first of all subjective whim...a really poorly socialized three-year-old thinks that.[265]

---

[265] https://youtu.be/HvgUtHNavsl

It's time to grow up and learn some new stories. Maybe even some old ones. I'll start: "In the beginning was the Word..."

STUDIES 'R' US

May 20, 2017

Of the responses I have gotten on campus to my blogging about Milo, the most revealing of the stakes in our current culture wars came to the fore this week: I threaten medieval studies. I threaten lots of other things, too, I am told: our students, my colleagues, the culture of diversity and inclusion that they would like to foster. But worst of all, I threaten medieval studies.

I know this because, as one of our graduate students explained this past Monday on one of the campus Facebook groups, "[many] graduate students and faculty have tried to step up and address this [*my endorsing (in her words) 'a known white supremacist'—who dates only black guys,*[266] *says 'white nationalism is not the answer' (his words),*[267] *and whom the actual alt-Right hates,*[268],[269] not that that *makes any difference* to the way

[266] https://www.thestranger.com/slog/2017/02/03/24847763/retraction-milo-yiannopoulos-is-not-a-white-nationalist

[267] https://www.breitbart.com/social-justice/2017/01/26/milo-white-nationalism-is-not-the-answer/

[268] https://www.breitbart.com/social-justice/2017/01/27/forced-glamour-magazine-admit-im-not-white-supremacist/

[269] https://www.breitbart.com/social-justice/2017/02/18/fake-news-cnn-smears-milo-white-supremacist-accuses-bill-maher-mainstreaming-hate/

the Left or Right talk about him], including holding conferences and workshops." (She is talking about the ones I mention here.[270]) Why the pressing need to shut me up? This is where things get interesting:

> We are doing our best to separate medieval studies from this AltRight neo-traditionalist trash. If you don't like this kind of speech, write your deans, and above all else, vote with your feet and take a different history class in the coming terms. You have the right to know.

Fair enough, the whole point of having a curriculum like ours is so that the students are free to choose from courses that they find appealing within the degree requirements set by the departments and studies programs for their majors. My courses count for a number of these degrees, including Medieval Studies and Religious Studies as well as History. It seems appropriate if students do not want to study with me that they take courses from my colleagues instead.

You would think this would solve the problem, but apparently not. To judge from the numerous panels and workshops that my colleagues in Medieval Studies (not my faculty appointment, we don't have faculty appointments in Medieval Studies at Chicago) have convened (there have been at least three this quarter that I am aware of, there may have been more), I am a threat not just to those who might want to take courses with me, but to the whole concept of studying the Middle Ages.

There have been similar reactions from colleagues who identify as medievalists elsewhere in the country, most notably the group sponsoring the session at the International Medieval Congress last weekend on "Whiteness in Medieval Studies."[271] As they see it, our field is not only too white in its faculty and student demographics, but too white in its methodologies, above all in its "lack of complex

---

[270] https://fencingbearatprayer.blogspot.com/2017/05/lady-wisdoms-school-for-snake-lords.html

[271] http://medievalistsofcolor.com/workshop/2017-workshop/

racial consciousness." In their view, having people like me who say things like "Some of the things that we value most in our contemporary culture were conceptualized and supported by white, a.k.a. European, men" (like, for example, chivalry, marriage by consent, and women's right to vote) only serves to attract white supremacists to the study of our field.

(Other than myself, Derek Black is their one example—and he abandoned his white supremacism thanks to his academic studies in medieval history.[272] Although I value greatly the contributions that Western civilization has made to the history of our species, I am not and have never been a white supremacist, not that saying so is going to convince them.[273] Milo knows how futile this exercise is.)

One of the things that Professor Peterson and his graduate students have been working on is understanding the personality dimensions associated with particular political affiliations, most notably conservatism and liberalism. Liberalism, they have found, is correlated strongly with openness, that is, being prone to fantasy, caring about aesthetics, ideas, and creativity (basically, me). Conservatism, on the other hand, is correlated strongly with conscientiousness, that is, being concerned with order, self-discipline, competence, and achievement (again, basically, me—I told you I was an Ent.[274])

Everybody in academia loves liberalism, right? We are all about ideas. Perhaps not so much aesthetics and creativity anymore, but definitely ideas, the more culturally diverse the better. Conversely,

[272] https://www.washingtonpost.com/national/the-white-flight-of-derek-black/2016/10/15/ed5f906a-8f3b-11e6-a6a3-d50061aa9fae_story.html?utm_term=.ofad14febc05

[273] https://fencingbearatprayer.blogspot.com/2016/01/the-unbearable-whiteness-of-west.html

[274] As Treebeard puts it: "I am not altogether on anybody's side, because nobody is altogether on my side, if you understand me." Except Milo and, I think, JBP. [I became less sure about Professor Peterson's side after January 2018. See below.]

academics hate order and discipline... No, wait. Something is wrong here. Politically speaking, as the Heterodox Academy has pointed out, there are almost no conservatives left in academia, but surely there are those of us who care about order and discipline, competence and achievement.[275] That is our whole point, after all: training young people to think. Isn't it?

I have never been wholly comfortable with "Studies" programs, and I think now I understand why. I love studying religion and the Middle Ages, even at times gender (I'll wait), but I have resisted our setting up a department or graduate degree program at Chicago in Medieval Studies, and I wish that I could teach in a Department of Religion, not Religious Studies, just as I teach in History, not Historical Studies. Gender Studies presents peculiar difficulties for me, as I have mentioned. But the problem, I now realize, is not with the "gender" part of the program so much as it is with "studies"—thus, I would argue, the ease with which such programs can be spoofed.[276]

It is also the reason that my colleagues in "medieval studies" feel so threatened by me. To coin a phrase: "There is no there there." "Studies," by their very nature, have no borders—or discipline. They depend utterly on feelings of belonging to a group defined only by mutual interest in particular periods, regions, sources, or themes, not any shared training or expertise. It is as if one wanted to have a program in sports—and refused to train the students in any particular sport lest they exclude anybody for not having that skill. Or a program in music in which nobody learned a particular instrument to play. Or a church where nobody had to confess any particular doctrine or understanding of God, that is, had no shared conception of worship or how to act in relation with the divine. In Professor Peterson's

[275] https://heterodoxacademy.org

[276] https://www.skeptic.com/reading_room/conceptual-penis-social-contruct-sokal-style-hoax-on-gender-studies/#.WSBD3YfJ-oI.twitter

terms, "studies" have no motivating story or star because they offer no training in what to *do*.

Sure, everybody in medieval studies likes studying the Middle Ages, but so what? Lots of people like studying the Middle Ages—including, quite possibly, a few white supremacists, who also like studying the history of Europe, the U.K., and the United States—but shared liking creates a different kind of community from shared discipline.

You cannot compete or excel in a game without structure and rules. It's the reason every child worth his or her salt hates P.E.[277] Not because they don't like being physically fit. But because there is no point in being physically fit *without being able to play a particular game.* (Arguably also why so many exercise programs fail.) The same thing applies to playing music. It doesn't work unless the musicians know how to play. It is part of the reason I converted to the Catholic church: I believe that liturgy follows creed, even as creed is given life in liturgy and service.[278]

Imagine a fencing tournament where nobody was supposed to know how to fence. Or a symphony played by musicians who had never trained in a particular instrument. How would you determine who got to play? Is it discriminatory to insist that fencers fence rather than, say, come to the strip wanting to have a tea party instead? We don't want people to feel excluded, my colleagues say. We want everyone to feel welcome. Another of our graduate students has argued in a piece published in *Sightings* this week (I have had quite an exciting week!) that medieval studies needs to forcibly diversify its faculty by purposefully hiring from underrepresented communities so as to counter the impression of "Whites Only" that persists in the field.[279]

---

[277] https://fencingbearatprayer.blogspot.com/2017/03/boys-with-tits.html

[278] https://fencingbearatprayer.blogspot.com/2017/03/trust-in-me.html

[279] https://divinity.uchicago.edu/sightings/denouncing-discrimination-enforcing-inequality

What he does not explain is why anyone would want to study the Middle Ages in the first place.

I do not teach "medieval studies." I teach history, particularly the history of Europe in the Middle Ages, but also the history of Christianity, because I believe that training students to think historically is a valuable discipline. To be sure, I also believe that it is important—*vital*[280]—to teach students the particulars of history, but this is the WHAT to my HOW and WHY.[281]

I do not teach the history of Europe in the Middle Ages because I want to create a community of medievalists, although I enjoy greatly the conversations of colleagues in my field. I teach the history of Europe in the Middle Ages because I believe this period of history made important contributions to the development of human civilization, above all in the development of Christian practice and thought, including the thought that all human beings, whatever their skin color, are made "in the image and likeness of God."

&❧

Which brings me to the importance of borders. According to Professor Peterson, another of the things that conservatives like is borders—and walls.[282] They like borders, he argues, because borders represent orderliness. Liberals, on the other hand, dislike borders and walls and want everybody to be able to come in. Contrary to what many of my colleagues would have you believe, there are good reasons to like both. The question is, as Professor Peterson points out, how do you know which is the right response at a given time? Sure, borders—and especially walls—are designed to keep people out, which makes it difficult to trade with and learn from them. But borders and walls are also designed to protect the people living within

[280] https://fencingbearatprayer.blogspot.com/2016/03/why-study-humanities.html
[281] https://fencingbearatprayer.blogspot.com/2016/01/my-why-how-what.html
[282] https://fencingbearatprayer.blogspot.com/2016/11/i-will-be-wall-for-them.html

from attack—and contagion. (Just ask the indigenous peoples of the Americas about smallpox, measles, and chicken pox. Oh, right, you can't. Most of them died.)

Here's where things get really interesting. Still following Professor Peterson: the best indicator of orderliness is not just a liking for discipline, but disgust. Those high in the personality trait of orderliness respond not with anxiety or fear to those they see as belonging outside their borders, but disgust. Much, you might say, as my academic colleagues in medieval studies are now responding to me.

The same student who made the Facebook post this last Monday was deeply concerned back in March that I mislabeled an image I had used to illustrate one of my posts (ironically, about all the insults I had been getting; I have since fixed the reference).[283] Such sloppiness, she insisted, indicated my complete disregard for the standards of scholarship to which, as a medievalist, I should be holding myself. "If you're going to embarrass us transatlantically," she told me, "please use correct reasoning about the illuminations you cite!"

What perplexed me at the time and still does is why she cared so much about *defending our field of study.* Somehow, thanks to the fact she and I were both medievalists, I was embarrassing *her.* You might almost think she was a conservative, so disgusting did she find what I had done. (The giveaway here is her emphasis on separating medieval studies from the "trash" she says I speak.)

Here's my theory. Our political labels of "liberal" and "conservative" are useless in explaining the tensions that we are experiencing over how to study the humanities on our college campuses. What we have is not a political crisis so much as a crisis of discipline. Ent that I am, I am so open to new ideas and ways of thinking that I drive my peer

---

[283] https://fencingbearatprayer.blogspot.com/2017/03/turning-other-cheek.html

reviewers nuts. They never know what box to put my work in—and tell me so.

But I also believe deeply in borders, that is, the distinction between disciplines, not as ways of keeping people out, but as ways of defining the skills that we need in order to be able to act and to think. I am not an "athlete" except insofar as I am a "fencer." I am not a "musician" except insofar as I am a "fiddler." I am not "spiritual" except insofar as I am "religious"—and Christian. I am not a "medievalist" except insofar as I am an "historian." Every skill I gain makes me more of a person. And less afraid. Having walls may be useful for keeping strangers out, but they are also places in which to train heroes—who will then have the courage to go out into the unknown and meet strangers, perhaps even make new friends.

☙

I said it back in September, and I will say it again. What our students need is not "safe spaces," but skills. This, I now realize, is why I have been wary of programs designed around "studies." It is also, I hypothesize, why my colleagues in medieval studies feel so threatened by me. Not the fencers, who just want to fence. Not the fiddlers, who just want to play music. Not the Catholics at my new church, who just want to worship God.

Not even most of my colleagues in History, although there are notable exceptions. But the medievalists, who have nothing to define their activity except their shared interest in a particular set of images, artifacts, stories, and texts. About which, as they have shown these past several weeks, they can be very possessive indeed.

THE UNBEARABLE WHITENESS OF MEDIEVAL STUDIES

May 23, 2017

I've been demoted from snake to low-hanging fruit. As University of Chicago Divinity School M.A. student Dr. Karl E. H. Seigfried argues in his recent *Sightings* piece:

> Few academics today openly support the Milo Yiannopouloses of the world, so denouncing the new breed of public hate monger can seem less like a brave stand than a signaling of virtue. By picking low-hanging fruit and standing against the most obviously bigoted targets, protesting professors avoid addressing parallel problems in their own disciplines.[284]

Cue outrage. I'll wait... Nothing yet? You do realize what just happened here? In one fell swoop, as befits a Viking, Dr. Seigfried renders both me and the colleagues who have been doing their best to distance themselves from me these past several months ridiculous. I can't decide whether I should be outraged or relieved. I rather enjoy being a snake, opening people's eyes. Just call me Lady Wisdom.

---

[284] https://divinity.uchicago.edu/sightings/denouncing-discrimination-enforcing-inequality

But according to Dr. Seigfried, I am not the real problem. (In truth, I am not. But, like Milo, I have learned how futile such protestations of association can be.) Rather, it is the field of medieval studies writ large, where the majority of faculty are white. In Dr. Seigfried's view, however much my colleagues in the field may decry the overwhelming whiteness of our profession, they are kidding themselves if they think, for example, that "broadening the curriculum to establish a 'multicultural Middle Ages'" will provide an effective counter to the racism historically attendant on the study of Anglo-Saxon language and literature.[285] Dr. Seigfried delivers the *coup de grâce*:

> If Old English really does have "a serious image problem," a full assessment of the issue requires reflection on issues of race in the hiring practices of the discipline itself.... To assert that white nationalism in the public sphere can be countered with white saviorhood in the academic realm is quite questionable.

His solution:

> The same scholars who criticize the alt-right, call for expansion of subjects covered, and declare support for various embattled communities need to openly address and diligently fight the lack of diversity of their own faculties. Until the institutions reflect the diversity of their wider communities, it's all too easy for the public to scoff at professors who decry prejudice while perpetuating systems of inequality in their own workplaces.

My guess is Dr. Seigfried (see author photo) will not be applying for academic jobs in Norse Studies any time soon. I have a harder time guessing how he plans to attract students from underrepresented communities to the study of Anglo-Saxon. Perhaps he does not want to. "Medieval England as a field is dead," one of my colleagues in medieval history asserted recently. Nor has it been particularly lively for the better part of my career. More precisely, nor has it been the

---

[285] https://daily.jstor.org/old-english-serious-image-problem/

field about which my colleagues in medieval studies allow themselves to be openly excited. That would be...in poor taste. Much better to wax breathless about...anything other than the history of medieval England—or anywhere else in northern Europe (unless it's pagan).

My colleagues' solution—dismissed by Dr. Seigfried as disingenuous—has been to include in their telling of the history of medieval England (and other points north) the stories of those who do not fit the nineteenth-century's celebratory image of the Anglo-Saxons, Vikings, and other northern European peoples, which, my colleagues worry, has been co-opted by newly nascent forces of white supremacism. (Again, not me, to give the futile but necessary liturgical response.) "Medieval Europe was not 'white,'" these colleagues insist (if not yet in print, then vigorously and vociferously on my Facebook wall). Nor, any longer, are the proper subjects of medieval studies "white." As Mary Dockray-Miller puts it in her article cited—and criticized—by Dr. Seigfried:

> Long before the Black Lives Matter movement on campuses across the country called for a more inclusive, more diverse curriculum, the discipline of medieval studies had been working toward the establishment of a "multicultural Middle Ages," a way out from under the field's reputation as thoroughly dead, white, and male. Since the 1980s, women authors, audiences, and subjects have been more frequently included in the field—part of the influence of second-wave feminism. Work on the Islamic Middle Ages has made its way from specialized journals into undergraduate textbooks. And the study of medieval Africa and the medieval Far East is on a similar, though slower, trajectory into recognition.[286]

Which is all well and good, insofar as all history is ultimately world history. No country, not even England, is an island in anything except geographical terms. But the elephant in the room...is still white, dead, Christian, and male. "Why study Europe in the Middle Ages?" I asked

---

[286] https://daily.jstor.org/old-english-serious-image-problem/

my Facebook salon. "Even those whose ancestors came from England don't care about it anymore. Why should anybody else?" My friends leapt into the fray.

A: Perhaps I'm wrong, but I think there must be many people who are hungry for a sense of roots and belonging to a civilization and a culture. For several years, I've been enchanted by Winston Churchill's idea of "the English-speaking Peoples," with its implication that English history is part of the heritage of English-speaking Americans (regardless of where their DNA came from). It's clear that even now, we Americans are shaped in part by the fact that our original colonies were founded by Britain, and by the English language. I dearly wish that the continuities between British and American culture were emphasized in our schools, rather than the idea that we Americans are utterly different from the British.

B: I can understand why Europeans still study the Middle Ages (assuming they do) because it explains their ethnogenesis—the Anglo-Saxons and the English, the Franks and France, and so forth, but why do Americans do it?.... [The] American Revolution was supposed to mark a break from All That.... In my view a central aim of the humanities is to broaden horizons, and whatever our heritage we should seek to learn something about Greece and Rome, about India, China, and Islam. Just reinforcing one's ethnic heritage seems provincial.

A: The American Revolution had some of its roots in ideas that were developed during the English Civil War. Nothing comes from a vacuum. I'm only beginning to learn about it, but it seems clear that there are good reasons why the American Revolution happened in the former colonies of Britain, specifically. We Americans are taught to think of ourselves as if we appeared like Athena, springing fully-formed from the head of Zeus, but in fact we have roots in English political, legal and cultural traditions.

C: Two words—Magna Carta!

B: Are not you folks, well, a bit defensive? It seems that the sole benefit of studying the Middle Ages is to reinforce anglophone chauvinism. Surely it must signify more than that. In my view the pivotal event of

Western medieval history is the Investiture Conflict, which had little to do with England and the English.

Test yourself: *A*, *B*, or *C*? To judge from the way my colleagues in medieval studies are embarrassed to claim an interest in medieval England *qua* medieval England—or northern Europe insofar as it was Christian—most of them would agree with *B:* the only reason to study the history of the English-speaking peoples—or Christianity—unapologetically is chauvinism. Even to suggest that Old English is worth studying as the root of our modern language smacks of provincialism. Better to study anything else—the history Greece and Rome, of India, China, and Islam—than to waste time, especially as Americans, on the history of the insignificant island from which the majority of our country's founding political, legal, religious, linguistic, and cultural traditions came.

I know, I know: not everyone in medieval England was what we would now call "white" or Christian. But most were (unless these categories are meaningless, too), and quite a few of them were male (ditto): Anselm of Canterbury (d. 1109), who went head-to-head with two kings (William II and Henry I) over the issue of investiture, not to mention writing some of the most beautiful prayers to the Virgin and her Son.

Stephen Langton (d. 1228), who went head-to-head with King John over his election as archbishop of Canterbury, thus embroiling John in the argument with his barons that led to Magna Carta. Geoffrey Chaucer (d. 1400), William Langland (d. ca. 1386), John Gower (d. 1408), and the *Pearl* poet, who together invented English as a literary language. The kings and members of parliament, the judges, lawyers, sheriffs, and clerks, who together over the course of centuries invented the common law. The monks, friars, and university scholars who wrestled with how to explain and embody the elements of their Christian faith. The burghers and craftsmen who built up the towns.

Of course, it's more complicated than a story of Great White Men. *Of course*, we need the stories of the women, the pagans, Muslims, and Jews, the foreigners, and the outcasts in order to appreciate the tradition in full. But if the only reason one would want to study literature written by white men is to reinforce one's sense of superior whiteness, how exactly, as per Dr. Seigfried's suggestion, is going into "the high schools in underserved communities to recruit for [bookish fields like religious studies]"—*his shift in terms*—going to work?

My colleagues in medieval studies would seem to want to have their rainbow-colored cake and eat it, too. They want to shed the image of medieval studies as predominantly white, Christian, and male by including in the rubric "medieval" the traditions of every part of the world other than the European (which is fine) without having to explain why someone who is not white—or Christian or male or dead—would want to study the traditions that came from the regions where the people were predominantly Christian and white (unless, as I said above, no one was, because no one now wants his ancestors to be identified as white, never mind Christian).

I would be more convinced by Dr. Seigfried's exhortation for my colleagues in medieval studies to commit themselves to hiring colleagues from underrepresented communities if he could explain why anyone from such a community would want to study what he does:

the mythology of the Norse.[287] If there are reasons for such study other than championing one's own whiteness, it would be good to know.[288]

---

[287] http://www.norsemyth.org/

[288] If it is not clear, I think there are, but at the moment the burden of proof lies on those who reject the reason I would give: that these traditions made important contributions to the history of humankind without which our present civilization would not exist. My guess from Dr. Seigfried's blog is that his argument would be in favor of paganism over against Christianity.

PERFORMING THE LOGOS

May 25, 2017

I laugh, make a joke about how much mischief I've caused. They're encouraged, it's safe to talk, I'm not going to get upset. And then it comes: "I don't understand what you see in him, he's just a provocateur. Why should we encourage such people to speak on our campuses?" I could answer a number of ways, insist that Milo bases everything he says on facts, even the jokes. "But that isn't the point," they say. "If he has an argument, why does he have to be so provocative about it?" But what they really mean is, why does he have to come *here*?

I wondered that myself at first. Why did Milo insist on giving his talks *on campus*? Why not avoid the protestors, rent a hall, sell tickets, give the talks, and put the videos up on YouTube? It is working beautifully for Jordan Peterson with his new series of lectures on the Bible.[289] But Milo always refused to back down and give his talks anywhere else. Today he gave a talk along with Pamela Geller to protest Linda Sarsour's invitation to speak at CUNY's commencement

---

[289] https://www.jordanbpeterson.com/bible-series/

exercises.[290] This morning he did a short video on Facebook explaining his plans:

> Unlike some of the other speakers, I don't want Linda Sarsour banned...I want her to debate in the open. I want her to come with facts and reason and logic. I want for her to be exposed. And so I'm going to be talking today about why I think she's wrong, not why I think she should be cancelled.

But people like Sarsour's supporters are not willing to debate Milo with facts, reason, and logic, as the protestors who showed up to protest his talk this afternoon proved by blowing whistles and yelling throughout his remarks. Milo is not going to change anybody's mind with his arguments if his audiences are already provoked. So what does he think he is doing? I think I know. He is embodying a myth. More precisely, he is embodying *the* myth at the heart of Western civilization: the myth by which, as Professor Peterson puts it, articulated truth brings the world into being. He is embodying the Word.

Milo describes his campus talks not just as speaking, but as *doing* something. Other conservatives, he insists, think that they can change people's minds by writing a column or publishing a book, but that isn't *doing* anything. And yet, it would seem, all Milo *does* is talk. (Or, occasionally, sing.) Why give the talks on college campuses? Partly, because Milo cares about education. And partly, because college campuses are the place where students are introduced to the arguments Milo is trying to expose in their most articulated form. But mainly because college campuses are the one place in our contemporary culture (other than places of worship) where people come together to speak *in person*.

I have been exhausted all quarter, which is not entirely surprising. I'm still on this low-carb diet, so my energy for explosive action like

---

[290] https://www.breitbart.com/tech/2017/05/25/milo-pamela-geller-protest-sharia-advocate-linda-sarsour/

speaking is limited. But I know what has been happening. I have been braced for attack. It is one thing to sit here writing about what I think. It is wholly another thing to stand up and speak it to a room full of other human beings. You try it. Stand up in front of a group of people and talk to them. Yeah, right.

It isn't about your words anymore. It is your whole being that is at stake, every muscle, every nerve ending, every emotion. Your whole body is screaming: "Danger!" Your body is right. It matters that Milo gives his talks before audiences of students who are in the same room with him. That is, whose bodies are in the same room as his. Whose bodies—and hearts and minds—will respond not just to his words or the sound of his voice, but everything about his physical presence. His movements. His gestures. His facial expressions. The force of his will.

What do you do when an audience is in the same room with you, listening? Do you speak in order to please them? Or do you risk conflict by speaking the truth? In Professor Peterson's words: "We use our bodies to represent things long before we understand what it is we are representing." We speak with our bodies. (Professor Peterson, like Milo, makes particular use of his hands.) We act things out before we are able to articulate them in words. Including the reason that it is so important to speak.

The single most important thing that Milo has done with his campus talks is stand up and speak the truth in the midst of the crowd. It helps that he has Navy Seals to protect him. But it is more important that he stand up, speak, and take the consequences. Like Christ. I have gotten into a lot of trouble—okay, mainly by way of the Internet—for comparing Milo to Christ. But Professor Peterson has done it, too. Okay, maybe not directly, but he talks about Christ-like figures like Milo all the time. Except that he calls them individuals who play out the archetype of the hero by being willing to speak.

"In the beginning was the Word. And the Word was with God. And the Word was God." What does this mean? Again, in Professor Peterson's words (I paraphrase):

> In the beginning was the Logos, that is, consciousness, because it is by no means obvious what there is, if there is no one to experience it. And this Logos or consciousness is associated with bringing reality into being.[291]

This, Professor Peterson explains, is what it means in Genesis that human beings—*both men and women*—are created in the image and likeness of God: with consciousness and the capacity to bring the world into being through speech. It's bloody mind-blowing! And it comes with enormous responsibility. A third time, in Professor Peterson's words:

> Don't underestimate the power of your speech! Now, Western culture is phallogocentric. Let's say it... It is predicated on the idea of the Logos. The Logos is the sacred element of Western culture. What does that mean? It means that your capacity for speech is divine. It is the thing that generates order from chaos. And then sometimes turns pathological order into chaos when it has to.
>
> Don't underestimate the power of truth. There is nothing more powerful [than the truth]. Now in order to speak what you might regard as the truth, you have to let go of the outcome. You have to think, alright, I'm going to say what I think. Stupid as I am. Biased as I am. Ignorant as I am. I am going to state what I think as clearly as I can, and I am going to live with the consequences no matter what they are.
>
> Now the reason that you think that, that's an element of faith. The idea is that nothing brings a better world into being than the stated truth. You might have to pay a price for that. But that's fine. You're going to pay a price for every bloody thing you do. And everything you don't do. You don't get to choose to not pay a price. You get to choose which poison you're going to take. That's it. So if you're going to stand up for something, stand up for your truth.[292]

[291] https://youtu.be/f-wWBGo6a2w
[292] https://youtu.be/6b_pWJkrhSg

Milo understands this. Seriously, it is why he wears a cross. Every word that we say matters because every word we speak either moves us closer to the truth or entangles us further in lies. Truths about the basis of our civilization, whether in the divinity of the individual or in the submission of the individual to God. Truths about the proper relations between women and men. Truths about speech and its effect on the world. We can choose not to speak and become, as Professor Peterson puts it, miserable worms. Or we can choose to speak, take the consequences, and bring a better world into being. Like God.

SIGNED WITH THE CROSS

May 27, 2017

What would Jesus do? Victorian pessimist and poet James Thomson (d. 1882) thought he knew.[293]

> This poor sexless Jew, with a noble feminine heart, and a magnificent though uncultivated and crazy brain, did no work to earn his bread; evaded all social and political responsibilities, took no wife and contemned his own family; lived [as] a vagabond, fed and housed by charity (if by miracle, it is clear that we cannot imitate him: would that we could!); uttered many beautiful and even sublime moral truths and more impracticable precepts; preached continually himself, and faith in himself alone as the one thing necessary; and died with the lamentable cry of womanish desperation, perhaps the most significant confession in history of a life of supreme self-illusion laid bare to itself at the point of death. My God, my God, why hast thou forsaken me? He founded a sect which holds him up as the Great Exemplar of mankind, and scarcely one member of which even tries to tread in his footsteps. I have much love and reverence for him as a man; but am quite certain that if everyone really set about following his example, the world (which is surely mad enough already) would soon be one vast Bedlam broken loose.

---

[293] http://www.victorianweb.org/authors/thomson/1.html

Did I mention Thomson was a pessimist? Nothing in what Jesus did—according to Thomson—was remotely admirable. Jesus never worked for a living or "engaged in trade of any kind." He never got married and had no children and "seems to have thought all sexual relations sinful, or at least inimical to holiness (Matthew 19:12)." He disowned his own mother and brothers (Matthew 12:46-50). He seems not to have understood that if the rich sell everything they have and give to the poor (Matthew 19:21), this would just make the poor newly-rich and therefore obliged to give everything they have to the formerly-rich newly poor. "It was of course easy for Jesus, who had nothing because he took care to earn nothing, to preach this absurd doctrine."

According to Thomson, it gets worse. Jesus' teaching "Render unto Caesar the things which are Caesar's (Matthew 22:21)" would seem to render "all political striving, all patriotism, and championship of liberty" contrary to his message, while his insistence that his followers should do better than the scribes and Pharisees in practicing what they preached (Matthew 23:2, 3) would seem to suggest that they should "observe the whole Mosaic ceremonial law," thus making "the Jews, in this respect,...the only orthodox Christians."

Much of his teaching was based on a delusion, that "the end of the world was close at hand." "Cherishing this delusion, it is no wonder that Jesus and his immediate followers had no care for thought of the morrow, for marriage and posterity, for patriotism; the wonder is how modern professing Christians dare to pretend that the delusion is not to be read clearly in the Gospels and Epistles." Thomson concludes:

> Had the biographies of Jesus shown that he worked hard, and got an honest livelihood as a carpenter; that he proved himself, under great difficulties, a good sweetheart, husband, father, citizen, patriot, making the best of the world as he found it; that he was modest and sensible while enthusiastic for the good of his fellows; that the sordid and

wearing circumstances of a life of toil and trouble left his mind serene and his heart noble, so that he was ever preaching lofty and liberal truth; that he died bravely as he had lived; then he would indeed have been a Great Exemplar for millions of poor men and women struggling to be good and true in all the natural and common i.e. nations of life.

Instead, Jesus was a bum. Or, perhaps more accurately, a socialist.

ॐ

It matters whom we take as our ideal. One of the things I like most about Jordan Peterson's lecturing is the way he is able to take apart complex ideas and build them back up. On the downside, however, it makes it difficult to summarize his arguments, much like Jesus' teaching. You get aphorisms: "Speak the truth. Develop your inner monster. Rescue your father from the underworld. Ascend the set of all possible dominance hierarchies. Sort yourself out." But unpacking them takes as much work as unpacking some of Jesus' sayings.

"Think not that I have come to abolish the law and the prophets; I have come not to abolish them but to fulfil them." (Matthew 5:17)

"Why do you see the speck that is in your brother's eye, but do not notice the log that is in your own eye?" (Matthew 7:3)

"Behold, I send you out as sheep in the midst of wolves; so be wise as serpents and innocent as doves." (Matthew 10:16)

"Whoever humbles himself like this child, he is the greatest in the kingdom of heaven." (Matthew 18:4)

"You shall love the Lord your God with all your heart, and with all your soul, and with all your mind. This is the great and first commandment. And a second is like it, You shall love your neighbor as yourself. On these two commandments depend all the law and the prophets." (Matthew 22:37-40)

Do you see what I just did there? Jesus said: "I am the way, and the truth, and the life; no one comes to the Father, but by me... If you love me, you will keep my commandments. And I will pray the Father, and he will give you another Counselor, to be with you for ever, even the Spirit of truth, whom the world cannot receive, because it neither sees him nor knows him; you know him, for he dwells with you, and will be in you." (John 14:6, 15-17) Thomson was right: Christians take Christ as their Exemplar. Where he was wrong—as are many who try to use Jesus as their social and political model—was in understanding what that means.

֍

I think Professor Peterson understands. We have to start with the fact that once we were apes, kin to the chimpanzees. And to the zebras. And to the lobsters, who like us live in dominance hierarchies. And would tell stories about what it means to be Top Lobster, if only they could speak. Human beings, unique among the animal kingdom, speak. That is, we tell stories about the past and the future, not just utter cries of alarm about the present.

We tell stories about what we imagine is going to happen not just today, but tomorrow, and the next day, and the next day, and the last day, which we imagine coming soon. And we hypothesize about how best to act, given what we know about the past. The more stories we tell, the more examples we have of how certain actions played out.

Over the millennia since we developed consciousness and speech—in the Christian tradition called *Logos*—we have told story after story about heroes who were able to ascend not just this or that dominance hierarchy—the hierarchy of strength (Hercules) or the hierarchy of good looks (Apollo) or the hierarchy of singing (Orpheus)—but the set of all possible dominance hierarchies.

The first hero to do this was the Mesopotamian god Marduk. Marduk was not just strong and handsome and mellifluous. He was all eyes, with which he could see everything. When the flood-monster Tiamut threatened to destroy the world for killing her husband Apsu, the gods elected Marduk Head God to do battle with her. Anshar, Marduk's grandfather, pled with him: "My son, who knowest all wisdom, quiet Tiamat with thy holy incantation." That is, with thy magic words. In the story Marduk kills Tiamut, cuts her body into parts, and makes the world from it. Professor Peterson explains:

> The mythic tale of Marduk and Tiamat refers to the capacity of the individual to explore, voluntarily, and to bring things into being as a consequence. The hero cuts the world of the unpredictable—unexplored territory, signified by Tiamat—into its distinguishable elements; weaves a net of determinate meaning, capable of encompassing the vast unknown; embodies the divine "masculine" essence, which has as its most significant feature the capacity to transform chaos into order. The killing of an all-embracing monster and the construction of the universe from its body parts is symbolic (metaphorical) representation of the central, adaptive process of heroic encounter with the undifferentiated unknown, and the construction or generation of differentiated order as a consequence.[294]

Yahweh, the LORD of Israel, was another such hero.

᪣

"Canst thou draw out Leviathan with an hook?" the LORD asked Job, "or his tongue with a cord which thou lettest down? Canst thou put a hook into his nose? Or bore his jaw through with a thorn?" Who was this Leviathan, and why should the LORD boast of drawing him out with a hook?

> I will not conceal his parts, nor his power, nor his comely proportion... His scales are his pride, shut up together as with a close seal... Out of his mouth go burning lamps, and sparks of fire leap out. Out of his nostrils goeth smoke, as out of a seething pot or cauldron. His breath kindleth coals, and a flame goeth out of his mouth... He esteemeth iron as straw, and brass as rotten wood. The arrow cannot make him flee: clingstones are turned with him into stubble.... He maketh the deep to boil like a pot: he maketh the sea like a pot of ointment. He maketh a path to shine after him; one would think the deep to be hoary. Upon

[294] *Maps of Meaning: The Architecture of Belief* (1999)

earth there is not his like, who is made without fear. He beholdeth all high things: he is a king over all the children of pride. (Job 41:1-2, 12, 15, 19-21, 27-28, 31-34)

In other words: he was a fire-breathing dragon of the sea. And Yahweh killed him, broke him into pieces, and gave him to the people to eat. Thus the psalmist sang to him:

> Yet God my King is from of old, working salvation in the midst of the earth. Thou didst divide the sea by thy might; thou didst break the heads of the dragons on the waters. Thou didst crush the heads of Leviathan, thou didst give him as food for the creatures in the wilderness. Thou didst cleave open springs and brooks; thou didst dry up ever-flowing streams. Thine is the day, thine also the night; thou hast established the luminaries and the sun. Thou hast fixed all the bounds of the earth; thou hast made summer and winter. (Psalm 74:12-17)

When Jesus' followers said he was God, this is who they meant. He was a monster-slayer who made the world.

❦

The key is in the psalms. "What do you think of the Christ?," Jesus asked the Pharisees. "Whose son is he?" They said to him: "The son of David." And he replied:

> How is it then that David, inspired by the Spirit, calls him Lord, saying: "The Lord said to my Lord, sit at my right hand, till I put thy enemies under thy feet" [Psalm 110:1]? If David calls him Lord, how is he his son? (Matthew 22:41-45)

Everything that was said of the LORD in the psalms, Christians read as pertaining to Jesus. At least, they used to, before the nineteenth century decided that only the Gospels and Epistles spoke directly of Christ. This was the Jesus whom medieval Christians like Thomas of Kempen thought they were called to imitate: not simply a man, but a hero who did battle with chaos in order to bring the world into being.

For to what angel did God ever say, "Thou art my Son, today I have begotten thee"?[Psalm 2:7] Or again, "I will be to him a father, and he shall be to me a son"? [2 Samuel 7:14] And again, when he brings the first-born into the world, he says, "Let all God's angels worship him." [Deuteronomy 32:43 LXX; Psalm 97:7] Of the angels he says, "Who makes his angels winds, and his servants flames of fire." [Psalm 104:4] But of the Son he says, "Thy throne, O God, is for ever and ever, the righteous scepter is the scepter of thy kingdom. Thou hast loved righteousness and hated lawlessness; therefore God, thy God, has anointed thee with the oil of gladness beyond thy comrades." [Psalm 45:6-7] And, "Thou, Lord, didst found the earth in the beginning, and the heavens are the work of thy hands; they will perish, but thou remainest; they will all grow old like a garment, like a mantle thou wilt roll them up, and they will be changed. But thou art the same, and thy years will never end." [Psalm 102:25-27] But to what angel has he ever said, "Sit at my right hand, till I make thy enemies a stool for thy feet"? [Psalm 110:1] —Hebrews 1:5-13

And how did he do battle with the dragon? By speaking the truth ("I am the way, the truth, and the life"), developing his inner monster (being wise as the Serpent), rescuing his father (Adam, the Law) from the underworld, ascending the set of all possible dominance hierarchies (he is seated at the right hand of the Father), and sorting himself out.

❧

What would Jesus do? In Professor Peterson's words:

Christ embodies the hero, grounded in tradition, who is narrative depiction of the basis for successful individual and social adaptation. As the Word "made flesh" (John 1:14) there "in the beginning" (John 1:1), he represents, simultaneously, the power that divides order from chaos, and tradition rendered spiritual, abstract, declarative, semantic. His manner of being is that which moves morality itself from rule of law to rule of spirit—which means *process*.[295]

Morality is not much in fashion these days. We talk about rights and get offended when other people do not respect them. We demand

---

[295] *Maps of Meaning: The Architecture of Belief* (1999)

that no one judge us while judging everyone else for the slightest misprision. We spend all of our time looking for the mote in our neighbor's eye while neglecting the beam in our own. And we claim dominance on the basis of our being offended, humbling ourselves before no one and no God.

It is hard to be a hero. It is hard to live according to the Truth, to put on the armor of God (Ephesians 6:10-17) and stand not for the crowd calling for the crucifixion of the sinner, but for wisdom and virtue and love. It means taking responsibility for ourselves and our own lives and orienting ourselves towards a goal. It means being willing to make sacrifices of the present for the future. It means understanding that it is we who make the world in which we live one word—and act—at a time.

It means fulfilling the law, not abandoning it; absorbing tradition so as to learn from it while not giving into nostalgia for something dead. It means humbling ourselves before our own ignorance and being willing to learn from our mistakes, like a child. It means being willing to speak and take the consequences for our speaking as well as being willing to listen when others speak so that we might learn from them.

It means loving each other as creatures of God, every human being made in the image and likeness of our creator, imbued with a spark of divinity revealed in our capacity for rational speech. It means putting on Christ and "speaking the truth in love" (Ephesians 4:15). Which means, sometimes, saying things that others find difficult to hear because it forces them to confront the most dangerous dragon of all: ourselves.

ST. MILO THE DANGEROUS AND THE DRAGON OF CHAOS

July 8, 2017

This time last year, I thought I had myself pretty well sorted out. I had gotten over my writer's block and was looking forward to getting my book manuscript finished.[296] I had qualified for the USA Veteran Fencing Team for 2016 and was going to Germany in October to compete in the World Championships. I was even making what felt like real progress in learning the fiddle. Sure, I was heavier than I liked, but all things considered I was doing well.

I was going to be on leave for the Autumn and Winter terms, which meant going to Germany would not cut into my teaching schedule, and I was reasonably confident that I would be able to finish the revisions on my book in time to submit my manuscript to my publisher before going back to the classroom in the Spring. It was going to be a relaxing nine months, or so I thought. Little did I know how dangerous—and exhilarating—my year would be!

---

[296] *Mary and the Art of Prayer: The Hours of the Virgin in Medieval Christ Life and Thought* (2017)

I have lost track of how many times I have told the story. About how our deans sent out the letter explaining to our incoming freshman that they should not expect to find "safe spaces" or "trigger warnings" at the University of Chicago. About how the letter made me curious to learn what all the fuss the previous Spring had been about, particularly with Milo's college tour. About how after three days of bingeing on the videos of his talks I wrote to Milo, introducing myself as a professor from the University of Chicago and telling him how much I admired what he was doing in his tour. About how I started writing for and about him on my blog... and he started sharing my posts with his fans on his Facebook page. About how I became, in some circles at least, famous.

Happily, as it turned out, I was able to finish my book manuscript months before I thought I would, leaving me time throughout the winter to follow Milo on his tour. Virtually, for the most part, along with the rest of his fans, but one evening in December, when the bus came through Chicago, in person. (For the full story, listen here.[297]) I have written in these pages about how much Milo inspired me and his fans.

No matter how hyperbolic my praises became, Milo would be sure to top his previous performance. First there were his talks. Then there was his appearance on the Bill Maher show after the Berkeley riot. Then there was the dignity with which he faced his detractors after losing his speaking engagement, his book contract, and (by his own gentlemanly decision) his job. That's what made me most famous these past few months—when I called his conservative detractors...a naughty name. Friends—yes, I still have some—have sympathized with me, how much I have had to go through. With the backbiting

---

[297] https://fencingbearatprayer.blogspot.com/2017/07/three-kraters-symposium-how-i-met-milo.html

from my fellow academics. With the refusals to take what I argued about the importance of Milo's tour seriously. With the petitions and Facebook gossip and the articles in the campus newspaper. Okay, yes, it's been hard. I have never had such vicious insults hurled at me, at least since I was a kid.[298] But—truth be told—I have been having the time of my life!

Are you kidding me? It is every writer's dream to have had the numbers of readers I have had this past year. Over 1.2 million hits on my blog since October. Articles in *Sightings* and *First Things*.[299],[300] Interviews with colleagues.[301] I've been on radio and in the newspapers.[302],[303] I have hundreds of new friends and followers on Facebook. I have received hundreds more emails and messages of support. I even got to meet Based Mom herself, Christina Hoff Sommers, after she tweeted about my adventures to her readers. And, of course, I got to meet Milo.

It has been a magical—better, a mythological year. Not only did I submit my book manuscript—a book I have been working on for the better part of fifteen years; it will be out in November. Inspired by Milo's own diet and fat shaming, I got myself back on my low-carb diet to lose the "book baby-weight" and since October have gone from a size 12 to a 6.[304] Inspired by Milo's warmth in talking about being Christian (and not a little by finishing my book on devotion to Mary), I took the leap I have been meaning to for years and converted to Catholicism.[305]

---

[298] https://fencingbearatprayer.blogspot.com/2017/05/dangerous.html

[299] https://www.firstthings.com/article/2017/06/the-quest-for-the-historical-mary

[300] https://www.firstthings.com/web-exclusives/2017/06/the-mystery-of-mary

[301] https://youtu.be/TTpMwpdzq_c

[302] https://fencingbearatprayer.blogspot.com/2017/03/fencing-bear-on-air.html

[303] https://fencingbearatprayer.blogspot.com/2017/03/another-fine-fix-bears-gotten-herself.html

[304] https://fencingbearatprayer.blogspot.com/2012/02/justification-by-fat-alone.html

[305] https://fencingbearatprayer.blogspot.com/2017/03/trust-in-me.html

Inspired by Milo's courage in standing up to the Social Justice Warriors among my colleagues in academia, I started writing about him and why I thought his campus tour was so important—and was published in *Breitbart*.[306] Every step was more exhilarating than the last; every day I found myself brimming over with things to write about him, about our culture, about what it means to be in the fray. And somehow, as Milo puts it, we kept winning, even when it seemed everything was lost.

What on earth was going on? It was like living in a dream—or a story. I kept trying to explain it, much to the consternation of my colleagues. After all, Milo was dangerous. Milo was saying things he shouldn't. Milo, for goodness's sake, liked Donald Trump! And I went and compared him to Our Lord Jesus Christ. Not as God—I never said that—but as Holy Fool, or if you prefer Professor Peterson's word, Trickster. What I meant, and Professor Peterson means, is that Milo seemed to be playing not just a political or cultural role ("provocateur"), but an archetype.

Tricksters live on the edge, on the borders between order and chaos, civilization and the wild. They do and say the things that everybody is thinking about, but are too well-behaved (or scared) to do or say. They make fools of themselves so as to point up the foolishness in the established order.

Jesus did this all the time. Just ask the money changers at the temple. Or the scribes and Pharisees who kept trying to trip him up with logic and the law. Everything tricksters do is calculated to have some specific effect—to ridicule those who have puffed themselves up with their own importance or to draw attention to the ways in which people try to hide their nakedness with lies. Professor Peterson talks

---

[306] https://www.breitbart.com/social-justice/2016/12/01/establishment-conservatives-guide-to-milo/

about the importance of telling the truth. Tricksters tell the truths that society has declared out of bounds. Truths about the tough things like money, prestige, and sex. Truths about the workings of the masses and the elite. Truths about God.

I read the manuscript of Milo's *Dangerous* for him back in January, when he still had the contract with Simon and Schuster. (I can tell you this now—I'm in the acknowledgments!) At first read, it struck me as it seems to have struck more recent readers, as essentially a re-telling of Milo's encounters with various opponents over the previous year.[307] "Why the Progressive Left Hates Me." "Why Twitter Hates Me." "Why Feminists Hate Me." "Why Black Lives Matter Hates Me." "Why the Media Hates Me." "Why Establishment Gays Hate Me." "Why Establishment Republicans Hate Me." "Why Muslims Hate Me." "Why Gamers *Don't* Hate Me."

But then, when in February he realized he needed to add another chapter so as to distinguish himself from the Alt-Right, it all snapped into place. These weren't just opponents in the Social Justice Wars. These were out-and-out Monsters. Milo wasn't just playing the Trickster, stirring things up with his harlequin antics. He was playing the Monster Slayer. The Hero. The Articulate Word. Even when he was dressing in drag.

It is why he made his comeback in May wearing the snake. Snakes are symbolically—as well as evolutionarily—the same thing as dragons. Heroes are the ones who slay the dragon and get the gold—or the virgin. Heroes are the ones who go out from the walls of the city, out from the boundaries of civilization into the wild to face the terrible dragon of chaos, the potential for disruption. It seems banal to say it so baldly; I much prefer the story that I told back in November,

---

[307] https://amgreatness.com/2017/07/08/milo-yiannopoulos-dangerous-manifesto-transgressive-right/

where I compared Milo to Po the Kung Fu Panda—and Jesus. But people seem to keep missing the point, so I will say it again, more plainly. Milo has tapped into the archetypes by which stories live.[308]

And in tapping into the archetypes, he brings them alive—and sweeps others up into the story as well. You saw the jacket he was wearing on Thursday at the party for the launch of his book? One-of-a-kind, custom Balmain, studded with gemstones. Could you imagine a more perfect treasure for a dragon to hoard? If in May, Milo appeared wearing a living snake, in July he came forth wearing its magical skin. Or maybe he was dressed as the Bride of the Lamb, the gem-studded Heavenly Jerusalem. Or maybe he meant the gemstones to recall the mosaics of the Hagia Sophia, the Church of Holy Wisdom once at the center of the Christian world.

Of course he's rude and says things that upset people. Sometimes people need upsetting. But he never doxxes anyone—or threatens to—unlike some others in the media (cough cough CNN). Despite what you may have heard, he isn't nearly as explicit about his sexual exploits as your average HBO blockbuster (cough cough *Game of Thrones*). And the only way he is able to perform as apparently effortlessly (and mischievously) as he does is because he has a loyal team of staffers working tirelessly behind the scenes (and occasionally on camera) to create the illusion of recklessness and mayhem in which the Trickster thrives. I know: I met them on the bus in December, before he was shamed.

They are with him still, months after his purported end. (I don't know in detail, but it can't have been easy for them in March; certainly, March took its toll on me, and I was only watching at a distance.) All you have to do is listen to the things that people were saying about him at the party—my friend Shelly Kennedy was there on the spot to

---

[308] https://fencingbearatprayer.blogspot.com/2017/06/self-authoring-meta-tale.html

report (forgive the sound in this video, we are still novices at doing these[309]): Milo gives people hope who have given up being able to speak their opinions in academia, in the arts, in politics, even in the media.

Just look what he has done for me. It is exactly what Professor Peterson says the Hero is supposed to do: go out into the wilderness to conquer the dragon and bring back its pieces for people to make things from. Or go down into the underworld and rescue his dead father—his tradition—from the belly of the whale. What makes Milo a conservative is not his lifestyle or his sense of style, but his belief in our Western Judeo-Christian tradition—which for some reason nobody, not even the so-called Establishment Conservatives, seems willing to defend, not at least as vigorously as Milo.[310] Not with any hope of actually, you know, *winning*.

Winning is not about being nice. It is not about being polite while the barbarians burn down your city. Winning is about putting on the armor of God—the breastplate of righteousness, the shield of faith, the helmet of salvation, and the sword of the Spirit "which is the word of God" (Ephesians 6:13-17)—and going forth into the fray, just as Milo goes forth onto our college campuses, wielding the Word. If it is politically incorrect to insist that Jesus is Lord, so be it. Milo is politically incorrect.

But he is also right. We can sit by and watch our civilization die, let the dragon in through the gate of the city to eat us. Douglas Murray has written about how many in Europe seem to think that being eaten is the only option.[311] Certainly, they seem unwilling to say that there are things about their own civilization that are worth

---

[309] https://youtu.be/TwGOzPQNinc

[310] [Now I would say simply, "our Western Christian tradition." It's been a long journey! See https://fencingbearatprayer.blogspot.com/2019/07/make-culture-christian-again.html]

[311] *The Strange Death of Europe: Immigration, Identity, Islam* (2017)

preserving, never mind fighting for, if only with words. Likewise, it seems, many here in the United States. Just look at the responses to the speech that President Trump gave in Warsaw this week. He says:

> Our own fight for the West does not begin on the battlefield—it begins with our minds, our wills, and our souls. Today, the ties that unite our civilization are no less vital, and demand no less defense, than that bare shred of land on which the hope of Poland once totally rested. Our freedom, our civilization, and our survival depend on these bonds of history, culture, and memory.[312]

They hear:

> In his speech in Poland on Thursday, Donald Trump referred 10 times to "the West" and five times to "our civilization." His white nationalist supporters will understand exactly what he means. It's important that other Americans do, too... The West is a racial and religious term. To be considered Western, a country must be largely Christian (preferably Protestant or Catholic) and largely white... In Trump and [Steve] Bannon's view, America is at its core Western: meaning white and Christian (or at least Judeo-Christian). The implication is that anyone in the United States who is not white and Christian may not truly be American but rather than an imposter and a threat.[313]

It is true that Trump emphasizes the Christianness of what we call, for lack of a better term, "the West." Peter Beinart, who words these are, would insist that the "Western values" of democracy and capitalism are not "Western" but "the universal aspiration of humankind"—begging the question of what to call those who do not accept the values by which those of us in "the West" would prefer everyone to live. Trump talks about people's interiors—their minds, wills, and souls—while Beinart talks about their skin.

---

[312] https://www.whitehouse.gov/briefings-statements/remarks-president-trump-people-poland/

[313] https://www.theatlantic.com/international/archive/2017/07/trump-speech-poland/532866/

What Beinart does not explain is how he proposes to defend democracy and capitalism in the absence of the tradition which gave these ideals birth. "Sort yourselves out, buckos!," Professor Peterson likes to say. "Never apologize. Work harder than everyone else. Stay humble. Be twice as funny as you are outrageous. Seek attention. Be hot. Have fun. Be dangerous," Milo says.

> Read all the books that your college is too afraid to stock in the library. Find the thinkers and writers and the artists who have been shamed out of the mainstream, and find out why.... Write a song you're not supposed to. Design a video game you're not supposed to. Start a blog you're not supposed to. Discuss ideas you're not supposed to. Get on social media and tell a joke you're not supposed to. Share a meme you're not supposed to. State some facts you're not supposed to. Be dangerous. Like that hot guy on the cover.[314]

The most dangerous things Milo has said all year have nothing to do with politics and everything to do with culture. And culture, as Professor Peterson has shown, has everything to do with the stories we tell and the heroes we admire. It may or may not be the case that the Dragon-Slaying Hero is a universal archetype. It is the case that it is an ideal that has been at the heart of "the West" since before it was "the West." And at the heart of the archetype of the Monster-Slayer is not someone who is white, but someone who is willing to risk death for his friends.

It is someone whose eyes are open and who is willing to speak the truth, whatever the costs. It is someone who refuses to lie even to save himself from humiliation and shame. It is someone who takes responsibility for his errors—as Milo did in the speech that he gave the Wednesday after the Monday he lost his (then) career—and does not play the victim in order to escape.

---

[314] *Dangerous* (2017)

It is someone who goes out from the safety of the city, of the socially-accepted crowd, in order to confront the monsters whom no one else is even willing to name. It is someone who is willing, whatever the risks, to be an Individual, to stand out from the herd, take the insults and accusations, and return only love. Such people are scary. But they are also lots and lots of fun to watch. They are even more fun to be. Just ask Milo. Or me.

FENCING BEAR'S DAY OUT WITH MILO AND THE BOYS

July 10, 2017

I got my wish! Remember how envious I was of Laurie Penny, getting to ride around with Milo in his "swank black trollmobile" last summer?[315] Well. Let me tell you about the day I had yesterday with Milo and his boys! It was just as Laurie Penny says. There was the "swank black trollmobile." There was the posse of twenty-something young men. There were the incessant jokes about how much expensive champagne the band of pranksters drank the night before. There were the endlessly replayed videos of the bottle-smashing (Milo is half-Greek, after all). There were the tales about going to strip joints and how beautiful the strippers were. There was... absolutely nothing that made me nervous about any of this.

I don't know Penny, but I have been writing about Milo for almost a year now, and I have never seen anything in him or his friends that she describes. Sure, they are boisterous. Sure, they are twenty-something young men. Sure, they spend time joshing each other—and

---

[315] https://medium.com/welcome-to-the-scream-room/im-with-the-banned-8d1b6e0b2932

Milo—and telling jokes. Perhaps it is because I am old enough to be their mother, old enough even to be Milo's mother, but nothing that they said or did at all alarmed me. It just made me wistful for when I was their age.

Milo being Milo, everything that we did was perfectly symbolic. We met at—you guessed it—Trump Tower (okay, that was my idea, but they stayed there Saturday night). We drove in the "swank black trollmobile" (Penny's words) up to the "best bakery in Chicago" (Milo's words; one of his friends knew the baker). We got on the CTA to look for Milo's book posters ("It's like a cab but there are so many people on it"—Milo).

We took photos with Milo's poster at Wellington Station and then got back in the car, which whisked us to DePaul, where Milo and the boys performed their most mischievous prank of the day: filming Milo pretending to give a book to the library. It was hellish! The humanity! They didn't even raise their voices, although Milo giggled a bit loudly when he slipped and fell while trying to sneak away from the book shelf. And then we went to a pub...where we talked about prayer.

You think I'm kidding, right? You would rather believe Penny's version of the story because she "knew Yiannopoulos before he was Yiannopoulos," and I only met him this year.[316] You think he is as dangerous and sick as she does for telling the jokes that he did about being abused as a teen-ager. You think he deserves the humiliation he got back in February and, like Penny, you think his pranks hurt more people than they help. You think his young men are "playing with a toy dictator" and need to grow up. You think they are all the more dangerous because they are frightened and out of their depth with an irresponsible troll as a mentor.

---

[316] https://psmag.com/news/on-the-milo-bus-with-the-lost-boys-of-americas-new-right#.8061cp4jc

Except she was writing about them in February just after they had been run out of town by the anti-fascists and cast off by the ::cough cough:: spineless c—s who had previously supported him. At the time when she—like practically everyone else other than me—was confidently predicting Milo's permanent downfall.[317] But five months later the core of his staff is still with him, and Milo's book launched on Amazon for the second time this year at number one. Perhaps Penny was wrong.

Penny wrote in February about how she almost felt sorry for the young men who told her their stories about "how they got lost" (she calls them "Lost Boys," with Milo playing the role of Peter Pan):

> I hear stories of strict religious parents, sexual misadventures, a feeling of drifting in a world which has not offered them a clear way to be heroes. A desperate longing for something to belong to, for adventure and friends and enemies to fight.

"It would be adorable," she opines, "if it weren't fundamentally chilling." I heard some of those same stories indirectly last December when I met Milo and his boys traveling on the bus. That time, a couple of them tried some of the same things on me they seem to have tried on Penny (e.g. trying to convince me Milo isn't gay or that they were when they weren't), but by the end of our visit, I was giving each of them a motherly kiss. (Yes, I'll be Wendy!)

Penny claims that Milo exploits these young men—not sexually, she is careful to admit—but "by whipping up the fear and frustration of angry young men and boys who would rather burn down the world than learn to live in it like adults, by directing that affectless rage in service to their own fame and power. This," she insists, "is the sort of exploitation the entire conservative sphere is entirely comfortable with." Oh, really? Penny clearly hasn't met any of my conservative friends. (I agree with her about the "conservative moral outrage" that

[317] https://www.thecollegefix.com/meet-milos-champion-conservative-professor-remains-side-post-scandal/

brought Milo down in February, but it has not affected his popularity with his fans. Conservatives, like liberals, have their own problems with their so-called elites.) I am not sure she has even met Milo. Certainly, she has not met the Milo I have.

Milo is not angry, nor are his young men. The ones I have met don't seem particularly frustrated; they certainly aren't afraid. Motivated, yes. Hard working, yes. Ridiculously talented memesters, yes. And, yes, like Milo, prone to jokes. Jokes which, by the by, are far from as childishly unscrupulous as Penny would like to assume. For example, the little video we shot yesterday at DePaul.[318]

You all remember what happened to Milo last spring at DePaul.[319] (If not, see p. 215 in *Dangerous*, his best-selling book.) The College Republicans had invited him to speak, but minutes into his talk, a Black Lives Matter activist took the stage, seized the student host's microphone, and proceeded to blow a whistle into it every time Milo attempted to recover the floor. Worse, the college police who were in attendance did nothing to remove the protestors, even when the protestors—not Milo—began threatening violence, one of them shaking her fist inches from Milo's face.

(It was watching this video that won me over utterly; Milo never lost his good humor throughout the event. The absolute best moment was when he invited the young black woman Kati Danforth up on stage—"Madam, you want to come up? You want to come up?"—so that she could tell her fellow students what she thought about their "protest." He later interviewed her and her fellow College Republican on his podcast.)

So, yes, Milo thought it would be a good joke to take a copy of his book to the library. He and the boys talked about it on the drive over

---

[318] https://youtu.be/6VLiQTHYCi8
[319] https://youtu.be/Pw-MnRyIoQY

from the train station. "Let's have me go into the library and go up to the librarians and tell them I am here to give them my book because I know they won't buy it," he proposed. We arrived, everyone piled out of the "swank black trollmobile" (Milo, ever courteous to the driver, made sure he understood our plans), and the boys went into the building to scope it out.

Meanwhile, Milo was rethinking what he wanted to do. "Maybe it would be better just to film me going into the library and reading the book. Or perhaps putting it into the shelves. It doesn't seem quite right to make fun of the people at the desk by putting them on the spot in that way." I know, can you believe it? The "Most Hated Man on the Internet" has a conscience about whom he involves in his jokes? Who'd've thunk?

At which point, the monstrous "lost boys" came back with their description of what the library looked like, and we all charged in... quietly, keeping our voices down, so as not to disturb the students who were studying. We worried for a moment about whether we needed to have library cards to get in, which, as it turns out we didn't. So we all filtered into the main lobby and had a seat.

Milo and Pizza Party Ben talked for a bit about what would be funniest, and then Will started directing Milo about how to play the different scenes they would need. I got to hold the iPhone for one shot—the one at the end where Milo and Ben are pretending to read. The most impressive shots were the ones Will did of Milo sneaking down the hallway to the library door and then, in reverse order, the one of the car driving up to the building and Milo getting out.

It was all so... professional. As if Milo and his team actually, you know, knew what they were doing. Milo sent the clips off to his cameraman for editing after he and Will talked over what would make the sequence funniest—what kind of music, how to use the outtake of

Milo falling. And then we all got back in the car, and Milo thanked the driver for his role.

No, I do not think Milo and his boys were on their good behavior just because I was there. There was no reason for me to be there other than that Milo appreciates the writing I have done for him this year. I had met his trainer Will in December, but the others did not know me. It was a little awkward in the first minute or so when they introduced themselves to me and clearly weren't quite sure who I was.

But then I handed one of them Fencing Bear (the toy), took a picture of the group, and handed out Fencing Bear prayer cards, after which I explained a little bit about how Milo and I met. Which seemed to satisfy them, particularly when Milo was so clearly attentive to me. Over the next few hours, I made the kind of small talk an older woman who happens to be a college professor makes with young men her students' age. I asked what they were doing: just out of school, in a band, in the army, working for Milo since last year.

And so it went until we got to the pub, and Milo and I started talking more seriously about some of the things I think he might like to read to prepare for the next edition of his college tour. I had been talking about the importance of Christianity for the argument that he and I need to make for the future of Western civilization, when I happened to glance to the side and saw one of the boys—no, young men—reading the prayer card I had given him. You know what it says if you know my blog; it's there on the side bar. It's the quotation from Augustine's commentary on the psalms:

> You grasp my soul, and topple my enemies with it. And what is our soul? A splendid weapon it may be, long, sharp, oiled, and coruscating with the light of wisdom as it is brandished. But what is this soul of ours worth, what is it capable of, unless God holds it and fights with it? Any sword, however beautifully made, lies idle if there is no warrior

to take it up... So God does whatever he wishes with our soul. Since it is in his hand, it is his to use as he will.

And the next thing I knew, this thoughtful young man was asking me about what I had learned from Jordan Peterson's descriptions of spiritual discipline (okay, my words, not his; he said it better) and telling me about the breath-control prayer practice he was learning. Lost boys? Yes, but not for the reasons Penny would insist. These boys—these young men—are lost (if they are) because our contemporary culture has abandoned them. Because women like Penny have told them over and over that they are the bad ones because they are men and because they like jokes and pranks and drinking and beautiful women. (I got a stern talking to from the whole group about how much money the strippers are able to make. "They're smart women," they insisted. My dad always used to say the same thing.[320])

These young men are not the problem. Penny is, along with all of the feminists who agree with her that it is masculinity as such that is toxic. That it is men to blame if they recognize—like Milo—that men and women are different, and say so. That it is the patriarchy to blame for things like women's desire for families and children—oh, sorry, do we desire such things? I do. And so, apparently, does Wonder Woman, even if she is a goddess. (The boys and I talked about her, too.)

I happen to like it when Milo teases me and says, "Oh, you are such a woman!" Because he is right: I am. But I like it because he is also a gentleman and treats me like a lady whenever we meet. And then he listens to me with the utmost respect when I speak to him not as a woman, but as a professor, because even more than he is a gentleman, he is a scholar, willing to learn. From me. A woman. Like,

---

[320] https://fencingbearatprayer.blogspot.com/2016/01/chivalry-our-lords-style-ca-ad-33.html

you know, his other great friends, Ann Coulter and Christina Hoff Sommers. Also, you know, women. Some misogynist, eh?

Milo thanks me in the acknowledgments to his book for "constant intellectual nourishment," which I have been more than happy to provide. Because when I wrote to him back in September after watching the video of what happened to him at DePaul and told him, "Dear Mr. Yiannopoulos, I teach at the University of Chicago," he wrote back instantly. Almost as if he knew how much he could learn from being in touch with me.

HATE SPEECH HOCUS POCUS

July 22, 2017

What was it we used to say when we were kids? "Sticks and stones can break my bones, but words will never hurt me." *Not!,* according to Lisa Feldman Barrett, professor of psychology at Northeastern University. (*She has a nice web page, maybe I should get someone to help me redesign mine....*) Words *can* hurt. Not directly like physical blows, but through their effects on our nervous system. In Barrett's words, published last Sunday in the newspaper of national record (*did that hurt?*), words can "make you sick, alter your brain—even kill neurons—and shorten your life."[321] We know this because science.

> Your body's immune system includes little proteins called proinflammatory cytokines [*NB fancy words!*] that cause inflammation when you're physically injured [*for example, with sticks and stones*]. Under certain conditions, however, these cytokines [*that fancy word again*] themselves can cause physical illness [*because they're, like, proteins, that is, physical. Try to keep up, 007*]. What are those conditions? One of them is chronic stress. [*Note bait-and-switch: stress as such may be a*

---

[321] https://www.nytimes.com/2017/07/14/opinion/sunday/when-is-speech-violence.html

form of violence, as opposed, say, to the necessary condition for learning. Jonathan Haidt and Greg Lukianoff have some words to say about this.[322]]

Your body also contains little packets of genetic material [*now we are invoking Darwin, which is how you know this is science*] that sit on the ends of your chromosomes [*those things that determine how you develop physically, which we get from our male and female parents—sorry, was that hate speech?*]. They're called telomeres [*another fancy word!*]. Each time your cells divide, their telomeres get a little shorter [*I didn't know this, should I be worried? Apparently, yes*], and when they become too short, you die [*mortality, the human condition; no, wait, we are supposed to be immortal, if only our telomeres didn't get shorter? I'm confused*]. This is normal aging [*oh, good*]. But guess what else shrinks your telomeres? [*Umm....*] Chronic stress.

Once upon a time, such stress was called "life." Do you remember? Not anymore. If words can cause stress, and if prolonged stress can cause physical harm, then it seems that speech—at least certain types of speech—can be a form of violence. But which types? Aha! You know exactly where this is going, don't you? Professor Barrett backpedals a bit here, perhaps anticipating the kinds of criticisms that Professors Haidt and Lukianoff would bring to bear on her words. It is not (her word) "offensiveness" that is the problem:

Your nervous system [*see, we're still talking bodies here, even though now we are talking about words*] evolve [*more science*] to withstand periodic bouts of stress, such as fleeing from a tiger, taking a punch or encountering an odious idea in a university lecture.

[*Pretty good going, evolution! Especially considering university lectures have only been around for, oh, thirty generations or so, and most people had no contact with them until, say, one or two generations ago. Just saying. Tigers and punches are older; even lobsters know about dominance hierarchies, and we separated from them millions of generations ago. Maybe evolution works faster in university settings. Sorry, I'm getting a little carried away. It must be the fancy scientific words.*]

---

[322] https://www.theatlantic.com/education/archive/2017/07/why-its-a-bad-idea-to-tell-students-words-are-violence/533970/

Rather, it is "abusive" speech that we should be wary of. What counts as "abusive" speech? You know! You don't? That's okay, Professor Barrett spells it out for us:

What's bad for your nervous system...are long stretches of simmering stress [*which, Professor Barrett is careful to point out, is different from the stress you experience when confronted with ideas that you find offensive*]. If you spend a lot of time in a harsh environment worrying about your safety [*for example, as a woman living in a community in which her male and female relatives insist she wear a veil or they will kill her—whoops! Is that hate speech?*], that's the kind of stress that brings on illness and remodels your brain. That's also true of a political climate in which groups of people endlessly hurl hateful words at one another [*What was it my colleagues in medieval studies called me? Oh, right, I started it by giving "three cheers for white men," "white" now being permissible only as a term of abuse*], and of rampant bullying in school or on social media. [*For some tips on how to deal with this kind of bullying, see above.*] A culture of constant, casual brutality is toxic to the body, and we suffer for it. [*Wait for it...*]

That's why it's reasonable, scientifically speaking, not to allow a provocateur and hatemonger like Milo Yiannopoulos [*touché!*] to speak at your school. He is part of something noxious, a campaign of abuse. There is nothing to be gained from debating him [*just what my departmental colleague Amy Stanley said about me!*], for debate is not what he is offering. [*How would Professor Barrett know? Has she heard Milo speak? Amy has known me for over twenty years, and she simply assumed I was not worth debating. She never asked me.*]

The political and legal arguments against this kind of "scientific" reasoning more or less write themselves. Or, at least, they should, if the First Amendment actually means anything, even for speakers like Milo, "stupid as he is" (*Really, NR? We used to be friends!*):

The First Amendment doesn't have a "stress" clause. And this is exactly why it exists. Totalitarian movements can always find plausible seeming excuses for censorship. That's why the First Amendment bans them from even attempting the exercise.—Daniel Greenfield, *Frontpage Mag*[323]

Barrett poses as a faithful interpreter of scientific evidence, determined to protect students from the words endangering their telomeres. But in reality, her argument would pave the path to the criminalization of unpopular speech. "Violence" is dangerous, after all, and it merits state violence to subdue and prevent it. By her logic, any controversial speaker could be grouped with a "campaign" of some sort and thus made into a contributor to something akin to physical violence in its effects.—Elliot Kaufman, *National Review*[324]

The left has spent decades successfully normalizing the intentionally vague term "hate speech" in the culture, even going so far as to insist that it should not be protected by the First Amendment. But what is "hate speech"? It's anything the left wants it to be, of course. When the media elites of CNN or HBO or *The View* or late night talk shows openly bash Christians or the traditional values of flyover Americans, it is never, ever condemned as hate speech; but those same elites leap to denounce virtually everything the right says as such. It is a brilliantly effective way to delegitimize conservatives and their ideas, and to exclude them from the public sphere. Now illiberals want to take the concept of hate speech to the next level, redefining the word "violence" to include emotionally hurtful language, and Barrett and the *New York Times* are attempting to legitimize this scientifically.—Mark Tapson, *Frontpage Mag*[325]

As Milo has repeatedly said, there is no such thing, legally speaking, as "hate speech." Even the Supreme Court agrees.[326] So why do we keep hearing about "hate speech" and its capacity for violence? In a

---

[323] https://www.frontpagemag.com/point/267291/new-york-times-makes-scientific-case-outlawing-daniel-greenfield

[324] https://www.nationalreview.com/2017/07/free-speech-censorship-paternalistic-condescending-dangerous/

[325] https://www.frontpagemag.com/fpm/267290/lefts-next-step-redefining-hate-speech-violence-mark-tapson

[326] https://www.washingtonpost.com/news/volokh-conspiracy/wp/2017/06/19/supreme-court-unanimously-reaffirms-there-is-no-hate-speech-exception-to-the-first-amendment/

word: transubstantiation. You know, the doctrine according to which the bread and wine of the Eucharist transubstantiate into the flesh and blood of Christ when the priest speaks the words "Hoc est corpus meum." (*Ha! Take that, anti-Christian elites!*) I'm serious, which is what makes the irony all the more delicious.

Professor Barrett thinks she is arguing scientifically, when what she is actually doing is arguing theologically. In, of course, the best medieval tradition—you know, what the universities were originally founded for, back when questions like whether you could change the substance of things simply by speaking about them were matters of real debate, not just weapons in a culture war. (*What? Did I hear you say something about accusations of heresy? Sorry, no heretics here, we're liberals. We welcome debate. Even from conservatives like Milo. I'm sorry, I'll stop. That must have been painful. What with, you know, your sides splitting and all.*)

But the debate is older than the universities. It goes back—wait for it—to the Dark Ages, when even Christians were not yet sure how to explain the mystery at the heart of their faith. (*Technically, I know, for everyone outside medieval studies the whole "Middle Ages" counts as "dark." Think Carolingians, if you know who they were. The first ones in western Europe to have to deal with waves of Muslim immigrants, just FYI. Plus Vikings, of course.*[327])

Back in the day, Charlemagne—you know him, it is his empire that the founders of the EU wanted to replicate—had spent decades trying to convince the pagan Saxons to convert. He had tried everything: sending his armies into their territory, destroying their sacred shrines, deporting masses of them into Frankia, herding them into rivers at sword point so that they could be baptized. Eventually, his advisors

---

[327] https://fencingbearatprayer.blogspot.com/2016/01/chivalry-year-1000-style-ca-989-and-1023.html

like Alcuin of York convinced him (or, at least, his son Louis the Pious) that these strong-arm tactics would not work. What was needed was not physical violence (*See? See? Even medieval barbarians could tell the difference*), but speech.

More specifically, reasoned speech to explain what the Saxons found most difficult to comprehend: how, exactly, the priest speaking words over the bread and wine could *do* something. In contrast, for example, with runes. (*I make this argument in detail in the first chapter of my book* From Judgment to Passion, *if you want it in full.*) Runes, you see, were a kind of magic words with which the Saxons—or their pagan ancestors—would have been much more familiar. You wanted to make something potent, like, say, a sword, you didn't just mumble some mysterious words over it; you carved the letters into the very substance of the thing.

These were the secret letters that Odin (or Woden) hung for nine days on the tree to bring back from the realm of the dead. If written correctly, they could, among other things, "cure illnesses, make fetters fly off, stop spears in flight, put out fires, reconcile strife between heroes, scatter witches, protect companions in battle, and inspire irresistible love in women" (*I'm quoting myself here, p. 38.*) But—and here was the catch—they had to be *written*, not just spoken aloud.

And then along came the Christians, insisting that the spoken—not written or carved—word had the power to transform the physical world. Here is the way the monk Paschasius Radbertus, writing sometime around 830 A.D., explained it to the Saxon novices at the monastery of Corvey:

> It is not to be doubted that the communion of Christ is his true body and blood, for every Catholic who rightly believes in his heart in righteousness and confesses by his mouth in salvation that God created all things out of nothing will never be able to doubt that it is possible that out of one thing another might be made, as if against nature, or

indeed by a law of nature, that did not previously exist. For the nature of all creatures does not exist of itself, nor of themselves again do they create all those things that are born from them; rather the nature of all things is authored by the will of God.

Sound familiar? Okay, maybe not, unless, of course, you have been reading Professor Barrett. Just substitute "evolution" for "the will of God," and you will start to see. So evolution—sorry, God—creates everything out of nothing—sorry, DNA. No, wait, now I'm confused. Because, you see, we are arguing reality, which we human beings perceive (as Professor Peterson has shown) always already through stories, that is, myths. And here, with Paschasius as with the clashes between elite liberals and flyover conservatives, we are dealing with competing mythologies, the one insisting that spoken words can wound, the other insisting that for words to hurt they need to be given actual physical form.

Except, of course, it is the flyover conservatives who tend to believe in the miracle that Paschasius was describing (we call it the doctrine of the Real Presence), and the elite liberals who insist they do not. (*Or maybe they do, I keep losing track of who is on whose side any more.*) Believe it or not, Paschasius was asking the Saxons to make quite a leap by insisting that they take his word or, rather, the word of the priest as transformative of physical reality in a way that previously they had expected only physical markings to be able to do. And yet, in the sixteenth century, along came the Protestant reformers to insist that the doctrine as Paschasius had described it was so much hocus pocus. Not scientific at all.

The idea of "hate speech" is a categorically similar heresy. I wrote about this back in February, as one person of the "unholy Trinity" of the Left. The idea of "hate speech" depends upon the idea at the root of Western civilization, that the Word—the Logos—took on flesh and entered into the world to suffer the infirmities of the flesh. This is likewise the idea behind the argument that Professor Barrett would make, that speech can be classed as violent because it induces physiological changes in the listener. One wants simply to say, "Duh. People are emotionally affected by things that they hear."

But we in the post-Christian West are still, at root, Christian in the mythologies by which we perceive the world (*I know! I will keep saying it, mischief-maker that I am!*), so arguments about words having a physical impact sound, well, *true*, in way that they would not, say, in a culture founded on the idea that God did not entangle himself physically in the world, where they might simply sound crazy—or blasphemous. (*You know what I mean. Try it yourself, say, in Paris, the birthplace of scholastic theology.*)

It is also the reason that what Milo is doing—taking his speech physically onto our college campuses—strikes so many of our liberal elites as physically dangerous: he is, as I have argued over and over again, performing a role, incarnating the Logos, as it were, by speaking the truth. Which, before you get all hot and bothered with me, is what Christians are supposed to do: imitate Christ. (It says so right here, in Paul's letter to the Romans, verse 13:14.) Of course Milo seems physically threatening when all he does is speak. What else would he seem in a culture in which the Word is believed to have become flesh?

It is also, of course, why Milo does what he does to make himself ridiculous. Because in a reality in which God himself entered into the creation which he made out of nothing through the womb of a woman, his own creature, there is nothing shameful about being a human being, nothing shameful about laughter or joy or longing to imitate the creativity of God. Unless, of course, you think it blasphemous to worship the Word.

QUEEN OF SPACE

July 23, 2017

Yesterday, Milo ascended into the heavens. (You knew I was going to say that, didn't you?) Okay, not in body, but in image and words. And, okay, he fell back to earth again, a modern-day Icarus on wings of helium. But he—or his authorial effigy—was up there above the clouds for over an hour, live-streaming his (book's) adventure on Facebook. Thousands of his fans joined in to watch; over 165,000 have now seen the video. In the livestream chat, some of them (trollishly?) insisted that the footage proved the earth was flat; others insisted that what we were watching was not actual footage captured in space, but only the book projected onto a green screen.

Some of us (myself included) even believed for a moment that what we were seeing was live. And why not? Do you realize how unspeakably cool it is that Milo—and a few other guys to help him—could do this? Launch a copy of his book up above the clouds, film the whole thing, and *get it back*? Ever so casually, just by following the GPS attached to the balloon. You know, as if it were an everyday occurrence. Which, I'm sure you realize, it is. The balloon that they used looked pretty simple, just a single balloon attached to a metal strut. The camera was a GoPro, which anybody can buy for a few hundred dollars, depending on the model you choose.

Things fell apart a bit when the assemblage hit the ground, but the guys were able to upload the footage so that thousands of us could watch Milo's book soaring above the clouds. And how did we watch? On hand-held or laptop or desktop devices with astonishing computing power. In color. With sound.

𝆕

Back in 1950, the pope exercised his infallible authority to pronounce ex cathedra on Christian doctrine for the first time in Church history. (I know, you thought he did this all the time, but most doctrine has been affirmed through councils, not issued ex cathedra. The promulgation in 1950 was the first since the articulation of the doctrine of papal infallibility by the First Vatican Council of 1870.) "By the authority of Our Lord Jesus Christ, of the Blessed Apostles Peter and Paul, and by our own authority," Pope Pius XII wrote,

> we pronounce, declare, and define it to be a divinely revealed dogma: that the Immaculate Mother of God, the ever Virgin Mary, having completed the course of her earthly life, was assumed body and soul into heavenly glory.[328]

This wasn't, of course, a new teaching. The tradition of Mary's bodily assumption into heaven goes back to antiquity. Its celebration had been a feature of the Orthodox liturgy since the beginning of the seventh century; the popes began observing its celebration soon thereafter. Throughout the Middle Ages, the feast of the Assumption was considered liturgically the same in rank as the greatest feasts of all: Christmas, Easter, and Pentecost. But exactly how Mary had been assumed remained something of a question, and no council had ever pronounced on the particulars of the doctrine.

[328] http://w2.vatican.va/content/pius-xii/en/apost_constitutions/documents/hf_p-xii_apc_19501101_munificentissimus-deus.html

And then came modernity, and the exploration of space. And—perhaps not coincidentally—the papal pronouncement to the effect that, yes, Mary was *bodily* assumed. Carl Jung was quite excited by the official pronouncement of the doctrine. "If the Assumption means anything," he wrote to the Dominican priest Victor White, "it means a spiritual fact which can be formulated as the integration of the female principle into the Christian conception of the Godhead. This is certainly the most important religious development for 400 years."

Feminist theologians like Mary Daly were unimpressed. "Although," she opined in *Gyn/Ecology: The Metaethics of Radical Feminism* (1978), "protestants were alarmed at the papal proclamation of this dogma in 1950, the catholic myth-makers undoubtedly sensed, as least subliminally, that this final gesture was no threat to the primacy of the self-mothered godman." Jung was wrong to hope that the dogma of the Assumption suggested the integration of the female principle into the Trinity. Rather, in Daly's view, it only completed the demolition of the goddess. But, according to Daly, there was worse to come:

> Having eliminated Mary, the ghost of the Goddess, [the religious rapism of traditional Christianity] sets up a unisex model, whose sex is male. Jesus, androcracy's Absolute Androgyne, is male femininity incarnate. Unlike Dionysius, whom he spiritually incorporates, he is not a member of a pantheon of female and male peers. He is the Supreme Swinging Single, forever freed from challenge by Forceful Furious Females. Moreover, the male-identified femininity of the unisex christian model does not negate male masculinity/sadism. Rather, it *accepts* this. This christian demolition of the Goddess and mythic establishment of male divinity has paved the way for the technological elimination of women through the application of modern medicine, transsexualism, cloning, and other forms of genetic engineering.

And you thought "I BATHE IN MALE TEARS" was bad! Daly famously refused to allow men even to take her advanced women's studies courses at Boston College, never mind speak. Wouldn't you love hearing her debate feminism with Milo? (She died in 2010, alas.)[329]

෪

I refuse to believe that something of this imagery was not in the back of Milo's mind when he and the guys decided to launch his book into space. Why else make such a big deal in his Facebook posts about being able to see the Great Wall, Amy Schumer, and Rosie O'Donnell from there? He was going to be the queen for the day, while they would remain hopelessly earth-bound—and fat.

Okay, he probably wasn't thinking in *exactly* these terms—about Jung and the role of the feminine in Christian theology and Daly's claim that Jesus was "androcracy's Absolute Androgyne." But, you know, close. Or maybe it's just that I have been thinking in more or less these terms for the past thirty years, ever since I read *Gyn/Ecology* while backpacking across Europe with my boyfriend and trying to figure about what being a medievalist meant.

You see, I had *meant* to become an astronaut. I'm serious. I was an undergraduate at Rice University in Houston, and Rice owns the land on which the Johnson Space Center was built. Although I didn't appreciate it at the time, I did my first ever research paper, back in fourth grade, on President John F. Kennedy. You know, the one who launched the manned space program in a speech that he gave on campus at Rice.[330] (I got a C+ on that paper, and my dad got really mad. Not about the C+. About the fact that I was writing about Kennedy, whom he loathed.)

The first real research paper I did, one snowy winter in eighth grade, was on the manned space program. As part of the assignment,

---

[329] And, yes, Daly is saying some very interesting things here about transsexualism. Too much to unpack in one go.

[330] https://www.jfklibrary.org/learn/about-jfk/historic-speeches/address-at-rice-university-on-the-nations-space-effort

we were supposed to write off for information. I wrote to NASA and got lots of wonderful pamphlets on the history of the program, plus some cool prints of the space shuttle which was then being built. I spent high school convinced that I was going to be able to go up—bodily—into space. Just like Princess Leia. Or Mary. Mary got me my junior year in college and has refused to let me go. But I miss those years of reading science fiction and OMNI magazine (cover-to-cover, every month). I miss geeking out over Robert E. Heinlein and Isaac Asimov and Frank Herbert. I miss the dreams of going into space. I miss the stars. Most of all, however, I miss the joy.

Do you remember when *Star Wars* first came out, how *fun* it was? OMG, the movies that we grew up with in the seventies! They were all so...depressing. Okay, I was little young to see some of the really depressing ones until I was older, but I have no memory of any movie before *Star Wars* affecting me in quite *that* way. Giving me hope that there were adventures to be had, even if only in a galaxy far, far away. I wanted adventures like that, with dashing, roguish pilots at my side, and civilizations at stake.

And then something happened, and it all went away. First, I was stronger at Latin than mathematics and physics, which was fine. Then, I got drawn into the study of the scriptures and the history of religion. But something changed culturally as well, after *Challenger* exploded in January of my senior year. It was as if the heart went out of our country when the crew of *Challenger* died. Although the space shuttle program came back—eventually—and some of my friends actually became astronauts (which was very cool), the magic was gone. We—the country—no longer believed.

❧

But *what* did we no longer believe? In ourselves? In America? In the adventure of aiming for the stars? Thirtysomething years ago, when my boyfriend and I were on our Grand Tour the summer before the *Challenger* blew up, we were all still convinced that the US and USSR might end up in a nuclear war. My friends and I knew that President Reagan was, if not a bad guy, then a fool. We knew it because the grown-ups told us so; plus, he was just so smooth-talking when you saw him on television. And he had that idiotic idea that we as a country could protect ourselves from nuclear missiles with lasers or some such. And then, three or four years later, the Berlin Wall came down—but the stars never came back.

It's odd, really. I am sitting here writing on a machine I could only dream of at that time. Sure, we had Macs, with—wait for it—all of 512k RAM. There was no public internet. You listened to music on cassette tapes or (wonder of wonders!) CDs. And HBO was still the best way to see movies, at least until rented tapes became the thing. Everything was new and fresh and exciting. And, okay, I was young. But the young people I know now don't seem to have the hope that we did. Certainly not the young people who have spent the past year protesting Milo's talks.

I blame Mary Daly. I really do. I blame her for the poison that has seeped into our culture, separating women from men. But even more I blame her and feminists like her for poisoning the images that we had of hope. Of the Mother of God being assumed gloriously into the heavens not because God wanted to rape her or obliterate her femininity, but because he loved her as his creature, mother, sister, and bride, and wanted her to be with him in heaven as his queen. Daly wanted none of that. Pick a passage, any passage, more or less at random from *Gyn/Ecology,* and you get the gist:

> The majority of those who believe themselves to be sophisticated would probably deny that taking christian [*NB lowercase*] myth "seriously" has had any controlling effect on their behavior or beliefs. The fact is that

the symbols of christian and prechristian patriarchy permeate Western culture and are actively promoted by Western technocracy. The messages of murderous misogynism are simultaneously superrefined and super coarsened. Moreover, the christian church prepared the way for post christian mental/moral dismemberment by morally coercing its members to believe the blatantly bizarre. The penalty for refusing such forced acts of "faith" was eternal damnation and hellfire. The descendents (*sic*) of christians (including former christians as well as those remotely controlled by the general heritage) have been trained to believe the unbelievable. Thus trained, they are ripe for the rapes of the professional bureaucratic and technological tyrants, the fabricators of texts and textiles that contort minds/bodies. In a particular way they are vulnerable to the violations of the media massagers, the sublimating ad-men.

It is hard to know where to start in unpacking such passages (the book is full of them). Was Daly a prophet or madwoman? Lunatic or seer? It all sounds so...*current*. Except for the part about who is controlling whom. Did I mention that Daly taught at Boston College, a *Jesuit* school? Of course, she is right about "the majority of those who believe themselves to be sophisticated" denying that they have been in any way influenced by Christian myth. But everyone who is anyone knows that the West promotes patriarchy and "murderous misogynism" and that Christianity is to blame. Plus, of course, that Christianity was all built on lies. Sorry, "the blatantly bizarre."

Like, for example, the belief that God loves the world and suffers when his children do. Or that he made them in his image and likeness to be makers of things, to be curious and artistic and willing to reach for the stars. Or that he gave them free will to obey or disobey his commandments, preferring children to robots whom he could control. Or that he made them both male and female to be companions and helpmeets. "Thus trained [in such beliefs]," Daly would contend, "[Christians] are ripe for the rapes of the professional bureaucratic and technological tyrants, the fabricators of texts and textiles that contort minds/bodies. In a particular way they are vulnerable to the violations of the media massagers, the sublimating ad-men."

⸘

Sending his book into space—literally, sublimating it—was a media stunt. Of course it was. "Seek attention," Milo tells readers of the book.

> We live in an age where the competition for attention is getting tougher and tougher. Half a century ago, everyone watched the same channels on TV because, well, there wasn't much else. Now there are thousands of channels, YouTube feeds, books, games, and websites competing for the public's eyeballs. If what you have to say is important, you have to know how to get people listening.

Even a thousand years ago, there were already too many books to read. It is the first rule of rhetoric. You must first capture your audience's good will. But how do you capture their good will when their minds are already filled with the fear of eternal damnation and hellfire? With the fear of being called racist or sexist or homophobic or Islamophobic or transphobic simply for affirming your faith in your own culture, including its technology and art? Milo knows: by having fun. And what could be more fun than sending your own book into space just because—thanks to the wonders of modern technology and our faith in ourselves as makers—you can?

RISUS ET BELLUM

September 21, 2017

Milo really needs to put this motto on a t-shirt: "Laughter and war."
It is what he called for back in November, when accepting the prize
for courage in journalism from David Horowitz's Freedom Center:

> So let us fight, but let our motto be *Risus et bellum*, Laughter and war.
> Because nothing stings our foes, foreign and domestic, more than our
> hearty laughter at their lies and nonsense. And also because nothing
> will better remind us what we're fighting for than the laughter of
> Chesterton, of Chaucer and of Shakespeare, and of course the God
> who inspired them all.[331]

I have to confess, I am quite weary today. It is taxing withstanding
a SJW attack.[332] My colleagues in academia have, over the past week,
used every weapon in the standard arsenal: long-running Facebook
threads in which they talk about how deplorable I am; an open letter
passed round the internet at the speed of light, garnering (at an
estimate) some 1,400 signatures from colleagues at large to be sent to
my Social Sciences Dean; an open letter just posted to be signed by

[331] https://www.breitbart.com/social-justice/2016/11/12/full-text-milos-annie-taylor-
award-acceptance-speech-david-horowitzs-restoration-weekend/
[332] [For my version of *Middle Rages*, see the posts collected in "MedievalGate," https://
fencingbearatprayer.blogspot.com/p/medievalgate.html]

colleagues at my university, although, to be fair, the call for signatures does not mention me, only advises (I paraphrase) "if you don't know why this is important right now, Google it"; Tweets declaring that I deserve to be raped (for advocating chivalry, mind you); alarmed articles in the Huffington Post[333] and elsewhere; and hints of plans for protesting a talk that I was scheduled to give in New York, withdrawn after the fact with the insistence that my critics should not give me the attention I so clearly crave.

You gotta laugh. I'm serious. There is nothing else for it. Just now, as I am writing, a friend on Facebook is messaging me, asking about a comment I made on my Facebook page (which you can see, even if you are just visiting; my Facebook salon is bathed in sunlight, unlike those of the colleagues who have spent the past week defaming me; they also seem to have a habit of taking posts and threads down, as well as deleting comments from friends who come into support me).[334]

I had posted the link to the open letter, with the observation that it was too bad the signatories were not including their academic fields, just their institutional affiliations, as including the former would have made "an interesting list to parse." By which I meant, I recognize some but very few of the names, making me suspicious of how many of the signatories are in any way affiliated with medieval studies. If the signatories had described themselves more fully, it would provide interesting data for a network analysis of how these kinds of lists spread.

But of course that is not what Twitter is now saying I meant. They took it as a threat to unleash my Twitter trolls (which I don't have; I barely use Twitter myself). Meanwhile, my friends on my Facebook feed are talking about cowboy boots. That's the problem with conservatives:

[333] https://www.huffpost.com/entry/whats-with-nazis-and-knights_b_59c0b469e4b082fd4205b98d?ncid=engmodushpmg00000003

[334] https://www.facebook.com/rachel.fultonbrown

we just don't care, even when our enemies are coming for us. We want to get on with our scholarship, raising our children, making art, clothing, homes, textiles, toys, all of the wonderful things that human beings have invented to make the world a more comfortable, enjoyable, and beautiful place in which to live.

They want to compose death threats about a woman whom they have never met. My favorite Tweet of the several I have seen (I don't go looking for the most part; I am relying on friends to relay things to me) has been this one by Karl Steel @KarlSteel:

> Apart from argumentative substance, a key difference between Rachel Fulton Brown & us is that she'll take support from ANY random layperson+.

I posted a screenshot to my Facebook page with the comment: "ROTFLMAO. He's talking about YOU GUYS!!! I have the best friends. All my friends are the best." Professor Steel subsequently Tweeted that I had called him an elitist. My friends are now designing name tags and t-shirts.

Of course what my academic colleagues who are distressed by my blog post[335] answering Dorothy Kim's blog post[336] about proving ourselves in medieval studies against advocating white supremacy are upset about is that they believe Milo is a white supremacist, although they are being careful to dodge round that in the most recent screenshots I have seen.

> But to clarify [*one colleague wrote in her explanation about why she had de-friended a colleague who is senior to us both and who was trying to organize some kind of conference session at which we could talk about the issues my blog post had raised*], I don't actually think RFB [*I'm "RFB"!*

---

[335] https://fencingbearatprayer.blogspot.com/2017/09/how-to-signal-you-are-not-white.html

[336] http://www.inthemedievalmiddle.com/2017/08/teaching-medieval-studies-in-time-of.html?m=1

Or as my friends call me, "The Notorious RFB"] is a "white nationalist" (that's an extreme position that even Milo Y. refuses to be affiliated with, and that's important to note, because so many of these terms are *not* interchangeable, and as good scholars, we need to get as firm a handle as possible on the different groups jostling alongside, and sometimes in conflict, with each other under the umbrella term "alt-Right").

So that's a relief! Maybe she actually read Milo and Allum's Guide![337] Or maybe not. She continues:

So, to recap, are RFB and her "friends" [*a.k.a. "Random Laypersons"*] white nationalists (in the vein of Hitler-worshipping neo-fascists?) [*sic*] Um, no. But are they (primarily) white, primarily (male) ethnocentrists? Um, yeah. And that characterization *will* hold up in the scrutiny of FRB's [*not sure who that is, I'm RFB!*] writings (public and more scholarly), interviews, and the like. It's called intellectual history.

So that's me told. Although not quite: the post goes on for some four-and-a-half screenshot pages, getting gloomier and gloomier. Somehow blaming me and all my non-SJW colleagues (there are still a few of us, especially in medieval studies, as my critical colleague makes sure to say—that takes nearly a full page, blasting us for believing in things like chivalry, the crusades as initially a defensive campaign, medieval Catholic ideals of celibacy as not in fact directly responsible for the recent pedophilia scandals, *you know*) for making *her* miserable, when, as she concludes, she and her colleagues in "Uppity Killjoy Medieval Studies" refuse to be bowed by "this racist, sexist, misogynist, homophobic, etc., Medieval Studies as Usual." (My guess is, she has been reading Mary Daly; if not, I have a guinea pig-chewed first-edition copy of *Pure Lust: Elemental Feminist Philosophy* that she can borrow.) (I had guinea pigs in grad school and not enough shelf space higher than they could reach.)

---

[337] https://www.breitbart.com/tech/2016/03/29/an-establishment-conservatives-guide-to-the-alt-right/

I want to go shopping for cowboy boots. Seriously, who has time for this kind of lamentation? I get it, they're upset. I used a rude word to make my point about what the real answer is to the anxiety about white supremacists taking over our field. (To coin a phrase, "Learn some f*cking medieval history!" My friends are working on the t-shirt design.) I posted a nice photo of the colleague whose post I was criticizing, to illustrate her point about her body being the proof that simply by being herself she is waving a "'highly ridiculously unlikely-to-be-a-white supremacist' flag in the classroom."

I pointed somewhat mischievously to the fact that one of the most senior historians in medieval studies for the past several decades is black and yet studies exactly the fields they say (political and crusade history) are most overrun by "white ethnocentrism." (New catch phrase; note how "white supremacist" doesn't work anymore). And I made an argument from my own scholarship about how studying some "f*cking medieval history" makes it ridiculous to try to claim that medieval Christians—or myself—were as focused on race as contemporary uses of Christian symbols by actual white supremacist groups would have us believe. (I am dependent on my colleagues for this information. I have never met a white supremacist; I have no idea what symbols they use.)

And for my pains, I have 1,400 colleagues in academia at large who think I am out to harm them. (There was the small matter of an image that MILO's team used to illustrate the article they did about me, which the authors of the open letter claimed to be a death threat against Asians. The image was meant to be a play on my avatar as Fencing Bear, using the *Game of Thrones* character Maege Mormont, known as "She-Bear."[338] I need to do another post on the problems of interpretation at stake. I am quite sure by now someone has figured

---

[338] http://awoiaf.westeros.org/index.php/Maege_Mormont

out a way to make my desire for cowboy boots sinister.) We talked about this whole furor in the Three Kraters Symposium last Friday, and Josh had something really important to say about laughter.[339]

> Laughter is the most readily available source of courage that a person has in the face of their own demise. What are you going to do? You're worm-food. You might as well just give up. What's the point? Everything you touch will be gone in a hundred years. Well, fuck it! (*laughs*) That's the readiest source of courage in the face of the inevitable. And it trickles down into every little tiny thing. You know. Like what's the deal with airplane food? What *is* the deal with airplane food? Why can't we fix this? We can land probes on comets but we can't fix airplane food. It's funny! It's absurd!

The random laypersons who have friended me in their hundreds over the past six months seem to get it. Why can't my academic colleagues? Milo makes jokes. I have been writing about his jokes for now over a year. He is not threatening anyone (except Dylann Roof and Islamic terrorists), although his jokes may certainly make some people uncomfortable. (Ben Shapiro, Leslie Jones, Amy Schumer, and Lena Dunham spring to mind.) But the *point* of his jokes is not to make people uncomfortable. They already are. The point of his jokes is to make people free.

Milo recorded the first episode of his podcast this week as a kind of interview with Chadwick Moore, his Director of Research.[340] I say "kind of interview" because sometimes it was hard to tell who was interviewing whom. The premise was that Chadwick had invited Milo over to his hotel room and they were drinking champagne, which wasn't champagne, but blanc de blanc, which Milo said was not real champagne. It didn't matter. They got tipsy and giggly and, at one point in the conversation, they couldn't stop laughing for a good minute or more, kinda like I was when I first read Karl Steel's Tweet.

[339] https://youtu.be/y9jo4TggO_g
[340] https://youtu.be/w5rG-e2n2-8

On Sunday, Milo and his team are going to attempt to walk onto Berkeley campus and put on a four-day Free Speech extravaganza. It is, as Milo likes to say, war. But it is war on the pearl-clutchers who would insist nice grandmotherly professors like me should not use naughty words. It is war on my academic colleagues who willfully misrepresent or misinterpret images or phrases to make it seem as if calls not to harass someone ("Be gentle, she's young") should be read as threats of rape.

It is war on the nannying professors at Berkeley who are planning on cancelling classes rather than having their students risk walking through campus on a day when speakers are talking about why feminism hurts women, the problems with not taking Islam seriously as a religion governed by its own system of laws, the threats to our access to information with the politicization of Silicon Valley, and the very real demise that we are witnessing to the First Amendment culture of freedom of speech. It is far from clear whether the speeches are even going to happen. And yet there are Milo and Chadwick in the podcast, laughing and laughing and laughing, till the tears come. What was it that Josh said?

> Laughter is the most readily available source of courage that a person has in the face of their own demise.

My friends in my Facebook salon know how to laugh. I wonder why my colleagues in academia are so dour.

THE POWER OF PRAYER

September 27, 2017

"Jesus Christ is the light of the world, a Light no darkness can extinguish." There is a little video going the rounds on Facebook which you may have seen.[341] It purports to show the power of the Eucharist driving away the forces of darkness—or, at the very least, purple—in the guise of two young women wearing "Left Action" t-shirts. The women are strolling along a covered walkway, when they encounter a procession led by a crucifer and bearing the Host. The women balk, back off, and scurry away, while choirs sing, "Gloria," and the subtitle shows a text from Proverbs 28:1: "The wicked flee when no man pursueth: but the righteous are bold as a lion."

I've had a tough last couple of weeks. Not that I'm complaining—much. Just that it is hard still receiving emails and messages from friends keeping me informed about the things that colleagues in medieval studies from around the globe now believe about me. That I "support racism, white supremacy, misogyny, etc." because I am friends with Milo—that well-known black dick-sucking supposed white supremacist about to get married to his black fiancé, *may they*

---

[341] https://www.facebook.com/watch/?v=1694384963966225

have many years of happiness together—and have been published in *Breitbart*, that alleged platform for the alt-Right staffed almost entirely by Catholics and Jews. As one of my colleagues in medieval studies put it in a recent listserv post:

> *Breitbart* is a racist and white supremacist, as well as misogynistic and otherwise bigoted platform. This is widely known, and all writers for *Breitbart* are therefore knowingly associating themselves with those ideologies; when they choose a website like *Breitbart* as a place to associate with, feed, lend their names to, use as outlet for their own ideas, etc., someone pointing out that their actions support the website, and therefore support racism, white supremacy, misogyny, etc., is not "name calling"; it is analysis. And there really is only one word to appropriately describe a person who actively supports racism. Using that word is not "name calling."

I am sure the editors at *Breitbart,* not to mention Milo, are used to this sort of thing, but it is wearing. I know I shouldn't be, but I am actually truly shocked. Not that my academic colleagues around the country have heard such things about *Breitbart* or Milo, which they now attribute to me, but because hearing about me, knowing who I am and where I teach, they seem to have been *not the slightest bit curious* to read what I have written about Milo or to wonder how I, a scholar of medieval Christianity and the devotion to the Virgin Mary, ended up becoming his friend.

Surely, *surely*, there must be a certain disconnect. A moment when they think, "I've known Rachel for over ten or twenty or thirty years. She always struck me as thoughtful if a bit forceful in her arguments. Maybe I'll go look at her blog and see." One colleague—*may the Lord rain blessings upon her*—did, and within hours changed her mind about what she had heard. She read my blog posts, read the screenshots I sent of her the longer conversations that had been going on about me for the past year and a half on Facebook, and even bought Milo's book on Kindle and started reading it. And found it "in many instances perfectly reasonable, however controversial his public performances may be."

This past week or so I have had the now-usual flood of Facebook friend invites from readers around the world, friends of friends who have seen my posts on Facebook that their friends have shared, people who have watched my interview with Jonathan Pageau[342] or the videos my friends and I have made in our Three Kraters Symposium,[343] people who saw the articles about me in the *Chronicle of Higher Education* and *Inside Higher Ed*.[344],[345] Others have written to me directly, thanking me for being (as one alum of my own institution put it) "a voice of reason in a time of shallowness and insanity" and urging me to "keep up the great job and keep your standards high!"

And then there were the nearly 1,500 colleagues (I use the term loosely) who signed the Open Letter sent to my Dean of Social Sciences and the Department of History in which I am described as ignorant of "the discourses of structural racism and white supremacy," not to mention employing "unconscionable and dangerous tactics in attempting to make [my] claims." By which they mean, I am friends with Milo and tagged him in my Facebook post. Oh, and I used a naughty word in urging my medievalist colleagues to do their jobs.

I had a dark night about this time last week, when I knew the letter had gone to my chair of department and dean. I could feel the forces of darkness closing in, tempting me to turn to the dark. I wrote to one of my friends who has been stalwart throughout my adventures with Milo:

---

[342] https://youtu.be/aQSLPmZQ8sI

[343] https://www.youtube.com/channel/UCum5ScIyxrlhTP6_luBGWBQ

[344] https://www.chronicle.com/article/A-Debate-About-White-Supremacy/241234

[345] https://www.insidehighered.com/news/2017/09/19/one-professors-critique-another-divides-medieval-studies

I am a little worried. Not that I did the wrong thing—I have well-meaning friends getting into my head, suggesting that if only I had been nicer.... But because I have touched evil, and I am scared of being sucked in.

I had a thought earlier this evening about how useful it might be to have amulets against the Evil Eye on me when I go into particular situations. The cross as a power against the Enemy, actually apotropaic, not just symbolic to remind myself of who I am. Needing to say blessings in order to protect myself against the onslaught of evil.

This spiritual threat, I have never felt anything like it.

I can't believe it is just in my head, just an effect of being so stressed and tired. There is a real force to it, that I have drawn Evil's attention. How can it be so powerful? Has Our Lord not defeated the Enemy? I understand that the demons get stronger the stronger you get, but that is partly a way of saying, the stronger you get, the greater the challenges you are able to take on. But this, this feels personal and alive and deadly, a force that would make everything I have ever touched or believed in ugly.

My well-meaning friends would say, you drew this to you, and they would be right. But also wrong: because their solution is to be mild, keep their heads down, and hope it passes them by. Let it work its slow poison, until everything is corrupted. As if, unless we fight actively, Evil will win. It tries to make us believe that we don't need to fight, but that doesn't mean it goes away. It just lulls us into apathy and inattention while it carries on growing and taking over our lives.

Until this past week, I confess, I had thought that these forces existed mainly as metaphors. Now they feel very, very real. As if I have never been so alive before, so sensitive to what is really at stake. Awake into a new reality, just like in the stories of the saints or Neil Gaiman's novels. My home is filled with images of Mary; it now feels like these are points of protection, guarding this place, but going out into the world, I need to arm myself with the cross—and it is NOT a metaphor. Not just a symbol. And that if I do not say my prayers... That I MUST say my prayers or risk attack.

That evening I was also anxious for Milo, knowing that soon he was going to be risking a repeat of the violence he encountered last February at Berkeley. As it turned out, Free Speech Week was cancelled and all he was able to do was bring a few friends onto campus on Sunday, where a handful of followers had been allowed past the barricades so that he could sign autographs and give a short speech.

But of course, being Milo, he did something more. He knelt in prayer. He framed it as a response to the football players' Take A Knee protest, but being as it were on the front lines with him, at least in my own small teapot of medieval studies, I immediately felt it as something more. Not just as a gesture to demonstrate that kneeling might mean many things, but as an actual exercise of prayer against the forces of darkness he—and I—somehow seem to have called forth simply by being willing to champion our culture and faith.

Milo said that he was praying for the protestors "who don't know what they are doing" in calling for a socialism they don't understand and "for each other for the strength and fortitude to carry on, to fight for free speech in the face of overwhelming odds, and for America, the greatest nation in the world." As he knelt, the protestors kept screaming and his supporters started singing. But Milo stayed silent, his head bowed in prayer. Theatrical? Of course. But also humiliating in the way prayer always is. A little bit silly, not quite the thing you expect. But what else can we do? That night, when I felt Evil tempting me, my friend wrote back:

> War changes people, and culture war is war, in the psychological if not physical strength. Something to think about: For a million years of human evolution, the *homo sapiens* who was outcast from his or her tribe died. To be shunned by the group was a death sentence: ostracization was murder. Only with the rise of civilization, a fairly recent development, did it become possible for us to survive the exclusion from our close-knit groups, to move, to find a new group.

But we still have a million years of evolution, deep traits embedded, that make us scream with terror and faint with stress from the pressure of our peer group. Psychologically, almost none of us can survive being truly alone.

I know that this is what my colleagues in medieval studies who circulated the Open Letter about me want to accomplish. They want to ostracize me, make sure that I have no village, no tribe, no home. They say so explicitly, that they want my department to somehow make sure that I am no longer part of the tribe because (they say) my words and friendship with Milo have placed others in danger. This is how the Devil works: by generating fear. (They are afraid of Milo, so they want me to be afraid as well.)

It is also why the demon names itself Legion. Because the demonic is what drives human beings to act in mobs, to shout down the dissenter and drive him—or her—from their midst. I understand now something that I have long prayed to understand. This—this evil—is what prayer is designed to counter. It is the darkness that Jesus, the light of the world, drives away. Because with Jesus Christ, none of us is ever truly alone, no matter how many voices may be raised against us, as Milo—kneeling alone in prayer—showed beautifully yet again. *"Jesus Christ is the light of the world, a Light no darkness can extinguish."* That, my friends, is the real power of prayer.

THE FEMALE OF THE SPECIES

September 30, 2017

A: I don't understand what fencing has to do with anything. I mean, I know she fences, but...what does that have to do with...any of this?

B: It struck me as reminding us of the boxer of last year's femfog.

A: Exactly. I can't help wondering if her (supposed) facility with weapons is supposed to be significant? Should DK expect a challenge at dawn, delivered by a beanie baby or wtf that is? (And anyway, modern foil fencing ain't no thing; show up with a rapier and dagger and we'll talk.)

C: I keep thinking of Frantzen and his boxing.

This time last year, I was looking forward to competing as a member of Team USA at the World Veteran Fencing Championships in Stralsund.[346] I had also just started blogging about what I had seen in Milo's campus tour, and I was eager to enter the fray on the side of the Dangerous Faggot. Little did I know what adventures my blogging would bring! The sense of being caught up in an archetypal story, playing a character I had never thought to be able to imitate. Watching a friend rise in popularity and fame, only to be brought

[346] https://fencingbearatprayer.blogspot.com/2016/07/gratitude-and-fellowship-of-sword.html

down by the betrayal and calumny of those whom he had called friends. The attention of the media, for good and ill. It has been quite the whirlwind of adulation and infamy, love and hate, all the while I have been attempting to chronicle what it feels like to be living a myth.

And you wonder what fencing has to do with it? Nothing—my competition year was more or less completely shot, so preoccupied have I been since Worlds with finishing my book and blogging about Milo. And yet, *everything*. It has nothing to do with weapons as such, but it has everything to do with competition. It has nothing to do with feeling physically threatened, but it has everything to do with being willing to put oneself at psychological risk. It has nothing to do with proving myself as a woman, but everything to do with training myself to be strong enough to take the worst that other women can throw at me. Including myself. After all, as the poet once famously put it, the female of the species is more deadly than the male.[347]

All of the speakers in the above conversation are women. Again, they are all younger than I am. All three are in English, not History, but only one is a student of medieval literature, so perhaps they may be forgiven for not understanding the spiritual significance of the martial arts. Certainly, it does not seem like any of them have experience as sport fencers, although I am intrigued at the suggestion that speaker number three is practiced in rapier and dagger. (Judging from her cv, she seems to work on Elizabethan tales of treason and murder, but that could just be Shakespeare's influence. Perhaps she knows my friend Greg Mele.[348])

And you thought I was just a silly teddy bear? I admit it, I am surprised at the vehemence of the response that my tagging Milo in my Facebook share of my blogpost about Dorothy Kim's blogpost

---

[347] https://www.bartleby.com/364/191.html
[348] http://www.fortezafitness.com/personnel/gregory-d-mele/

has provoked.[349] Sure, I thought to get Professor Kim's attention. She has, after all, been paying close attention to me for over a year.[350] But to get almost 1,500 signatures on an Open Letter sent to my dean and department? That takes a special level of outrage, far beyond what my telling my medievalist colleagues to "learn some [expletive] medieval western European Christian history" would seem to warrant.

I am reminded of a scene from Terry Pratchett's *Lords and Ladies* (1992), in which the Elf Queen is attempting to shame Magrat Garlick into submission. The Elf Queen has kidnapped Magrat's soon-to-be-husband the Fool, and Magrat has sallied forth wearing armor under her wedding dress to rescue her man. Before getting engaged, Magrat had served as the younger witch of the not-quite-coven of Lancre, in which she was subject to the steely eye of Granny Weatherwax and the ribald teasing of Nanny Ogg. In Granny's formulation, Magrat was a "wet hen," too soppy and sentimental ever to be a proper witch, not to mention bring down the glamorous Elf Queen.

But when Magrat shows up to challenge the Elf Queen, both Granny and Nanny have been overpowered, and it is up to Magrat to defeat her. Magrat makes the first move and grabs the Elf Queen, whom she discovers to be almost weightless, physically insubstantial. But then the Queen launches her counterattack, "exploding into [Magrat's] uncertainty like a nova."

> She was nothing. She was insignificant. She was so worthless and unimportant that even something completely worthless and exhaustively unimportant would consider her beneath contempt. In laying hands upon the Queen she truly deserved an eternity of pain.
>
> She had no control of her body. She did not deserve any. She did not deserve a thing.

[349] https://fencingbearatprayer.blogspot.com/2017/09/how-to-signal-you-are-not-white.html

[350] https://fencingbearatprayer.blogspot.com/2017/09/why-dorothy-kim-hates-me.html

The disdain sleeted over her, tearing the planetary body of Magrat Garlick into pieces.

She'd never be any good. She'd never be beautiful, or intelligent, or strong. She'd never be anything at all.

Self-confidence? Confidence in what?

The eyes of the Queen were all she could see. All she wanted to do was lose herself in them...

And the ablation of Magrat Garlick roared on, tearing at the strata of her soul...

...exposing the core.

She bunched up a fist and hit the Queen between the eyes.

Back a lifetime ago, before I had ever made the medal round at a national veteran event, I was in tears yet again, talking with my friend Ed. "You are too nice," he told me. "You need to be willing to win." The taxi driver who picked me up last Sunday to take me to New York where, I had heard, some of my opponents were planning to protest the seminar I was scheduled to give, told me much the same thing. I was fired up and anxious and ready to fight, but he looked straight at me and said, "You find it hard to be the one who has to be mean."

I hate mean girls. I hate the gossiping and the backbiting and the sneering about how ugly other women are. I hate the impulse women seem to feel to bring each other down, to rip and tear at each other's reputation—to slut-shame and slander. I hate the preening and the prancing and the bitchiness that seems to be the stuff of women's conversation about other women. I hate the way in which women refuse to compete on the basis of skills, and go after each others' souls instead. It is almost worse when academic women do it to each other.

The women in the above thread were not, in fact, talking primarily about me. They were talking about my dear friend and senior colleague Jane Chance, professor of English at Rice when I was an undergraduate there, and a fellow lover of Tolkien. Two weeks ago, when Jane first heard of what I had written about Dorothy Kim and wondered what on earth had happened to me to say something, in her experience of me, so out of character, she wrote to me, asking for my side of the story.

I told her, and to her great credit, she went back out into the wilds of social media, attempting as a good senior colleague to mediate. She was shunned. As she told my friend Andrew Holt, when he interviewed her about her experience in the online fray:[351]

> I felt there had to be some way of convincing [Rachel and Dorothy] both to apologize for any hurt and shake hands, at least virtually.

> Returning to Facebook, where the debate had become more heated, I truthfully said, "I stand for both Rachel Fulton Brown and Dorothy Kim." Although this got the attention of the FB posters, it immersed me even more deeply in chastisement. Some of my medievalist Facebook friends and others who don't know me very well personally were aghast that I could support Professor Fulton Brown, period. The more I insisted both had said uncivil things to the other, the worse it became. The supporters of Kim refused to believe anything I said about Fulton, largely because of defamatory comments about Fulton Brown's friend, Milo Yiannopoulos, whom she had come to know initially as a Catholic writer.[352] Having herself recently converted to Catholicism, she began to follow Milo's other posts and writings, often published in *Breitbart*.[353] He has been accused of white supremacy, pedophilia, rape threats, and any number of things, which he has countered with lawsuits that he has won. However, Kim followers and other Fulton Brown critics falsely accuse Milo's supporters of reacting violently at public meetings, for which she is blamed for associating with him.

---

[351] https://apholt.com/2017/09/28/reflections-on-the-state-of-medieval-studies-an-interview-with-dr-jane-chance/

[352] Not quite true, although Milo's Catholicism shone out to me from the first when I started watching his talks. I told Jane I have read back through his archive of articles into the reviews that he wrote as a beginning journalist for the *Catholic Herald*.

[353] Again, not quite true: I converted this year, in the midst of my blogging about Milo, after decades of studying the medieval devotion to Mary. It was time.

The more Jane tried to make peace, the uglier the responses to her mediation became, until she began to despair for our field as a whole.

> I have always liked to think being part of a community of medievalists is a haven because we are often so misunderstood both by other academics and non-academics. Kalamazoo [our annual International Medieval Congress] has served as a retreat from university politics. I now deeply regret having already reserved a flight to Kalamazoo for 2018—I am afraid to go. Some of these friends have said things that are hard to forget.

For example, from the above thread in which the young women were talking about Jane's interview:

> Frankly, being familiar only with JC's writings on race in Tolkien—which I wouldn't really dignify with the term research—I'm disappointed but not surprised by the utter shitness of her not argument.

I know this young woman's work. I was a peer reviewer for one of her books. (She didn't know that, I'm sure. Now she does.) I liked her book and learned a great deal from it. I do not understand why she feels the need here to bring Jane down simply for trying to defend me. The things that Jane has shown me that our younger colleagues, many of them women, said about her on her own Facebook page are even worse.

You will say, so why did I say the things that I did about Dorothy? (Note, please, that throughout *that* blogpost I call her "Professor Kim," and the only thing I said about her looks was a direct quotation from her own article.) Because back in January 2016, when she and I first engaged online,[354] I had said this:

> Thank you, Dorothy Kim, for starting this thread. This has been an enormously helpful conversation for me and I am deeply grateful to all of you who have engaged in it today. It is my firm belief that this is exactly the kind of conversation we need to be having as scholars of the

---

[354] https://fencingbearatprayer.blogspot.com/2015/06/talking-points-three-cheers-for-white.html

Middle Ages but that it has become so very difficult to have because of the justifiably strong feelings on all sides. You have all given me a great deal to think about in how to frame what I have been trying to say, particularly in helping me understand how what I have said might be misunderstood. It is only through such engagement that we learn how to express ourselves better, and these are issues that I have not had anybody to talk about with in quite these terms. It is almost certain that Fencing Bear will take up some of the things you have raised, but her custom is not to name names under such circumstances (except, today, to give a shout out to Dorothy for starting this thread). If you would prefer me to cite you by name in any response I give, please let me know. Otherwise I will cite anonymously as a good medieval scholar should ("a certain friend"). ::salute::

To which, Professor Kim replied: "^^I have no issues in you citing anything I have said in this thread."

Today, the CBC ran an interview in which another of my medievalist colleagues David Perry commented on the controversy in our field.[355] I say, controversy, but in fact it is a controversy of one (me) as against the majority of my colleagues who have no clue what the Society for Medieval Feminist Scholarship and In the Middle Facebook groups have been saying about me. Or had no clue, until recently.

> "I think that in the last few months, the academic community has really begun to show itself as engaged in this fight in really powerful and important ways," Perry says. But he admits not all scholars are onside. "There are fault lines. There's a medievalist who is a friend of Milo Yiannopoulos. So it's not unified, but in general I think the mainstream body of medieval scholars have joined the people who have been calling for this for years."

Note how I have achieved She-Who-Must-Not-Be-Named status. I am simply the medievalist who is Milo Yiannopoulos's friend. Which

---

[355] https://www.cbc.ca/radio/day6/episode-357-little-rock-nine-historians-vs-neo-nazis-tabatha-southey-fired-robots-yuval-harari-and-more-1.4309188/medieval-history-scholars-are-suddenly-on-the-front-lines-in-the-fight-against-white-supremacists-1.4309219

means it is more or less pointless to try to explain how this does not put me on the side of the white nationalists or white supremacists, as Milo himself has repeatedly shown. (See chapter 2 in *Dangerous*, "Why the Alt-Right Hates Me.") What matters is that I am, effectively, to become a non-person. Nothing. Insignificant. So worthless and unimportant as to be beneath contempt.

One of the things that you learn as a fencer, particularly a veteran fencer, is to take all fencers seriously, whatever their age. Someone my age can easily be taken down in a bout by a fencer of fourteen (the age at which fencers can compete in the open Divisions). Someone my age can also take out fencers much younger than I am. What's the saying? "Old age and treachery will always beat youth and exuberance."[356] Not in fencing. And not in academia, either.

When I engaged Dorothy Kim a year and a half ago, I saluted her as a worthy opponent. I was sincerely grateful for the challenge that she presented my original "Three Cheers for White Men" post, and I was energized at the thought of making my argument better. What I did not expect was to spend the next year and a half receiving screenshots from colleagues showing me what she was saying about me. I appreciated that she had friends who supported her in her arguments (I met many of them in that first Facebook exchange), but what I did not anticipate was the general unwillingness of the scholars in my field to read the primary sources. To come to my blog and see what I had written about Milo. Perhaps even, like Jane, to change their minds about what they had heard.

I say general unwillingness, but of course that's not true. I have no idea how many people from my field of study or academia more generally have visited my blog in the last couple weeks. I do know that my salon of Random Laypersons continues to grow and that I have

---

[356] https://www.brainyquote.com/quotes/david_mamet_478663

received letters of thanks from around the country, indeed around the world, encouraging me in taking a stand against the glamour. But the glamour is strong, as is the mob. Which is where, if you are still curious, fencing comes in.

Three years ago, I quit this sport, dramatically, hysterically, humiliatingly when I lost in the direct elimination round not once but twice in the same weekend to less experienced fencers than myself after coming out of the pools both times in the top 8.[357] Everything that the Elf Queen threw at Magrat, I threw at myself after losing the second of those bouts in two days. The pit opened up and all I could see was my utter worthlessness. And then it got worse as I fell in. And in. And in. Disdain? I knew it. Contempt? I was it. Ugly? I had never seen anyone uglier, less able to control her emotions, more despicable and humiliating than me.

I cried for almost a whole day, so overwhelming was the humiliation, not at losing, but at not being able to lose well. And so I quit. Took the summer off. Worked on other things. And waited to receive the peer review reports on my book. Which, when they came, told me that there was no book there. That I had humiliated myself all over again by thinking I could write anything that anybody would want to read. Self-confidence? Confidence in what?

Here is my theory about what is happening in my junior colleagues' response to Jane and me: they are in the grip of terrible writer's block, and they are taking it out on us. Jane has published twenty-three books, both edited collections and monographs, and over one hundred articles. She has out-published almost everyone in our field, including the men with whom she has had to compete throughout her career. My publication record is nowhere near as impressive in quantity, partly because I write such long books. But even I am amazed at how

---

[357] https://fencingbearatprayer.blogspot.com/2014/04/why-i-choked.html

much I have managed to write just on my blog this past year, and I did finish my second book.

Writing is hard. It takes you out into the wilderness and confronts you with all your inadequacies. It is the Elf Queen telling you over and over and over again, "You suck." It is extremely tempting to take it out on others, to blame them for your not being able to find the thing that you most want to say. But the Elf Queen is insubstantial and the glamour is in part of our own making, our willingness to succumb to the lies about what it means to create.

I started this blog over nine years ago as a way of helping me get started on writing my second book. I began with a prayer because I had no idea what I was going to be able to say, nor was I sure that I would ever figure out how to write my book. I started fencing because I wanted to understand the metaphors that my monastic sources were using about the role of military discipline in shaping the soul. And I kept writing on the blog because it was the one place that the writer's block did not seem to hold sway.

This was the context for that first post I wrote about Milo and the response to his talks: "A few words of advice to Trigglypuff—and her teachers." Because I've been there. I know what it means not to be able to sit with your emotions. I know what it means not to be able to find that sweet spot between anxiety and boredom. I know what it means to confront the Elf Queen—all the previous scholarship in our field—and have it tell you nothing that you write will ever be as insightful, profound, well-received, important as what older scholars have said. I have been there, with the Devil bearing down on me, telling me to burn my own book.[358] And I have been there with the other girls telling me I suck.[359] And believing them.

---

[358] https://fencingbearatprayer.blogspot.com/2013/09/sister-mary-devil-and-me.html
[359] http://fencingbearatprayer.blogspot.com/2017/05/dangerous.html

"You did well there, girl," [Nanny says to Magrat after she battles the Elf Queen to a draw.] "Didn't think you had it in you to survive an attack like that. It fairly had me widdling myself."

"I've had practice," said Magrat, darkly.

So have I.

CONSENTING ADULTS

October 1, 2017

I know that this is going to be difficult for many of you to hear, but the Catholic Church (that is, the Church taking the Pope as its institutional head) has not always recognized marriage as a sacrament. Yes, yes, I know that that is what it says in the Catechism, that Scripture "speaks throughout of marriage and its 'mystery,' its institution and the meaning God has given it," but until the twelfth century, Latin theologians weren't convinced.[360] (I don't know the Greek argument as well as I know the Latin, so we're going to go with Peter Lombard & Co. here. Maybe some of my Orthodox friends can help with the Greek side of the story.)

The argument is more or less an open secret among historians of canon law, that is, the law of the Church, but judging from the comments on my Facebook feed under my share of Milo and John's wedding photo, my guess is the priests aren't telling. So let me tell you, for Milo and John's sake, because I know some of you are mad at them.

---

[360] http://www.vatican.va/archive/ENG0015/__P51.HTM

Just to review, do you all remember what the Catechism says about what makes a marriage? *Hint*: It isn't sex. Yes, the Catechism says things about the man and the woman being made for each other and it being good that they love each other (which it is!), but the actual sacrament, the thing that makes them married, is not that they were made for each other. It is their consent.[361] Here's what the Catechism says:

> The Church holds the exchange of consent between the spouses to be the indispensable element that "makes the marriage." If consent is lacking there is no marriage. [*Which, by the by, excludes marriage by rape. Just saying.*]

> The consent consists in a "human act by which the partners mutually give themselves to each other": "I take you to be my wife"—"I take you to be my husband." This consent that binds the spouses to each other finds its fulfillment in the two "becoming one flesh." [*NB: The consent is still what makes the marriage, it is simply fulfilled in the union of the flesh.*]

> The consent must be an act of the will of each of the contracting parties, free of coercion or grave external fear. [*Again, no rape, no parents telling you that you have to get married, no threats to your life if you don't say yes.*] No human power can substitute for this consent. If this freedom is lacking the marriage is invalid.[362]

And that's it. Nothing about having children, although that can be one of the blessings of marriage. Nothing even about proving that the couple has had sex (not unheard of in other traditions). Solely the *voluntary consent of the contracting parties*. They don't even have to take communion, although that is nice, too. You'd almost think the Church was a little embarrassed about it all.

Well—before the twelfth century—it was. You've heard of the Church Father Jerome, right? I'm sure you've heard of him. How he enraged all the pious Romans in the fourth century by convincing

---

[361] http://www.vatican.va/archive/ENG0015/__P52.HTM

[362] http://www.vatican.va/archive/ENG0015/__P53.HTM

good Roman matrons like Paula and her daughter Eustochium to vow themselves to celibacy and virginity?[363] He was corrupting the family, they said. He was killing women, they said. When Eustochium's sister Blaesilla died of her asceticism because she had been following Jerome's advice, they ran him out of town.

But, of course, in the long run, Jerome won. As the Protestants love to point out, the medieval Church was all about repressing people's sexuality. All those monks and nuns, vowing themselves to lifelong virginity, or, if they couldn't manage virginity, lifelong guilt about their sexual desires.

For the greater part of the Latin Church's first thousand years, the ideal was not Married-with-Children but Married-to-God. During these first thousand or so years, marriage, insofar as the laity insisted on getting up to it, was a matter for the family, not the Church, although some couples might go to church afterwards for Mass or to ask for a blessing. But the elements of the marriage ceremony—the dowry, the bride's veil, the feasting, and, above all, the joining of right hands (*dextrarum junctio*) and the exchange of consent—came not from the Church of Rome, but from Rome. That is, ancient pagan Rome. Because, after all, this was about property—and sex.

And then something amazing happened, around about the year 1100. Canon lawyers started talking about marriage as if it might be a matter not just for the family, but for the individuals involved. Above all, they started talking about it as if the consent of the woman mattered. (See, I told you "white men" were a good thing.) Noble families hated it, particularly the kings. Here were the priests insisting that brides ought to have a say in whether their fathers and brothers handed them over to men their families had chosen for them. Popes started telling kings who their wives actually were. And the theologians

---

[363] http://www.newadvent.org/fathers/3001022.htm

started arguing about what exactly it was that made a marriage a marriage, and whether even it might be counted as a sacrament.

Some, like the Bolognese canon lawyer Gratian, argued that it was consummation, that is, sexual intercourse that made the marriage. A couple might be betrothed in words, but it was the sexual act that made them married. Others, like the Parisian theologian Peter Lombard, insisted rather that it was the moment of consent—the "I do" of the individual parties, who would be truly married even if they never had sex. The argument continued for the better part of a century, but (as we have seen) the consensualists won out. After all, you wouldn't want to argue that Our Lady and Saint Joseph were living in sin, now would you?

This was the sticking point for the argument from consummation. It said so, right there in the Gospels, that Joseph and Mary had gotten married, after the angel convinced Joseph it was okay to go ahead with Mary pregnant (Matthew 1:24). But of course—*of course*—Mary and Joseph never actually *had sex!* (We're talking Mary's perpetual virginity here, not Mary and Jesus's brothers standing outside trying to see him; Jerome took care of that argument.[364]) But Mary and Joseph must have had a perfect marriage, nevertheless. So clearly marriage could not be only about sex. Or even primarily about sex. It had to be about consent.

Other exciting things happened in the twelfth century. The troubadours began singing more and more about love. Commentators on the Song of Songs explained the way in which Solomon's love song might be read as the story of Christ and Mary's love (yes, you read that right, as a love song between the Mother and her Son). Great ladies and queens like Eleanor of Aquitaine and her daughter Marie patronized artists and singers telling tales of courtly love (a much

---

[364] http://www.newadvent.org/fathers/3007.htm

contested topic then as now—I'm sure my colleagues in medieval literature will have much to say about this!) Love was in the air—and it became associated more so than ever before with marriage. But the Church stuck with consent, the free exercise of the will.

Fast forward to the sixteenth century, when yet again the kings—or, at least, one king—came into conflict with the Pope over whether he could put away a wife for another woman, and many things changed, including the place that virginity was to have as an ideal. (You think our contemporary political rhetoric is divisive? You should read what Luther said about the Pope![365])

Nor, of course, is marriage considered a sacrament by those who protested against the sacramental system established by Peter Lombard in his *Sentences*. (Oh, did I not say? Peter Lombard is the one who came up with the list of the canonical seven; before Peter there were any number of lists.) But even Christians who do not recognize the authority of the Pope still recognize the solemnity of the "I do."

What does any of this have to do with Milo and John's exchange of vows? I just said it. They said it to each other. "I do." "I consent to be your husband until death do us part." (Knowing Milo, I'm trusting that they said something like this; it certainly looks from their photo that this is what they said.) Not because saying so somehow makes the sex okay—it doesn't, not even for a woman and a man. But precisely because the only way for there to be the possibility of virtue in sex is for it to be protected by the marriage vow.

How was it the Apostle Paul put it (1 Corinthians 7:8-9)? "Better to marry than to burn." Better to stay faithful to one person than to burn with lust for many. The argument, of course, is rather different in the Greek Orthodox Church, less infected than the Latin tradition with Augustine's arguments about original sin. But in the Latin West,

---

[365] https://fencingbearatprayer.blogspot.com/2016/10/hate-trump-blame-luther.html

and indeed in the twelfth century, when the theologians and canon lawyers were arguing about whether Mary had married Joseph or only married God, this was the question: how could you declare something a sacrament that was, in effect, about sex?

So they dodged. Marriage wasn't about sex, it was about consent, and it was a sacrament not because it was about sex but because it was about the free exercise of will. Sex, now, that was another matter, because sex after the Fall is always to a certain extent out of our control. Always, that is, somewhat sinful, even when sanctified with love.

I know that Milo has written previously against the argument that (sacramental) marriage is for gays and lesbians as well as for heterosexual couples.[366] He is also sincerely concerned about what it means to try to force the Church to change its teaching about marriage—and rightly so. If it was only in the twelfth century that the priests managed to wrest control of marriage out of the hands of noble families and kings, it was because the State is always interested in the way in which property changes hands, and whatever it may be sacramentally, marriage remains a concern of those who would like to be able to hand their property on to their kin.

But as a sacrament, the whole point is that marriage is not about the State or even families, but about the freedom of the will. And what could be more sacred than pledging oneself to be faithful to the love of one's life? In the modern world, we talk a lot about love as if it excuses all things, but love without virtue is still sin. Milo and John have now pledged themselves to live together virtuously, just as heterosexual couples pledge themselves to live. If it is hard for a man and a woman to keep faith together, it is no less challenging for two women or two men.

---

[366] https://web.archive.org/web/20120510090344/http:/yiannopoulos.net/2012/03/16/the-lingering-stench-of-gay-marriage/

Faithfulness is always in short supply, and true friendship is arguably even rarer than true love. Most heterosexual couples struggle with it, and we are supposed to be the ones made for each other by God. Perhaps we should worry more about our own propensity to sin than what it means for others to make such promises unto death.

SOLA SCRIPTURA

October 7, 2017

We are living through an interpretive crisis. Perhaps we should have seen it coming. The Christian world, after all, is now celebrating (if that is the right word) the five hundredth anniversary of being ripped apart by a similar challenge to its interpretive frame, started when a certain obscure lecturer in theology nailed (or not) Ninety-five Theses to the door of the university chapel in Wittemberg hoping to initiate a debate about indulgences.[367] (Trigger warning: talk of Scriptural exegesis to come!)

Back then, Martin Luther and his fellow reformers (some of whom he vehemently disavowed, and yet who still get lumped together with him as anti-Catholic) came up with the idea that readers of Scripture should be able to interpret the texts themselves, without any necessary input from the Magisterium or the tradition. As Luther put it: "A simple layman armed with Scripture is to be believed above a pope or a council without it."[368]

Be careful what you wish for—to coin a phrase. Surely even Luther would be surprised at the way some read Scripture today. You've

[367] https://www.luther.de/en/95thesen.html
[368] http://mluther.ccws.org/vessel/4.html

heard about the *Buzzfeed* article, I'm sure.[369] You will also know, if you read it carefully and not just for the juicy bits (see below), that I have been in touch with Milo for over a year, sending him things to read and suggesting ideas for his campus talks. On December 9, 2016, he wrote to me under the subject line "So here's something I could use help on":

> I want to make my big Christmas talk about "How the Catholic Church has been right about absolutely everything ever".

In the same thread we talk about making arrangements to meet in person for the first time in Chicago—I was hoping to meet at Trump Tower, but as it turned out, the weather made us change venue because Milo's drivers were wimps not used to dealing with the snow; we got to meet at Trump Tower in July—and I tell him I have been brainstorming for just such an argument. We talked by email more over the next week. I suggested various books for him to look at, including Diane Moczar's *Seven Lies About Catholic History: Infamous Myths About the Church's Past and How to Answer Them* (2010). (As I told him: "This book is a quick read, but as I remember does a good job answering some of the more persistent fables. The opposite of the Church getting everything right—things that everyone tends to get wrong about the Church!" To which he replied: "ah, excellent").

And we came up with a list of themes: consensual marriage, education (he added this one), science, the separation of Church and State, and (my favorite) the rejection of identity politics in favor of a willingness to see *all* human beings as made in the image and likeness of God. My proof? A passage from Scripture, from the Apostle Paul's Letter to the Galatians (3:23-29):

---

[369] https://www.buzzfeednews.com/article/josephbernstein/heres-how-breitbart-and-milo-smuggled-white-nationalism#.rgQv6m8l6

392

Now before faith came, we were confined under the law, kept under restraint until faith should be revealed. So that the law was our custodian until Christ came, that we might be justified by faith. But now that faith has come, we are no longer under a custodian; for in Christ Jesus you are all sons of God, through faith. For as many of you as were baptized into Christ have put on Christ. There is neither Jew nor Greek, there is neither slave nor free, there is neither male nor female; for you are all one in Christ Jesus. And if you are Christ's, then you are Abraham's offspring, heirs according to promise.

In the talk as he gave it at Minnesota State, Milo quoted only the central part of this passage, which I had highlighted for him. From the script to his talk:

No lecture on Christmas would be complete without at least one bible quote. And here it is, Galatians 3:28:

There is neither Jew nor Gentile, neither slave nor free, nor is there male and female, for you are all one in Christ Jesus.

The bible is arguing against the identity politics that has gripped western civilization in the last few decades. Identity doesn't matter, because we are all human beings. The most vibrant places on earth for the catholic church are in South America, Africa, and even China. Hardly what you'd expect from a religion painted by the left as evil and white.[370]

In his own words, from the video of his talk (at 9:30, with his ad libs in italics):

...Well, the bible is arguing here against identity politics. (Audience murmurs) No, it is! It is! Now, they didn't know about it then, but what they are effectively arguing for is a world not that dissimilar from the one envisaged by Martin Luther King. Identity doesn't matter because we are all equal human beings. Now in their case it is equal human beings under God. But it might similarly be equal human beings freed from the shackles of identity politics that insist on dividing us all by race, gender, sexuality. The most vibrant places on earth for the catholic church are in South

---

[370] https://www.breitbart.com/social-justice/2016/12/15/full-text-merry-milo-christmas-minnesota-state-university/

America, Africa, and China. Which isn't really what you'd expect from a religion painted by the left as evil and white. *It isn't. Why? Because of that (pointing to the slide with the verse).*[371]

Because, as I had told Milo several times over the course of our email exchange:

It is actually the same with "race/class/gender": the current identity politics are a kind of Christian heresy (as is Marxism[372]): Paul says in Galatians 3:28: "There is neither Jew nor Greek [i.e. race], there is neither slave nor free [i.e. class], there is neither male nor female [i.e. gender]; for you are all one in Christ Jesus." The identity fanatics want to pull us apart.—September 23, 2016

History is a huge one. What most Americans think they know about Catholicism are myths created largely in the nineteenth century by popular writers like Walter Scott, Washington Irving, and Mark Twain. Twain has an astonishing account in "Connecticut Yankee" about how the Catholic Church invented slavery (he seems to be thinking mainly about Anglo-Saxon England, to the utter neglect of the ancient Romans!). Slavery is a complicated issue: the main thing Christianity does is recognize even slaves as human beings (Galatians 3:28), which meant throughout the Middle Ages, the Church recognized an obligation to preach to all the people—and to hold the nobility to account for the way in which they treated the peasantry. I did a blog post in my Chivalry series on the difference between the Vikings (whom everybody celebrates in modern popular culture as murderous thugs) and the crusaders (whom modern popular culture like "Kingdom of Heaven" vilifies) with the giant difference between the two being the Peace of God movement of the early eleventh century.[373] I can send links!—October 13, 2016

Galatians 3:28: this should be common to all Christians, that we do not seek to divide each other into groups by sex, race, or class. I think you can point to the Catholic Church in the global south, as they like to call it: the Church is much more vibrant in places where there are

[371] https://youtu.be/W5q4u1nE6tI

[372] https://fencingbearatprayer.blogspot.com/2017/02/the-church-of-left.html

[373] https://fencingbearatprayer.blogspot.com/2016/01/chivalry-year-1000-style-ca-989-and-1023.html

lots of brown and black people (Latin America, Africa, even China under threat of persecution) than it is where there are lots of white people now. Not all of these churches are Catholic, of course: lots of Anglicans in Africa creating problems for Lambeth Palace, lots of Pentecostals everywhere. And liberation theology, oh, my! Not the Church's best moment. A good essay by Michael Novak that has been sitting in my browser waiting for this moment to send it to you! (I need to read it carefully, but the gist looks sound): http://www.nytimes. com/1984/10/21/magazine/the-case-against-liberation-theology. html?pagewanted=all–December 14, 2016

Knowing that sunlight is the best disinfectant, yesterday I posted this status on my Facebook page.

"Rachel Fulton Brown, a University of Chicago medievalist, sent Yiannopoulos dozens of emails about the history of Christianity, the Crusades, and the righteousness of the West."

Here is some of what I wrote him, in Milo's words. (His team added the slides). You may recognize some of the themes from my blog. I was particularly proud of the way he used Galatians 3:27-28:

"For as many of you as were baptized into Christ have put on Christ. There is neither Jew nor Greek, there is neither slave nor free, there is neither male nor female; for you are all one in Christ Jesus."

Take that, identity politics.

(Astute fans of Milo and Fencing Bear will recognize the argument about education from my "Sightings" piece. This was not a point that I thought to suggest for the Christmas talk, but I wish I had!)

I gave chapter and verse from the Letter of Paul to the Galatians and–because we live in an age of easy reference to what people say from their own mouths, no need to rely on hearsay–a link to the video in which Milo uses this verse. By evening, I had received this screenshot from one of my friends:

Rachel Fulton Brown has kindly provided some of the content of her emails to Jesus Milo on her FB. It's as insane, anti-semitic, etc. as you might expect.

I can only assume that the speaker here never clicked on the video. Somehow, I have no idea how, she has made Paul's Letter to the Galatians "insane" and "anti-Semitic." What are my colleagues teaching their undergraduates these days? Do they (my colleagues) not know who Paul was? That he was originally the devout Jew Saul of Tarsus, active in the early effort to suppress the followers of Jesus, to whom the risen Jesus appeared in a blinding light as he was traveling to Damascus and asked him, "Saul, Saul, why do you persecute me?" "Who are you, Lord?" Paul asked. And Jesus answered: "I am Jesus, whom you are persecuting; but rise and enter the city, and you will be told what you are to do" (Acts 9:1-9). After this vision Saul, blinded for three days, became known as Paul, the Apostle of the Gentiles. In Paul's own words, as recounted in the Letter to the Galatians (1:11-24):

> For I would have you know, brethren, that the gospel which was preached by men is not man's gospel. For I did not receive it from man, nor was I taught it, but it came through a revelation of Jesus Christ. For you have heard of my former life in Judaism, how I persecuted the church of God violently and tried to destroy it; and I advanced in Judaism beyond many of my own age among my people, so extremely zealous was I for the tradition of my fathers. But when he who had set me apart before I was born, and had called me through his grace, was pleased to reveal his Son to me, in order that I might preach him among the Gentiles, I did not confer with flesh and blood, nor did I go up to Jerusalem to those who were apostles before me, but I went away into Arabia; and again I returned to Damascus.

> Then after three years I went up to Jerusalem to visit Cephas, and remained with him fifteen days. But I saw none of the other apostles except James the Lord's brother. (In what I am writing to you, before God, I do not lie!) Then I went into the regions of Syria and Cilicia. And I was still not known by sight to the churches of Christ in Judea; they only heard it said, "He who once persecuted us is now preaching the faith he once tried to destroy." And they glorified God because of me.

Paul is more famous now for the things that he wrote about men lying unnaturally with men (Romans 1:26-27), but in the history of the Church he is more important as the one who insisted that *both* Jews and Gentiles might be followers of Jesus, as against some of the other apostles (the "circumcision party") who argued that Jesus had been sent only to the people of Israel (Acts 11). This is why Paul was so insistent in the Letter to the Galatians that there was "neither Jew nor Greek" after baptism. Not because he hated the Jews, but because he wanted *both* Jews and Greeks (a.k.a. Gentiles) to be part of the same Church.

Richard Spencer would not agree. (In his own words, about Milo: "Ignore him. Milo is not Alt-Right or an identitarian or nationalist of any kind. Why should we demonstrate loyalty or kindness to a man who fundamentally does not agree with our basic premises?"[374]) I know this. Milo knows this. And I know that Milo knows this because we have talked about it. Milo wants nothing to do with Spencer and his ilk, as he has repeatedly said throughout the course of the past year and half since he and Allum published their article for *Breitbart* on the alt-Right.[375]

In the article, they famously put Spencer in the group of "Intellectuals" (as opposed to the "Natural Conservatives," "The Meme Team," and "The '1488rs'"). Wondering about this, I asked Milo, did he really believe, as they had put it in the article, that Spencer was "dangerously bright"? Because, I said, when I read one of Spencer's talks it sounded dangerously loopy. Or, as I put it in the subject line to the email I sent: "Okay, no, he's a goofball." To which Milo replied: "Yeah not very smart."

---

[374] https://altright.com/2017/05/02/what-to-do-about-milo-a-strategic-assessment/
[375] https://www.breitbart.com/tech/2016/03/29/an-establishment-conservatives-guide-to-the-alt-right/

In contrast, Sarah Posner, reporting for *Rolling Stone*, seems to have been thoroughly taken in.[376] Milo is the one who wants us not to look at race ("Jew or Greek") or class ("slave or free") or gender ("male or female") as we define what it means to be American. Milo is the one who wants America to be the "land of the free and the home of the brave." That is why he enjoys singing our national anthem so much.[377] Spencer along with actual white supremacists like Andrew Anglin[378] are the ones who fantasize about such historical Never Never Lands as "white ethno-states" empty of blacks and Jews.

Milo may be physically nearly blind—he is![379] All you have to do is watch how his eyes cannot track people at a distance when he is talking with them; it is also why he has to have his nose nearly touching his smartphone screen in order to be able to read it—but at least he knows how to read Scripture in context. Which is more than I can say for those in the media and academia who have spent the past year and

---

[376] https://www.rollingstone.com/politics/politics-features/meet-the-alt-right-spokesman-whos-thrilled-with-trumps-rise-129588/

[377] Milo has explained why he did not see Spencer's supporters in the karaoke bar: he is nearly blind. They sold the video in which Milo sings "America the Beautiful" for $10k so that it could be used in exactly the way that the clips in which Milo described his being abused as a teenager were: to take Milo down. Why should white supremacists like Spencer and Anglin want Milo taken down if Milo is on their side?

[378] Here is Anglin, miffed at not being included in Allum and Milo's article, explaining why Milo, whose mother is of Jewish descent, is dangerous: "Beware of anyone who isn't talking constantly about Jews. They are probably up to something. They are at best useless. Any attempt to downplay the Jew role in the destruction of Western civilization should be looked at as subversion. This Breitbart article is the first large-scale attempt to co-opt the movement and remove the Jews. I expect Breitbart to do follow-ups, pushing this same narrative. Probably, they've been awarded this task by other Jews. The Jews have their schemes. But we also have schemes. And God, the universe and the spirits of our ancestors stand with us against the darkness of the eternal Jew."

[379] https://youtu.be/Uhs1j1NKrYM

half trying to label him as a white supremacist because he refuses to put people into the boxes that they do.

MILO IN THE DOCK

October 12, 2017

You've read the *Buzzfeed* article. You love Milo, but you have questions. What was he doing in the karaoke bar with Richard Spencer and friends? Why was he so mean to Allum Bokhari? Why was Steve Bannon so mean to him? Why did he write those things in the emails that *Buzzfeed* published? Is he really friends with Devon Saucier? You don't want to believe what the media are saying about him—that he is secretly a white supremacist even though he just married his black husband; that he is a misogynist, racist, xenophobic bigot—because you have read his book and listened to his college talks, and nothing that he has published or said on camera fits with this description.

But now that you know that he has had help writing those talks and that Allum was his ghostwriter for *Dangerous*, you are worried. Who is Milo? Can we trust him? Short answer, as emphatically as I can put it without being on camera myself: *YES*. Yes, you can trust him. Yes, I have trusted him from the first moment I started watching his talks just a few weeks ago this past year. Yes, we can trust him, even if there are further leaks, which you can guarantee there will be because his enemies, our enemies, are *NOT GOING TO GIVE UP*.

You can trust me on this, too. The first talk I watched was the one that he gave in September 2016 in Lubbock at Texas Tech, and I saw instantly that his vision is bad. Every time he looked at the audience, he had to squint, even with his glasses on. (He explains his condition in part here.[380] Here in June 2016 he tries to try on contact lenses with Pizza Party Ben's help.[381] He failed.) After that video, I went back through his archive, beginning with the talk he gave in February 2016 at Rutgers. In the version I saw, the camera stayed focused on him throughout the greater part of his talk. There was an odd moment when the audio carried the sounds of people shouting, but Milo just smiled and looked a bit vague until things settled down.

It turns out, as he explained later in one of his podcasts (I'm sorry, I forget which one), that he never saw the women smearing themselves with fake blood. They were too far away. Watch him in the video that Richard Spencer's friends made that night in Dallas (it was in the wee hours of April 3, 2016).[382] As Milo is singing, he never looks at the crowd. Indeed, his eyes are for the most part closed, and his gaze never points in the direction of Spencer. He never makes the salute that Spencer and friends do. He waves his hands about expressively, but the only gesture he makes at the end is to point his finger "Number One!" (Listen also to the voices in the background: there were women in the crowd, whom the bartenders who were there that night do not mention.[383] And Milo most certainly never had the same haircut as Spencer. Just saying.)

---

[380] http://web.archive.org/web/20120904050316/http:/yiannopoulos.net:80/2011/05/24/eye-robot-2/

[381] https://youtu.be/DWi7F51iLMo

[382] https://youtu.be/XLNLPIRS62g

[383] https://www.dallasobserver.com/news/interview-with-bartender-who-kicked-milo-yiannopoulos-out-of-karaoke-9948271

Why should he have been in the bar in the first place? Even the *Buzzfeed* article makes this clear: he and Allum had been researching their article for *Breitbart* (published March 29, 2016) on the different elements of the alt-Right, a term which Spencer claims he invented in 2010. In their article, famously—I say, famously because this is the one part of the article every media outlet quoted over the whole of the summer of 2016 to prove that *Breitbart* approved of the white nationalist alt-Right—Milo and Allum included Spencer in a group they called "The Intellectuals" and whom they described collectively as "dangerously bright."[384]

Given that even *Rolling Stone* seems to have been impressed with Spencer's academic record (B.A. at University of Virginia, Master of Arts in the Humanities at University of Chicago, admitted to the Ph.D. program at Duke University),[385] Allum and Milo may perhaps be forgiven the description as moderately accurate. (I have my doubts about Spencer, as I have explained.[386] But then I teach at the University of Chicago. I am far more than "dangerously bright." Just saying.)

In their article Milo and Allum also talk about how surprised they were that these "dangerously bright" white nationalists were willing to talk with them. All "hacker and white nationalist" Andrew Auernheimer (a.k.a. weev) would say to them was: "The tireless attempts of you Jews to smear us decent Nazis is shameful." This alone would have been sufficient cause for Milo to refer in his emails to Devon Saucier as his "best friend" and to make promises to him if Saucier would give him and Allum the information they needed for their articles. When you are a journalist, such sources—enemies though they may

---

[384] https://www.breitbart.com/tech/2016/03/29/an-establishment-conservatives-guide-to-the-alt-right/

[385] https://www.rollingstone.com/politics/politics-features/meet-the-alt-right-spokesman-whos-thrilled-with-trumps-rise-129588/

[386] https://fencingbearatprayer.blogspot.com/2017/10/sola-scriptura.html

be—are indeed your "best friends." As Milo (a Jewish gay) and Allum (a mixed-race *Breitbart* reporter) noted in their article, you might even attend their "secret dinner parties."

Milo and Allum also explained why the alt-Right had gained the purchase that it had: because the "establishment conservatives" to whom their article was addressed (thus its title) had done nothing to oppose it. In their words:

> The Establishment bears much of the blame. Had they been serious about defending humanism, liberalism and universalism, the rise of the alternative right might have been arrested. All they had to do was argue for common humanity in the face of black and feminist identity politics, for free speech in the face of the regressive Left's censorship sprees, and for universal values in the face of left-wing moral relativism.

But Establishment Conservatives didn't.

> Instead, they turned a blind eye to the rise of tribal, identitarian movements on the Left while mercilessly suppressing any hint of them on the Right. It was this double standard, more than anything else, that gave rise to the alternative right. It's also responsible, at least in part, for the rise of Donald Trump.

What did I call the conservative establishment when they turned their backs on Milo back in February? Oh, right. It wasn't ladylike. And you wonder that Milo uses edgy passwords and rejoices when Bannon suggests that there is a way to fight back? I do not know Devon Saucier, nor was I aware of Milo's contact with him. I have, however, met numerous members of his team, including some of those mentioned in the *Buzzfeed* article. I met Mike Mahoney (a.k.a. Mike Ma), Hayden Newton (a.k.a. @sadieisonfire), Will Magner (Milo's personal trainer), and Matt Perdie (Milo's cameraman) in December when they brought the Dangerous Faggot bus through Chicago en route to Milwaukee.[387]

I met Pizza Party Ben along with some of his friends when Milo was here in Chicago in July. And I have spoken at length with Tom Ciccotta (who interviewed me for *Breitbart* last month when I was being called a white supremacist by my academic colleagues in medieval studies)[388] and Allum Bokhari (who helped me publish my article about Milo at *Breitbart*, under the title "An Establishment Conservative's Guide to MILO," in homage to Allum and Milo's piece).[389]

It is true. Milo can be bitchy. I can well imagine him saying the things that the *Buzzfeed* article quoted him saying in his emails. But what you cannot hear in the emails is the way he says these things, nor can you get the proper context, which *Buzzfeed* most certainly does not want you to have. For example, about Allum. Allum and Milo have been working closely together for some time under fairly stressful circumstances.[390] You tell me if you could write at the volume that Allum does. Right. Now add the fact that you are trying to cover some of the most culturally and politically charged topics of the day

---

[387] It was *very* romantic! Milo's driver—a.k.a. Hayden—was worried about getting stuck in the snow that hit Chicago that afternoon, so instead of meeting at Trump Tower as we had planned, I drove all the way out into the suburbs. Milo met me at a Weber's Grill! And bought me wine and made me eat cheesecake. After which, I was in no condition to drive back home (40 miles in the still-worsening snow—I may have lived in Chicago for almost 25 years, but even I was worried by that time), so Milo offered to let me stay overnight with him on the second bed in his hotel room. He took me to the Dangerous Faggot bus and introduced me to Hayden and Mike Ma, who then spent the next hour trying to convince me that Milo wasn't gay. They failed! I drove home the next morning after the snow had stopped.

[388] https://www.breitbart.com/tech/2017/09/26/university-chicago-supports-medieval-studies-scholar-accused-encouraging-white-supremacy/

[389] https://www.breitbart.com/social-justice/2016/12/01/establishment-conservatives-guide-to-milo/

[390] https://www.breitbart.com/author/allum-bokhari-milo-yiannopoulos/

405

on one of the most trafficked sources on the internet. And that any mistakes you make will be the topic of articles across the internet for months, not to mention putting your job at risk. And you thought worrying about your grades was hard. You might feel a little unstable at times, don't you think? I sure do.

I wrote to Allum the day the *Buzzfeed* article posted: "HOW ARE YOU? How are all of you and Milo's team doing? This must have been a truly awful week for all of you." He wrote back: "Haha yes, I am doing fine! Thank you for checking in. As you'd expect buzzfeed made everything sound worse than it actually was." That same day, Milo wrote on his Facebook page:

> About my colleague, Allum Bokhari: Allum has been a trusted friend and colleague of mine for many years. We have done tremendous work together. He has always been a source of reason, urging caution and balance when we cover sensitive topics, as we have done on many occasion. As you'd expect, the vultures at Buzzfeed news have grossly misrepresented our relationship. He has not on any occasion "spied on me," nor I on him. We had a brief falling out over the use of a password and credit card information (which I myself provided to him), but as is often the case, this was a result of miscommunication, not malice, and was quickly resolved.

> Despite the fact that we were both in a bad mood at the time (for different reasons), we still managed to produce a brilliant piece of journalism on the alt-right, one which even made Bloomberg's list of 40 top stories from 2016. The media continues to be obsessed and enraged by this piece, because they can't tell the difference between analyzing a movement and endorsing it. Allum continues to be one of my most intelligent and capable colleagues, and we continue to trust each other. We wouldn't still be working together otherwise.

As you know from the *Buzzfeed* piece, Milo trusted Allum so much as to hire him for $100,000 to ghostwrite *Dangerous*, hardly the thing you would expect Milo to do if he didn't trust Allum—and hardly the thing you would expect Allum to accept if he did not want to be working with Milo anymore. But what does it mean that Allum has written so much for MILO? Only this: that Milo is not just an author, but MILO, much as Rubens the painter was not just Sir Peter Paul Rubens (d. 1640), but a whole studio of painters producing artwork under the supervision of the Master.

Yes, Steve Bannon hired Milo as a writer, but he also hired him—as, again, the *Buzzfeed* article makes abundantly clear—as a face. Milo has a beautiful face. He also has an extraordinary speaking ability, which makes him even more valuable as, quite literally, a spokesman for the argument that Bannon, Allum, and he want to get across. What is their argument? That America is the greatest country in the history of human civilization, not because it is "white" (it never has been), but because it is founded on particular values: freedom of speech, freedom of religion, capitalism, property rights, and what we used to call liberalism.

The same values that Establishment Conservatives purport to believe in, but consistently, persistently, pusillanimously refuse to support (what was it I called them?), preferring instead to cede more and more of our liberties to the Left rather than risk their own careers. Do you wonder that so many of us have been writing to Milo over the past year (as evidenced by the *Buzzfeed* article) THANKING him?

Aggrieved by the encroachment of so-called cultural Marxism into American public life, and egged on by an endless stream of stories on Fox News about safe spaces and racially charged campus confrontations, a diverse group of Americans took to Yiannopoulos's inbox to thank him and to confess their fears about the future of the country.

He heard from ancient veterans who "binge-watched" his speeches on YouTube; from "a 58 year old asian woman" concerned about her high school daughter's progressive teachers; from boys asking how to win classroom arguments against feminists; from a former NASA employee who said he had been "laid off by my fat female boss" and was sad that the Jet Propulsion Lab had become "completely cucked"; from a man who had bought his 11-year-old son an AR-15 and named it "Milo"; from an Indiana lesbian who said she "despised liberals" and begged Yiannopoulos to "keep triggering the special snowflakes"; from a doctoral student in philosophy who said he had been threatened with dismissal from his program for sharing his low opinion of Islam; from a Charlotte police officer thanking Yiannopoulos for his "common sense Facebook posts" about the shooting of Keith Lamont Scott ("BLUE LIVES MATTER," Yiannopoulos responded); from a New Jersey school teacher who feared his students would become "pawns for the left social justice campaign"; from a man who said he had returned from a deployment in "an Islamic country" to discover that his wife was transitioning and wanted a divorce (subject line "Regressivism stole my wife"); from a father terrified his daughter might attend Smith College; from fans who wanted to give him jokes to use about fat people, about gay people, about Muslims, about Hillary Clinton.[391]

And you wonder why *Buzzfeed* was so eager to launch its attack? Milo *is* dangerous. Not because he makes jokes that you would not make about blacks (whom he loves, particularly John) or Jews (because he has a tense relationship with his mother, who is of Jewish descent) or women (because he is gay and handsome and young and bitchy) or other young men (ditto). But because he tells the truth about our country and our tradition and the importance of standing up for Western civilization *when no one else will.*

Expect more attacks. Expect them to get more and more and more vicious. And remember with every attack what you heard Milo say in his talks. Over and over and over again. "Laughter and war."

> So let us fight, but let our motto be Risus et bellum, Laughter and war. Because nothing stings our foes, foreign and domestic, more than our hearty laughter at their lies and nonsense. And also because nothing will better remind us what we're fighting for than the laughter of Chesterton, of Chaucer and of Shakespeare, and of course the God who inspired them all.

---

[391] https://www.buzzfeednews.com/article/josephbernstein/heres-how-breitbart-and-milo-smuggled-white-nationalism#.rgQv6m8l6

Laughter and war. The Left hates being made ridiculous because the Left is totalitarian, and totalitarians hate laughter. But it is not just the Left. The establishment Right hates Milo just as much as the Left because he makes them ridiculous, too. And both hate us—Milo's supporters—because, thanks to Milo, we have learned to laugh at them. And for that they will never forgive us because laughter shows what they really are. *Nothing.*

LIES, DAMN LIES AND PEER REVIEW

November 2, 2017

My academic colleague and long-time friend Carol Symes (Associate Professor of History, University of Illinois; PhD, Harvard 1999) posted this article on the American Historical Association website this morning. She, of course, mentions me.[392]

> To date, the only tenured historian of medieval Europe to have found an audience for her views on these issues is Rachel Fulton Brown (Univ. of Chicago), a columnist for *Breitbart* who has used her privileged position and powerful allies to deride, bully, and persecute a junior, untenured medievalist of color. In a blog post published in mid-September, and in subsequent interviews, she has explicitly justified these attacks by invoking her authority as a historian (PhD, Columbia 1994). "If you teach the history," Fulton Brown told *Inside Higher Ed*, "everybody basically learns that it's a very complicated story, and there's nothing to support the white supremacist argument in it." According to her, proving that "you are not a white supremacist" simply means showing that you can find some black people in medieval Europe: an essentialist exercise tantamount to noting the existence of

---

[392] https://www.historians.org/publications-and-directories/perspectives-on-history/november-2017/medievalism-white-supremacy-and-the-historians-craft

medieval women without any critical analysis of pervasive misogyny and the workings of gender and power.

"The history" that Fulton Brown professes to teach (which "everybody basically learns," as though by osmosis) is "medieval western European Christian history, including the history of our field." In other words, it is a fictive, hermetically sealed, and fiercely policed "western European Christian" space. It is not the history of a multiethnic, culturally diverse, religiously pluralistic, interconnected medieval world. Nor does it include the story of how that world was narrowed down by "western European Christian" historians. In a subsequent statement cited by the *Chronicle of Higher Education*, Fulton Brown again insisted that "medieval white supremacy [. . .] is not a narrative that makes any sense if you know anything about our field."

It will certainly come as news to *Breitbart* Editor-in-Chief Alex Marlow that I am "a columnist for *Breitbart*," given that *Breitbart* has only ever published one of my articles and that that article was explicitly marked as republished from my blog. (Nor was I paid. Not that I would mind being a columnist for *Breitbart*. I would be in excellent company.[393]) It is true that I have invoked my authority as an historian in the on-going argument in medieval studies, but since when did having scholarly expertise in a field become unmentionable as a basis for making comments to the press?

But I *never* said that "proving 'you are not a white supremacist' simply means showing that you can find some black people in medieval Europe." What I *said* was that in order to prove you are not a white supremacist to your students in the classroom (as Professor Kim said I should[394]), *if* you are white (as am I, like Carol; I would show you her photo, but I got in big trouble for doing that last time; no, it is only fair that I share, here is the photo from her professional home

---

[393] https://www.breitbart.com/people/

[394] http://www.inthemedievalmiddle.com/2017/08/teaching-medieval-studies-in-time-of.html?m=1

page[395]; I'll share mine, too, just so you know what I look like[396]), what you need to do is *do your job* and "learn some f*cking [*sic*, Carol left that bit out] medieval western European Christian history, including the history of our field." Because, if you do, you will learn that the narratives that white nationalists like Richard Spencer have invented are *lies*.

But of course the Left loves Richard Spencer because he fits their narrative. Unlike me. NB that Carol could find nobody to fit her narrative about the white supremacism allegedly rampant in academic medieval history *except me*, which is inconvenient to say the least, if she wants to make her case about how dangerous I am. I admit I am privileged; I have known *that* all my life. As I said a year ago, before I had ever published in *Breitbart*:

> *White privilege.* Of course I have it. I've always known I have it. I grew up in the South, after all, where you hear about it every day. "You kids are so lucky," the grown-ups would say to my siblings and me.[397]

Meaning, as I explain in that blogpost, *you have a responsibility to stand up* for those who are not so lucky, even as you take the abuse for being one of the lucky ones.[398] But of course academically the great privilege that I have is to teach at the University of Chicago, the one university in the country whose president has been consistently willing to stand up for what we used to call academic freedom.[399] I'm not quite sure what we call it now. "Bullying," perhaps, if we disagree with colleagues in our field.

---

[395] https://history.illinois.edu/directory/profile/symes

[396] https://home.uchicago.edu/~rfulton/index.html

[397] https://fencingbearatprayer.blogspot.com/2016/11/white-privilege.html

[398] https://fencingbearatprayer.blogspot.com/2017/10/the-niceness-cosmopolitan-creed.html

[399] https://www.nytimes.com/2017/10/20/opinion/robert-zimmer-chicago-speech.html

I wonder what you call some 1500 colleagues being willing to sign an anonymously-authored Open Letter calling for a colleague's institution to "publicly acknowledge and *act on* your responsibility to protect vulnerable colleagues—within and without the University of Chicago—when your senior faculty violate basic norms of professional behavior and place those less powerful in the path of harassment and other forms of violence" (my emphasis).[400] A group hug? I'm just guessing here.

(Just for the record, I have never called Professor Dorothy Kim anything other than "Professor Kim," nor have I attributed to her anything other than her own words. I shared what I thought was a flattering picture of her that I found online with one of her interviews solely to demonstrate why she would say what she said about herself not having to signal the unlikelihood that she is a white supremacist.[401] You may draw your own conclusions about why she said what she did. I have written to one of the other signatories of the Open Letter asking for references to the harassment that he predicted would follow upon my blogpost.[402] I have yet to hear back.)

Do I have powerful allies? It is true, I have several hundred Random Laypersons who have friended me on Facebook over the past ten months thanks to my willingness to stand up for Milo when even the conservative establishment would not. (What was it I called those spineless c*nts? Oh, right. Bullies. Random Laypersons can get their t-shirts here![403]) But other than Milo, none of these people are remotely what you would call powerful (no, I do not know Steve Bannon), and

---

[400] https://www.dropbox.com/s/mk2ifzv34803zlo/chicago_open_%20letter.pdf?dl=0

[401] https://hortulus-journal.com/kim/

[402] https://www.huffpost.com/entry/whats-with-nazis-and-knights_b_59c0b469e4b082fd4205b98d

[403] https://fencingbearatprayer.blogspot.com/p/shop.html

the only reason Milo is so important is, you guessed it, his own army of Random Laypersons, a.k.a. fans.

None of whom is the least bit interested in trolling a university professor in medieval studies, however self-important she might feel. Guess what? Academia has become a joke—just as Milo says. Soon even Hollywood won't be worth trolling either. And for that, we academics, like Hollywood's denizens, have no one to blame but ourselves. My friend Carol makes some more specific arguments about what we professors in medieval history need to teach:

> The task of the medievalist, from the earliest days of history's institutionalization as a modern academic discipline, was to construct the nationalist narratives that bolstered the claims to territory, patrimony, and sovereignty on which 19th-century European states and aspiring states depended. The most obvious example is the *Monumenta Germaniae Historica* [MGH], founded in 1826 to catalogue all "monuments of German history" in advance of a unified German imperial state: that is, texts and artifacts produced by any people that could be considered "Germanic" (those of Anglo-Saxon England and Visigothic Spain, for example) or in any region open to German territorial aspirations (Poland and the Low Countries, for example). In the 20th century, the eminent medieval historian Charles Homer Haskins helped to devise the intellectual framework for the WWI doctrine of national self-determination on the basis of such claims. His star pupil, Joseph Strayer, helped to advance the cause of "Western" (white) supremacy during the Cold War. Strayer's own students went on to populate the history departments of many prestigious American universities. (I myself am heir to this legacy.)

In lieu of peer review, I asked my Random Laypersons on Facebook what they thought of these claims.

> What. The. Actual. Hell?! Does she seriously believe that the best way to counter a 19th century subversion of history is with Marxism—a 19th century subversion of philosophy and economics? Your position has always been "scientia gratia scientia." There are also some glaring omissions of facts. While the Roman Empire may not have been

monochromatic, the barbarian invasions certainly were. And what was the response to this sudden influx of a foreign culture? Walls. The people in the Veneto created artificial islands to preserve their identity and created a society that valued not skin color but familial lineage. Then, as now, the native population was worried about being raped, slaughtered, and replaced—which happens no matter who it is walking in with a sword.

The entire argument is built on a straw-man: insufferable 18-19th century Europeans seeking myths rather than history created a label for a past epoch, and therefore their claims taint that period's history for all time. The black American historian (me) says: this strawman is actually a claim to European supremacy over understanding the Christian western past. It is a claim to white racist power to determine reality; this claim is not only problematic, the power it presumes is nonexistent: they cannot make the past in their own image. The blogger might realize this if she actually understood the argument of Dr. Rachel Brown.

It's disingenuous for the writer to suggest that the efforts of German nationalist historians in 1826 to construct an ancient German identity, using ancient and medieval texts (principally, of course, Tacitus' Germania), were typical of historians generally.

This is absurd. *Some* medievalists were interested in national origins, others busied themselves [with] quite different matters. Strayer was interested in defending western democracy *against Stalinism*, but that is not at all the same as defending "white supremacy." With this kind of logic, I could just as easily argue that Symes wished for the victory of Stalinism during the cold war.

The attack on the Monumenta, one of the great scholarly achievements of modern times, is disgusting. It is part of a many-sided effort to reveal the genesis of the modern nations of Europe. There are many analogues. When, for example, Polish scholars discussed the emergence of the Polish state under the Piast dynasty at the end of the first millennium. they were scarcely arguing for the "whiteness" of the country. They were against Russification, and wanted Poland to be Poland.

That there was a nationalist agenda driving the foundation of the MGH is not a revelation. That it was a "white supremacist" agenda is ridiculous. The article further implies that there are "suppressed" sources about lots of people of color around medieval Europe. No doubt there were such, but the insinuation of the field suppressing documentation of them is atrocious.

So, in case I am missing something (I really only glanced at the piece because of the MGH cover, sorry), they are calling the outlook of scholars in 1826 evidence that the Middle Ages were hell-bent on shaping a white/national agenda. This means, therefore, that we should not use those source collections or editions? This is shameful. I have spoken with plenty of German academics who *still* consult works on the Teutonic Order and the Baltic crusades written by German historians during the 30s and 40s (you can all make the connection there). Why do they still use them? Not because of the authors' worldviews, but because the source analysis and editions were so damned good that there haven't been better ones since then. They are not focused on the opinions of the scholars, but rather the quality of scholarship. I could be missing the point that they are making about the MGH, and if I am, please correct an ignorant monk.

The study of the Middle Ages in the 18th and 19th century has nothing to do with the racialization of slavery (which did not exist in the German lands) or imperialism (since Germany did not exist, not even as a country, before 1871). At the very least, Symes's point of view is ethnocentric—she is only thinking of the British Empire, as if all ideas were invented there and nowhere else. That, to me, is exactly the same disease of which she accuses others.

Symes does not know the history of history writing, and apparently no Latin either. The title of the series is not "monuments of German history," but "historical monuments of Germania." That's not Germany, but Caesar's (and the medieval) Germania, i.e., the territory outside the Roman empire either chronologically (post-Roman) or geographically (territories that did not belong to the Roman Empire). Now, one could of course discuss the issue of the lack of a German state, which shifted the emphasis of German historiography from State to Nation (Volk). But to say that the project itself was run "in advance of a unified German imperial state" is to say that Heinrich Friedrich Karl vom (and zum) Stein was able to anticipate in 1820 what would happen in 1871. Or, if you wish, that he was some kind of shaman capable of "talking" to Bismarck as German chancellor. This is not just preposterous. It is anti-historical, and shows, more than anything, the true Bolshevik colors of this piece. History does not matter. Kommissar Symes can forward and rewind history as she pleases in order to get the idea.

La crème de la crème: "His star pupil, Joseph Strayer, helped to advance the cause of 'Western' (white) supremacy during the Cold War." Were there any racial conflicts during the Cold War? Doesn't Symes know that Russians are also "white" people?

Does that mean that Joe Strayer's Dictionary of the Middle Ages was a nationalistic enterprise? You know, the one for which Bill Jordan (his student) was an assistant editor and cites frequently in his work?

One more detail. Symes got the Herbert Baxter Adams award of the AHA in 2008. Adams was a student of Johann Kaspar Bluntschli in Heidelberg. A historian of international law, Bluntschli is the author of a pamphlet published in 1871 under the title "An impartial opinion on the Alabama question and the manner of settling it." In that pamphlet, Bluntschli defended the Confederacy and argued that under international law, rebels were to be regarded as a belligerant party, and refuted the Union's accusations against Britain for having sold warships to the South. So, Bluntschli—by Symes's logic—was a racist, because he supported the Confederacy. Adams, his American student, never condemned Bluntschli, so Adams must have been racist too. Symes should return the prize to AHA in protest against the role of "systemic racism."

This puts the MAA...in a bind. How can they award the Haskins Medal for the best medieval book now—he is complicit in the WS takeover of the field!!!

I have the best Random Laypersons. All my Random Laypersons are the best.

I know what Carol and my other colleagues in medieval studies are actually upset about. I have challenged their interpretive frame. Carol says so. What (Carol thinks) I have suggested about the complexities of understanding the historiography of our field and the way in which I signaled that I am not a white supremacist (*I know, I know, good luck with that!*) is, in essence, "an essentialist exercise tantamount to noting the existence of medieval women without any critical analysis of pervasive misogyny and the workings of gender and power."

I have told you already what I think about gender. (TL;DR: It is *boring* as an analytic in comparison with the relationship that medieval Christians talked about between the human and the divine.) I have also explained *at length* what I think about chivalry.[404] But it makes no difference. I refuse to adhere to the prevailing orthodoxy of the field, and for that I must be silenced and shamed.

Thanks to Christian Smith (Professor of Sociology, the University of Notre Dame), I now understand this dynamic better than I had before. Carol and I are both historians, but she works in a much more sociological frame of interpretation than do I. (Mine is more psychological, but with heavy doses of mythology and rhetoric.) From within her frame of interpretation, I should not exist, much like Milo. How can I, a woman, not use gender theory?

How *dare I* not acknowledge that society is constructed primarily for the perpetuation of structures of power? How *dare I* suggest that there are ways to read the devotion to the Virgin Mary other than through the lenses of race and gender? (As I said to my departmental colleagues just last week, I think we should be paying greater attention, even in American history, to class, if only because academics are by profession such snobs.) I am, in a word, that most dangerous of thinkers: a heretic.

Professor Smith details the practices in which those committed to the sacred project of sociology are trained.[405] There are twelve steps in all. Here are a few of the most essential. *Step 1:* "Undertake a long apprenticeship of demanding training in graduate school to learn

[404] https://fencingbearatprayer.blogspot.com/2015/06/talking-points-three-cheers-for-white.html

[405] *The Sacred Project of American Sociology* (2014)

the right ways of seeing the ultimate truth about reality, to learn to transcend ordinary understandings of lay men and women, to correctly re-describe the world of appearances in the approved worldview, and to pass the tests of discipline that finally admit one as an approved disciple into the fold of the enlightened ones."

Step 4: "Through an arduous program of research, writing, teaching, attending meetings, presenting papers, writing and publishing articles and books, and traveling the land to speak and listen, tell near and far the bad news of society's evils that must be overcome and the good news of the promise of salvation through personal conversion, social transformation, and the eventual collective realization of justice, equality, and mutual affirmation."

Step 12: "Remain alert and ever vigilant against false sheep, heretics, and traitors within the fold who threaten to betray the project, and against wolves, philistines, and conservatives outside of the fold who threaten to cut the project's funding—be prepared if dire need arises to sacrifice one's own standards of reason and fairness to eliminate the former and obstruct the latter."

As I said in the other article of mine that *Breitbart* linked, we in academia are living through a religious crisis.[406] Such crises are not simply crises of what we think about the supernatural or the after-life. They are crises of how we define reality through the stories that we tell. They are crises of mythology—tales about the transcendent—but they are also crises of history—the stories that we tell about ourselves and our communities. I am not surprised that Milo's talks on college campuses attracted the protests that they did; it is one of the reasons I started writing about him.

---

[406] https://www.breitbart.com/social-justice/2017/02/17/u-chicago-milo-scares-students-faculty-even/

Milo, as I hope I do, understands that it is more than just our academic standards of objectivity that are at stake in the current political correctness. It is our very apprehension of reality. My colleagues like Carol are willing to lie about me—and about Milo—over and over and over again for as long as it takes (they hope) to shut us up because, as they see it, everything we say is a lie. Luckily for us, in Milo's words, "nobody can resist the truth wrapped in a good joke." We are not going to shut up. This is America, where for the moment we still believe in freedom of speech.[407] Even for academics like me.

---

[407] https://www.cato.org/blog/poll-71-americans-say-political-correctness-has-silenced-discussions-society-needs-have-58-have

V. MILO WILL DIVIDE US.
R. THANKS BE TO GOD.

November 4, 2017

Remember the Good Old Days, when the worst thing you could be called was a white supremacist? That was *so* last season! Yesterday, *The Daily Caller* published what was supposed to be the first article in a weekly op-ed column by a well-known journalist.[408] The author, himself a victim of abuse at the hands ::ahem:: of older men when he was a young teenager, talked about the accusations coming out against Hollywood actor Kevin Spacey and excoriated the star for his (Spacey's) attempt to cover himself in the cloak of his newly-acknowledged identity as a gay man.

The author went on to cite the recent CATO Institute Free Speech and Tolerance Survey, which reports, among other things, that 58 per cent of Americans, including 73 per cent of Republicans and 58 per cent of independents "believe the political climate today prevents them from saying things they believe."[409],[410] (Conversely, 53 per cent

---

[408] https://dailycaller.com/2017/11/03/a-round-of-applause-for-kevin-spacey/

[409] https://www.cato.org/survey-reports/state-free-speech-tolerance-america

[410] https://www.cato.org/blog/poll-71-americans-say-political-correctness-has-silenced-discussions-society-needs-have-58-have

of Democrats "do not feel the need to self-censor.") The author then gave two examples of the kinds of things that conservatives feel it is impossible to say without risking reprisal: that homosexuality is a sin ("not worth losing your soul over") and that the Left-wing press worries more about "Islamophobia" than the effects of actual terrorist attacks. He concluded:

> This week I have been accused of causing "pain and divisiveness." I should hope so. A terminal disease in contemporary American culture is niceness. Appropriateness and earnestness are this country's cardinal sins. For three decades, conservatives have been scolded, reprimanded, backed into toothless, diluted positions, robbed of their effectiveness and browbeaten out of their zeal by language-policers demanding "civilized discourse." Well. Daddy Trump did not win the presidency through gingerliness—nor did I amass millions of fans by being scrupulously conciliatory. The progressive Left is dedicated to the annihilation of America and every surviving libertarian and conservative person in it. The Left's gratuitous vandalism of American institutions and its hostility to the principles that have made this country great cannot be fought with essays in magazines. The Left can only win by forcing us onto the uneven playing field of political correctness and constructive dialogue. I choose war.

Today, his column was cancelled. It is almost as if he had a crystal ball. (Don't blame me if your mind goes there, it is hardly my fault!) Look, he calls out the Right for constantly giving ground to the Left by being *nice*—and they fire him for calling them out. Milo being Milo rallied fairly quickly. I, on the other hand, am feeling tired and sick, and not just because I was looking forward to having a regular column from Milo to read.

This is exactly what the Left wants: to divide us, make us— Republicans, libertarians, conservatives—back shamefaced from the room while they talk constantly about how America was founded on racism and there has never been a time in which academia was not infected with violence. (Trust me on this, I have screenshots.) And then they accuse *us* of being divisive. One of my academic colleagues tried to make nice yesterday by suggesting that perhaps what we as medievalists need is a chance to sit down together and talk. He posted this call for a session on one of the medieval listservs:

> The AHA takes late-breaking sessions. Would anyone in this community like to sit down with Rachel Brown for a collegial, in-person, moderated discussion? I envision a format like presidential debates: There would be mutually agreed-upon questions such as the place of online media in academic discourse, the purpose of the study of history, the political ramifications thereof, the limits of academic freedom, the place of theory, and the decolonization of the field (and NOT about Milo, doxing, or anything else that might lead to personal attacks). Each respondent would have a set amount of time to respond with a prepared or impromptu answer.

The take-down was swift and sharp. No, he was told, this is a terrible idea. And how dare you believe that you can be considered an ally when you make such a horrible suggestion? He withdrew it within twenty-four hours.

The Left talks all the time about how important it is to be inclusive, but only at a price: to be included in their community, you must accept the terms of their debate. You must, if you are white, admit that you are the beneficiary of privilege, regardless of your class. (Just for the record, again, I have admitted mine, but I say it depends on my class, too.[411]) You must admit that the United States was founded not on universal values, but on racism, genocide, and slavery, and supported by racism to this day.

You must not believe in "reason" or "civil discourse" as if there were ever a Golden Age of academia in which such standards were upheld. And you must never, ever suggest that someone like me—or Milo—be allowed a platform to speak. And if you are on the Right?

[411] https://fencingbearatprayer.blogspot.com/2016/11/white-privilege.html

There is nothing you can say that will not be taken as evidence that you do not believe what the Left says you believe. Because they are always right.

You'd think that would make us immune. I have been wracking my brains (what little is left of them after Thursday's post) trying to understand what it is that the conservative establishment hates so much about Milo. I don't think that it is that he is gay; they seem to like Peter Theil.

I am not convinced that it has anything to do with the endorses-pedophilia charge. It can't be that they sincerely believe he is anti-Semitic, although they seem more than willing to use both charges against him. What it seems to be is what he said in his one-and-only *Daily Caller* column: he refuses to make nice, which makes him, as the insult-du-jour puts it, *divisive*. For which they cannot forgive him. But why? This is what Robert Mercer said in withdrawing his support from Milo.

> Without individuals thinking for themselves, society as a whole will struggle to distinguish the signal of truth from the correlated noise of conformity. I supported Milo Yiannopoulos in the hope and expectation that his expression of view contrary to the social mainstream and his spotlighting of the hypocrisy of those who would close down free speech in the name of political correctness would promote the type of open debate and freedom of thought that is being throttled on many American college campuses today. But in my opinion, actions of and statements by Mr. Yiannopoulos have caused pain and divisiveness undermining the open and productive discourse that I had hoped to facilitate. I was mistaken to have supported him, and for several weeks have been in the process of severing all ties with him.[412]

Exactly what was Milo supposed to be able to do, without causing pain? Our opponents refuse to engage with us in reasoned, civil

---

[412] https://www.bloomberg.com/news/articles/2017-11-02/rentech-s-robert-mercer-to-resign-as-co-ceo-of-hedge-fund-firm

discourse. Again, I have screenshots—*hundreds* of them—in which my academic colleagues call me names, accuse me of willfully putting people in danger, chastise anyone who dares to defend me or even to suggest that I might be given the chance to debate. They do not want me to have a platform or a voice. They want me silenced. Like Milo, they want me shamed. *Because I have disagreed with them.*

There is no answer to this argument that will not be taken as divisive or causing pain. There is absolutely nothing I can say that will not be taken as an attack. I cannot convince my academic colleagues that they are in precisely *zero* danger from Milo or me. I cannot convince them that my friendship with Milo is based on the values he champions and the virtues he preaches (even if he does not yet live them). They want to see me as the enemy. They *need* to see me as the enemy. And because I am the enemy, they can call me any name they please. But if I call them out for calling me names, *I am the one causing pain.*

Mr. Mercer did not specify which of Milo's actions and statements have occasioned the "pain and divisiveness" that now puts Milo beyond Mercer's pale, although the timing suggests that his re-evaluation has something to do with the *Buzzfeed* piece. That piece, as you all know, attempted, yet again, to make Milo out to be a white supremacist, as Mercer himself, by his own admission, has been accused of being. But that is not why Mercer changed his mind about Milo. He is worried that Milo is too *divisive*. I know someone else who was accused of being *divisive*. And said so. "Do not think," Our Lord told his disciples,

> that I have come to bring peace on earth; I have not come to bring peace, but a sword. For I have come to set a man against his father, and a daughter against her mother, and a daughter-in-law against her mother-in-law; and a man's foes will be those of his own household. He who loves father or mother more than me is not worthy of me; and he who does not take his cross, and follow me is not worthy of me. He

who finds his life will lose it, and he who loses his life for my sake will find it.—Matthew 10:34-39

Conservatives and libertarians are deluding themselves if they think that they can get out of this culture war without being divisive or causing pain. Try it. Tell someone you love who has had an abortion that life begins at conception, and do not budge. Tell someone you love that it is not possible to have free medical care or free education or a guaranteed income for everyone regardless of whether he or she works without creating a coercive, dysfunctional state, and do not budge. Tell someone you love that class differences are more important than gender or race—and beauty even more so—and do not budge.

Tell someone you love that you are bothered by the theological differences between Christianity and Islam, and do not budge. You. Will. Cause. Division. And pain. Lots of it. I've said it before and I will say it again, Milo can be bitchy. (Yes, he is sometimes bitchy even to me. It was endearing. He told me how badly I dress. And teased me about my driving. And those are just the ones I am willing to tell you. So there.) I am certain that there have been times in his life that even he would rather forget. Things he has said that have hurt people he loves. Comments that he has made that have come out sharper than he intended. Behaviors that he has indulged in that have caused others pain. He is a sinner; he admits it. (As do I.[413])

But I do not get the sense from Mercer's letter that these are the kinds of things he was upset about. He seems to be upset that Milo was not able to do what he, Mercer, wanted him to do—"[spotlight] the hypocrisy of those who would close down free speech in the name of political correctness"—*without causing division and pain.* Too bad.

---

[413] https://fencingbearatprayer.blogspot.com/2017/06/signal-virtue-beauty-and-beast.html

V. MILO WILL DIVIDE US.R. THANKS BE TO GOD.

Division and pain come with the territory when you are speaking the truth. Just ask Our Lord.

FOR THE LOVE OF MILO

December 24, 2017

This is the season for wonders. In a special issue of the *Medieval Feminist Forum: A Journal of Gender and Sexuality,* Jennifer Edwards, Associate Professor of History at Manhattan College, has published a thoughtful reflection on the ongoing argument in medieval studies over what is—and is not—appropriate for us as scholars to say about feminism. In her essay "#Femfog and Fencing: The Risks for Academic Feminism in Public and Online," she talks in detail about my blogging this past year and a half. While she most certainly does not endorse anything that I have said about feminism or Milo, she describes me with a generosity and compassion I had long ago despaired of in interactions with my academic critics. On my intervention in the Society for Medieval Feminist Scholarship (SMFS)[414] Facebook thread that Dorothy Kim hosted about my "Talking Points: Three Cheers for White Men" in January 2016, Edwards notes:

> To her credit, Brown responded calmly, with some humor, and with a willingness to learn from her critics.

More generally, she remarks:

---

[414] http://smfsweb.org

Clearly Brown is deeply serious and sincere in her writing about faith and her connection to conservative politics.... Her blog, and other writings on these subjects, demonstrates deep reflection and eagerness to engage others in expressing her perspectives. As her participation in the January 2016 SMFS conversation and her responses on her public Facebook posts show, she is generally temperate, patient, and persistent in dealing with criticism. She has not, as far as I can tell, deleted any of these engagements or made any effort to hide them. [*I haven't, with one exception, when I became worried about the joking tone one comment thread started by a student on one of my own posts had taken. I deleted it because it was clearly upsetting her, even though it was on my own Facebook page.*] She has linked to critical posts and responded to them with greater respect than we see from typical online responses. [*Fencing Bear salutes.*]

This is not to say that Edwards does not have concerns:

[Brown] has, however, grown increasingly comfortable with "blatantly offensive and demeaning language," as Libby Anne put it, since her devotion to Yiannopoulos began.[415] Even her defense of his "spineless c[——]" comment [*my only use of that word on my own part, just saying*], added as an update to the "Bully Culture" post, in which it appears, references Yiannopoulos's influence. Rather than using her platform to draw attention to conservative causes or participate in debates as a conservative interlocutor [*I am not sure what she means here; to my mind I talk about them all the time*], she has embraced the language of trolls and harassers to marginalize and demonize those with whom she disagrees [*I am not sure what she means here either; I called the conservatives who cancelled Milo's speaking engagement and book contract "spineless cunts," no one else. I have referred to my academic colleagues throughout by their professional titles, not epithets*]. There is a celebratory atmosphere on her Facebook page as interlocutors are chased away by a salivating throng of friends and devotees [*a.k.a. my Random Laypersons. I'm not sure whom they are supposed to have chased away; I actively work to make sure that all feel welcome, just ask my friend Paul*].

And yet:

---

[415] https://www.patheos.com/blogs/lovejoyfeminism/2017/02/university-of-chicago-professor-uses-c-word-in-defense-of-milo-yiannopoulos.html

What is palpable in these discussions, however, is that none devolved into a call for anyone to be assaulted, or otherwise harassed [*except, to the best of my knowledge, me—rereading the screenshots I have from this past September is bracing, to say the least!*], and there was clearly articulated concern *not* to allow the conversation to become harassing, particularly among SMFS members. [*Edwards notes elsewhere that she was writing before September 2017 when I responded to Dorothy Kim directly about her accusations against me. For the record, when I posted about this debate on my Facebook page, I explicitly called for my Random Laypersons not to harass Professor Kim. This exhortation to gentleness was taken by some as a rape threat.*]

So far, so good. And yet.... There is still a problem. Not—as Edwards is gracious to point out—with my interactions with my colleagues directly. Rather, it is the way I talk about Milo:

Brown's defense of Yiannopoulos centered on his "truth-telling" in a way that is reminiscent of [Allen] Frantzen's writings about feminism. [*Frantzen became famous about the time I did for his comments on his own blog about the effects of feminism on men.*[416] *Like Milo, Frantzen is gay; like me, he is a martial artist, in his case, a boxer. Edwards treats the controversy over his blogging in an earlier section of this same article.*] Just as Frantzen wanted to clear space and build courage for "FUM" [*Fogged-Up Men*] who were unable to risk criticizing feminism, Brown claimed she admired Yiannopoulos for doing just that—making the criticisms that "nobody has been willing to say lest they get shamed, shouted down, and told to shut up." Over a series of blog posts [*a whole book's worth!*] and public Facebook posts, Brown articulated a devotion that reached the level of hero worship of Yiannopoulos (even declaring love for him) for saying things she felt others were too cowardly to say. Many of her interlocutors suggested that this "cowardice" was because such things were harmful and inappropriate, but Brown questioned all such limitations on speech.

"A devotion that reached the level of hero worship": you don't say! Yes, I love Milo. I have said so on numerous occasions, both on my own behalf and that of his fans. I am proud to acknowledge him

[416] https://www.chronicle.com/article/Prominent-Medieval-Scholar-s/235014

as my "vile boyfriend" (as one of my liberal friends calls him on my Facebook page—one of those whom my salivating throngs of Random Laypersons have somehow not chased away, just saying). I was, in fact, relieved when *Buzzfeed* outed me as one of Milo's advisors, so that I could explain more fully how much contact I have had with him. He acknowledges me in *Dangerous* as one of his two main sources of "intellectual nourishment." He has been over the past year and a half a constant friend.[417]

What is so wrong about saying I love him? Edwards would say, because Milo encourages hate, but as all those who actually watch his talks know, this is not the way in which his fans hear him. (The media seem incapable of changing a narrative once they get hold of it, thus the continuing slander about what Milo said on Twitter about Leslie Jones. In sum: "Ghostbusters is doing so badly they've deployed @ Lesdoggg to play the victim on Twitter. Very sad!" "Barely literate. America needs better schools!"—for which Jones had him blocked. At which Milo responded: "Rejected by another black dude!" Not exactly the slavering incitement to harassment that you have doubtless heard about.)

Yes, Milo tells jokes that make even some of his supporters uncomfortable—including, most recently, Andrew Bolt[418]—but the atmosphere at his talks is not one of hate, but of joy.[419] I am hardly the only one to call Milo a hero or to thank him for speaking when others will not. Just look at the videos on his YouTube channel from his recent tour in Australia. Over and over again, his admirers say, "Thank you. Thank you for speaking up." Which, I am guessing, for my academic critics only makes things worse.

---

[417] https://www.milo.net/37598/fulton-brown-my-university-protects-free-speech-and-dissident-voices-yours-doesnt/

[418] https://youtu.be/OqCxWk-xMA4

[419] https://youtu.be/W2xDX2gA8BQ

Academics nowadays are not supposed to love. Not our subjects. Not our culture. Not—it would seem—ourselves. Love pollutes. Love corrupts. Love compromises our objectivity. Love is simply a cover for the oppression it should be our mission to expose. Edwards's implication would seem to be that my love for Milo makes me blind to his real effect rather than—as I have argued—better able to see him for what he is. Try it in any academic context. Say that you study what you do—the history of Christianity, for example, or devotion to the Virgin Mary—out of love, and watch the response. People get nervous. They look around at each other for reassurance. They start saying things about how "we need to be very careful here" and about the importance of being "inclusive." They ask questions about the way in which whatever you have said you love—a text, an image, a person, a culture—has been harmful.

They do everything they can to avoid acknowledging that they, too, have taken pleasure from the subjects of their own work or that what they study is for themselves an object of love. They declare themselves on the side of justice and against hate. But they never say the word "beautiful." And they will not use the word "love" except as a way to claim that your love for your subject is tainted by your sexism (always assumed of conservatives, even if, like me, you are a woman) or by your race.

Maybe I am simply having the wrong conversations. Maybe there are academics out there who are unembarrassed to claim that they do the work that they do not out of a sense of righting injustices, but out of love. Tony Esolen is one, but my sense is that he is fairly isolated.[420] For the most part, the academics I know are a depressingly joyless lot, even many of those who call themselves Christian. I wonder why.

---

[420] http://www.ncregister.com/blog/pjsmith/anthony-esolen-in-his-own-words-why-i-left-providence-college-for-thomas-mo

Edwards remarks on the comments that I have made about feeling isolated in academia as a Christian, with the suggestion that I should suck it up since I have tenure, while in the same breath insinuating that my Christian beliefs are beyond the pale because they "appear to promote limitations on women's rights and the imposition of so-called traditional values." (How was it Milo put it? Oh, yes: "Abortion is murder.")

According to Edwards, "[what] Brown does not like is that the unpopularity of her ideas means they are not accorded the position of power she would like them to have." In Edwards's words:

> It is not only the extreme Right positions that concern her colleagues— such as those that deny women equality [*I have no idea what she is talking about, nor would Milo*], control over their bodies [*as I put it on Facebook recently, I believe that a woman's right to choose begins with whether to have sex—the ultimate control over her own body*], or freedom from body- and slut-shaming [*I have written about this issue at length, just not recently, so my colleagues may be forgiven for not knowing about these posts*[421],[422],[423]]; it is the implication for Brown's scholarship if her vision of medieval culture is so narrow [*where have I heard this before?*[424]] and short-sighted [*my published scholarship is all listed on my homepage, if you want to read more; it is not clear to me how many of those involved in this debate over the past year and half have looked further than my blog*[425]]. Brown defends herself by emphasizing that the blog is a casual space without the standards of an academic publication [*so much for peer review!*]. But it reveals patterns of thoughts and methods of reaching conclusions that, again, trouble those who emphasize evidence, logic, and argumentation in the classroom and in scholarship [*I'm sorry, I think I just hurt myself laughing at what Milo would say*].

---

[421] https://fencingbearatprayer.blogspot.com/2009/04/daughters-of-eve.html

[422] https://fencingbearatprayer.blogspot.com/2011/08/plus-size-gorgeous.html

[423] https://fencingbearatprayer.blogspot.com/2012/03/skinny-bitches.html

[424] https://fencingbearatprayer.blogspot.com/2008/07/isnt-that-bit-narrow.html

[425] https://home.uchicago.edu/~rfulton/

What have I or Milo said that is so wrong? We have argued for love, not of victimhood but of responsibility. Not of death, but of life. Not of a culture in which homosexuality is punishable by death and women are blamed for being raped, but of a culture in which marriage is defined through mutual consent and women are held to be the equals of men. We have argued for beauty and creativity and imagination and joy. And for doing so we have been called the worst names our critics can possibly conceive. Racist, because we believe in challenging individual human beings to excel.

Sexist, because we see fertility as a blessing. Misogynist, because we argue that women need fathers and husbands and brothers and sons as much as they need mothers and sisters and daughters. Xenophobic, because we argue in favor of a civilization defined by its openness to other cultures like no other in human history. Nazis, because we argue in favor of limiting the power of the state. Islamophobic, because we argue that differences in religion actually affect the way in which people see the world.[426]

I have written before about how I understand my privilege and my responsibilities as a professor with tenure.[427] I am fully cognizant of the power that I have thanks to my position at the University of Chicago. I have hundreds of emails and Facebook messages from readers of my blog, thanking me much as Milo's fans thank him for standing up in the face of the criticism my blogging about him has received. I do not think of myself as a victim in the slightest. I think of myself as a warrior on the side of joy.[428]

I have never had so much fun in my life as I have had this past year, even when I was writing in Milo's defense last February, even when 1,500 or so of my academic colleagues called for me to be censured

[426] https://fencingbearatprayer.blogspot.com/2017/08/piss-christ-and-son-of-allah.html
[427] https://fencingbearatprayer.blogspot.com/2016/01/blogging-with-tenure.html
[428] https://fencingbearatprayer.blogspot.com/2016/01/how-to-be-happy-warrior.html

for refusing to be called names. What makes me sad is not that my ideas "are not accorded the position of power [I] would like them to have," but that my ideas about Christianity and Western civilization and its benefits do not bring my academic colleagues more joy.

Milo gives conservatives permission—and reason—to laugh, not just at the names they have been called ("spineless cunts"), but at themselves ("A fool and a teddy bear take on the world. You gotta laugh!"). If only we could persuade others to join us, think of the fun we could have celebrating the beautiful things that we love in our culture—and in ourselves.

'HE SAID, SHE SAID': MILO'S LIVELIER STYLE IN REVIEW

December 26, 2017

Now that we've celebrated the birth of Our Lord, it is time to review the lies that have been told about his servants this past year. One servant in particular. You know whom I mean. My colleagues in medieval studies can't stop talking about him!

> Just a reminder, since apparently people have recently been writing MY is not so bad and also white supremacy is just not so terrible for medieval studies. TW: for terrible awful things.

The above Facebook post links to an article published back in September 2017 by another of my medievalist colleagues arguing that "to target Milo at a fellow human being"—which he implies I did by writing about the things others have been saying about me on social media and tagging Milo on my Facebook share—is "a solicitation for harassment, including likely violent threats."[429] His proof? A list of things that he says Milo has said, with helpful links to his (my colleague's) sources.

---

[429] http://www.thismess.net/2017/09/milo-and-livelier-way.html

This same colleague has recently challenged me on Twitter—where I cannot respond, he has me (the "Famous Medievalist") blocked!—with a link to his original article (see below for the full piece, along with the beginning of the Twitter thread). He tweets as @Lollardfish (with blue checkmark!), but his name in real life is David M. Perry.

> Dear Famous Medievalist: Here's a brief reminder of Milo's history of abuse, including racially based abuse.
>
> I'm not weighing in on the other arguments until we get this clear: To take the side of Milo is to take the side of the most vile types of abuse, including the encouragement of sustained racist harassment.
>
> And to all those who think Famous Medievalist is defensible because those SJW scholars are so super annoying...you too can read what Milo has said and done and make a choice.

Okay, then. Let's read what Milo has said and done, according to Perry's list. You have most certainly heard Milo say many of these things. But have you heard them in context? I give Perry's account of what he says Milo has said in italics. My comments follow.

1. Perry says Milo *"singled out a Jewish reporter and called him: 'a typical example of a sort of thick-as-pig-shit media Jew,'"* linking to an article written by Daniel J. Solomon for *Forward*.[430] Here Milo was talking about Joe Bernstein—you remember Joe Bernstein! You know, the writer for *Buzzfeed* who published the exposé about Milo in October 2017 where he tried to prove Milo is sympathetic to the white nationalists.[431] Back in January 2017, Milo had this to say about Bernstein (as reported in full by Solomon):

> Yiannopoulos told fans at Minnesota State University that Joe Bernstein...represents "a typical example of a sort of thick-as-pig shit

---

[430] https://forward.com/fast-forward/358909/milo-yiannopoulos-slams-thick-as-pig-st-media-jews/

[431] https://www.buzzfeednews.com/article/josephbernstein/heres-how-breitbart-and-milo-smuggled-white-nationalism#.dpQwGx8bLm

media Jew, who has all these sort of right, P.C. politics." Bernstein and his ilk, Yiannopoulos continued, have "Totally predictable opinions on absolutely everything. But really stupid. And seems to be driven by social acceptance and political correctness, rather than actually telling an interesting story or doing anything worthwhile."

Perry wants you to believe that Milo's comments about Bernstein make him anti-Semitic. What Milo actually was saying is somewhat more complicated: that there are Jews like Bernstein who side with P.C. politics rather than, as does Milo, support for Jewish causes like the defense of Israel.[432]

2. Perry says Milo *"defended the racist and sexist invective aimed at Leslie Jones,"* linking to an article written by Terry Moran, Emily Taguchi, and Claire Pedersen for *ABC News*.[433] This is one of the stories that the media loves to tell, but—as Milo's followers know—is a confection of lies. Yes, Milo told *Nightline*, that he thinks *"trolling is very important... I like to think of myself as a virtuous troll, you know? I'm doing God's work."* But as Milo explains at length in his book *Dangerous*—published in July 2017 and therefore available to Perry in September 2017 when he compiled his list of Milo's sayings—it was Jones, not Milo, who started the argument on Twitter about why *Ghostbusters* was doing so badly at the box office.

To reiterate: Milo had written a review of the movie on its release, in which he argued that the scriptwriters had done Jones a disservice by casting her in such a stereotypical role—in his words, "worthy of a minstrel show." According to Milo, not only was the film insulting to Jones, its "petty two-dimensional feminist posturing" demeaned the entire female cast.[434] No wonder it tanked at the box office, as

---

[432] https://youtu.be/1XKEeEEi_Jk

[433] https://abcnews.go.com/Entertainment/leslie-jones-twitter-troll-regrets-attacking-ghostbusters-actress/story?id=41808886

[434] https://www.breitbart.com/tech/2016/07/18/milo-reviews-ghostbusters/

Milo predicted it would.[435] It was in this context that Jones began tweeting and the twitterers responded in swarms. As Milo tells the story in *Dangerous*:

> Media reports say I was the one who led these swarms. This couldn't be further from the truth. Jones was engaging in running battles with her detractors on Twitter for hours before I got involved, actively trading insults with them and provoking them.
>
> I criticized Jones, tossing a few jabs her way. The reason lefties in the media saw me as ringleader of the trolls is that it's hard for them to imagine people moving collectively *without* a leader. It's their authoritarianism showing: for them, a herd must have a shepherd. The idea of people thinking and acting independently frightens them.
>
> My only crime was daring to criticize a black woman, itself seemingly proof of racism today. I tweeted that Jones was playing the victim, that her character in *Ghostbusters* was an unfunny racial stereotype, and that her tweets were barely literate. All are true. (Despite calling people "bitches" all evening, she had the audacity to report me for that last one.)

Even if Perry had not read *Dangerous* by September, I had written in detail about this exchange back in February 2017.

> *Full transcript for those who missed the spat:*[436] Jones had been Tweeting about the bad reviews *Ghostbusters* was getting, one of which Milo wrote, "Teenage Boys with Tits: Here's My Problem with Ghostbusters." Milo jumped into the Twitter fray with: "If at first you don't succeed (because your work is terrible), play the victim. EVERYONE GETS HATE MAIL FFS." Jones reported Milo to Twitter and called one of his fans a "racist b*tch" for saying "how sad that a comedian would want to limit free speech. Lenny Bruce is rolling over in his grave." Milo responded to Jones: "Ghostbusters is doing so badly they've deployed @Lesdoggg to play the victim on Twitter. Very sad!" "Barely literate. America needs better schools." At which point, he was blocked

---

[435] https://www.breitbart.com/social-justice/2016/05/05/heres-left-desperate-defend-new-feminist-ghostbusters/

[436] https://www.breitbart.com/social-justice/2016/07/18/ghostbuster-leslie-jones-reports-milo/

from linking to her account. To which Milo replied: "Rejected by yet another black dude." And that was it.

If Milo is to be blamed for everything that people on Twitter said about Jones, then I wonder what that says about Perry encouraging my colleagues to believe that "To endorse [Milo] is to endorse bigotry. To summon him into a dispute is to ask for escalation"?

3. Perry says Milo *"took the stage at UW [Milwaukee] and put up a picture of a trans student. He later repeated the attacks on the student at a second event. Yiannopoulos proceeded to attack the student's physical appearance, using an anti-transgender slur and adding, 'The way you know he's failed is I can still bang him,'"* linking to a blogpost at *Media Matters* written by its staff.[437] The *Media Matters* blogpost gives Milo's comments at the second event in full:

> I've become a feminist icon. Do you want to know why? So at my previous date at UW Wisconsin, I happen to put on the screen, the image, a picture of a nice young man who think he's a lady and used the law—because of course progressives always when they don't get what they want or want to get in somewhere that they don't belong, invoke the great patriarchal force known as the government—to try to get into the women's locker rooms. This young man was desperate for a bit of tit and minge.

> So he tried, via the government, to get himself into the women's locker rooms at UW Milwaukee. Now he created a terrible fuss, an awful fuss, when I put his name up there and so did the president of that university. But it turns out, he's going to quit the university. So I have become a sort of second wave feminist icon, protecting women from men in their locker rooms. Well, you're welcome, feminism.

> Now, this young person—sometimes they think, sometimes they say I'm mean, sometimes they say it's too much. Sometimes they say you're too vindictive, it's too cruel. But the point of doing this, is that, you know, they invoke the government, they use the government to get

---

[437] https://www.mediamatters.org/blog/2016/12/16/breitbart-s-milo-yiannopoulos-doubles-down-harassing-transgender-university-wisconsin-student/214849

a variety of things through that ordinary, normal people would not permit. And then this person, Justine or Adelaide, or whatever he calls himself this week—[*audience laughter*].

It's Christmas, I don't care anymore!

Adelaide, good lord, went to the press and said I had used violent words as though violent words were a thing. What the fuck is a violent word? If you can't take a joke, how are you going to deal with having your dick cut off?

Of all the insults thrown at him, this is the one that Milo has said he will own: "transphobe." Milo has spoken out regularly against the use of gender reassignment surgery as a treatment for gender dysphoria, but in this context he is supported by Dr. Paul McHugh, the inventor of the surgical treatment—meaning that if Milo is a "transphobe," so is the inventor of trans people. In a report published in *The New Atlantis* in September 2016, Dr. McHugh and his co-author Lawrence Mayer concluded that the procedure has not had the beneficial effect that McHugh himself had originally hoped it would and that he could therefore no longer recommend it as a treatment:

> The scientific evidence summarized suggests we take a skeptical view toward the claim that sex-reassignment procedures provide the hoped-for benefits or resolve the underlying issues that contribute to elevated mental health risks among the transgender population. While we work to stop maltreatment and misunderstanding, we should also work to study and understand whatever factors may contribute to the high rates of suicide and other psychological and behavioral health problems among the transgender population, and to think more clearly about the treatment options that are available.[438]

Milo has been particularly vocal about using such treatments on children, but in the case at Milwaukee, he was also speaking out against the claim that allowing individuals who are biologically male to use

---

[438] https://www.thenewatlantis.com/publications/executive-summary-sexuality-and-gender

women's dressing rooms is without risk to the women involved. In this particular case, at the time he made the application to use the women's dressing room in January 2017, Justin/Justine Kramer still had male genitalia—and the legal name "Justin"—thus the complaints when he tried to use the women's sauna.[439],[440] Kramer went on to sue the school, thus Milo's comments about Kramer's use of the government to force his way into the women's locker room.

4. Perry says Milo *"referred to women as 'cunts'"* in a talk at West Virginia University. Here Perry's source is an article by Erin Beck for the *Pittsburgh Post-Gazette*.[441] In her account, Beck refers at this point only in paraphrase to the things Milo said in his talk:

> Mr. Yiannopoulos made a variety of sexist and other comments rooted in bigotry during the speech, which mostly celebrated Donald Trump winning the presidential election, according to prepared remarks published on Breitbart. Among them: calling women "c——" and suggesting that people who call out racism and sexism are actually targeting "political preferences."

The remarks published by *Breitbart* are somewhat fuller.[442] In Milo's own words, commenting on the responses to the election:

> Others have felt a negative effect, like Matt Harrigan, who lost his job as CEO of a company called PacketSled after threatening to assassinate Trump with a sniper rifle.[443] He claims it was a joke. Maybe he should write for Amy Schumer—it seems they're both fans of being unfunny,

---

[439] https://www.dailywire.com/news/5419/man-angry-university-not-letting-him-show-his-junk-amanda-prestigiacomo

[440] https://www.washingtontimes.com/news/2016/may/3/transgender-student-denied-entry-women-locker-room/

[441] https://www.post-gazette.com/news/education/2016/12/04/Breitbart-writer-uses-slurs-to-attack-WVU-professor/stories/201612040131

[442] https://www.breitbart.com/milo/2016/12/01/full-text-milo-west-virginia-university-trump-means/

[443] https://www.washingtontimes.com/news/2016/nov/15/matt-harrigan-packetsled-ceo-resigns-over-trump-as/

unoriginal and total cunts. The thing about Daddy is, positively or negatively, you're gonna feel him!

In other words, it wasn't "women" whom Milo called "cunts," it was *one* woman—Amy Schumer—along with a man, Matt Harrigan, specifically for their remarks about President-elect Donald Trump. Biting my tongue here on how to parse this one!

5. Perry says Milo *"referred to a professor as a 'fat faggot'"* in the same talk at West Virginia University. Again, his source here is the *Pittsburgh Post-Gazette* article by Erin Beck.[444] According to Beck:

> Mr. Yiannopoulos, whose supporters often heap hatred on his targets, slipped in his remarks that Daniel Brewster, who is gay, is "still on Twitter" after showing a slide that called Brewster a "fat f———."

By now, you should be getting fairly suspicious. Why did Milo call Professor Brewster a "fat faggot"? Because Brewster had scheduled a seminar at the same time as Milo's talk specifically in order to discourage his own students from listening to Milo. In Milo's words, again from the *Breitbart* transcript on which Beck relied:

> There is one thing I don't like about this college though. Professor Daniel Brewster. Now, Professor Brewster teaches sociology, which comes in just above gender studies in my rankings of "burger flipping majors"—but not very far above. I hear he's fond of bullying conservative students, who often find themselves compelled to leave his class mid-lecture. I hear he's hosting a, and I quote, "multicultural LGBTQ event" at this very second.

> What's more, I heard he informed students this week that if they attended his event—which just so happens—just so happens!—to overlap directly with mine—they would get extra credit! In other words, students who opt for my event over his will get a lower grade. Students told me he specifically did this to deter people from my event, and when we emailed him for his side of the story, he didn't deny it.

---

[444] https://www.post-gazette.com/news/education/2016/12/04/Breitbart-writer-uses-slurs-to-attack-WVU-professor/stories/201612040131

Professor Fatass's Twitter profile contains this quote: "I welcome the fact that students feel safer knowing that I will be an advocate for them and that I am willing to fight for their rights and their inclusion." Well that's not true, is it Professor Stuff-Your-Face-With-Froot-Loops? In fact, the opposite is true. If student testimony is correct, he actively works to exclude students—conservative and libertarian students—from his class, and clearly has no respect for the right to consider and discuss different, dangerous points of view.

He is the personification of the cancer eating away at universities: preaching tolerance in public and practicing censorship in private. But Mr. Brewster aside, I'm impressed with West Virginia. If I do eventually found a department of men's studies, this might just be the place to do it. In the meantime, let's get down to business.[445]

Let us recall Milo's own name for himself, emblazoned on the bus that he used for the tour: "Dangerous Faggot." "Faggot" is not an insult for Milo in the way that "fatass" is. Is it bigotry for one gay man to call out another gay man for being fat? You decide.

6. Perry says Milo *"argues that trans folk are 'disordered'."* Here Perry's source is an article published by German Lopez at *Vox* about Milo's appearance on the Bill Maher show in February 2017.[446] Lopez summarizes the exchange that Milo had with comedian Larry Wilmore, ending with Wilmore's injunction to Milo to "Go fuck yourself":

The exchange began when Yiannopoulos made some anti-transgender remarks—by misgendering a trans activist, perpetuating a myth that allowing trans women into women's bathrooms will put women at danger, and arguing that trans people have a mental disorder.

Wilmore responded: "I just think it's sad, because the same arguments that were used against gay people—treating them like aliens who just wanted to fuck anything that moved and that's why we should avoid them at all costs—[are] being used [against trans people]."

---

[445] https://www.breitbart.com/social-justice/2016/12/01/full-text-milo-west-virginia-university-trump-means/

[446] https://www.vox.com/identities/2017/2/18/14659650/larry-wilmore-milo-yiannopoulos-bill-maher

Here, as noted above, Milo is dependent upon the research published by Dr. McHugh for his understanding of transgenderism as a "disorder"; the "trans activist" in question is Justin/Justine Kramer. Lopez sides in his analysis with Wilmore, claiming that Milo was simply playing the troll to no purpose, thus Wilmore's response:

> Yiannopoulos, however, didn't seem too interested in Wilmore's points. As he usually does, he quickly reverted to trolling by the end of the segment—arguing that gay people may be disordered because he, as a gay man, feels "really disordered," before calling the other guests on Maher's show stupid. Wilmore, in the face of this trolling, replied, "You can go fuck yourself."

What Lopez does not describe, however, is what happened afterward. From my own account of the episode, back in February 2017:

> Do you think it was an accident that Milo suggested in the midst of the give-and-take with comedian Larry Wilmore over Milo's opinions on transgenderism and gays that Maher should invite guests with higher IQs on his show? To which Wilmore replied, right on cue: "First of all, you can go f*ck yourself alright... If your argument is that these people are stupid, you didn't hear a word that this man said earlier in this segment because he can talk circles around your pathetic, douchey little ass." The audience loved that! But so did Milo, as you can see from his grin.

> Maher is right. Milo is an imp—and he relishes it. He is an imp, a clown, a fool. Or, as I prefer to call him, a holy fool. He is dangerous not because he incites violence (again, he never does, except against Dylann Roof), but because in being willing to make himself a fool, he forces others to recognize their own foolishness. Who really came off better in the exchange between Milo and Wilmore? Wilmore, who lost his cool and started cursing Milo? Or Milo, who thereafter happily egged all the other panelists on? Particularly after Wilmore responded to Milo's description of how everyone both on the far Left and on the far Right hates him (no offense, but it's true!): "I think you're leaving out a lot of people." "You see," Milo said after everyone laughed, including himself, "this is the perfect example of how humor can bring people together."

As Milo likes to say, "Nobody can resist the truth wrapped in a good joke"—including the jokes that he makes about himself.

7. Perry says Milo *"says that grabbing women's genitals is not sexual assault."* His source here is a tweet by The Reagan Battalion (@ ReaganBattalion) with a link to Milo's appearance on the Joe Rogan Show.[447] The Reagan Battalion, if you don't know the story, was directly responsible for Milo's losing his invitation to speak at CPAC, his job at *Breitbart*, and his contract with Simon & Schuster in February 2017.[448] What Milo actually says in this clip is, of course, rather different from what the tweet wants you to believe:[449]

> Milo: This sexual harassment craze right now, it's really just a way for women to tell you they've been hit on, isn't it?

> Joe Rogan: It's a way to get money.

> Milo: It's not just that, [it's a way to say] somebody was expressing sexual interest in me. All of these quote unquote rape stories from campuses that don't actually involve any sex. Um. Of course the ones that do involve sex-rape stories are all frauds and hoaxes. Um. The ones that don't involve sex or [are all] O, hideous! Someone touched my breast, how awful!—what's the woman really telling you there? She's telling you that someone was sexually interested in her. It's a sort of bragging, isn't it?

> Rogan: Well, it is unless someone does really touch your breast in an unwanted way.

> Milo: How are you supposed to know now?

> Rogan: But if some guy comes up and grabs your tit, that is actual sexual assault.

---

[447] https://twitter.com/ReaganBattalion/status/833700767475331072

[448] https://www.mic.com/articles/169118/exclusive-meet-reagan-battalion-the-anonymous-squadron-that-destroyed-milo-s-career#.gvL3J5iGr

[449] [As of July 20, 2019, the clip is no longer available on YouTube. Full video: https://youtu.be/LnH67G7vAu4]

Milo: Our parents' generation would have turned around and said, "Keep your fucking hands to yourself," and moved on with their lives. They wouldn't have gone into university administrators and tried to destroy the guy's reputation and life over it. It's not that big of a deal. If someone touched your tit, get over it.

Rogan: That's a really big deal. That's a rude person who doesn't have any respect for anybody else's body.

Milo: It's rude, but when you enlarge...

Rogan: You should take those people out of campus, you shouldn't be allowed to do that.

Milo: That's ridiculous.

Rogan: You shouldn't be allowed to grab someone's pussy.

Note what happened in this conversation. Milo brought up the question of the sexual harassment craze, and Rogan egged him on. It was Rogan, not Milo, who talks about pussy-grabbing. All Milo mentioned was having someone touch your breast—to which, if the attention is unwanted, he suggests the response, "Keep your fucking hands to yourself." As a woman of his parents' generation who has had her breasts grabbed more than once by men in whom I was not sexually interested, I agree. Having your breast grabbed is not the moral—or criminal—equivalent of rape. I reserve the right to slap any man's face who presumes to touch me without my consent.

8. Perry says Milo is *"also a plagiarist."* Perry's source here is an article published in January 2015 by Jef Rouner at the *Houston Press* in the midst of the #GamerGate controversy.[450] Rouner's reference is a collection of poetry entitled *Eskimo Papoose* that Milo self-published in 2007 under the pen name Milo Andreas Wagner (—which should already give you a clue; everyone knows how much Milo loves Wagner's operas).

---

[450] https://www.houstonpress.com/music/gamergate-journalist-milo-yiannopouloss-self-published-poetry-book-contains-unattributed-tori-amos-lyrics-6497169

The poems are a pastiche of references to some of Milo's favorite singers and characters including Tori Amos, Britney Spears, Mariah Carey, and *Buffy the Vampire Slayer*. Far from pretending that the lyrics are all his own compositions, Milo has openly acknowledged that he was quoting from other authors, as Rauner notes:

> When confronted with accusations of plagiarism on Twitter Yiannopoulos freely admitted that the collection was made up of other people's words, and that it was an example of "sampling" like in music.

> "There isn't a line in the whole thing that isn't from somewhere else. That's obviously the point," said Yiannopoulos. "You actually, really believe that it could possibly be anything but a giant piss-take? That it could be 'deception'? Really?"

Milo won't tell you how old he is, but these poems were published over ten years ago—about the time he would have been, say, twenty-two or twenty-three. They are, if you will excuse the term, juvenilia. They are also no longer for sale, suggesting rather that Milo has not attempted to make any money off of them. The worst that can be said is that they are somewhat pretentious, like much poetry written by young men and women before they have found their own voice. If he did not write the poems, he almost certainly wrote the description of the book that appears now on Google Books:

> Milo Andreas Wagner's second volume of poetry. Milo Andreas Wagner was born Milos Yiannoppoulos [*sic*] in Athens in 1983. His family settled in Britain while he was still a child, and it is here that he attended schools in Canterbury and Knightsbridge. He is an accomplished musician, listing among his greatest passions Richard Wagner, Friedrich Nietzsche and Arthur Schopenhauer. He has also travelled extensively, and is currently reading philosophy. His literary and philosophical areas of interest include eschatology, repetition, semiotics and confession.[451]

---

[451] https://books.google.com/books/about/Eskimo_Papoose.html?id=O_-LAAAACAAJ

I had thought that I had photographs of the poems sent to me by one of Milo's fans, but I can't find them. Rauner quotes lines from several of the poems, but as best I can tell, none of them in full. One poem, entitled "Confession," contains the following lines:

> How do we learn
> But by theft?
> Nothing in this book is true
> I made it all up.

My suspicion is that Milo had been reading a little too much James Joyce. Or maybe the Psalms.

9. Perry says Milo *"coordinated some Gamergate activities via Breitbart, helping to lead to rape and death threats for numerous individuals, many of whom are still being harassed."* Perry's source here is an article by Kristen V. Brown published at *Splinter* in October 2015.[452] Like the accusation that Milo's tweeting about Leslie Jones was the immediate cause of the Twitter storm that her own tweeting occasioned, the claim that Milo was the leader of—rather than the first major reporter on—#GamerGate is one of the media's favorites. Unusually, Brown (no relation) gives Milo a comparatively fair hearing. In her own words:

> Perhaps the most shocking thing about Milo Yiannopoulos is that he is utterly charming... After all, you don't amass 85,000 Twitter followers, become the conservative torch-bearer in a gaming industry civil war, attract a cult following among young, Internet-savvy men, and become a figurehead of the Men's Rights movement without knowing a little something about exploiting the human psyche....

> "People have this idea that I'm a misogynistic monster," Yiannopoulos tells me, "But as soon as they meet me they say, 'Oh, you're so nice in person!'"

Brown even gives his views on feminism a fair hearing:

---

[452] https://splinternews.com/the-ultimate-troll-the-terrifying-allure-of-gamergate-1793852307

"Women's rights is one of the great successes of our society. But it seemed like we were taking a retrograde step," he told me. "We were going backwards. We were giving people like feminists podiums to bully people. A lot of what I have done since is purposely ridiculing that, getting under the skin of people I have decided are bigots."

What she does not mention are the rape and death threats that Perry (following the usual narrative) claims Milo's journalism about #GamerGate provoked. For these, Perry would have had to go elsewhere, for example, the Wikipedia entry on the controversy.[453] But as everyone on reddit knows, the Wikipedia entry on Gamergate is famously biased:

I don't think it's exactly a secret that the Wikipedia article about GamerGate is biased. What's strange is how, when I searched through a great many other articles and studied the language used on each topic, what I've discovered is that GG's article on Wikipedia is UNIQUELY biased in that the tone of the article is completely, utterly in disregard for Wikipedia's policy of Neutral POV, and in such a way that I could not find any other article on Wikipedia that is biased in this particular way.[454]

Milo talks in detail about his experiences with #GamerGate in chapter 10 of *Dangerous*: "Why Gamers *Don't* Hate Me." He credits #GamerGate with his rise not just as a journalist, but as a supervillain:

My supervillain origin was GamerGate, a bitter war between gamers, anonymous internet trolls, hectoring feminist scolds, and left-wing journalists. If you only follow mainstream media, you probably only know GamerGate as grown men playing video games all day and harassing women on the internet. In reality, it was the first battle in an anti-leftist, culturally libertarian, free speech movement that led directly to Trump's election.

---

[453] https://en.wikipedia.org/wiki/Gamergate_controversy

[454] https://www.reddit.com/r/KotakuInAction/comments/35t4dc/discussion_the_gamergate_article_on_wikipedia_is/?st=jbo5h6cf&sh=6c74691c

tl;dr: The rape and death threats were hoaxes; the GamerGaters included women; and gaming journalism was just as corrupt as the gamers said. But you don't have to take my word for it. If you want the full story, read *Dangerous*.

10. Perry says Milo *"led a smear campaign against black journalist Shaun King, claiming he wasn't black (King is black)."* Perry's source here is an article by Jack Mirkinson published in August 2015 at *Salon*.[455] Mirkinson was writing in response to an article published by Milo at *Breitbart,* itself responding to accounts published by Vicki Pate on her blog.[456] For Mirkinson, the only explanation for Milo's, *Breitbart*'s, and Pate's interest in the story is that "white people" are crazy:

> Let's be very clear about why *Breitbart* decided this was a worthy story to pursue. It's the same reason that Fox News was so reluctant to call Charleston shooter Dylann Roof a racist. Some people in America find the idea that there is such a thing as white supremacy—or that white people are in any way to blame for the racism in our society— so terrifying that they would rather concoct a huge racial conspiracy theory wherein ghoulish black activists run roughshod over a cowed white populace. To *Breitbart*, the Shaun Kings of the world are the ones with all the power, exploiting a weak and politically correct society for their own personal gain.
>
> It is all self-evidently insane, of course, but white people have been deluding themselves about the racial state of play in America for centuries, so why stop now?

Why should Milo, a white man who has just married his black husband John, be so interested in a story about a Black Lives Matter activist who may not, in fact, be black? Perhaps because, in his own words, Milo cares more about black people than he does about being

---

[455] https://www.salon.com/2015/08/21/the_plot_to_destroy_shaun_king_how_
breitbart_turned_a_ludicrous_conspiracy_theory_into_national_news/
[456] https://www.breitbart.com/politics/2015/08/19/did-black-lives-matter-organiser-
shaun-king-mislead-oprah-winfrey-by-pretending-to-be-biracial/

politically correct about Shaun King. From chapter 5 in *Dangerous*, "Why Black Lives Matter Hates Me":

> Many of the most cherished people in my life are black men. Because I love and respect them, I believe they deserve truth, not lies, in the face of the harsh reality of black America today. It's a reality that includes problems created and sustained by the Left, and by the black community itself—as well as real problems of enduring racism. The Left, by contrast, seeks to patronize minorities by preventing them from coming into contact with anything that might offend them....

> Black Lives Matter hates me, and I hate them. But I don't hate them because they pose a threat to white people. I hate them because they do precisely the opposite of what they claim to do. They cause more black lives to be lost, not less. And they do so by attacking the one group of people trying to help their communities [the police]. The people who really ought to hate Black Lives Matter are black people.

And you wonder that I say I love him? It must be wonderful to be John.

&❧

In Perry's words:

> The thing about Milo is that he does not hide his racism, sexism, anti-Semitism, incitement to harassment against trans and undocumented students [*not referenced by Perry*], and other despicable actions. There's no subtext here, just text.

You don't say. How can Famous Medievalist support someone like Milo? Because I read the primary sources, Milo's own words, rather than relying on media hearsay. Funny that I have such a different impression of him, don't you think?

2018

THE WRONG JOKE IN THE WRONG PLACE: MILO AND M*A*S*H

January 1, 2018

My father served as a surgeon in the US Air Force for two years during the Vietnam War. Stateside, he was stationed from 1970 to 1971 at Offutt Air Force Base in Omaha; in Thailand, he was stationed from 1971 to 1972 at Udorn. We stayed in Omaha while he was abroad. I was only five when we moved to Omaha, so my memories of those years consist primarily of swimming lessons, skating, giant snow drifts, and being baptized[457],[458]—but there is another memory that sticks out that is somewhat less usual.

There was a party for the doctors and their families out by a lake. After dinner, we kids—there were lots of us, all fairly young—had been shooed outside to play in the gloaming, but after exploring the grounds and exhausting the potentials of tag, we got curious about what the grown-ups were doing. We snuck back inside. The lights were down. They were watching a movie! On screen, there were surgeons in their

---

[457] https://fencingbearatprayer.blogspot.com/2012/06/my-baptismal-home.html
[458] https://fencingbearatprayer.blogspot.com/2016/02/that-old-time-religion.html

greens standing over a patient, a woman. As we watched, her belly started swelling and swelling under the sheet, until it was so big that it burst, spraying confetti!

As one kid, we ran horrified from the room, more terrified by what the grown-ups had done when the woman's belly exploded than by what we had seen. What had the grown-ups done that was so frightening? They laughed. And laughed. And laughed. Great big male laughs—most of the doctors were men—but the women laughed, too. They were laughing for eons before we could flee. It was horrible!

I have no idea whether the grown-ups knew we were there. I have a vague memory of someone trying to comfort us, so maybe we screamed when we ran. But I am not sure. They were laughing so loud, all I remember is seeing the confetti burst and not understanding how—*how!*—the grown-ups could think it was funny to see someone suffering like that. It was years before I could process what I had seen and realize the joke.

∽

You have doubtless read some of the January 13, 2017 draft of *Dangerous* that Simon & Schuster's lawyers have filed as evidence in the lawsuit that Milo has brought against the publishing house for cancelling their contract with him. As Andrew Buncombe reported for *The Independent*,

> There is barely a sheet among the 264-page draft that does not contain comments, edits, annotations and entire sections struck through. Written alongside the book's prologue, titled The Art of the Troll, Mr Ivers wrote: "Careful that the egotistical boasting that your audience finds humorous doesn't make you seem juvenile to other readers—especially here."[459]

---

[459] https://www.independent.co.uk/arts-entertainment/music/news/milo-yiannopoulos-book-edits-annotations-simon-schuster-editor-tears-apart-a8132351.html

THE WRONG JOKE IN THE WRONG PLACE: MILO AND M*A*S*H

Over and over again in his editorial comments, Mitchell Ivers called Milo to task:

> Avoid parenthetical insults—they just diminish your authority. Throughout the book you're [sic] best points seem to be lost in a sea of self-aggrandizement and scattershot thinking.

> In a book that will be read by people who don't share your POV, avoid gratuitous insults. They detract from the overall point you're making. In a lecture or a Breitbart column, the audience already shares your POV and sense of humor.

> This section is very well argued but dry. Mixing in humorous quips only works when the quip is genuinely funny to all readers—and not when it diminishes your authority.

> This section is superfluous. After the long dry explanation of Gramsci, it would be better to go to the next section, which is "Why the Left Hates YOU [the reader]."

> These points are stronger without gratuitous insult and teat reference.

> Too important a point to end in a crude quip.

> When you discuss Leslie Jones in this book—AND YOU MUST—don't resort to jokes about her looks.

> Don't start chapter with accusation that feminists=fat. It destroys any seriousness of purpose in a chapter that will (obviously) be closely scrutinized by your critics. If you troll them, they won't listen. You will be speaking ONLY to the already initiated.

> Three unfunny jokes in a row. DELETE.

> This joke feels OLD.

> Dumb joke.

> Gratuitous.

> Inappropriate place for humor.

> Deleting this. It's clearly the wrong joke in the wrong place. At a certain point, you have to decide that the importance of your message is more important than your irreverent side.

This chapter ["Why Black Lives Matter Hates Me"] is so well researched and well argued that you should reconsider the supercilious jokes in it. They detract from what might otherwise be your best chapter.

Sarcasm and sexual humor get in the way of your point here. DELETE.

This whole section has to go. Too much ego at a point when you've had truly eye-opening insights into contemporary media. The ego stuff just trivializes everything.

Too silly to sustain the serious argument you are making.

These abrupt changes in tone in this particularly [sic] chapter do NOT lighten your message with humor. They simply diminish your authority.

This is not the time or place for another black-dick joke.

And so on, for 598 comments in total. Not all of Ivers's comments are critical:

Expand on the idea of trolling as truth-telling—that's something your critics have never considered.

This point about institutionalized racism is very important—it is a distinction that conservatives and liberals can agree on. Racism still exists, but it was legal then [before the Civil Rights Act].

This is a good point [about virtually all art as cultural appropriation]—maybe include in at a later point in the book.

But for the most part, Ivers seems to have seen his role as bringing Milo the Jokester to heel. The argument that Milo was wanting to make—and, therefore, presumably the reason that Simon & Schuster originally agreed to publish his book—was *too serious*. Joking would only diminish Milo's authorial authority. Playing MILO too much would make it impossible for readers to absorb what Milo Yiannopoulos had to say.

荤

I sometimes wonder what my father's patients would think about that movie that made the doctors and their wives all laugh so hard.

Would they be willing to go under his knife knowing that he—and his fellow surgeons—thought it was funny watching a woman's belly explode? Certainly, we kids thought it was "the wrong joke in the wrong place." The last thing we wanted to believe was that our parents—*our parents!*—might find something so—let's face it—*mean* cause for laughter. That woman was suffering! Her belly blew up!

Except, of course, it didn't. And, of course, my father and his colleagues had all seen much, much worse. Dad never talked much with us kids about what he saw while he was in Thailand. He used to show us slides of the golden temple roofs in Thailand, and he brought back wonderful presents—statues of elephants, wicker-work balls, rice-patty hats, a dancing doll. But only once did I catch a glimpse of the *other* slides that he had. Slides of hospital beds. Slides of the men whose bodies had actually blown up and whom he had operated on. You tell me whether it was inappropriate for him and his fellow surgeons to be making jokes.

There was something my father did tell me. One evening when he was at Udorn, the medical staff got a treat. They were going to get to see a movie about—you guessed it—themselves! Except it wasn't exactly themselves. It was about the medical personnel serving a Mobile Army Surgical Hospital during the Korean War, although of course everyone who watched the movie when it came out in 1970 knew it was about the Vietnam War.

As my father told it, everyone on the base was really excited when they heard they were going to get to see the movie. They had all been too busy in the operating room to see the movie in the theater stateside and were delighted that they were going to get to see it on screen. They knew it was a comedy, and they could use a good laugh, especially about the situation they were in. And then the movie started. And the helicopters flew in. And everyone sobered up. I bowdlerize, that

463

is not quite what my father said, but it was close. NOTHING about the movie was in the least bit funny to the surgeons and nurses and other staff at Udorn.

Look at what the poster says: "*M*A*S*H* is what the new freedom of the screen is all about!" "The funniest...you will be bowled over by its wit!" "*M*A*S*H* is the best American war comedy since sound came in." "*M*A*S*H* is a cockeyed masterpiece—see it twice."[460] My siblings and I loved the television series *M*A*S*H*. We loved imagining our father as an *alter Hawkeye*, the heroic and principled surgeon joking his way through saving the soldiers' lives and criticizing the blunders of his superior officers. (Dad was a bit like that.)

Dad hated the show. He hated Alan Alda, whom he saw as a poseur, perhaps for his support of the Equal Rights Amendment (can you say, "male feminist"?), although Dad never said. He hated the way in which the show criticized the war without making a proper argument about why the U.S. had gotten involved. And he hated the jokes, which he thought were unfunny. And yet, he and his fellow surgeons had laughed when the woman's belly blew up. What gives?

❧

This time last January I read the same draft of *Dangerous* that Mitchell Ivers marked up. Milo's more careful readers will recognize that the book published in July had gone through numerous revisions, many taking Ivers's criticisms about Milo's jokes on board. My criticisms were more stylistic. I made lots of suggestions about how better to frame the argument and to set up the narrative Milo wanted to tell. I could tell that what I was reading was a rough draft, and Milo had told me that Simon & Schuster would be doing the copy-editing, so I didn't worry overmuch about his jokes. What I worried about was

---

[460] https://en.wikipedia.org/wiki/MASH_(film)

whether anyone would read his more substantive argument without them.

Do I find all of Milo's jokes funny? Sometimes—I admit it—I cringe, but most of the time I laugh. Not because I think it would be funny if, say, a woman's belly actually burst and spewed forth confetti, but because context matters. And in context, what Milo is saying is deadly serious. As Ivers realized in his editorial comments, in humor audience-POV is everything. Test yourself. Did you think Alda's character Hawkeye was funny? I did—until my father explained the argument behind Hawkeye's jokes. That Hawkeye's position was deeply anti-American, not generically compassionate. That the surgeon Alda played was telling only part of the story. That the men whom my father had been operating on included allies of the United States as well as our own soldiers who were depending on the United States to help them.

Do you think it is funny living in North Korea now? Or that it was funny when the U.S. pulled out of Saigon and the North Vietnamese took over the South? Do you think it is funny when women who have had abortions find themselves plagued for life with guilt? Or when women who are morbidly obese die of the complications of being fat? Do you think it is funny when certain young women ruin certain young men's reputations with false accusations of rape? Or when some young black men shoot other young black men and there are no police to be found?

Do you think it is funny that all criticism of the United States as a country that focuses on the way in which it has failed to live up to its ideals is considered worthy of prime time television, but that any attempt to point to the way in which the United States has been instrumental in furthering those ideals is taken as proof of its systemic racism? Milo doesn't. Nor do I.

֍

There is a word for the kind of jokes that my father and his fellow surgeons laughed at that night by the lake. Gallows humor. A year ago, who knew what 2017 would bring? Not Milo. He had no idea that by February he would have lost his book contract, speaking engagement, and job thanks to a video that showed him making jokes about his own experience of abuse. He had no idea that by September he would have lost even some of his staunchest supporters thanks to an exposé of certain emails that he had written making jokes about issues that he considers deadly serious.

He had no idea that by November all but one of his speaking engagements in the U.S. would be cancelled by threats of violence against the venues he had booked so that his fans could come hear him tell a few jokes about how difficult our cultural situation has become. What he did know, and said even in that early draft of his book, was that somehow the Left had persuaded conservatives that it was *too dangerous to laugh* and that it was his purpose to give them license to push back. Even Ivers seems to have believed that Milo had something serious to say. Why, then, didn't he like Milo's jokes? You decide.

THE TRICKSTER AND THE SHADOW

January 2, 2018

Quick, think of a joke, a really funny joke! I know, it's hard, isn't it? Like, really, really hard. Almost as if it is *wrong* to make jokes, even mild ones, never mind the kinds of jokes that Milo likes to make. I'm sure you've heard about Milo's jokes.[461],[462] Everyone has.[463],[464]

[461] https://www.telegraph.co.uk/books/news/milo-yiannopoulos-lawsuit-documents-do-reveal-book-wasnt-published/

[462] https://www.pastemagazine.com/articles/2017/12/the-editors-notes-on-milo-yiannopoulos-rejected-ma.html

[463] https://www.washingtonpost.com/blogs/erik-wemple/wp/2017/12/28/leave-the-lesbians-out-of-it-who-wants-to-edit-milo-yiannopoulos/?utm_term=.e8383b1d8823

[464] https://www.vulture.com/2017/12/milo-yiannopoulos-book-editor-comments.html

Particularly how unfunny they are, according to some.[465],[466],[467],[468],[469] Here are some of the jokes that Simon & Schuster's copy-editor Mitchell Ivers found particularly unfunny in the first draft of Milo's *Dangerous* (Ivers's comments in italics):

> I can practically hear science fiction authors currently suffering an incursion of social justice feverishly writing stories about traveling through time to bump off [cultural Marxist] Antonio [Gramsci] before he wrote anything influential.—*Unclear, unfunny, delete.*

> Did you notice, by the way, that these stroppy [*whiny*] celebs uniformly threatened to move to [*overwhelmingly*] white countries? ... If it wasn't Canada, it was New Zealand, Australia or another [*primarily*] white, English-speaking country. Why not Mexico or the Gambia? It turns out that the Hollywood Left is even more racist than the high level Nazis, many of whom settled in—shock, horror!—South American compounds after fleeing Germany.—*I don't like using Nazi analogies. Ever. Let other people do that.*

> Apparently I'm more dangerous to women than Charlie Sheen, who accidentally shot women, pulled knives on them and put them at risk of HIV. What am I going to do to a woman, tell [*her*] them to drop 10 lbs and get better highlights?—*Not worth the weak joke.*

> Incidentally, why is it that America's nanny state never controls the really unhealthy behaviors that plague our culture? They will ban large sodas, but not put a waiting period on blue hair dye. They check ID for alcohol purchases if you look younger than 35, but do they weigh feminists before serving them venti frappuchinos? Put a warning label

[465] http://digg.com/2017/milo-yiannopoulos-book-editors-comments-simon-schuster-mitchell-ivers

[466] https://mashable.com/2017/12/28/milo-yiannopoulos-book-notes-edits/#2jdYHf15yOqf

[467] https://www.washingtonpost.com/news/the-intersect/wp/2017/12/28/not-even-funny-editors-markup-of-milo-yiannopoulos-manuscript-draws-ridicule-ire/?utm_term=.da822e8aea94

[468] https://www.theguardian.com/books/2017/dec/28/unclear-unfunny-delete-editors-notes-on-milo-yiannopoulos-book-revealed

[469] https://slate.com/arts/2017/12/the-best-editor-comments-from-milo-dangerous.html

on cigarettes but not on a Bikini Kills record.—*Three unfunny jokes in a row. DELETE.*

According to 2014 figures, American woman have an average life expectancy of 81.2 years. For men, it's 76.4—and it's not just because women are nagging men to death.—*This joke feels OLD.*

Do men's lives matter? Apparently only if they're good-looking enough to make a feminist flip the bean.—*Dumb joke*

Rather than being a twenty-first century version of Amazons, the mythical Greek warrior-women like Xena, modern day feminists are more like a revamped version of the Donner Party. They'll eat their own at any point if they sense their ideology is in trouble.—*Dumb joke*

Rape is terrible. Well, I assume it's terrible for most people. Personally, I've never gotten off faster than when I've had a gun to my temple. My boyfriend will tell you I can't even get hard these days without a knife to my throat. That's just me though.—*Deleting this. It's clearly the wrong joke in the wrong place. At a certain point, you have to decide that the importance of your message is more important than your irreverent side.*

I know, that last one went too far for me, too. Has he made *you* laugh yet? No? Here's a few more:

Despite [my] the obvious degeneracy, I consider myself pretty right-wing. I like to mess with leftists' heads by dressing up in drag and bragging about cum-soaked gay orgies on one evening, and unloading a pump-action shotgun into a placard marked "feminism" while "The Star-Spangled Banner" plays in the background on the next. If Madonna can do it, why not me?—*Joke falls flat here.*

For far too many young black adults in America the only dream they have of escaping a life of poverty is playing professional sports, [or] becoming a music artist, or dating me.—*Again, joke falls flat here.*

You know, if I was fed a constant stream of articles telling me that the world hated me because of the color of my skin, I might burn down a city or three too. I would of course do it much more elegantly than Black Lives Matter. Why is it that no left-wing protestor knows how to rock a good pair of aviators? And why can't they carry their Molotov cocktails around in a Louis Vuitton instead of a drab black rucksack?

For God's sake, lift your pinky when you're throwing rocks at the riot squad! Act like a lady! My goodness, at least the political street thugs of the 1930s had a sense of style! I'd also have the good sense to burn down someone else's neighborhood instead of my own. There's nothing worse than having a good riot only to return home and find that your neighbors burned down your house too, not to mention the pharmacy where you pick up your grandma's medicine.—*Attempts at humor here are too weak and too long.*

Over a million Muslims poured into the Mediterranean to cross into Europe, but rather than opening the gates, the EU should have airdropped soap, shampoo, and conditioner into the sea and then shipped them right back.—*Stupid ethnic joke diminishes any authority.*

They would have at least returned smelling better than the French, Italians, or Greeks.—*Gratuitous*

Of all the groups the Left desperately protects, Islam is the most inherently hilarious. I mean, even their outfits are hilarious. Ridiculous. Is there anything more comically sinister than the sight of a herd of women swathed in black bedsheets?—*This isn't funny enough to be used here.*

Islam preys on the most vulnerable in society, offering them a sense of higher purpose. It's no wonder that gingers convert to Islam in such high numbers, and it might explain Lindsay Lohan, too.—*These abrupt changes in tone in this particularly [sic] chapter do NOT lighten your message with humor. They simply diminish your authority.*

They have especially high conversion rates in jails, [which should be especially concerning to the left but is not.], making Islam and black dick the two things most likely to penetrate new inmates.—*This is not the time or place for another black-dick joke.*

Too much? Yes, I thought so. Here's the thing: *why?* Is Ivers right about these jokes being unfunny? Or is it that they are simply too dark, so that laughing seems wrong, even as you stifle the guffaws?

❧

I have written before about Milo's jokes and asked my Random Laypersons about what they think of them. You may remember what one of them said:

> Milo uses humor to force us to examine our deeply held beliefs—often erroneous beliefs. If you actually listen to him, that is. Those who don't listen cannot possibly understand either what he's saying or what he's doing. Yes, he's a troll, but he's a self-aware troll. And he's funny. It's unfortunate that progressives have no sense of humor, no sense of fun, no notion of the absurd. They miss so much—in life and art.

Or what Milo himself has said about why it is so important to laugh:

> Laughter is one of the first things to leave us when the authoritarians take hold. The thing that tyrants hate the most is the sound of laughter because it means somebody somewhere has gone off script. Someone has gone off message....

> It's often said that in order to find out who has power, who has control in a society, you have to find out who you're not allowed to laugh about. Today that's feminists, Black Lives Matter and Islam. Those are the groups that will get you into trouble if you crack jokes about them. You'll have your newspaper column taken away. You'll be banned from Twitter. Of all these groups, Islam is the most inherently hilarious....

> It's easy to bleat about Christianity. It's low-hanging fruit. It's more difficult, and it takes more bravery, to criticize Islam with sincerity and seriousness. And with jokes.

Look at the jokes that Ivers marked as unfunny, weak, flat, dumb, and OLD. Can you rewrite them so that they would be less offensive? Say, if Milo were making fun of Christians for preying on the weak in society? Or if he said men were nagging women into early graves? Notice that Milo says nothing about the ethnicity of the Muslims swimming the Mediterranean, although Ivers assumes he is making an ethnic (as opposed to a religious) joke.

It is the ethnic Europeans—French, Italians, and Greeks—whom Milo says smell bad. What if he accused male chauvinists of only caring about good-looking women? Or Christian women of looking ridiculous for refusing to cover themselves? What makes a joke funny—and what not? Try it this way: can you think of a joke that is funny while at the same time offensive to *nobody*? Can you think of a side-splitting joke that is *nice*? Of course you can't. There aren't any. Laughter is always at *somebody's* expense. The question is, whose?

§♦

Back in February, now almost a year ago, Jordan Peterson was asked what he thought about Milo.[470] His response: Milo is playing an archetype, that of the Trickster. I said, holy fool, but it amounts to the same thing.[471] But what is a Trickster? In Professor Peterson's words:

> Trickster figures emerge in times of crisis. And they point out what no one wants to see. And they say things that no one will say.... Carl Jung regarded the Trickster as the precursor to the Savior.... It's a very complicated idea. What it basically means is that in order to find your genuine voice or even to move the truth forward, you have to be willing to be a fool. Because you don't know enough really to speak on behalf of the truth. By even attempting to do so you're going to put yourself in an awkward position and make mistakes.... And so you have to be willing to do that. And so that's really Milo's position. He's a provocateur...a comedian.... And comedians say what everyone is thinking but won't say. And that's why people laugh.

So the Trickster is a kind of truth-telling hero, which sounds rather nice, yes? What Jung said was somewhat darker. Indeed, he associated the Trickster directly with the darkest elements of the human psyche, what he called the Shadow. In Jung's words:[472]

---

[470] https://youtu.be/sv17aouIX2Y

[471] [I don't think this anymore; there are important differences between Tricksters and Holy Fools. Milo is playing a holy fool, not a trickster as Professor Peterson describes it, but the similarities are still riveting.]

[472] "On the Psychology of the Trickster-Figure," in *The Archetypes and the Collective Unconscious*, trans. R.F.C. Hall, Collected Works of C.G. Jung 9.1, Bollingen Series XX (1968)

The so-called civilized man has forgotten the trickster. He remembers him only figuratively and metaphorically, when, irritated by his own ineptitude, he speaks of fate playing tricks on him or things being bewitched. He never suspects that his own hidden and apparently harmless shadow has qualities whose dangerousness exceeds his wildest dreams. As soon as people get together in masses and submerge the individual, the shadow is mobilized, and, as history shows, may even be personified and incarnated.

And what happens when the Shadow is incarnated? He shows people who think themselves civilized things they would rather not know about being human:

A minatory and ridiculous figure, [the Shadow] stands at the very beginning of the way of individuation, posing the deceptively easy riddle of the Sphinx, or grimly demanding answer to a "quaestio crocodilina" [a question to which there is no answer other than death]. If, at the end of the trickster myth, the saviour is hinted at, this comforting premonition or hope means that some calamity or other has happened and been consciously understood. Only out of disaster can the longing for the saviour arise—in other words, the recognition and unavoidable integration of the shadow create such a harrowing situation that nobody but a saviour can undo the tangled web of fate.

In a word, the Trickster is *dangerous* because he shows human beings what they look like *to themselves*.

§⚭

Do you still think Milo is simply being mean? Let's look again at the targets of his jokes: cultural critics like Antonio Gramsci who believed that Western civilization ought to be destroyed, celebrities threatening to move to another Anglophone country if Trump won the election, celebrities like Charlie Sheen now infamous for their treatment of women, politicians who institute some legislation on health grounds but not others, feminists who make comments about killing all men, or feminists who go after other women who challenge their interpretation of society.

Or people who assume anyone thinks rape is good, people who try to put each other in boxes and expect them to behave only in certain ways, activists who seem not to care about their own neighborhoods or the effects of their activism on the people they purport to want to help, Leftists who insist that wearing a burka is liberating, Europeans who do not want to acknowledge the change that their culture is going through. Still not funny? Again, why? More than likely, because you see none of these targets as actual threats. You think Milo is making a big deal out of nothing. But what if you're wrong? Here's my theory. To be funny, jokes rely on tapping into the Shadow. They touch on things that we would rather not see about ourselves, that, as Jung says, we have relegated to the unconscious, believing ourselves *better than that.*

If we laugh at a joke—and laughter is almost always involuntary, it is very difficult to make yourself laugh—it tells us something about ourselves that more often than not we would rather not know. That we are cruder than we would like to think. That we are meaner than we would like to believe. That we are as much animals as we are divine. Again, Jung, on the Trickster-myth:

> Anyone who belongs to a sphere of culture that seeks the perfect state somewhere in the past [*he means a Golden Age*] must feel very queerly indeed when confronted by the figure of the trickster. He is a forerunner of the saviour, and, like him, God, and, and animal at once. He is both subhuman and superhuman, a bestial and divine being, whose chief and most alarming characteristic is his unconsciousness.

> Because of it [in the stories] he is deserted by his (evidently human) companions, which seems to indicate that he has fallen below their level of consciousness. He is so unconscious of himself that his body is not a unity, and his two hands fight each other. He takes his anus off and entrusts it with a special task [*thus the black-dick jokes?*]. Even his sex is optional despite its phallic qualities: he can turn himself into a woman [*remember Ivana Wall?*] and bear children. From his penis

he makes all kinds of useful plants. This is a reference to his original nature as a Creator, for the world is made from the body of a god.

On the other hand he is in many respects stupider than the animals, and gets into one ridiculous scrape after another. Although he is not really evil, he does the most atrocious things from sheer unconsciousness and unrelatedness. His imprisonment in animal unconsciousness is suggested by the episode where he gets his head caught inside the skull of an elk, and the next episode shows how he overcomes this condition by imprisoning the head of a hawk inside his own rectum. True, he sinks back into the former condition immediately afterwards, by falling under the ice, and is outwitted time after time by the animals, but in the end he succeeds in tricking the cunning coyote, and this brings back to him his saviour nature.

The trickster is a primitive "cosmic" being of *divine-animal* nature, on the one hand superior to man because of his superhuman qualities, and on the other hand inferior to him because of his unreason and unconsciousness. He is no match for the animals either, because of his extraordinary clumsiness and lack of instinct. These defects are the marks of his *human* nature, which is not so well adapted to the environment as the animal's but, instead, has prospects of a much higher development of consciousness based on a considerable eagerness to learn, as is duly emphasized in myth.

Can you believe the trouble Milo has gotten into just this past year? Riots cancelling his talks, journalists calling him the most appalling names, his friends abandoning him, his investors pulling out. Talk about being bewitched! And yet, throughout—by my own witness—he has been unfailingly eager to learn.

❧

I have said it before, but I will say it again, just to be clear: I do not think Milo is anything other than a gifted young man, however much he may be playing with myth in the characters he assumes. But I do think that his gifts include an uncanny willingness to confront the Shadow both in others and in himself. How he came to this

475

willingness is a question even I do not know him well enough to answer, although my motherly intuition tells me that it was not easy. Milo himself would most likely point to his being gay, never able, as he has often said, to make children with the person he loves. In his book manuscript, of course, the way he put it was somewhat darker, as befits the archetype he is playing:

> Gay men are chaos incarnate. We are gods of mirth, mischief, danger and subversion....

> We have an energy and power over everyone else, a dark, innate perversion and malevolence that other would-be rebels like goths and punks would kill to have. Gay sex is a dark act. It is black magic— especially the way I like it. It defies biology, and as much as I enjoy it in every room of the house, the club or the public bathroom, it belongs in the closet....

> When gay men exercise risk, they have an advantage—as the chosen ones on the outskirts willing to be the outlet for anyone and everyone's fantasies. As society's subversive rebels, we can go further than anyone else....

> I do consider this part of myself to be wrong. But I also *like* being wrong. I get off on being a degenerate. And that's why I don't get angry when the alt-right use the phrase—on the contrary. I encourage it! Because society needs purity, and society needs degeneracy. As an agent of chaos, I'll defend the agents of order, because I know I need them to exist.

Milo the Degenerate knows that he needs us, his civilized friends, in order to exist. Are we willing to admit that we need him, too?

JORDAN, MILO AND THE BITCH QUEEN

February 2, 2018

I've told you how I saw the interview between Jordan Peterson and Cathy Newman as a Christian and as a fencer.[473],[474] Now it is time to tell you how I saw it as a woman. Cathy Newman is a bitch. Of course she is, that is her stock-in-trade. It was on display a year ago when she interviewed Milo, and it was there in spades when she was talking with Jordan. She was not interested in having a productive conversation with either Milo or Jordan. She—as an empowered woman—wanted to take them both out.

She had a harder time with Milo.[475] He just laughed at her accusations, incredulous at how she twisted what he said into purported evidence that he did not believe in equality for women or that he believed women had no place in the workforce—or on the internet. Jordan, however, she got to—big time.[476] Yes, there was that moment when

[473] https://fencingbearatprayer.blogspot.com/2018/01/a-cheek-for-cheek.html

[474] https://fencingbearatprayer.blogspot.com/2018/01/why-jordan-peterson-lost-that-bout-to.html

[475] https://youtu.be/eJiNeCBpCHQ

[476] https://youtu.be/aMcjxSThD54

he turned on her and pointed out how willing she was to be offensive and how uncomfortable it made him.

But for the most part, he played the gentleman, turning the other cheek to her accusations and trying to make his argument without offending her. (Good luck with that!) Even after he achieved his "gotcha" moment he wasn't trying to dominate her, quite the reverse. He was holding firm against her attacks, but he did *not* want to hit her back. She did. She wanted to *hurt*. Oh, she had no intention of physically challenging either Milo or Jordan. But she wanted to hurt them. You can see it in her eyes, hear it in her voice. "Answer me," she demands of Milo. "Should women just give up trying and go play with their Cindy dolls?" she challenges Jordan. Classic bitch queen tactics, to which there is no polite answer.

Honey Badger Radio has an outstanding analysis of the way in which Newman played her hand against Peterson, turning his desire to keep from hurting her into a victory for her after the fact.[477] Men—at least, chivalrous men, which in the West means most men; other cultures arguably have other standards—do *not* like hurting or dominating women. It is, if you will, their kryptonite, which women like Newman use against them all the time. I say, women like Newman, but we've all done it at some point, haven't we, ladies? You've heard yourself use questions like Cathy's against your husband or boyfriend. You know *exactly* what she was doing. *Own it.* And be more compassionate. It's what women are supposed to be good at, right?

Caring. Yeah, right. Even Jordan falls into that stereotype when Cathy is badgering him about what women-led companies might be like. Sure, he suggests, you might run the experiment and make a company more "compassionate" and "caring" towards its workers and see how that turned out. "Why not?" When all the while he is having

---

[477] https://youtu.be/akpHo67e-ik

a conversation with a woman who is the antithesis of compassionate and caring towards him.

How on earth did men ever get the idea that women are compassionate and caring in the first place? Because without us, they have nothing to live for. Okay, maybe not Milo—he has John—but men like Jordan? He talks about it all the time! Women are what inspire him: his daughter, his wife. He cares about them deeply and wants to make a good life for them. Which means taking on the sacrifices that he needs to in order to grow the hell up and succeed. But it terrifies him. You can see that, too. Just look what he says about Adam and Eve. There was Eve, tempted by the snake to eat the fruit, and there was Adam, the poor dope, going along with her. She eats the fruit and gets self-conscious, so she gives some to him—and he gets even worse. He gets conscious of *her* judging *him*. In Jordan's words:

> Now, no clear-seeing, conscious woman is going to tolerate an unawakened man. So, Eve immediately shares the fruit with Adam. That makes *him* self-conscious. Little has changed. Women have been making men self-conscious since the beginning of time. They do this primarily by rejecting them—but they also do it by shaming them, if men do not take responsibility. Since women bear the primary burden of reproduction, it's no wonder. It is very hard to see how it could be otherwise. But the capacity of women to shame men and render them self-conscious is still a primal force of nature.[478]

"So are you saying," the Cathys of the world would reply, "that women should be meek and sweet just because men are afraid of them?" No—but we should not be hypocrites about it either. They *are* afraid of us, just look at them. Working all hours of the day and night to make us more comfortable, out there in the street laying gas lines, out on the oil rigs risking their lives to get us energy, staying up

---

[478] *12 Rules for Life: An Antidote to Chaos* (2018)

late into the night writing managerial reports and legal briefs. Work, work, work, work, work.

Men do the most physically dangerous jobs so that women like Cathy—and me—can sit around writing lengthy tomes about how oppressed women are because they aren't in charge of enough Fortune 500 companies or head of more academic institutions. Give me a break. Do you want to know why I have always hated gender studies? Because the only question that anybody seems to care about in gender studies is why women don't have more power. Over and over again. "How did women exercise authority?" "How did women assert control?" "Why aren't women more in charge?" You'd almost think we were back in the Dark Ages.

Remember the Wife of Bath's tale? We read it in high school, and it took me a long time to figure out what the punchline meant, probably because at that time the thing that I wanted most was a boyfriend and there were no takers. Except there were—I just wasn't interested in the young men who were interested in me. What is it that women most desire according to the Wife of Bath? *Sovereignty.*

We want to rule over our men, shame them into growing the hell up so that they will be good husbands and fathers and take care of us when we have children. The stakes are high—as Jordan acknowledges. You want to risk having a child with a man who won't be there to fight off the dragons? Not me. But the choice is the woman's, as it should be. And men know it and fear us because they are nothing unless we say yes. *No wonder Milo finds it a relief to be gay. Who wants to be subject to a Cathy?*

WHY FEMINISM IS CANCER

February 8, 2018

Feminism is cancer because it is built on a lie. Actually, it is built on a whole pyramid of lies, but there is one gigantic one at its base. Here it is in its most diabolical form. The author is Ludwig Feuerbach, his translator the novelist George Eliot, the work his *Essence of Christianity*, published in English in 1854:

> But here it is also essential to observe, and this phenomenon is an extremely remarkable one, characterising the very core of religion, that in proportion as the divine subject is in reality human, the greater is the apparent difference between God and man; that is, the more, by reflection on religion, by theology, is the identity of the divine and human denied, and the human, considered as such, is depreciated.... To enrich God, man must become poor; that God may be all, man must be nothing....

> The monks made a vow of chastity to God; they mortified the sexual passion in themselves, but therefore they had in heaven, in the Virgin Mary, the image of woman—an image of love. They could the more easily dispense with real women in proportion as an ideal woman was an object of love to them. *The greater the importance they attached to the denial of sensuality, the greater the importance of the heavenly virgin for them: she was to them in the place of Christ, in the stead of God.*

Do you see what Feuerbach did here? Do you see how he foreshadowed almost every argument made ever since about the meaning of Mary, God's mother? About how she was, in effect, the monks' pin-up girl because they were deprived of the company of actual women? About how, whatever devotion they had to her, it must have been about sex—and putting a woman in place of God? Do you understand why this argument is literally diabolical? Do you understand the pride in insisting that God takes away from man his identity, making man poor so that God—in Feuerbach's formulation, the abstraction of all human values projected onto the imaginary object which is then imagined as acting as a subject back on man—might become rich?

Do you understand how it undercuts everything in the proper relationship between the sexes, not to mention between God and man? Satan himself could not have phrased it better—or more deceptively. Do you see the lie yet? No? Let's fast forward then to 1949. Here it is, even more explicitly, in the founding manifesto of modern feminism, Simone de Beauvoir's *The Second Sex*:

> Paradoxically, it was Christianity that was to proclaim the equality of man and woman on a certain level. Christianity detests the flesh in her; if she rejects the flesh, she is, like him, a creature of God, redeemed by the Savior: here she can take her place beside males, among those souls guaranteed celestial happiness....

> Of course, the divine Savior who brings about Redemption is male; but humanity must cooperate in its own salvation, and perversely it will be called upon to manifest its submissive goodwill in its most humiliated figure. Christ is God; but it is a woman, the Virgin Mother, who reigns over all human creatures. Yet only marginal sects restore the great goddesses' ancient privileges to the woman. The Church expresses and serves a patriarchal civilization where it is befitting for woman to remain annexed to man. As his docile servant, she will also be a blessed saint....

For the first time in the history of humanity, the mother kneels before her son; she freely recognizes her inferiority. The supreme masculine victory is consummated in the cult of Mary: it is the rehabilitation of woman by the achievement of her defeat. Ishtar, Astarte, and Cybele were cruel, capricious, and lustful; they were powerful; the source of death as well as life, in giving birth to men, they made them their slaves. With Christianity, life and death now depended on God alone....

Nature is originally bad, but powerless when countered with grace. Motherhood as a natural phenomenon confers no power. If woman wishes to overcome the original stain in herself, her only alternative is to bow before God, whose will subordinates her to man. And by this submission she can assume a new role in masculine mythology....

As a servant, woman is entitled to the most splendid apotheosis.[479]

Yet again, it is God who is the thief, here, however, acting in the service of "patriarchal civilization," according to which the only value—horror of horrors!—that women have is in being an object for men. Mary supplants Christ in reigning over human creatures, but God still reigns over her, the Son forcing her to kneel before him. Christianity—or so de Beauvoir insists—is the author of the lie keeping women in second place. The pagan goddesses were divine in their own right, enslaving men even as they gave birth to them. Mary, on the other hand, is a mere servant in her elevation.

You believe de Beauvoir, don't you? You believe that Christianity has been bad for women. You believe that Mary, in humbling herself before God, lost everything that made her a potential model for women. You believe that Christianity stripped the goddesses of their rightful womanhood—and that Christianity honored women only insofar as they were subordinated to—or became like—men, rational and purified of the flesh. Of course you do. Erich Neumann said so in *The Great Mother*, his magisterial account of the archetypal feminine published in 1955. Here is the lie again, in Neumann's words:

---

[479] Trans. Constance Borde and Sheila Malovany-Chevallier (2011)

Thus the spiritual power of Sophia [Wisdom] is living and saving; her overflowing heart is wisdom and food at once. The nourishing life that she communicates is a life of the spirit and of transformation, not one of earthbound materiality.

As spirit mother, she is not, like the Great Mother of the lower phase, interested primarily in the infant, the child, and the immature man, who cling to her in these stages. She is rather a goddess of the Whole, who governs the transformation from the elementary to the spiritual level; who desires who men knowing life in all its breadth, from the elementary phase to the phase of spiritual transformation.

In the patriarchal development of the Judaeo-Christian West, with its masculine, monotheistic trend toward abstraction, the goddess, as a feminine figure of wisdom, was disenthroned and repressed. She survived only secretly, for the most part on heretical and revolutionary bypaths.[480]

There it is again! The claim that Christianity—or, rather, the Judeo-Christian West—was "patriarchal," hellbent (to coin a phrase) on repressing the "feminine figure of wisdom." Elsewhere—Neumann points to "the Orient"—the goddess managed to hold her own. But here in the West, she was pushed into the shadows by the "masculine, monotheistic trend toward abstraction" (see Feuerbach, above) to return, according to Neumann, only as a witch. Have you spotted the lie yet? Here's a hint: it has to do with God.

How do you know that Christianity is "patriarchal" and concerned more with monotheistic abstraction than with the flesh? How do you know that it suppressed the feminine and made Mary a figure of submission for women? How do you know the only reason medieval monks devoted themselves to Mary was because they were not allowed to have sex? How do you know that Mary's submission to God represents the victory of the masculine over the feminine? How do you know that Christianity made women the second sex? I'll tell you. Because enlightened idiots like Feuerbach and de Beauvoir and

---

[480] Trans. Ralph Manheim (1963)

484

Neumann told you so—and lies, as Satan knows, are always easier to believe than the truth.

∾

The medieval Christians whom modern philosophers, feminists, and psychoanalysts loved to despise had a much more sophisticated understanding of the feminine—and of God—than their cultured despisers ever allowed. Not only did they *not* "disenthrone and repress" the Virgin; neither did they use her as a kind of porn. (They had God for that.[481],[482]) Quite the reverse. Medieval Christians put Mary on a magnificent throne, elevated high above every creature in Creation, because she herself was a throne for God.

"Come, my chosen one," they imagined Christ saying to her, "and I will place my throne in you because the king has desired your beauty." And what a throne she was! "O truly blessed, O truly stable throne," the Franciscan preacher Conrad of Saxony (d. 1279) hailed her in his popular *Mirror of the Blessed Virgin Mary*, a commentary on the Ave Maria,

> just as it is said in 3 Kings 8:13: Thy most firm throne for ever. This most high throne is in the intellect, raised up on the affections; it is most high over men, raised up over angels.... On this throne, Mary, on this throne, I say, of her mind, the Lord was seated, and the house of her body was full of the majesty of the Incarnate Word.... Therefore, it is said in 3 Kings 8:11-12: The glory of the Lord had filled the house of the Lord. Then Solomon said: "The Lord said that he would dwell in a cloud." Therefore, the house of the Lord, Mary, was filled with the glory of the divine majesty by the cloud of the humanity assumed by God; that cloud, I say, of which it is said in Ecclesiasticus 43:24: The medicine of all is in the speedy coming of a cloud. And again in Ecclesiasticus 50:6: [He shone in his days] as the morning star in the midst of a cloud. For like the star in a cloud is the Word in the flesh assumed by him.

---

[481] https://fencingbearatprayer.blogspot.com/2017/01/gods-vagina.html
[482] https://fencingbearatprayer.blogspot.com/2017/01/lies-of-left-gender-fluidity.html

Far from rejecting the flesh assumed from the Virgin—as de Beauvoir would have it—God reveled in it, taking her flesh and glorifying it in the flesh of her Son. Likewise, far from denying the spiritual power of the feminine—as Neumann would have it—medieval Christians like Conrad and his contemporaries Richard of St. Laurent (d. ca. 1250) and pseudo-Albert the Great (the heroes of my new book on Mary, if you haven't guessed) identified her explicitly as Wisdom and the Mother of Wisdom, her mind the most perfect mirror of the divine in which the Lord took up his throne. In pseudo-Albert's words:

> That the most blessed Virgin was wiser than any other creature, is indicated by the fact that the book which is entitled *Wisdom* is especially interpreted concerning her: the Church interprets what is said of the Lord's wisdom as if it is said of her, as is evident in the epistles [that is, the lessons for the Office and Mass] which are read of her. In wisdom, however, there is nothing of stupidity or ignorance: therefore the most blessed Virgin was full of wisdom. But in faith, wisdom is not full, but only in part, as it is said: *For we know in part, and we prophesy in part* (I Corinthians 13:9). Therefore, the most blessed Virgin did not have faith, but full knowledge.

And what did the Virgin know? According to pseudo-Albert, *everything*: all the arts, all the sciences, the whole of the law, both canon and civil; everything in the book of the *Sentences* (the textbook of theology used in the schools); everything pertaining to the Trinity, to angels, and to the six days of Creation; everything pertaining to the Incarnation of the Word, the sacraments, and the Resurrection, to the past, present, and future, and to the kingdom of God. (How's that for an empowered woman? STEM fanatics take note.) Indeed, Richard insisted, so perfectly was Mary illuminated by the Divinity whose dwelling she was, that

> ...in God, so to speak, she was deified (*deificata*), made a participant in divine eternity, without corners or turnings. *From behind* [Richard is commenting on the description of Solomon's throne, 3 Kings 10:18-

19] means the end of the body: because in life there is no perfect happiness, but only in the life to come. Then the likeness of the divine image (*divine imagines similitudo*) will shine forth in our mind or understanding through our memory, reason, and will.

Feuerbach would insist that God exists only insofar as human beings, having consciousness of themselves as a species, see themselves acted upon by the object of their abstraction. In his words:

> The divine being is nothing else than the human being, or, rather, the human nature purified, freed from the limits of the individual man, made objective—i.e. contemplated and revered as another, a distinct being.

In Feuerbach's thinking, God exists insofar as the attributes of human nature exist; man mirrors God because God mirrors man. For Richard, it was Mary who was the most perfect mirror, the one in whom Wisdom saw Wisdom made flesh:

> Mary is an *unspotted mirror* for the souls of the faithful, in which they ought to gaze continuously. For so great is her purity that anything greater [than she] under God cannot be thought, just as blessed Anselm says; for she was worthy to conceive him, as Jerome says, who reformed in us the image deformed by the old Adam, when through her love and obedience the wax of human nature was made warm and pliable and was impressed once again with the seal, that is, the Son of God, in her virginal womb.

Mary, the Mother of the Word, was herself the most perfect human being because in her body and soul was realized the most perfect reflection of the divine. Far from being subjected to her Son by her love and obedience, Mary became his most perfect likeness. As woman, in other words, Mary realized—made real—God. Some pin-up girl, eh?

❧

This is the great lie of feminism, the cancer at the heart of modernity: the claim that Christianity made less of humanity, made less of woman in its meditation on the relationship of Mary to God. All the lies on which the modern critique of the "patriarchy" rests are metastases of this great cancer. The lie that in Christianity the created, material world was considered evil or worthless. The lie that in Christianity only the masculine virtues were valued. The lie that because God became incarnate as a man motherhood was demeaned.

The lie that God demands our subjection because Mary humbled herself to serve the Lord. No wonder the feminists are so angry. Everything they believe about the relationship between women and men, humanity and God, is based on a lie about Mary's relationship with her Son. I wonder where that lie came from. Or from whom.

ALMA MATER, OR WHY MILO SITS ON A LION THRONE

February 11, 2018

I never set out to teach like a woman, but somehow it happened anyway. Back when I was a beginning teacher, my great hero was Erich Auerbach, more particularly, Erich Auerbach as the author of *Mimesis: The Representation of Reality in Western Literature* (1953). His whole method seemed to me to be genius. He would start each chapter with a lengthy block of text, which he would then use as a key to unlock the underlying patterns of Western culture, wondrously made visible through his close reading of the text.

You can see how I use this technique in my blog posts, but it comes from my teaching.[483] In effect, I encourage my students, "Submit yourself to the word, and let it teach you. If you read carefully, thinking about what the text tells you about why the author was writing and paying attention to what it can tell you about the circumstances in which the author found it important to write, that is when it becomes a proper historical source, something in which you are able to ground an argument."

---

[483] https://home.uchicago.edu/~rfulton/Masterclass.pdf

My goal in training to students to read this way is to give them confidence in their ability to interpret the evidence, while at the same time encouraging them learn to read the texts for their own sake. I see myself in the classroom not so much as an authority in the sense of the one who knows everything—although, by this stage in my career, I know a hell of a lot!—but rather as a guide.

What I want is to provide a frame in which texts that the students have previously found boring, irrelevant, or otherwise inaccessible become *possible* to read. To paraphrase the Lorax: I speak for the texts. I am, as it were, their advocate. Through me, I want to help the texts come to life. Through me, I want to make what they say visible to the world. Kinda like—dare I say it?—Mary, who gave birth to the Word.

৵

Have you ever wondered why we call colleges our "alma mater"—"nourishing mother"? The Wikipedia entry notes that the epithet goes back to antiquity as applied to certain mother goddesses, but that in an educational context, it first appears around 1600 when the Cambridge printer John Legate began using it in his emblem for the university press.[484] But before that, in a Christian context, it referred, of course, to the Virgin Mary. "Alma Redemptoris Mater," sang the eleventh-century monk, mathematician, and astronomer Hermannus Contractus ("Herman the Lame"):

> Nourishing mother of the Redeemer, star of the sea who holds open the gate of heaven, help your people who have fallen to rise again: you who to the amazement of nature gave birth to your Creator, virgin after as before, you who received the Ave from Gabriel's mouth, have mercy on us sinners.

I have blogged already about the way in which, in the Middle Ages, Mary was seen as the one who made God visible to the world,

---

[484] https://en.wikipedia.org/wiki/Alma_mater

the temple in whom the Lord became present in his Creation.[485] And I have blogged about how medieval Christians saw her as Wisdom and the Mother of Wisdom, the most perfect mirror of God.[486] Now I would like to tell you about how she gave birth to the universities. It had to do with her relationship to texts. Particularly texts talking about her and her Son.

According to the Protestants (long story—it has to do with changes to the Hebrew on which the Protestants based their translations of the Old Testament), the scriptures that they inherited from the medieval tradition spoke very little about Mary; only the Gospels had any real information about her. But according to the medieval tradition going back to the Orthodox interpretation of the scriptures in Greek, not only the Gospels, but all the texts of the Bible, including the Old Testament, spoke about Mary just as they spoke about her Son: *all the time*. This is the way one twelfth-century author put the puzzle in his *Speculum virginum* or *Mirror of Virgins*:

> If I tried to say anything about the Lord's Mother it would be an act of reckless presumption rather than learning. For the magnitude of grace divinely granted to Mary exceeds my faculty of speech, since she was chosen before she was born to conceive the eternal Word, and crowned once born with the perfection of all blessings.

Nevertheless, he would try:

> She then is the bride of the eternal king; she is daughter, mother, and virgin; dove, sister, and beloved; unique mother of the unique Son of God, foreordained in heaven before she was born to be the Mother of God's Son....

> She is the dawn, the sun, the moon, and the star: the dawn preceding the Sun of justice in its rising; the sun in whom the Creator himself set the tabernacle of his body, and came forth like a bridegroom from his

---

[485] https://fencingbearatprayer.blogspot.com/2018/02/your-mother-wants-you-home-jordan-and.html

[486] https://fencingbearatprayer.blogspot.com/2018/02/why-feminism-is-cancer.html

chamber; the moon radiant from its Creator's splendor...; and the star of the sea, because she is the path, the harbor, and the life of sailors in this worldly darkness. In paradise she is the flower and fruit of trees that exude the finest balsam, and the green shoot of all spices....

Since she is mother and virgin, she is revealed by a mystic figure in the bush that burned and was not consumed. In the tabernacle of Moses, fashioned with such variety of materials and such marvelous art, she is supremely figured in the branch of Aaron and the golden urn. She is the dry branch that flowered among the other dry branches, bearing flower and fruit before the whole mass of humankind which had withered in sin....

The golden urn which preserved the manna symbolizes the purity of her mind and body in its gold, displaying the manna—that is, the Word of God, "the food of angels" [Wisdom 16:20]—to all the faithful. Do you see that all the labor of the wondrous tabernacle and its most precious hangings—"in gold and silver, purple and linen, twice-dyed scarlet" and every precious stone [Exodus 25:3-4]—pertained to those four things [the tabernacle, the ark, the golden urn, and the branch of Aaron] in which the future mysteries of the Mother and Son were chiefly hidden for our future age?....

Indeed, you will find many things proclaiming and bearing witness to the Lord's Mother in the prophets' writings and miracles, and if we were to scrutinize and discuss every one of them, our dialogue would exceed all bounds. For what speech can contain her whom the Son of God chose from before the commencement of time to be his temple... who alone was preserved to redeem humankind? .... All these things, wrapped and veiled in symbolic foreshadowings, have been revealed to our age more clearly than light by the gracious gifts of heaven....

If then you seek Mary with a subtle understanding, you will find her in heaven before all creation; you will see her in paradise and in Noah's ark in the flood; you will see her among the patriarchs and wandering with the people of God in the desert; you will find her among the judges and kings coming forth from the royal stock and blooming among the Jews like a rose among thorns.[487]

---

[487] Trans. Barbara Newman, in Constant Mews, *Listen Daughter* (2001)

Would you like me to explain what our author—he calls himself Peregrinus or "Pilgrim"—is saying in this text? Not just the quotations taken verbatim from the scriptures (Wisdom, Exodus), but all of the images that Peregrinus invokes are allusions to titles of Mary that her ancient and medieval devotees found in scripture. She is the bride, daughter, and mother of the king found in Psalm 44 (45). She is the dove, sister, and beloved found in the Song of Songs. She is the dawn, sun, and moon of Song of Songs 6:9, and the tabernacle of Psalm 18 (19):6. She is the tree of life giving forth flowers and fruits of Revelation 22:2; and she is the tree giving forth balsam of Ecclesiasticus 24:20-21.

She is the burning bush from which the Lord spoke to Moses (Exodus 3:2) and the tabernacle fashioned according to the pattern shown to Moses on the mountain (Exodus 25). And she is the ark in which the rod of Aaron and the golden urn of manna were stored (Numbers 17:2-8; Exodus 16:33-34; Hebrews 9:4). The only image that is not strictly speaking taken from scripture is that of Mary as the star of the sea (*stella maris*), but even this was simply a pun on her name (*Maria*).

What should we do with such a myriad of names? Erich Neumann—if, that is, he knew anything about the ancient and medieval Christian tradition[488]—would point to the way in which such titles were applied

---

[488] Really, he didn't: "This patriarchal consciousness that says, 'The victory of the male lies in the spiritual principle,' devaluates the moon and the feminine element to which it belongs. It is 'merely of the soul,' 'merely' the highest form of an earthly and material development that stands in opposition to the 'pure spirit' that in its Apollonian-Platonic and Jewish-Christian form has led to the abstract conceptuality of modern consciousness. But this modern consciousness is threatening the existence of Western mankind, for the one-sidedness of masculine development has led to a hypertrophy of consciousness at the expense of the whole man." Note how Neumann blames the "patriarchal" Judeo-Christian tradition as a whole. My guess: Neumann had been reading too much Nietzsche.

to the Great Mother. Vessel, tree, oven, ship, city, mountain, gate, temple, house: all were images of Mary that ancient and medieval Christians found in the scriptures, above all in the books of Wisdom and in the psalms. In Neumann's words:[489]

> The abundance of manifestations is a characteristic of the archetype and the plethora of names by which the powers are invoked among all peoples is an expression of their numinous ineffability.

Even the lion was associated with Mary, as her Son, the true Solomon, sat on his lion throne (3 Kings 10:18-20), that is, on her. Again, Neumann:

> The enthroned Mother Goddess lives in the sacred symbol of the throne. The king comes to power by "mounting the throne," and so takes his place on the lap of the Great Goddess, the earth—he becomes her son. In widespread throne cults, the throne, which was originally the godhead itself, was worshiped as the "seat of the godhead."

As, for example, in the magnificent ivory triptych at the Walters Art Museum in Baltimore, in which Christ is enthroned in majesty on the lap of his mother.[490] Everything in Creation was contained by the Virgin, she—as her medieval devotees sang—who enclosed the Creator of all things in her womb. To know the Virgin was to know everything because it was through her that the Creator of everything became visible to the world. Again, Neumann, speaking of the Great Mother archetype:

> In its entire phenomenology, the elementary character of the Feminine appears as the Great Round, which is and contains the universe.... Now that we have gained some idea of the full scope of the Great Mother, who in truth encompasses almost everything—heaven, water, and earth, while even fire is her son—it becomes evident that the Feminine cannot be identified with the telluric-chthonic, the lower, earthly principle, as the later patriarchal world and its religions and philosophies would

---

[489] *The Great Mother*, trans. Ralph Manheim (1963)

[490] https://art.thewalters.org/detail/36652/opening-madonna-triptych/

have it. The totality of the Archetypal Feminine goes far beyond the projection in which she unites the elements of earth, water, air, and fire.

Mary's medieval devotees would agree! "Not only heaven and earth," or so one anonymous preacher commenting on the antiphon *Salve regina* put it,

> but also other names (*aliis nominibus*) and words of things (*rerum vocabulis*) fittingly designate the Lady. She is the tabernacle of God, the temple, the house, the entry-hall, the bedchamber, the bridal-bed, the bride, the daughter, the ark of the flood, the ark of the covenant, the golden urn, the manna, the rod of Aaron, the fleece of Gideon, the gate of Ezekiel, the city of God, the heaven, the earth, the sun, the moon, the morning star, the dawn, the lamp, the trumpet, the mountain, the fountain of the garden and the lily of the valley, the desert, the land of promise flowing with milk and honey, the star of the sea, the ship, the way in the sea, the fishing net, the vine, the field, the ark, the granary, the stable, the manger of the beast of burden, the store-room, the court, the tower, the castle, the battle-line, the people, the kingdom, the priesthood,

Nor was this all.

> She is the sheep, the pasture, the paradise, the palm, the rose, the river, the draught, the dove, the column, the clothing, the pearl, the candelabra, the table, the crown, the scepter, the bread, the oil, the wine, the tree, the rod, the cedar, the cypress, the plane tree, the cinnamon, the balsam, the myrrh, the frankincense, the olive, the nard, the crocus, the reed, the pipe, the pen, the gum, the sister and mother.

"Indeed," the preacher apologized, "that I might briefly conclude, all scripture was written concerning her and about her and because of her, and for her the whole world was made, she who is full of the grace of God and through whom man has been redeemed, the Word of God made flesh, God humbled and man sublimed."[491] This, according to Neumann, is what the Great Mother does: she gives voice

---

[491] *Sermon on the Salve Regina*, trans. Fulton Brown, *Mary and the Art of Prayer* (2017)

to the poets, words to the flesh, transforming the Son who enters into her that he might go forth into the world as a hero and savior. In Neumann's words:

> We have repeatedly referred to the spiritual aspect of the feminine transformative character, which leads through suffering and death, sacrifice and annihilation, to renewal, rebirth, and immortality. But such transformation is possible only when what is to be transformed enters wholly into the Feminine principle; that is to say, dies in returning to the Mother Vessel, whether this be earth, water, underworld, urn, coffin, cave, mountain, ship, or magic cauldron....
>
> [She, in the guise of the seeress,] is the center of magic, of magical song, and finally of poetry. She is the source from which Odin received the runes of Wisdom; she is the Muse, the source of the words that stream upward from the depths; and she is the inspiring anima of the poets....
>
> This transformation presents a typical opposition to the Masculine, whose transfiguration appears as an illumination of the head— solification, coronation, and halo. True to her feminine nature, Kore [the goddess of the Eleusian mysteries] becomes a "bearer" of light. Her luminous aspect, the fruit of her transformative process, becomes the luminous son, the divine spirit-son, spiritually conceived and spiritually born, whom she holds on her lap, or who is handed up to her by her creative Earth Mother aspect.

Neumann could almost be describing our ivory. Look! It opens to reveal the suffering, sacrifice, and resurrection of the Word made flesh in Mary's womb, he who filled her mind with wisdom even as he took from her the flesh in which he entered into the world. Ultimately, Neumann is right about the power of the Great Mother, but for the wrong reasons. He insists that she survived in Christianity only on the margins, in spite of the "patriarchal" masculinity of her wordy Son.

But Mary was known in her guise as Great Mother throughout the Middle Ages, not because the medieval Christians were crypto-pagans, but because they knew how to read the scriptures about her according to the tradition going back to the temple as recorded in the psalms.

(If you want the full story, it's in my book! For a shorter version, go here.[492]) Mary was the *alma mater* of the medieval theologians, poets, commentators, and artists because in her the Creator of all things took his rest (Ecclesiasticus 24:14-15). She was the throne of Wisdom and the Mother of Wisdom, the one through whom God spoke his Word, and therefore the patroness of the trivium, the arts of language taught in the schools.[493]

The masters of the theology faculty at Paris took her as their patroness on their seals, and the students at Eton College said Matins in her honor while making their beds. As even Henry Adams realized, although again for reasons he did not understand, she was the Muse inspiring the construction of the great Gothic cathedrals as well as the Lady to whom the troubadours sang. Without Mary, Western medieval art is inconceivable, not to mention the study of the natural world, all of whose creatures she framed. (Yes, I show this in *Mary and the Art of Prayer*, too!)

&❧

"O splendid jewel," the Benedictine abbess Hildegard of Bingen (d. 1179) sang to Mary,

> ...serenely infused with the Sun! The Sun is in you as a fount from the heart of the Father; it is His sole Word, by Whom He created the world, the primary matter, which Eve threw into disorder. He formed the Word in you as a human being, and therefore you are the jewel that shines most brightly, through whom the Word breathed out the whole of the virtues, as once from primary matter He made all creatures.

> O sweet green branch that flowers from the stem of Jesse! O glorious thing, that God on His fairest daughter looked as the eagle looks on the face of the Sun! The Most High Father sought for a Virgin's candor, and willed that His Word should take in her His body. For the Virgin's

---

[492] https://www.academia.edu/20444220/MARY_IN_THE_SCRIPTURES_THE_UNEXPURGATED_TRADITION_The_Theotokos_Lectures_in_Theology_7_
[493] https://home.uchicago.edu/~rfulton/Trivium.htm

mind was by His mystery illumined, and from her virginity sprang the glorious Flower.[494]

How the Christian tradition lost sight of the Virgin infused with the Sun is a story I do not entirely understand yet. It begins in the sixteenth century and reaches its apex in the eighteenth century with such Enlightened *philosophes* as Casanova and his friend Voltaire. But somehow the Mother of Wisdom with the Word enthroned in her lap was forgotten—banished to margins of Christian thinking, exiled from the study of the arts of language to which, as her ancient and medieval devotees believed, she had given birth.

She survived in memory in the seals of some universities, and she sits in her guise as Alma Mater on the steps of the campus in New York City where I did my doctoral work. But she is otherwise forgotten, diminished to the status of a lowly housewife, a peasant girl chosen for no particular reason to bear a son by God. And yet, without her, Wisdom cannot come into the world. *Have you figured out now why Milo sits on a lion throne?*[495]

---

[494] *Scivias*, vision 13.1, trans. Mother Columba Hart and Jane Bishop (1990)

[495] https://fencingbearatprayer.blogspot.com/2018/01/i-spy-milo-on-set.html

THE GOOD THIEF

March 31, 2018

Would you be ashamed to be crucified next to a thief? Never mind the tenderness of your body, the injustice of being condemned to death for speaking the truth, the betrayal by your friends, the wracking of your entire body and all of your senses with agony, the mocking and scorn of the mob.[496] Would you be *ashamed* to be crucified *next to a thief?* This is what the thirteenth-century Dominican Jacobus de Voragine said about the pain of Christ's passion:

> The pain of the passion was of five kinds. The first was its shamefulness. It was shameful because it happened in a place of shame, namely, on Calvary, where malefactors were punished. The mode was shameful, because he was condemned to a most ignominious death, the cross being the instrument of punishment for thieves... The Lord's passion was shameful because of the company in which he suffered. He was reckoned with thieves and robbers who were criminals to begin with; but later one of them, Dismas, who was crucified at Christ's right side, was converted...and the other, Gesmas, on the left side, was condemned.[497]

---

[496] https://fencingbearatprayer.blogspot.com/2018/03/mob-justice.html
[497] "The Passion of Christ," in *The Golden Legend*, trans. William Granger Ryan (1995)

Do you remember what Jesus said to Dismas, according to the Gospels? "Truly, I say to you, today you will be with me in paradise." *A thief! But of course. Isn't paradise where thieves belong? You know, because they rob from the rich and all. And the rich deserve to be robbed. Because property is theft.*

YouTube has been suggesting some interesting videos to me this past week, ones that somehow in my study of Milo's oeuvre I had not previously seen. There was one in particular that blew me away. I am sure you have seen the stills from the event. Milo is dressed in a dark purple leather jacket with a dashing floral scarf around his neck. His hair is dark and tousled (be still, my heart!), and he is speaking with slides but without notes. He commands the stage—he looks daring and mischievous.

The red backdrop makes it look as if he is speaking from Hell, the very image of the "clickbait provocateur who [hates] the Left more than he [loves] anything" (as *The Guardian* would put it).[498] But what was he talking about? Until this past week, I did not know. Judging from the photograph, it could be anything. The event was in June 2013 when Milo was working as a tech journalist. He mentions at the beginning of the talk that *The Kernel* is going to be up and running again, so it was after some financial difficulties but before his first massive public shaming.

The event organizers who appear in the video joked comfortably with him, and the audience responded warmly to his talk. But of course they did—because he was already trolling them. The title of his talk? *10 Reasons Why the Sharing Economy is Bollocks.*[499] The joke? The whole conference was about the "sharing economy" in tech. And there was Milo with a warning about how it could all go horribly wrong.

[498] https://www.theguardian.com/world/2017/feb/21/milo-yiannopoulos-rise-and-fall-shallow-actor-bad-guy-hate-speech
[499] https://youtu.be/ZeSkWeSkuSc

"Owning stuff is awesome," he told them. "I don't feel guilty about being a capitalist. I feel quite nice about it. I rather like the things I can buy. I like having nice things. I don't want other people touching them. And I think that I'm probably in the majority for most kinds of purchase." Think about it. *Do* you want people touching your things?

I don't. I like having house guests, but I do not want strangers in my home while I am elsewhere, unless they are there specifically to take care of my things. The whole thought of Airbnb makes me queasy, never mind what Milo says about how it is actually serving only the upper middle class who can afford to take holidays and rent out their homes. Or how—as he notes—it puts prostitutes and drug dealers in your living room.

But with the sharing economy in full swing, I am now wrong not to want to share out my home or my car. It isn't even clear, as Milo points out, that those things belong to me at all. At least not morally. At least not according to the ideals of "sharing" on which rental arrangements like Airbnb purportedly depend. I posted the video to my Facebook page, and my good friend—and stalwart British socialist—Paul immediately responded, "Read the Bible FFS," followed by a string of scriptural citations.

> Come now, you rich, weep and wail over your impending miseries. Your wealth has rotted away, your clothes have become moth-eaten, your gold and silver have corroded, and that corrosion will be a testimony against you; it will devour your flesh like a fire. You have stored up treasure for the last days. Behold, the wages you withheld from the workers who harvested your fields are crying aloud, and the cries of the harvesters have reached the ears of the Lord of hosts. You have lived on earth in luxury and pleasure; you have fattened your hearts for the day of slaughter. You have condemned; you have murdered the righteous one; he offers you no resistance.—James 5:1-6

> He casts the mighty from their thrones and raises the lowly. He fills the starving with good things, sends the rich away empty.—Luke 1:52-53

Do not store up for yourselves treasures on earth, where moth and decay destroy, and thieves break in and steal. But store up treasures in heaven, where neither moth nor decay destroys, nor thieves break in and steal. For where your treasure is, there also will you heart be.—Matthew 6:19-21

They devoted themselves to the teaching of the apostles and to the communal life, to the breaking of the bread and to the prayers. Awe came upon everyone, and many wonders and signs were done through the apostles. All who believed were together and had all things common; they would sell their property and possessions and divide them among all according to each one's need. Every day they devoted themselves to meeting together in the temple area and to breaking bread in their homes. They ate their meals with exultation and sincerity of heart, praising God and enjoying favor with all the people. And every day the Lord added to their number those who were being saved.—Acts 2:42-47

How can you call yourself a Christian, my friend seemed to be suggesting, if you don't want to share? How can you call yourself a Christian if you claim anything is yours? How can you call yourself a Christian if you believe—horror of horrors!—in private property as something *good*? There followed a second string of links to articles about how Milo's current business is failing,[500] including the "privilege grant" that he set up to aid young white men going to college.[501],[502] Milo, you see, is not a good thief, even when he gives money away. He *likes* owning things. Unlike, say, Robin Hood. Milo—according to most mainstream journalists, not to mention not a few of my colleagues and friends—*belongs in Hell.*

---

[500] https://www.advocate.com/media/2018/3/30/more-terrible-things-are-happening-milo-yiannopoulos

[501] https://thehill.com/blogs/blog-briefing-room/news/380821-milo-yiannopoulos-charity-for-white-men-closes-with-questions

[502] https://www.nbcnews.com/business/business-news/milo-yiannopoulos-charity-white-boys-winds-down-mystery-remains-over-n860756

THE GOOD THIEF

What is Hell like? Primo Levi knew. He lived there for almost a year.[503] Hell is where nothing belongs to you, not even your name. "Consider," Levi asked his readers, describing what happened to him and his fellow prisoners within 24 hours of their arrival in Auschwitz,

> what value, what meaning is enclosed even in the smallest of our daily habits, in the hundred possessions which even the poorest beggar owns: a handkerchief, an old letter, the photo of a cherished person. These things are part of us, almost like limbs of our body; nor is it conceivable that we can be deprived of them in our world, for we immediately find others to substitute the old ones, other objects which are ours in their personification and evocation of our memories.

> Imagine now a man who is deprived of everyone he loves, and at the same time of his house, his habits, his clothes, in short, of everything he possesses: he will be a hollow man, reduced to sufferings and needs, forgetful of dignity and restraint, for he who loses all often easily loses himself. He will be a man whose life or death can be lightly decided with no sense of human affinity, in the most fortunate of cases, on the basis of a pure judgment of utility. It is in this way that one can understand the double sense of the term "extermination camp", and it is now clear what we seek to express with the phrase: "to lie on the bottom."

What did it mean "to lie on the bottom"? It meant becoming a thief in order to stay alive. As Levi and his fellow prisoners learned, everything in the camp was useful—but everything could be stolen. Including their bodies—and wills. I dare you to say that it was because Levi was Jewish that he thought property was important to his sense of humanity, to his sense of self. I dare you to say that if he had been Christian, he would have experienced the camp as a great experiment in sharing. I dare you to say that he experienced learning to steal as a good thing, that watching his fellow human beings reduced to phantoms without possessions or names was a lesson in not clinging to silver and gold.

[503] *Survival in Auschwitz*, trans. Stuart Woolf (1996)

I dare you to say that the Nazis were the good guys for forcing him and his fellow prisoners to learn this lesson in selflessness. Of course you would not, it is beyond despicable even to think as much. And yet. Think about the way we valorize thieves. We reward them for their daring. We ridicule those from whom they steal for caring so much about things. We celebrate the Robin Hoods of our government for coming into our homes and demanding, at the point of a gun, that we *share*. We scold capitalists for wanting to make nice things that others might want to buy. We talk glibly about how "property is theft." We shame each other for wanting to protect what is ours. I say "we," but of course politically the shaming tends to go only one way.

Back in the Middle Ages, before Robin Hood became romantic, Dante put thieves in Hell.[504] Property is *not* theft. Owning things is *not* theft. You will say that this is not what Jesus meant when he argued against storing up treasures on earth. But note why he argued against them: because these are the kinds of treasures that *thieves* can break in and steal. Almost as if he knew how National Socialists would behave.

The sharing economy is bollocks, according to Milo, because it denies our need not just for emotional and intellectual health, but also for security (e.g. a home) and autonomous mobility (e.g. a car). In his words: "My worry is that these sorts of businesses [promoted by the sharing economy] rob us of that because they make us think that nothing really belongs to us anymore. And we've seen some pretty horrible examples in history of what happens when government or when business starts to behave like this."

Like thieves. There is a further reason, Milo argued, why the sharing economy is bollocks. "Number 9," he insisted, "the best things in life can't be shared." Because the best things in life aren't things: "It's the memories. The look on a child's face. So, holidays, for example.

---

[504] https://digitaldante.columbia.edu/dante/divine-comedy/inferno/inferno-25/

It seems weird to me that we would try to make holidays less special through this grubby sharing of space...so that holidays become this occasion of you engaging in someone else's life somehow."

And how do you feel about the fact that Facebook now owns our memories? In an age when businesses own more and more of the things that we use to distinguish ourselves as persons, Milo concluded, "I think it would be nice if they left our personal property alone." *Would you still be proud to be crucified next to someone who tried to steal other people's property? Next to a thief?*

'YOU ARE ALL BEAUTIFUL, MY LOVE'

April 7, 2018

There is a reason that women need Mary, and it isn't just because she is the Mother of God. It is because a) Mary is the most beautiful woman God ever made. And b) women are bitches about other women—especially beautiful ones. Let me explain. Beautiful women (or, at least, women who want to think they are beautiful) can be consummate bitches about other women whom they want to make feel less beautiful than they. Trust me on this, I've been on the receiving end.

But less beautiful women—we might, if we were being uncharitable, call them ugly—can be even uglier about beautiful women. Just look what they write about Mary! As a myth—or so Marina Warner argued in *Alone of All Her Sex: The Myth and the Cult of the Virgin Mary* (1976)—the Virgin Mary deserves to die because, in her excellence and beauty, she is an insult to all other women:

> [The] adulation of the Virgin excludes other women.... In a celebrated English tenson, or discussion, written in the thirteenth century, a

misogynist thrush attacks the regiment of women. The nightingale in reply cites the Virgin Mary, the supreme example of feminine perfection. Its defence is spirited and generous:

Man's highest bliss in earthly state

Is when a woman takes her mate

And twines him in her arms.

To slander ladies is a shame!

The thrush admits defeat and flutters off disgraced.

But the nightingale's argument—that all women resemble the Virgin Mary—is very rare, for every facet of the Virgin had been systematically developed to diminish, not increase, her likeness to the female condition. Her freedom from sex, painful delivery, age, death, and all sin exalted her ipso facto above ordinary women and showed them up as inferior.... The Queen of Heaven became the staple antidote to love on earth. She was feminine perfection personified, and no other woman was in her league.

Certainly, Warner did not feel she was in Mary's league—and so wrote a bitter and dismissive book about how deceived she felt at being encouraged to model her childhood self on Mary. Subsequent feminist scholarship has tended to follow suit, regularly insisting that descriptions of Mary that laud her for her beauty detract from the status of all other women. If medieval poets and preachers lamented that they could not find the words to praise her and so applied every metaphor they could, it was because they could not bear to see the beauty or value of other women.[505] In Helen Phillips's words:

The result [of such poetic efforts] may be a deeply mysterious, powerfully attractive, and reverent splendour, but the verbal artifice, semantic alienations and dichotomies that play a part in creating the particular type of jewelled and mentally dazzling hyperbole to which writers of late medieval marian praise are so often drawn could be seen also as expressions of unresolved contradictions in the elevation to so

---

[505] http://maryandmariology.blogspot.com/p/ave-virgo-mater-christi.html

high a place in theology and devotion of a woman, in a society that gives women and female qualities in general little power or respect.[506]

Damned if you do, damned if you don't? Recognize Mary's beauty—Warner and Phillips claim—and you are denigrating all other women. Notice where such arguments lead when applied to other beautiful women. Beauty pageant queens, for example. Just think of the way other women talk about them. How jealous they are that *she* gets to be beautiful, and they don't. Or women athletes. Or actresses. Or any woman lucky—or unlucky—enough to find herself in the public eye for her beauty.[507] I've gotten it myself—no, not exactly for my beauty, but for photos that my husband took for my book and which I posted on my Facebook page.

It was telling that, when my (female) colleagues in medieval studies wanted to take me down for my support of Milo, they focused on my looks. Other women even do it to Milo, a gay man, especially when he dresses in drag. Writes Tanya Gold of Milo's costume for last summer's Coming Out Conservative party:

> In a fusty pink room in Chelsea, Milo is made into a woman. He wears a red and black dress. He is silent, transported somewhere I cannot reach. Miss Veronica Vera is the Dean of Miss Vera's Finishing School for Boys Who Want to be Girls. "We weren't sure," she says, "if he wanted to go very over the top big bouffant drag queen look. That was what I was told initially. But when we got here we decided that he wanted to be more real—and pretty."

> "This look is festive because Milo's femme self—who we will call for now Mila—will be hosting a party. It's a long gown and it's kind of a combination of a gothic look but it's also very kind of Miss Kitty dance hall girl look. Mila sees herself as a curvy girl so we have built in curves."

---

[506] "'Almighty and al mercible queene': Marian Titles and Marian Lyrics," in *Medieval Women*, ed. Jocelyn Wogan-Browne et al. (2000)

[507] https://www.thelily.com/feminist-attacks-on-taylor-swift-reveal-something-very-ugly-about-the-movement/

Finally he speaks. "It's fantastic", he says, "There's enough bad girl in there, isn't there?" There is, yes; he looks like he'd do anything. I ask him if he feels different. "Not really," he says, "but I live my whole life in character." I think that is the second most truthful thing he has told me. He climbs down from the mirror and sashays towards me. He has added a red ribbon to his wig and looks like a ruined Dorothy Gale. He looks like his mother.[508]

Do you wonder that women who think of themselves as feminists do everything they can to make themselves less threatening ...to other women? It is the only way that they can keep from being savaged—for being pretty. This is why women need the Virgin Mary: *Mary saves women from each other by being the most beautiful one in the room.* I know, I am one of them. I know what women are like.

You think men are hierarchical? Men are perfect lambs compared with women when it comes to hierarchy. Men willingly arrange themselves in hierarchies—think every military organization ever, not to mention every men's club, sporting league, business, and university (before they let all us women in). Men recognize authority in other men and know what it means to challenge it. They are overt about the challenges—and about standing up to each other when the challenge comes. (Except, of course, when they aren't, but then they tend to take revenge on each other as traitors.)

Not women. We women always fight dirty. We pretend that we do not create hierarchies, but we do, and every woman knows it. I read somewhere, I don't remember where, but you can always tell with a group of women who is the dominant one in the group: all the other women turn their feet towards her. They look to her to set the tone in the group, to know whom to include and whom to exclude. Often it is the one that the others acknowledge as better looking, but not necessarily.

---

[508] https://spectator.us/fall-milo-yiannopoulos/

Sometimes the alpha bitch manages to turn the others against the most beautiful one. Why? Because the most beautiful one is the greatest threat to other women's ability to attract men. Again, I've been there as the ugly one, completely overshadowed by my beautiful sister. I have also been the beautiful one, although I am less proud of how that played out.[509] Ask any woman, and if she is honest with you (unlikely), she will admit to sizing up—more often than not, quite literally—every other woman in the near vicinity, placing herself in the immediate hierarchy.

It is safest in the middle of the pack. Too far to the bottom, and you are going to be sitting by yourself eating glazed cinnamon buns by the dozen. (*I call that "junior year in high school."*) Too near to the top, and either the alpha bitch will have her eye on you and/or all the other women will, just waiting for her cue to take you out. (*I call that "senior year in high school." I have never been very good at staying in the middle.*) But one way or another, you will end up ranking yourself and ranking the others—and woe to her who tries to go against the ranking of the group.

(NB: This is also why it is a huge mistake for men to think that they will be welcomed as "male feminists." All it does it make them subject to the hierarchy determined by the alpha bitch.)

Nor does it work for women to pretend that there is no such hierarchy. If the first great lie of feminism is about how it is "the patriarchy" keeping women down, the second great lie is that "sisterhood" will save them. "Sisterhood" is just a way of saying, "Don't you dare challenge me, bitch." Never believe another woman when she claims that all women need to stick together as sisters. She will stab you in the back before you can even turn around. The only

---

[509] https://fencingbearatprayer.blogspot.com/2017/06/signal-virtue-beauty-and-beast.html

reason she said it was that she felt threatened by you and wanted to bring you down to her level. Again, why feminists all end up ugly: for all women to be "sisters," no one can be prettier than any of the others. Except when one woman clearly is. "Thou art all beautiful, O my love," medieval Christians heard Christ the Bridegroom tell Mary, his Bride,

> and there is not a spot in thee…. Thou art beautiful, O my love, sweet and comely as Jerusalem, terrible as an army set in array…. One is my dove; my perfect one is but one; she is the only one of her mother, the chosen of her that bore her. The daughters saw her and declared her most blessed, the queens and concubines, and they praised her.—Song of Songs 4:7; 6:3, 8

Women need an alpha bitch. If you prefer, they need a Queen. Perhaps she is the one who is most beautiful. Perhaps she is the one who is most willing to stand up to the other women when they attack each other. Think Granny Weatherwax or Queen Magrat in Terry Pratchett's Discworld stories. Think Veronica (the "true image") in *Heathers* (1988). But a group of women without a Queen soon becomes a mob, willing to follow the one who tells them to attack the outsider—the new girl, the threat, the one who makes the others look bad. Or the one to whom the men pay too much attention. The one who might steal their husbands.

Mary trumps all these hierarchies. She is not only the most beautiful—how could God's Mother be anything but? She is also Bride to the most fabulous Bridegroom. Daughter of the most loving Father. Sister of our first mother Eve. Virgin of virgins, Mother of mothers, and Queen of queens.

Nor is she meek—just ask those who have attempted to attack her cities. There is a reason the Bridegroom of the Song of Songs describes her as "more terrible than an army set in array." And yet, she is so humble that no woman could hate her—because she does not strive to be alpha bitch at all. Try to put yourself above her and the best you can do is look foolish. Serve her—and you become more beautiful than you could imagine in your wildest dreams.

"Feminism is cancer," Milo likes to say, "because it hurts women." It is cancerous because it makes women ugly, denies them the joy of being beautiful, brings them down to a level at which none of them is attractive to men. Mary is the antidote to this poison. *Pace* Warner, the adulation of Mary does not "exclude other women." It saves them from having to compete to be the most beautiful one in the room. If all women take Mary as Queen, then no woman has to denigrate her sisters in order to be beautiful. All she needs to do is turn her feet towards Mary—and Mary will make her like her, a bride of God.

WHAT WOULD MILO DO

May 5, 2018

I am finding it difficult to stay cheerful of late. I could blame the hot flashes, which have been wearing me down for the past several months, but it isn't just the hot flashes. It is the whole wretched culture war that—human nature being what it is—we are never going to win. It is the relentless pressure in academia to conform to the prevailing narrative of victimization and oppression that would cast one group as demons (white males, especially Christians) and the other as innocent (everyone else).

It is the unwillingness on the part of establishment conservatives to credit what Milo has shown are the stakes in our fight against the death of our Western ideals.[510] It is the feeling of being muffled and silenced for speaking out against the mischaracterization of my own field of medieval studies as riven with white supremacism and neglect of the Other.[511] It is the disappointment in not being able to do more

---

[510] https://www.newsmax.com/markbauerlein/milo-yiannopoulos-ucla-republicans/2018/02/27/id/845707/

[511] https://fencingbearatprayer.blogspot.com/p/medievalgate.html

to make a difference in the way in which the argument goes.[512] It is enough to make you want to quit.

And then I look at Milo and what he has been through trying to get his new business off the ground. The cancelled speeches. The loss of investors. The death threats to the venues where he was planning to speak. The ongoing ridicule in the media. I long ago lost track of the number of times he announced a talk only for it to not happen. All the talks for Free Speech Week, cancelled because *someone* convinced the administrators at Berkeley that the whole event was never meant to happen.[513]

All but one of the talks for the Troll Academy (American Edition), even those scheduled for commercial venues,[514] cancelled when the venues pulled out of their contracts after receiving threats of violence.[515] *The MILO Show* muffled by Facebook's on-going efforts to shut conservatives down.[516] And to top it all off, the death of his newest potential investor days before closing the deal.[517] Seriously, wouldn't you just quit? Milo won't. He won't even tell you about what he and his company have been through this past academic year—the year of the Troll Academy Tour that never happened. Because that would be playing the victim, which Milo never does.

---

[512] https://fencingbearatprayer.blogspot.com/p/the-lady-and-logos.html

[513] https://www.mercurynews.com/2017/09/23/uc-berkeley-free-speech-week-officially-canceled/

[514] https://depauliaonline.com/29754/nation/milo-denied-patio-theatre-cancels-troll-academy-tour/

[515] https://www.azcentral.com/story/news/local/scottsdale/2018/03/02/milo-yiannopoulos-scottsdale-event-canceled-venue/388339002/

[516] https://www.washingtonexaminer.com/red-alert-politics/milo-yiannopoulos-team-indicates-facebook-censorship

[517] https://www.politico.com/story/2018/04/27/yiannopoulos-business-implodes-after-death-of-crypto-billionaire-557456

Michael Brendan Dougherty has an insightful article in *National Review* about the culture war, although he doesn't call it that.[518] He calls it a religious crisis—just as I did a year ago last February in my *Sightings* article about Milo and the importance of his Dangerous Faggot campus tour.[519] Dougherty's argument: the reason that victim politics take on such a religious tone is because they are ultimately not political, but religious in character. What I said:

> The violent response to Milo's tour of our college campuses, culminating in the riot at Berkeley [in February 2017], is evidence of a deep crisis in religious thinking. If students cannot practice these difficult conversations in school, there is nothing to stop them from spilling into the streets.

What Dougherty says:

> The premise of victim politics is like a mirror image of devotion to the Suffering Servant. Just as in Christianity, so in social-justice politics: The wounds of the primordial victim testify to the broken state of human nature and society at large.... Putting this Victim at the center of the social order, in ritual or in preaching, begins the redemption of all humanity. The faithful confess to the ways their sins contributed to the fate of the victim. The ritual is meant to moralize and inspire those who witness it and motive them to more fully participate in the effort of redemption. It can also provide its adherents with a demonology that fills the world with invisible oppressors and tormentors, making them oversensitive and fearful....

> Depending on your disposition, you can take this mimicry of the Christian myth and ritual and its transmutation into politics as either a perverse compliment about the endurance of Christian thought or a kind of demonic parody. Either way, we are not here contending over something exclusively political. Once the explicitly political claims are filtered out, what is left over in victim politics is a churchly way of being

---

[518] https://www.nationalreview.com/magazine/2018/05/14/victim-mentality-identity-politics-dominate-modern-left/

[519] https://divinity.uchicago.edu/sightings/why-milo-scares-students-and-faculty-even-more

in a world that has escaped the bonds of religion. We are contending with a longing for recognition and esteem and for a mission that has a transcendent horizon; no form of human governance can ever satisfy such desires.

I have spent the past year and a half writing about the way in which I see Milo participating in these patterns of Christian ritual and myth, much to the chagrin of my academic colleagues who think I am crazy for suggesting that he is in any way imitating Christ. But this, of course, is the whole point. Given who he is—gay, of Jewish descent, in love with a black man—Milo *ought* to be playing the victim. And he won't. Because he actually believes in Christ, not just in imitating Him. Because we are not in a war about culture. We are in a war about God.

MONKEYSHINES

June 3, 2018

Comparing human beings to apes is all the rage these days.[520],[521] Certainly, it seems to spark a greater degree of outrage than any other human-animal comparison. Just look at Bill Maher's comparison of Donald Trump to an orangutan![522] Oh, wait, that was in 2013, when apparently such comparisons were called "jokes" and celebrities like Mr. Trump were supposed to be able to laugh them off.

Not anymore. We all saw what happened in summer 2016 when Milo... no, wait, Milo never made any comparison of Leslie Jones to a simian, but everyone still believes that he did. Nothing he could say will convince Twitter otherwise, so toxic has even the insinuation that someone might make such a comparison become. (To reiterate, Milo never compared Jones to any animal, never mind an ape, but he

---

[520] https://www.foxnews.com/entertainment/bill-maher-says-his-trump-orangutan-jokes-are-not-the-same-as-roseannes-ape-tweets

[521] https://www.nytimes.com/2018/05/29/business/media/roseanne-barr-offensive-tweets.html

[522] https://youtu.be/WdEiCGyLlGk

was permanently banned from Twitter anyway—go, look! Everyone is talking about it now.[523])

The outrage! The scandal! The cries of "Heresy!" and "Burn the witch!" It's all, well, so *medieval*. You knew I was going there. That is, after all, where you find all the best apes. Here's one of my favorites.[524] Do you like him? I call him "Milo" in honor of the first post that I did about our fabulous trickster. Here's another one from the same manuscript.[525] It seems apes were quite talented back in the Middle Ages, almost human, you might say. They could hunt with falcons, drive horse carts, play the bagpipes, capture birds in cages, blow bubbles, spin thread, and look at themselves in a mirror.[526]

Not at all like the apes that we have today, none of whom we want (apparently) to be related to. Darwin must be so disappointed.[527] You all know that I have had my own deal of trouble convincing my colleagues in medieval studies that I did not say certain things that they are convinced I did, much like Milo with Leslie Jones. I recently learned how to search for myself on Twitter—*I know! It is inconceivable in 2018 that I should not have known how!*—and have discovered a whole new treasure trove of comments about myself. (*Waves at all her new friends!*)

Building on the animal theme, one recent post explicitly compared me to an animal that first implants on a rock and then digests its own brain "often taken as an analogy to what happens at universities when professors get tenure." The OP was about Jordan Peterson's use of

---

[523] https://twitter.com/search?f=tweets&vertical=default&q=milo%20leslie%20jones&src=typd&lang=en

[524] http://www.bl.uk/manuscripts/Viewer.aspx?ref=add_ms_42130_fs001ar (go to fol. 38r)

[525] http://www.bl.uk/manuscripts/Viewer.aspx?ref=add_ms_42130_fs001ar (go to fol. 162r)

[526] https://blogs.bl.uk/digitisedmanuscripts/2012/04/monkeys-in-the-margins.html

[527] https://en.wikipedia.org/wiki/Scopes_Trial

lobsters to talk about hierarchy, and the subsequent discussion was about how ridiculous it was to compare humans to lobsters.[528] Much better to compare us, the participants in the thread suggested, to tunicates—"and you don't see humans ramming headfirst into a rock and consuming their own brains."[529] Except, it would seem, with me.[530]

wow sick burn — Sarah Taber @SarahTaber_bww (23 May 2018)

This explains Rachel Fulton Brown.—Jonathan Paul Katz @ JonathanPKatz (May 24)

pearl clutch —Sarah Taber @SarahTaber_bww (May 24)

I am so glad you know exactly what I am referring to. —Jonathan Paul Katz @JonathanPKatz (May 24)

My guess is that nobody is going to be outraged by this comparison. I wonder why.

---

[528] https://twitter.com/SarahTaber_bww/status/998385720992595968
[529] https://twitter.com/vikxin/status/998901500079325185
[530] https://twitter.com/SarahTaber_bww/status/999493618984538114

WORD ON THE TWEETS

June 4, 2018

My friends are so embarrassed at me. Here it is 2018—and I have only just learned how to search Twitter for comments about Milo and me. It has been quite the education. Twitter is a different country from Facebook, I have learned. They do things differently there. On Facebook, or so I have experienced it, it is about making friends and creating community. I call my Facebook profile page my "salon" after the salons of the eighteenth century, where wit and scholarship were deployed to discuss the great philosophical questions of the day.

Twitter is, well, more like the Wild Wild West, complete with gunslingers and showdowns at the OK Corral. I can see why Milo misses it. I have learned so many things about myself in the past few days! For example, that I think I am Jesus.[531] Wrong! That would be Milo. I think I am Mary, the Mother of Wisdom. (One day I am going to have to explain the difference between Milo's[532] *imitatio Christi* and worshipping Milo as God. Milo is not the one in danger of starting

---

[531] https://twitter.com/GuyEmersonMount/status/834060355609427969
[532] http://fencingbearatprayer.blogspot.com/2016/11/kung-fu-milo.html

a cult, just saying.[533]) Or that somebody out there thinks, contrary to all evidence, that I and Jordan Peterson have "a thing going on."[534]

(I think not, especially after I spent the past month on Twitter calling him,[535] Ben Shapiro,[536] and Dave Rubin[537] out for refusing to acknowledge Milo's role in clearing the ground where they have now comfortably taken their stand as champions for freedom of speech. Some IDW. Just saying.) Or that I have, metaphorically speaking, rammed my head into a rock like a tunicate and consumed my own brain for standing up for Milo and against the implication that my academic field is complicit in promoting white supremacy.[538] (At least, I think that is why Sarah Taber clutched her pearls at the mention of my name. Maybe this was a reference to oysters and poetry?[539])

But of course these Tweets were only the tip of the iceberg, as it were. (Picture me sitting on an ice flow; I am a white bear, after all. Polar bears were quite the exotic animals back in the Middle Ages. Perhaps that was before people realized how cruel they can be to baby seals.) The most, ahem, vigorous were posted back in September and October 2017. Here is a sample of some of the livelier contributions.

> TFW you're trying to catch up on the latest Rachel Fulton Brown controversy & accidentally navigate to her blog. —Kalinah @kalinah (16 Sep 2017), with GIF of Judge Judy closing her laptop

> Thread. Basic humanity and common decency are at stake here, not to mention professional ethics. —Jonathan Hsy @JonathanHsy (15 Sep 2017)

---

[533] https://fencingbearatprayer.blogspot.com/2018/02/who-wants-to-be-heretic.html
[534] https://twitter.com/public_archive/status/1003147809955012609
[535] https://twitter.com/RFultonBrown/status/996167978398945285
[536] https://twitter.com/RFultonBrown/status/996374373350207488
[537] https://twitter.com/RFultonBrown/status/996090984147628034
[538] https://twitter.com/SarahTaber_bww/status/999493618984538114
[539] https://fencingbearatprayer.blogspot.com/2009/01/pearl-of-great-price.html

Yes, predictable yet despicable, unethical and not so much badly argued as not argued at all. — Helen Young @heyouonline (15 Sep 2017)

There is no actual argument here. The whole point is to lash out & disparage a junior POC scholar. The degree of obsession is so disturbing. —Jonathan Hsy @JonathanHsy (15 Sep 2017)

Do you think @UChicago's Dept. of History is aware of Rachel Fulton Brown's malicious and inflammatory remarks? They should be. — Jacquelyn Clements @peripatesis (15 Sep 2017)

I'm disgusted that tenured R1 professor Rachel Fulton Brown has attacked untenured Dorothy Kim for her antiracism work in medieval studies / And in such a way and medium as to knowingly direct a community of racist and misogynist bullies at Kim. —Anna Wilson @ annapwilson (16 Sep 2017)

Apart from argumentative substance, a key difference between Rachel Fulton Brown & us is that she'll take support from ANY random layperson. / Only someone who no longer cares about scholarly substance would be so eager to seek the approval of nonscholars. —Karl Steel @KarlSteel (18 Sept 2017)[540]

I wrote about Rachel Fulton Brown and why saying "well, actually" to white supremacy never, ever works: —Donna Zuckerberg (blue checkmark) @donnazuck (5 Oct 2017), with link to her article about me in *Eidolon*[541]

The friends who taught me how to search Twitter this past week (with much mocking and Tweet-shaming, which arguably I deserved— seriously? And I called myself social media savvy? ;)) also helped me search for evidence—*any* evidence—that either my blogging or Milo's staff writer's article about my blogpost attracted any attention from the much anticipated trolls.[542] These are friends who have lived on

---

[540] [I also learned last June that Professor Steel had written quite a series of Tweets about me and Milo over the years. See https://fencingbearatprayer.blogspot.com/2018/06/through-twitter-glass.html]

[541] https://eidolon.pub/learn-some-f-cking-history-94f9a02041d3

[542] https://www.milo.net/30878/lady-with-a-sword-beats-down-fake-scholar-with-facts-and-fury/

Twitter for years, since giants walked the earth (R.I.P. @Nero). They know its ways and how to track them. Following the Tweet trails into their darkest recesses. Parsing the @'s and #'s for clues. Their report from the hunt?

Nothing. Nada. Zero. Zilch. NOT ONE POST attacking the junior colleague whom so many insisted my blogging and tagging Milo threatened. NOT. ONE. So much for the much-fabled Milo Troll Hordes. Perhaps they are as fictional as the claim that he harassed Leslie Jones. In contrast, I have learned from searches on Google (where I am more practiced) that my colleagues have continued to talk about me this past year as a "white supremacist" and "neo-Nazi medievalist."[543,544,545]

At least I think they mean me; it is always so hard to tell when one isn't able to attend their lectures without being accused of harassment for sitting in the audience.[546] I am not quite sure what to make of what I have learned from my foray into the Twitter wilds. To say that I was unaware of the degree of vitriol my colleagues had expended on my behalf—albeit behind my back—would be disingenuous. Friends have been sending me screenshots all year. But it is quite an experience to find your name used over and over and over again as a kind of curse. I am going to need to think on this. What's in a name? Clearly, it depends on whom you tweet.

---

[543] http://feature.politicalresearch.org/war-on-the-ivory-tower

[544] https://stroseenglish.wordpress.com/2018/03/19/a-target-of-the-alt-right-vassar-medievalist-dr-dorothy-kim-to-speak-at-english-symposium/

[545] https://www.timeshighereducation.com/features/long-view-scholars-assess-state-history

[546] http://www.strosechronicle.com/fresh/english-symposium/

MAEGE MORMONT AND THE THREAT OF ART

June 8, 2018

I do not watch *Game of Thrones*. I have no idea who this character is, whether I would like to be compared with her or not. I learn from *A Wiki of Ice and Fire* that her name is Maege Mormont, the Lady of Bear Island, and that she is "a short, stout, grey-haired woman, and a fierce warrior."

> She dresses in patched ringmail, and her favored weapon is a spiked mace. She is dedicated to the old gods, and loyal to House Stark. According to her brother, Jeor, she is stubborn, short-tempered, and willful.[547]

Apparently, she carries the title of House Mormont because her brother's only heir is an outlaw, while she herself has five daughters of mysterious paternity. Perhaps she changes shape and mates with a bear? Well, I am a bear in one of my guises, but I don't have any daughters. And thanks to Milo's fat shaming, I am not exactly stout. But grey-haired? Check. Fierce warrior? I prefer "hot and happy," but okay. You could say I am dedicated to the Old God—the God of

---

[547] https://awoiaf.westeros.org/index.php/Maege_Mormont

the Psalms, the one modernity rejected as too unsophisticated and replaced with the trinity of Science, Reason, and Humanism. [548]

And, of course, I am loyal to House Milo. According to my brother... check, check, check! (*Waves at beloved younger sibling! Trust me. He knows all about spiritual warfare.*) So, we'll go there. I am a Bear Lady of a Certain Age. This is not what my colleagues in medieval studies saw last autumn when Milo's staff writer used this image to illustrate her article about my blogpost on the on-going controversy in our field over what to do about the use of medieval imagery by certain white supremacist groups, including some of those interviewed by Milo and Allum Bokhari for their piece in *Breitbart* about the alt-right.[549,550,551] (*Got all that? Good.*)

As they put it in the Open Letter that 1,500 or so academics signed against me and sent to my provost, executive vice provost, and dean, my medievalist colleagues were deeply concerned that:[552]

a) I do not argue on the basis of critical race theory when I suggest that the best way to counter the arguments of the white supremacists is to "learn some f*cking medieval Western European Christian history, including the historiography of our field" (*I think it was the "f*cking" that got them; funny, I have been listening to them* talk dirty about Christianity for decades);

b) I used an image of Professor Kim that I found on the Internet with one of her interviews to illustrate her argument that she does not need to signal to her students that she is not a white supremacist

---

[548] https://fencingbearatprayer.blogspot.com/2018/05/training-soul-in-virtue-lessons-from.html

[549] https://www.chronicle.com/article/Medievalists-Recoiling-From/240666

[550] http://www.inthemedievalmiddle.com/2017/08/teaching-medieval-studies-in-time-of.html

[551] https://www.historians.org/publications-and-directories/perspectives-on-history/november-2017/medievalism-white-supremacy-and-the-historians-craft

[552] http://www.bryanvannorden.com/new-page-27/

while all those of us who are white do (*It was my fellow white colleagues to whom I directed my instructions to learn some "f*cking...history," not Professor Kim*); and

c) I tagged Milo in my Facebook share of my blogpost, thus "[exposing] Professor Kim to one of the most racially violent contingents currently operating." (*Seriously? Does none of these people ever watch Milo's videos? You'd think as scholars they would want to do the primary research.*)

But it was the article on *Dangerous* that convinced my colleagues that I had put Professor Kim in the greatest danger of "virtual harassment or actual harm." In their words:

> Indeed, one day after Professor Fulton Brown's post appeared, Professor Kim began receiving hate mail [*proof of which Professor Kim has yet to publish*], and Yiannopoulos himself [*Milo was not the author; it was one of his staff writers*] created a post for his followers describing Professor Kim as having been "beat[en] down" by Professor Fulton Brown and her sword.

> That post is not a mere Facebook folly. It contains an image from "Game of Thrones" of a female figure holding a metal-spiked club. Her weapon bears resemblance to the barbed-wire-wrapped bat used to kill an Asian-American character in "The Walking Dead" by bashing in his head. A post by another social media user accompanies the picture of Professor Kim with an assertion that Professor Fulton Brown "gets medieval" on her; the violent meaning of this familiar phrase from "Pulp Fiction" is well known.

> This country's sense of license to inflict violence upon people of color is considerable; we do not deem it unreasonable to fear for our colleague's safety as a result of your colleague's actions.

The article at Dangerous.com no longer shows the images, but you can read what Milo's staff writer penned.[553] I spoke with her on the phone after the article posted—there were some corrections that

---

[553] https://www.milo.net/30878/lady-with-a-sword-beats-down-fake-scholar-with-facts-and-fury/

I wanted her to make to my name—and she told me about the classes she had taken in college on the Bible and how much she admired my work. Based on the account of her piece given in the Open Letter— that, according to the headline, I had "beaten down" Professor Kim "with facts and fury"—the reader is primed to expect the worst. This is what the article actually says about my furious facts:

> Dr. Fulton Brown dismisses the obvious accusation that she could be a witch (witches make false oaths all the time) and denounces white supremacy, as did the authors of the Bible. While denying accusations of occultism, Dr. Fulton Brown nevertheless refers to "chants, puzzles and references to glass artifacts" to demonstrate that white European Christians do not appear to have been terribly interested in Mary's identity group orientation, and instead appear interested in the fact she gave birth to the Son of God.

> Citing scripture in Latin and English, narratives depicted in stain-glassed windows of medieval Cathedrals in Europe, fellow medieval scholars and chants and liturgy from the era, Dr. Fulton Brown demonstrates that the only person surprised that the Virgin Mary was a dark-skinned Jewess appears to be Dorothy Kim. As all good professors will do, Dr. Fulton Brown then guides Kim through the process of understanding that dark-skinned Jewesses are unlikely to be objects of abiding admiration for either Nazis or white supremacists.

Snarky? Well, a bit. But calling down Milo's fabled Troll Hordes to descend with threats of bodily harm? Give me a break. (*News flash: THEY DON'T EXIST.*) How did my colleagues manage to convince themselves that I had done what they claimed? That I had placed Professor Kim in physical danger?

My take: it was the image. Look at the way in which they argue in the letter: because Maege Mormont is shown holding a spiked mace, and there is another character in a completely different story world that uses a barbed-wire-wrapped bat to kill an Asian-American character, Milo's staff writer must have meant to encourage my Facebook followers (the source of "another social media user") to "get medieval" on Professor Kim. I shared the image on my own Facebook page, with this explanation.

> About that image that Milo's team used for the article that they did about my blog post... It is Maege Mormont, known as the She-Bear. Get it? "She-Bear," Fencing Bear...oh, never mind. The picture that they used was done by Emile Denis.

> Here is what my friends (a.k.a. Random Laypersons) said:

> Well the open letter was written to appeal to a constituency that is triggered by the word "Breitbart." It is no surprise then that they were triggered by an image of a tough, resilient mature woman, no matter its provenance. For a generation of boomer academics, and Gen Y students that do not agree to any distinction between words, imagery, and actual violence, this is unfortunately par for the course.

> What kind of medievalist doesn't know the difference between a mace and a baseball bat...geez.

> She-Bear is not as lovely as Fencing Bear. But, like the fierce imagery.

> Jorah Mormont's aunt. They are among the most steadfast and honorable of the Houses.

I have said before that we are living through a crisis of religion. Based on my colleagues' reaction to the image of the Lady of Bear Island, I would also argue that we are living through a crisis of symbolism and art. Thanks to the Enlightened emphasis of the past 200 years, particularly in academia, on "science, reason, and humanism," we have utterly lost the capacity to think in metaphor and analogy—the ground on which much religious thinking depends.

This, of course, is why Jordan Peterson's lectures have captured so much attention. It is also the reason, as I keep saying, that I wish he would read my book.[554] It isn't the Logos that we have forgotten. It is the Lady—and with her, the real reason that art is so threatening:

_____
[554] https://fencingbearatprayer.blogspot.com/2018/03/lady-day-invitatory.html

because, like Milo in his provocative costumes and characters, it points us to God.

MILO, THE HEATHERS, AND THE NEW SHERIFF IN TOWN

June 17, 2018

Back at the end of January, Jordan Peterson, Ben Shapiro, and Dave Rubin got together on Dave's *Rubin Report* to talk about how popular they all were.[555] Okay, that's not the title of the episode. It is "Frontline of Free Speech." And, to be fair, it has had almost 3.4 million views to date. So you could justifiably say that our three free speech heroes have every right to be a bit...*ahem*...proud of themselves.

Except. After spending a good hour and half congratulating themselves for being on the frontline of free speech, they started taking questions from the SuperChat audience. Here was one of the first ones that Dave read (at 1:33.20): "Quick one for Ben. I think we've already hit this, but any chance of a future discussion with Milo?" Ben's response was utterly predictable for those who know how ritualized this question has become: "No. Waste of time [*reaches for his water glass*]. I'd rather talk with people who have something say."

---

555 https://youtu.be/iRPDGEgaATU

Jordan's response was somewhat more interesting. He looked at Dave while Dave was reading the question, then turned to look at Ben to hear Ben's answer. As Ben spoke, Jordan nodded by lifting his chin. And then Dave moved onto the next question. Hardly the explosive response one might expect if one were looking for tells. Except *this* is what Jordan said a year ago last February, only days after Milo's shaming, when asked about the role that provocateurs play in the battle for freedom of speech:

> Milo's a classic example. He's an amazing person.... He's a trickster figure, archetypally speaking... He's a provocateur and a comedian... The funny thing about comedians. They're like jesters in a king's court. The jester was the only person who could tell the truth because he was beneath contempt....
>
> Trickster figures emerge in times of crisis, and they point out what no one wants to see, and they say things that no one will say.
>
> You can say all the terrible things about him. He's a provocateur, he's an egomaniac.... I don't think he's narcissistic because he has some real capacity for self-reflection.... And he's brave as can be.... And he's unstoppable on his feet. He just amazes me. I've never seen anyone I don't think—and I've met some pretty smart people—I've never seen anyone who can take on an onslaught of criticism and reverse it like he can.[556]

Funny, don't you think? How Jordan could admire Milo so much immediately after the Reagan Battalion released their video...and then less than a year later do nothing but nod when Ben implied that Milo has nothing to say?[557],[558] Things got even cozier with our three heroes

---

[556] https://youtu.be/v3gC2OJkx_A

[557] https://www.dailydot.com/layer8/reagan-battalion-milo-yiannopoulos-never-trump/

[558] https://dailycaller.com/2017/02/21/notorious-never-trump-org-funded-group-behind-milo-controversy/

when Ben had first Jordan, then Dave on his new Sunday show in May.[559],[560] Somehow, yet again, Milo's name kept coming up.

"If I'm not an alt-right fascist like Hitler—or Milo Yiannopoulos—that's how I was characterized in Canada, because the radical Leftists can't even get their bloody insults straight. [They say,] 'He's like Hitler—or Milo Yiannopoulos.' Because there's no difference between them," Jordan exclaimed, shaking his head at the idiocy of the Left. "It's just another attempt to pillory, as far as I can tell. I think it's dreadful, it really is." And yet, no word about how unfair it is to Milo to be lumped with Hitler.

"We're all rising together," Dave enthused when Ben jokingly credited him for "inventing" the YouTube interview format. "I love the idea that Shapiro is doing a show and more of these guys are connecting." Having thus established their camaraderie, Dave and Ben then talked about how they belong to a group of other provocative thinkers who relish the conversation but do not go out of their way to attack people—unlike the Left. "Look, people were upset when I had Milo on," Dave remarked. "I do not regret having Milo on."

Ben: "He was a big personality at the time." Dave: "Yes, he was a cultural phenomenon, for good or bad. And look, where is Milo now? You know, pretty much irrelevant." Ben: "Out in the wash, yeah." Dave: "But I have no regrets for anything that I did with him.... We had two gay people who had really different takes on things, really going into some issues that don't get discussed that often."

Things that don't get discussed that often? Like, say, what it is like sitting around talking about how popular you are and enjoying the fact that someone who used to be popular isn't any more (or so you hope)? I wrote last summer about how much I admired Jordan

---

[559] https://youtu.be/WTombNvaT6Y

[560] https://youtu.be/iGJx4qyc7mM

for what he had said about the Logos and Milo's role as Trickster. I spent a good six months or so listening to both his lecture courses and stuck with him all the way through the summer as he was working through the Biblical stories. I never expected him not to stand up for Milo after what he had said in February 2017.

And there he was in January 2018, *nodding* when Ben suggested that Milo had nothing to say. I tweeted at him and Dave and Ben in May. More to the point: I *learned how to tweet* in order to tweet at him and Dave and Ben in May in order to call them out.

> Hey, @jordanbpeterson @benshapiro and @RubinReport! Man up! You know very well that without have Milo Yiannopoulos to use as your despicable shield they would be coming after YOU. – Rachel Fulton Brown @RFultonBrown (14 May 2018)

No response. So I pushed a little harder.

> How to know you've become a Heather: when your conversation is more about who is part of the in-crowd than about ideas. @RubinReport @benshapiro @jordanbpeterson – Rachel Fulton Brown @RFultonBrown (15 May 2018)

Oh, yes, I am a *Heathers* (1988) fan. I watched it obsessively in graduate school, knowing that I was destined to be Veronica. I had the requisite crush on Christian Slater—he had, after all, also been in *The Name of the Rose* (1986), one of the two or three best movies ever about the Song of Songs. (Oh, you missed that bit? Watch the scene in the kitchen.) But also because I knew what it was like to be the bookish one in middle school desperate for the attention of the Heathers.[561] But I hate bullies. And I hate those who use their popularity to ostracize other people even more. Did you ever wonder why Winona Ryder's character is called "Veronica"? Because she is the true icon of Christ, the one who stands up to the bullies who

---

[561] I know the movie is set in high school, but the Heathers I knew were in middle school. I was too busy studying in high school to know who the Heathers were.

are destroying the society of the school with their status games. The scribes and the Pharisees who want to control who gets to see the face of God. Sure, Milo gets a bit salty with his insults sometimes.

But have you noticed what he has *not* done this entire year as Antifa and the Reagan Battalion and *Buzzfeed* and even his former colleagues at *Breitbart* have come after him either directly (*Buzzfeed*) or indirectly (*Breitbart*) over and over and over again?[562] Said anything against those who used to be his friends. Only of late has he started calling out Ben on his Instagram, but then he and Ben go way back—as Ben himself acknowledges.

I have yet to hear Milo say a word about Dave, and he said just the other evening on his podcast how he likes Jordan, even if he finds Jordan's *12 Rules* difficult to read. Meanwhile, the Heathers sit around congratulating themselves on their skill at croquet.

---

[562] https://www.breitbart.com/tech/2017/12/29/breitbarts-top-5-lgbt-2017/

'LIKE HITLER, OR MILO YIANNOPOULOS'

June 30, 2018

Back in November 2017, Lindsay Shepherd, a graduate student at Wilfred Laurier University in Ontario, was taken to task by two of her professors for showing a clip of a television show in which Professor Jordan Peterson talked about the problems he saw with Canada's proposed Bill C-16 and the effects it would have on freedom of speech. Her professors' complaint? That showing the video clip was tantamount to putting the students in her discussion section at risk of doxing, harassment, and physical threat because—they alleged—Professor Peterson had engaged in similar activities directed at his own students.

In her supervising professor Nathan Rambukkana's words:

> [Peterson] is a real person. But he is a real person who has engaged in targeting of trans students, basically doxxing them, if you know the term, giving out their personal information, so that they'll be attacked, harrassed, so that death threats will find them. This is something that he has done to his own students, that he has done to other students, and this is something that the students are aware of. So this is basically like playing—Not to kind of do the thing where everything is compared

to Hitler—*But this is like neutrally playing a speech by Hitler or Milo Yiannopolous [sic] from Gamergate...* To just present information like this neutrally, it can help cultivate an environment where these kinds of opinion, alt-right opinions, white supremacist opinions, anti-trans opinions, anti-gay opinions, anti-women misogynist opinions. Where those can feel like it's a space where those kinds of opinions can be nurtured and created.[563]

Because, of course, Milo Yiannopoulos is just like Hitler—just ask Twitter this past week.[564] Twitter's premise being, it would seem, that it is easy to spot when someone is likely to become a mass murdering monster based on the jokes that he makes. If only there were a way of telling the monsters from the rest of us.

Let's try a little test. If you had been alive back in 1933, would you have seen Hitler's rise for what it was—the beginning of one of the worst state-supported mass murders in human history? Are you sure? Because, you see, not everyone did. Some even thought Hitler was a bit of a joke. Here is the way one reporter for *Time Magazine* described him in February that year, just after he had been sworn in as chancellor in President Hindenberg's new cabinet ("Hitler Into Chancellor," 2/6/1933, Vol. 21 Issue 6, p. 22).

Except for beer, which few Germans consider alcoholic, Adolf Hitler touches no alcoholic tipple. Neither does he smoke. Hot water he calls "effeminate." Last week, on the biggest morning of his life, this pudgy, stoop-shouldered, tooth-brush-mustached but magnetic little man bounded out of bed after four hours sleep, soaped his soft flesh with cold water, shaved with cold water, put on his always neat but never smart clothes and braced himself for the third of his historic encounters with Paul von Beneckendorf und von Hindenburg, Der Reickspräsident.

---

[563] https://pastebin.com/2k3jjGKJ

[564] https://www.splcenter.org/hatewatch/2018/06/27/milo-wants-vigilantes-start-killing-journalists-and-hes-not-being-ironic

At their first meeting last August, upstart Herr Hitler was not so much as invited to sit down, despite the fact that he represented 230 Reichstag Deputies, by far the largest party in the Fatherland.

"With what power, Herr Hitler," growled Old Paul, "do you seek to be made Chancellor?"

"Precisely the same power that Mussolini exercised after his March on Rome!" chirped cheeky Adolf. (One scowling bust of Il Duce, two portraits of Frederick the Great adorn Herr Hitler's office.)

"So!" bristled Der Reichspräsident with the air of a Prussian schoolmaster about to squelch an urchin. "Let me tell you, Herr Hitler, if you don't behave, I'll rap your fingers!"

Note the adjectives! *Pudgy, stoop-shouldered, magnetic, cheeky.* Is Adolf Hitler someone you would describe as "chirping"? Would you worry about whether he wore "neat but never smart clothes"? Would you imagine him as a urchin about to have his fingers rapped by a Prussian schoolmaster? If only evil were so easy to spot.

Professor Peterson describes his "Maps of Meaning" university lecture course as, among other things, an introduction to evil.[565] Okay, he doesn't put it quite that way. What he says, and reiterated this past week in his interview with Bari Weiss at the Aspen Ideas Festival, was that he wants to show his students how, if they had been alive in 1933, just like the author from *Time Magazine*, they would *not* have seen Hitler coming.[566] In the interview with Weiss, Professor Peterson bristles at the comparison that the professors at Wilfred Laurier made of him with Hitler *and Milo* because, he says, professors should be more precise in their speech (at 30:00):

They said that playing a clip of Jordan Peterson was like playing a clip of Hitler or Milo Yiannopoulos. And I thought, well, let's go a little easy on the Hitler comparisons there, guys; we might want to save that for when it's really necessary... Because...it's sacrilegious to use an insult

---

[565] https://www.jordanbpeterson.com/maps-of-meaning/
[566] https://youtu.be/v6H2HmKDbZA

like that except in situations where it's justified. It's not appropriate to use a catastrophe like that casually, especially when you're doing it under the guise of moral virtue. There's no excuse for it.

And then, the second thing is, you're a professor, both of you. Get your damn words straight. Which is it? Am I Hitler or Milo Yiannopoulos? Seriously, those are not the same people. In case you didn't notice. One of them was the worst barbarians in the 20th century, with the possible exception of Stalin and Mao. And the other one is a provocateur trickster who's quite quick on his feet and...and...is...what would you say? Is stirring things up in a relatively non-problematic way. They're not the same creature.

And so to combine them in a single careless insult during an administrative investigation which was entirely unwarranted, and which was predicated on an absolute lie—there hadn't been a student complaint, as the university admitted—there's no excuse for that, and if they weren't professors, then, well, it wouldn't have been so bad, but they were.

Worst barbarian in the 20th century or provocateur trickster "stirring things up in a relatively non-problematic way"? To coin a phrase, *get your damn words straight*. Or, as Professor Peterson puts it in his *12 Rules for Life: An Antidote to Chaos* (2018): *"Rule 10 Be precise in your speech."* Because it is when you are not precise in your speech that the lies creep in. And along with the lies, the monsters. In Professor Peterson's words (*12 Rules,* p. 281):

> If you shirk the responsibility of confronting the unexpected, even when it appears in manageable doses, reality itself will become unsustainably disorganized and chaotic. Then it will grow bigger and swallow all order, all sense, and all predictability. Ignored reality transforms itself (reverts back) into the great Goddess of Chaos, the great reptilian Monster of the Unknown—the great predatory beast against which mankind has struggled since the dawn of time. If the gap between pretence and reality goes unmentioned, it will widen, you will fall into it, and the consequences will not be good. Ignored reality manifests itself in an abyss of confusion and suffering.

Be careful with what you tell yourself and others about what you have done, what you are doing, and where you are going. Search for the correct words.... The past can be redeemed, when reduced by precise language to its essence. The present can flow by without robbing the future if its realities are spoken out clearly. With careful thought and language, the singular, stellar destiny that justifies existence can be extracted from the multitude of murky and unpleasant futures that are far more likely to manifest themselves of their own accord. This is how the Eye and the Word make habitable order.

Don't hide baby monsters under the carpet [*here alluding to the children's book by Jack Kent,* There's No Such Thing as a Dragon—*FB*]. They will flourish. They will grow large in the dark. Then, when you least expect it, they will jump out and devour you. You will descend into an indeterminate, confusing hell, instead of ascending into the heaven of virtue and clarity. Courageous and truthful words will render your reality simple, pristine, well-defined and habitable.

So that is where the monsters come from. They are the Chaos waiting to swallow us whenever we do not pay careful attention to our speech. This, as Professor Peterson argues, is where monsters like Hitler and Stalin and Mao come from as well: from the little lies that we allow to grow into big ones, until they have taken over our whole lives.

Milo's name came up a second time in Weiss's interview with Professor Peterson. He was talking about the current difficulty that we have with defining who is to be excluded from polite conversation on both the Left and the Right. Unlike the Left—which he said was very difficult to set bounds for—the Right is simple (at 1:24:10).

JBP: We have a problem. We know how to put a box around the extremists on the right. Basically, we say, "Oh, you're making claims of ethnic or racial superiority. You're not part of the conversation anymore." .... With the radical right, you can kind of lay it down to one dimension: "Racial superiority." Nope, sorry, you're out of the conversation.

BW: [interrupting] But that's Milo. Who you mentioned before.

JBP: Well, I didn't say I was a fan of Milo.

BW: No, but you called him a prankster[567].

JBP: Well, he is a prankster mostly[568].

BW: Yeah, but he's also a racist.

JBP: Well, possibly. Yeah. [nods]

BW: [nods]

JBP: I haven't followed Milo that carefully...

BW: Okay. [nods]

JBP: It's possible that he is. I mean, it's hard to tell what Milo is exactly. He's a very complicated and contradictory person. Destined to implode, which is exactly what happened. Well, there's just no way you can be that contradictory a person and manage it. It's just not possible. He was just too many things happening at the same time for anyone to ever manage.

BW: [smiles]

Something evil happened in this exchange. Did you catch it? It was just at the moment when Professor Peterson turns his head to look at Weiss. The moment when she says, catching him off guard: "But that's Milo...." Whom she then describes in one word: *Racist*. Thus, by Professor Peterson's own criterion, removing Milo from the conversation. *Unpersoning him for the purposes of his own argument— without the slightest shred of proof*. At which, confronted with the unexpected, Professor Peterson struggled to choose the correct words:

First denial: "Well, I didn't say I was a fan of Milo." *I don't have sympathy for him.*

Second denial: "Well, possibly. Yeah." *You could be right about him.*

---

[567] https://www.youtube.com/watch?v=6b_pWJkrhSg
[568] https://www.youtube.com/watch?v=sv17aouIX2Y&t=8s

Third denial: "I haven't followed Milo that carefully...." *I don't know him.*

Peter didn't mean it either, when he denied Our Lord. But he did it anyway—three times—because he was scared.

> But Peter sat without in the court: and there came to him a servant maid, saying: Thou also wast with Jesus the Galilean.
>
> But he denied before them all, saying: I know not what thou sayest.
>
> And as he went out of the gate, another maid saw him, and she saith to them that were there: This man also was with Jesus of Nazareth.
>
> And again he denied with an oath, I know not the man.
>
> And after a little while they came that stood by, and said to Peter: Surely thou also art one of them; for even thy speech doth discover thee.
>
> Then he began to curse and to swear that he knew not the man. And immediately the cock crew.
>
> And Peter remembered the word of Jesus which he had said: Before the cock crow, thou wilt deny me thrice. And going forth, he wept bitterly.—Matthew 26:69-75

I have called Jordan out on Twitter and this blog over the past month or so for not standing up for what he said about Milo a year and a half ago when Milo's enemies first came after him in force. Friends tell me I am being too hard on him—that Professor Peterson is bearing a terrible burden being so much in the public eye. That he has been helping people over the past year through his lectures and books, and that any good he is doing would be jeopardized if he were to be too closely associated with Milo, who—they say, agreeing with Professor Peterson in his recent interview—was "destined to implode" anyway, because, well, that is "exactly what happened."

Or was it? Was Hitler "destined" to oversee the murder of millions of people because that is "exactly what happened" after "cheeky

Adolf" came to power? Or would it have been possible to prevent Hitler growing into a monster if those alive in 1933 had been able to recognize the lies? Tell one little lie, especially one specifically designed to put someone beyond polite conversation—"Milo is a racist"—and you open the door to all the monsters of hell.

Milo may make taboo-breaking jokes, but he stands by his words and does not lie.[569] Meanwhile, the journalists who speak and write about him lie *all the time*.[570],[571],[572] Think on that the next time you hear Milo compared with Hitler thanks to a joke.

---

[569] https://www.milo.net/44762/milo-i-regret-nothing/

[570] https://theschpiel.com/culture/exclusive-milo-says-new-york-observer-going-to-have-to-pay-for-false-reporting/

[571] https://observer.com/2018/06/milo-yiannopoulos-encourages-vigilantes-start-gunning-journalists-down/

[572] https://www.advocate.com/commentary/2018/6/27/milo-yiannopoulos-i-hope-journalists-are-murdered

SIR MILO OF LOCKSLEY

July 6, 2018

You've all heard what Milo wrote to the journalists who were pressing
him for comment about a restaurant he is said to frequent in New
York and his recent decision to join UKIP. You have also heard about
how Davis Richardson at *The New York Observer* and Will Sommer
at *The Daily Beast* reported his comment as an actual incitement to
violence.[573],[574] And you have heard about how PayPal and Venmo
closed his accounts after some 250,000 Tweets accused him of being
responsible for the deaths of five journalists thanks to the headline
that *The New York Observer* ran on Richardson's article about his
comment.[575]

"Dear Milo Yiannopoulos," the PayPal service bot wrote,

> We have recently reviewed your usage of PayPal's services, as reflected
> in our records. Due to the nature of your activities, we have chosen to
> discontinue service to you in accordance with PayPal's User Agreement.
> As a result, we have placed a permanent limitation on your account.

[573] https://observer.com/2018/06/milo-yiannopoulos-encourages-vigilantes-start-gunning-journalists-down/

[574] https://www.thedailybeast.com/far-right-youtube-stars-plan-takeover-of-ukip

[575] https://bigleaguepolitics.com/exclusive-milo-yiannopoulos-talks-his-lawsuit-against-newspaper-that-blamed-him-for-5-deaths/

Translation: *You are now outside the law.* Certainly, that is what many of those who tweeted about Milo's comment thought.

> Looks like Milo Yiannopoulos got his fucked up wish. Throw his ass in jail.—Scott Dworkin @funder

> This cannot be overstated on any day, but especially today. Milo Yiannopoulos is a terrorist.—The Sassiest Semite @LittleMissLizz

> Hey Milo Yiannopoulos—two days ago you called for "gunning journalists down." Today it happened. Enjoy prison.—Palmer Report @PalmerReport

> Arrest Milo. He's as responsible as the shooter.—Teddy Brewster @whatdidyoutwit

> If the Capital Gazette shooter turns out to be a fan of Milo Y, an arrest warrant should be issued for that asshole by the end of the day. Then arrest the president.—iResist @ThomboyD

> I swear to goddess that if what that piece of shit Milo Yiannopoulos said about gunning down journalists led directly to today's shooting in Annapolis, I will be relentless in lobbying my elected officials to have Yiannopoulos charged with inciting terrorism.—Paula @PaulaBonaFide

> It's ok to demonize Donald Trump and Milo Yiannopoulos because they are demons.—Roland Scahill @rolandscahill

The response from the conservative media was hardly better.

> Milo's shooting comment confirms it's time conservatives rid ourselves of him for good.—Cillian Zeal, *The Conservative Tribune*[576]

And yet, mysteriously, Milo's fans—including myself—stuck by him. I wonder why that would be. For one, because we know he is innocent. The shooting had nothing to do with his comment—and his comment was never intended as incitement to anything other than laughter at the stupidity and venality of the press. But also because we know what story we are in—and it isn't the one that the media—liberal or

---

[576] https://www.westernjournal.com/ct/milos-shooting-comment-confirms-its-time-conservatives-rid-ourselves-of-him-for-good/

conservative—would have you believe. We are, after all, Americans. At least, many of us are. (*Waves to readers in the U.K., Canada, Australia, and New Zealand—and everyone else who lives under the tradition of English common law!*) We know who the hero of the story is—and it isn't the ones who are calling for the head of the outlaw who has done nothing but stand up to the tyranny of the king.

I taught a course this past spring on "Medieval England," the first such course I have taught in my career.[577] My previous courses have tended to focus on questions of culture (e.g. war, travel, monasticism, scriptural exegesis, liturgy, animals, cities and towns—syllabi on my homepage[578]), but with this course—or so I thought—I wanted to focus on questions of nation-building, history, government, and law, above all to help myself understand what all the fuss was about when pundits bang on about our political and legal tradition.

Perhaps I should not have been surprised to discover that law is itself a question of culture, almost as gripping as religion and God! What did it mean to be "English" in the so-called "Middle Ages"? This was the question I posed to the class at the outset of the quarter. By the end of the term, we had learned some of the things that it most certainly did *not* mean, most importantly, that it was not about "race" in the sense in which that term in used now.

In the Middle Ages (roughly, from the departure of the Roman legions in A.D. 407 to the defeat of Richard III in A.D. 1485), being "English" was as complicated—and yet straightforward—as being "American" is today. Britons, Angles, Saxons, Danes, Normans: all thought of themselves as "English," their identity based not on race, but rather on the land where they lived, the language they spoke, and the laws under which they recognized their king. Even

---

[577] https://home.uchicago.edu/~rfulton/Medieval%20England.pdf

[578] https://home.uchicago.edu/~rfulton/

the eleventh-century King of England, Denmark, Norway, and "part of Sweden" Cnut—conqueror though he was—realized that he could not rule England solely by force of arms.

As he wrote to the English people from Rome, where he had gone "to pray for the forgiveness of my sins, and for the welfare of my dominions, and the people under my rule" (and, by the by, to attend the coronation of the Holy Roman Emperor Conrad II):[579]

> Be it known therefore to all of you, that I have humbly vowed to almighty God himself henceforth to amend my life in all respects, and to rule the kingdoms and the people subject to me with justice and clemency, giving equitable judgments in all matters; and if, through the intemperance of youth or negligence, I have hitherto exceeded the bounds of justice and clemency, giving equitable judgments in all matters: and if, through the intemperance of youth or negligence, I have hitherto exceeded the bounds of justice in any of my acts, I intend by God's aid to make an entire change for the better.
>
> I therefore adjure and command my counselors to whom I have entrusted the affairs of my kingdom, that henceforth they neither commit themselves, nor suffer to prevail, any sort of injustice throughout my dominions, either from fear of me, or from favor to any powerful person.
>
> I also command all sheriffs and magistrates throughout my whole kingdom, as they value my regard and their own safety, that they do no unjust violence to any man, rich or poor, but that all, high and low, rich or poor, shall enjoy alike impartial law; from which they are never to deviate, either on account of royal favor, respect of person in the great, or for the sake of amassing money wrongfully, for I have no need to accumulate wealth by iniquitous exaction.

Fancy that! A king promising to rule with "justice and clemency," cautioning his counselors not to engage in graft or currying favor, and commanding his sheriffs and magistrates to administer the law

---

[579] [Medieval sources cited from *Medieval England 500-1500: A Reader*, ed. Emilie Amt and Katherine Allen Smith (2018)]

impartially, without regard for social status or wealth! It sounds like a fairy tale, say, *The Return of the King*! Nor did the Normans, bastards that they were, find it any easier to rule the English with castles rather than courts of law. The Peterborough Abbey chronicler recorded that William the Conqueror made

> good peace...in this land, so that a man of any account might go over his kingdom unhurt with his bosom full of gold. No man dared slay another, no matter how much evil he had done to the other; and if any peasant had sex with a woman against her will, he soon lost the limb that he played with.

William's son Henry I specifically promised at his coronation to do away "with all the evil customs by which the realm of England was unjustly oppressed," which he then listed so that everyone would know to hold him to account. King John was just one in a series of kings to be brought to heel for his usurpation of the law and customs by which the English expected a king to be bound.

And when Parliament deemed Edward II "incompetent to govern in person," they did so on the basis that he had not willed to do "the justice to all" to which he had been bound by the oath that he made at his coronation. Likewise, Richard II. As the Articles for his deposition put it:

> 16. Also, the king refused to keep and defend the just laws and customs of the realm, but according to the whim of his desire he wanted to do whatever appealed to his wishes. Sometimes—and often when the laws of the realm had been declared and expressed to him by the justices and others of his council and he should have done justice to those who sought it according to those laws—he said expressly, with harsh and determined looks, that the laws were in his own mouth, sometimes he said that they were in his breast, and that he alone could change or establish the laws of his realm. And deceived by this idea, he would not allow justice to be done...

Kings of other realms, say, France, might have deemed themselves above the law, but the kings of England were kings only so long as they kept it. How much the stranger, therefore, is it that one of the great national heroes of the English should be someone living outside the law? Except, of course, in the stories, that is not the reason that he is the hero.

> The daylight had dawned upon the glades of the oak forest. The green boughs glittered with all their pearls of dew. The hind led her fawn from the covert of high fern to the more open walks of the greenwood, and no huntsman was there to watch or intercept the stately hart, as he paced at the head of the antler'd herd.

> The outlaws were all assembled around the Trysting-tree in the Harthill-walk, where they had spent the night in refreshing themselves after the fatigues of the siege, some with wine, some with slumber, many with hearing and recounting the events of the day, and computing the heaps of plunder which their success had placed at the disposal of their Chief.

> The spoils were indeed very large; for, notwithstanding that much was consumed, a great deal of plate, rich armour, and splendid clothing, had been secured by the exertions of the dauntless outlaws, who could be appalled by no danger when such rewards were in view. Yet so strict were the laws of their society, that no one ventured to appropriate any part of the booty, which was brought into one common mass, to be at the disposal of their leader.

This is the version that most Americans know, thanks to the romantic invention of Sir Walter Scott.[580] The scene is the forest where Robin of Locksley and his men have gathered after rescuing the Lady Rowena and her father Cedric from the clutches of the Normans De Tracy and Front-de-Boeuf. Outlaws to Prince John and his henchmen they may be, but (as Scott tells it) they are true Englishmen and so live, even in the greenwood, according to the law.

---

[580] http://www.gutenberg.org/files/82/82-h/82-h.htm

Thus, when they come to divide up the spoils they have taken from Torquilstone Castle, they do so not like thieves, but as men living under the law that the king, if he were truly king, would himself observe:

> Locksley now proceeded to the distribution of the spoil, which he performed with the most laudable impartiality.
>
> A tenth part of the whole was set apart for the church, and for pious uses; a portion was next allotted to a sort of public treasury; a part was assigned to the widows and children of those who had fallen, or to be expended in masses for the souls of such as had left no surviving family.
>
> The rest was divided amongst the outlaws, according to their rank and merit, and the judgment of the Chief, on all such doubtful questions as occurred, was delivered with great shrewdness, and received with absolute submission.
>
> The Black Knight was not a little surprised to find that men, in a state so lawless, were nevertheless among themselves so regularly and equitably governed, and all that he observed added to his opinion of the justice and judgment of their leader.

The media has spent the past two years doing its best to cast Milo as the villain in our national morality play, whether for mocking celebrities on Twitter, telling the truth about his own adolescence, singing *America the Beautiful* in a karaoke bar where he couldn't see what others were doing, or making jokes about how much everyone in the country hates journalists for lying to them. But we, his fans, know that they are lying to us, if nothing else thanks to the lies that they tell about Milo. Over and over and over again. Even when they say that they are going to give him the chance to publish his own version of events, they string him along—and then balk.[581]

Our national elites in journalism, academia, Hollywood, and politics may fancy themselves champions of the poor and oppressed, but all of us who voted for Trump know that they are not to be trusted

---

[581] https://www.milo.net/44762/milo-i-regret-nothing/

to do anything but lie in order to preserve the status to which they have become accustomed as arbiters of the realm. Just like Prince John while his brother King Richard was imprisoned—and even if Richard (a.k.a. the Black Knight) was not the great king Walter Scott would have us believe. Milo, on the other hand, says things like, "No more dead babies," and refuses to bend. Do you really wonder why we, his fans, have stood by him as our Chief?

MIDDLE RAGES

July 31, 2018

Three years ago, in June 2015, I wrote a blog post in praise of the values that undergird our culture in the West, particularly those which support women. I entitled my post "Three Cheers for White Men" to poke fun at the way "dead white males" had become the villains in modern academic culture, but my purpose was serious: to point to the ways in which women in Western civilization have been protected, supported, and encouraged by men from the Middle Ages to the present.

The response came in forms I had never expected—including in the guise of my champion. This is his telling of my story and its significance for my academic field. With thanks to all my colleagues in academia who were willing to go on record talking with Milo, especially Carol [Symes], in the hopes that we can put this chapter behind us. Fencing Bear salutes—and welcomes the conversation to come. Read on...[582]

---

[582] https://www.milo.net/45111/middle-rages/

MYSTERIUM TREMENDUM ET FASCINANS

August 15, 2018

What would you do if you found yourself in the presence of the divine? Last Friday, my friends from Three Kraters Symposium and I gathered together in a secret location—we rented a house—for a special anniversary episode of our show.[583] To mark the occasion, we decided to dress up—in togas. Our show is, after all, titled after the drinking vessels used in ancient symposia, and we open each episode with a toast to our health ("Ymas!") and to the truth that we hope to imbibe through our conversation ("In vino veritas!").

Little did my friends know that I had something even more special in store for them than just a chance to meet each other in person! Only I and a few helpers were in on the secret. As far as most of my friends knew, we were going to be recording that evening, so we would need to spend the day setting up, rearranging the furniture, getting the cameras and lighting ready, making sure everyone would be in costume for when we started filming the show. But then came the crisis: would I be able to sneak in my surprise without the others

---

[583] https://youtu.be/rRnD4bq8tf8

seeing? An inspiration! One of my helpers had been designated official photographer for the evening. She and I arranged that at the appointed time—as determined by the text messages I was receiving from another of my secret team—I would take the company out to the back of the house to the pool, where we would "practice" staging photos for when we were all in costume.

"We want to honor our friend who helped organize our weekend," I told them. "I kept her up late last night talking, so she is asleep now." She wasn't—she was in the car on the way back from the airport, bringing the Surprise! But my friends believed me (for the most part), and they gamely went along with the pantomime. First we practiced Raphael's *School of Athens*—we were going to be playing the part of philosophers on the show, after all. (We got out our cell phones to look up the reference.) Then we practiced Da Vinci's *Last Supper*—the second scene being necessary because the Surprise was not yet inside, and I needed to buy some more time. (I think someone joked at that point about how we should have Milo in the middle as Jesus. *Little did they know!*)

At last, the longed-for text message came. I thanked and congratulated everyone, and ran upstairs. He was there. My helpers and I had gone through the list of things that he requested year before last on his first tour.[584] We had the sparkling water, the Skittles sorted by color into cups, a token Husky puppy, the full-length mirror, the champagne, all to honor him for coming to play with us and share in our celebration. I hadn't seen him in person in nearly a year, although his voice has been in my ear all that time, and he spent the past month writing about me—16,000 words about me, to be precise, not to mention the

---

[584] https://thetab.com/us/2016/08/30/revealed-milo-yiannopoulos-outrageous-tour-rider-50906

time that he spent researching the article. You might say I was a bit overcome. Just a bit.

We put on our costumes and drank the champagne and began plotting how to effect his entrance onto our symposial stage. The house had a balcony out to the front with a door just outside the door of the bedroom where we were dressing. I instructed my helpers to get everyone outside for the group photos we had been practicing, as well as to have the appropriate music cued. He had requested "Entry of the Gods into Valhalla" from Wagner's *Das Rheingold*. Of course. One of my friends, concerned that I was taking so long to get ready, came knocking on the door. "Rachel! Where are you? We are all waiting outside."

"Go back down, Lewis!" I told him, somewhat sharply. "Now!"

It was time. I walked out onto the balcony, iPhone in hand with my text at the ready. Somehow, my friends still had no idea of the surprise to come. In Lewis's words,

> Little [had we known] that [the afternoon's] undressed rehearsals for our pictures were a ruse, a diversion worthy of an Early Modern English comedy. The stage was set perfectly, we were in front of our rental home arrayed along the driveway and perhaps getting odd looks from the neighbors. After all, with ladies in our group looking fetching in Neo-classical garb and we men in togas, it did look like the more family-friendly pictures from *Playboy*'s Midsummer Night's Eve mansion parties.

> My knock on Rachel's door telling her we were waiting and the sharp response from her still did not raise any suspicions, I know what a perfectionist she can be. It also seemed well worth the wait. When she made her appearance she was Lady Wisdom herself. Dressed in a silver gown as lovely and avant-garde as Sargent's *Portrait of Madam X*, but contrasted with a shawl of modesty and a reading from Proverbs.

> Then it all took a turn for the bizarre...

My dress was Ralph Lauren. ("Size 8," I told him. "Of course," he said.) The cloak-shawl came from the Bristol Renaissance Faire. My jewelry was costume, from Macy's. My text came from Proverbs 8:1-11. I blame the text for what happened next. "Wisdom's Call," I read in my best Shakespearean voice, my arms spread wide to embrace the words.

Does not wisdom call out? Does not understanding raise her voice?

At the highest point along the way, where the paths meet, she takes her stand; beside the gate leading into the city, at the entrance, she cries aloud:

"To you, O people, I call out; I raise my voice to all mankind. You who are simple, gain prudence; you who are foolish, set your hearts on it. Listen, for I have trustworthy things to say; I open my lips to speak what is right.

My mouth speaks what is true, for my lips detest wickedness. All the words of my mouth are just; none of them is crooked or perverse.

To the discerning all of them are right; they are upright to those who have found knowledge.

Choose my instruction instead of silver, knowledge rather than choice gold, for wisdom is more precious than rubies, and nothing you desire can compare with her."

I am not unaccustomed to public speaking, but I was still somewhat surprised at the effect as I read Solomon's words. It was as if my voice became the voice of Wisdom, crying out to her children to turn away from the lies towards the truth, inviting them to her instruction, promising them rewards beyond their wildest imagination. "Thank you, my friends, for being here," I said. "I am so happy that we have this house together.... The House that Wisdom has now built for herself (Proverbs 9:1)." Looking down from the balcony, I noticed that my friends all seemed puzzled, not happy, as I had anticipated. Josh started looking round for the Candid Camera crew. The others seemed upset. Perhaps even a little bit frightened. What was Rachel doing? And what was that text she had just read?

"But what would we be, in holding our Symposium together, if not for the God who inspired us all?" I concluded. And then Wagner's great finale started playing, and Milo came forth. I couldn't see him except out of the corner of my eye, even as I turned at his approach. I could sense my friends' astonishment, as they wondered who this terrible character might be. None recognized him as he strode onto the scene, although they rightly guessed the character he was playing. One thought perhaps he was an actor, smuggled into the household in the guise of the pool boy who had come earlier in the day to clean the pool. The others looked even more troubled and stunned than they had when I was speaking Wisdom's call.

"Holy moly, the neighbors are shitting in their pants!" one exclaimed. "I thought the 'pageant' on the balcony was corny and a little creepy," he later told me. "I didn't see the value in the theatrics." Another suggested: "I saw it all as Studio 54, and Warhol showed up. We were the cool kids there, some intelligentsia, some artists, some musicians, some beautiful people. It was the '70s and culture was a-changing."

Another described the scene as something from the *belle époque*— "the gilded four decades between the Treaty of Frankfurt in 1871 and the Guns of August in 1914." In his reading, our "crazy-quilt pageant of historical nostalgia, pop culture, and modern politics" partook of the films of George Méliès and his "moving tableaux of the art nouveau." Another told me that when she saw me come out on the balcony, it looked like I was wearing a communion veil, and that when I started reading from Proverbs it seemed appropriate given my work on the Hours of the Virgin.

I knew in part what they were seeing. While we were dressing, Milo had practiced with the mask before a mirror, saying, "This is the face for this character," and holding his mouth in a terrifying pout. Keith Johnstone describes this effect on his actors doing mask work.[585] Properly primed—as, for example, Milo had primed himself with the mirror—the masks assert their own characters. When he learned that we expected everyone coming to the party to appear in costume, Milo found the mask first and built his costume around it.

"Not Nero," he insisted. "That would be too obvious. A god. Neptune. No, the Symposium is Greek. Poseidon." *Out he came to join her: tall, clad in a suit of black scales, a mantle of feathers around his neck wafting in the light breeze like kelp beneath the sea, a trident in his hand, and face covered in a golden mask.* My friend Shelly recalled her reaction:

> I was surprised to see a dark, tall masked figure, carrying a trident, come out with black gauntlets in a dark feathered capelet. Is this the devil?—I wondered at first. The mask looked more like Loki to me, but this [figure] for sure had a trident, nor did [Loki] have feathers. So this must be Poseidon or some kind of tribal god. I didn't know who it could be under the mask.

Milo is tall, much taller than I am. He is commanding—at least, he often commands me, when I am not in character as his Professor. (More prosaically, Milo gives me very good advice.) I love him, as I have said. But even I was astonished at what I did as he stood beside me on the balcony, with Wagner playing, and my friends standing down below. I knelt.

I had not planned that gesture. In my mind, I was Lady Wisdom, welcoming her Son. I was the one who had brought this group of friends together over the past several years, as we bonded through our appreciation for what Milo was doing in his writing and his talks. I had just read Wisdom's words and invited my friends to the banquet. What was I doing *kneeling* before Milo *as if he were a god?*

---

[585] *Impro: Improvisation and the Theatre* (1987)

Until I converted to Catholicism this past year, I had never spent much time kneeling. At my old church, we knelt occasionally for prayer, but being Anglican (okay, Episcopalian) there was never a clear sense whether anyone other than ourselves was present during Mass. At my new church, we kneel before the tabernacle as we enter the pews, we kneel at the consecration of the host, and we kneel after we have received communion. We kneel because we know ourselves in the presence of God. And there I was—having spent the day keyed up with the anticipation of giving my friends a surprise—kneeling beside Milo in spite of myself. My heart pounding with excitement, all sorts of thoughts raced through my head, but the strongest was this: *Thanks to our play-acting, I have just experienced a taste of the mysterium tremendum et fascinans. This is what holy awe feels like.*

At which point, Milo stamped his trident in signal. Then he took off his mask and flourished it—gayly, you might say—and suddenly it was no longer Lord Poseidon, god of the waters and lord of the deeps, standing beside me, but my friend who had come to our party to do a video with us, not a god at all. I stood up, feeling foolish, only to find that my dress was soaking wet from the rain that we had had earlier that day. But Milo embraced and kissed me, and I was happy again.

And yet, for a moment, as I knelt beside him, Milo had been more than just a human being, just as I had become more than myself while reading the words of Wisdom. Christians talk about "putting on" Christ at baptism; we become Christians when we are baptized and anointed with the holy oil, cleansed of our sins and reborn into the royal priesthood. But how often do we think about what this anointing really means?

As Christians, we are invited to become godlike, transformed through our anointing into children of God, washed clean of our sins to stand before the throne of God, singing with the angels in his praise. I have written before about how I see Milo performing a kind of *imitatio Christi*, both in his willingness to speak the truth in the face of great censure and in the guises that he takes in his performance art. But it is not only Milo who is called to realize him or herself made in the image and likeness of God. It is all of us—and not just those who have already been baptized.

We are called to put on the mask of Christ and mirror him, to become like Wisdom the "unspotted mirror of God's majesty and the image of his goodness" (Wisdom 7:26), and to be transformed from glory to glory into his likeness as we behold his face "as in a glass" (2 Corinthians 3:18). This is what it means to be baptized into Christ, and this is why it was appropriate for me to kneel beside Milo, my fellow Catholic, as if in the presence of God—as in fact we are whenever we participate in that other great pageant, the liturgy. So I knelt. After which, I laughed and invited my friends to the party. Wouldn't you?

THE OLD VOICE OF GLAD AND ANGRY FAITH

September 10, 2018

"to say nothing of all the stuff I do behind the scenes I can never tell you about."

Not sure why you're defending the indefensible.

—JustJinxed, commenting on Three Kraters Symposium, *Episode 58: Politicon Caves to Twitter Outrage and Pulls Milo from Lineup*[586]

I get this kind of comment a lot from my academic colleagues, even those who are otherwise sympathetic to me. They don't know how much I am in contact with Milo or the kinds of things he and I have been talking about, and they tend to assume that Milo is as he has been portrayed in the mainstream media or by *Buzzfeed*: an agent provocateur, someone who is outrageous purely for material gain, a grifter, not a serious interlocutor, doing what he does for the sake of publicity and nothing else.[587]

---

[586] https://youtu.be/AX1JEgReL6s

[587] https://www.newyorker.com/magazine/2018/07/02/how-social-media-trolls-turned-uc-berkeley-into-a-free-speech-circus

How is it possible for me to defend such a person? Surely doing so, as one friend recently put it, is at odds with everything I am as an intellectual. Well. My first response must be of course, "Have you read much of my blog?" But I know that that is asking a lot of colleagues who are busy doing their own research and who tell me, bluntly, "I don't usually read blogs." But even those who write their own blogs have a hard time being sympathetic, particularly with my insistence that the crisis we are in as academics has anything to do with religion.

One, commenting on my *Sightings* article about what Milo's campus tour demonstrated about our culture on campus, noted that he found my argument "distressing on several grounds, most notably Fulton Brown's criticism that secularism is an inadequate substitute for religious ideals."[588] At least he got my argument right! And, to be fair, he does defend my—and Milo's—right to speak when invited to do so on campus, even if he disagrees with what we have to say. But—as a professor of evolutionary biology, not to mention the author of a book entitled *Faith vs. Fact: Why Science and Religion Are Incompatible* (2016)—he is already in the other camp, as it were. The camp that finds whatever I say about faith and the importance of Christianity for our culture ridiculous.

And you ask how I can defend Milo? How can I not? You may say, as does Professor Jerry A. Coyne, that "a Catholic [like Milo] who is gay is somewhat of a hypocrite," but it is saying something if that is the worst accusation you can bring. Which it is—everything else you have heard about Milo are lies. Milo has threatened no one, doxxed no one, called down internet trolls on no one.[589],[590] Neither is he a white

---

[588] https://whyevolutionistrue.wordpress.com/2017/05/17/u-chicago-divinity-school-students-call-for-curtailing-free-speech/

[589] https://fencingbearatprayer.blogspot.com/2018/07/sjws-converge-on-medieval-studiesin.html

[590] https://fencingbearatprayer.blogspot.com/2018/07/galgenhumor.html

supremacist or a Nazi. Nor, for the gazillionth time, does he "support pedophilia"—quite the reverse.[591] What Milo is, as everyone knows who watches even one of his talks all the way through, is a Christian dedicated to defending the soul of Western civilization. Don't believe me? It says so right on his website Dangerous.com:

> Dangerous is owned and operated by Milo, Inc., a 360-degree media company conceived of and founded by Milo. Milo, Inc., is dedicated to leading the battle for the soul of Western civilization by harnessing Milo's unique blend of laughter and war.

Why laughter and war? Milo explained at the conclusion to his acceptance speech for the Annie Taylor Award for Courage in Journalism in 2016:

> So let us fight, but let our motto be Risus et bellum, Laughter and war. Because nothing stings our foes, foreign and domestic, more than our hearty laughter at their lies and nonsense. And also because nothing will better remind us what we're fighting for than the laughter of Chesterton, of Chaucer and of Shakespeare, and of course the God who inspired them all.[592]

Here he was inspired by a passage from G. K. Chesterton's *Heretics* (1905):

> The usual verdict of educated people on the Salvation Army is expressed in some such words as these: "I have no doubt they do a great deal of good, but they do it in a vulgar and profane style; their aims are excellent, but their methods are wrong." To me, unfortunately, the precise reverse of this appears to be the truth.
>
> I do not know whether the aims of the Salvation Army are excellent, but I am quite sure their methods are admirable. Their methods are the methods of all intense and hearty religions; they are popular like

---

[591] https://www.breitbart.com/politics/2015/09/21/heres-why-the-progressive-left-keeps-sticking-up-for-pedophiles/

[592] https://www.breitbart.com/social-justice/2016/11/12/full-text-milos-annie-taylor-award-acceptance-speech-david-horowitzs-restoration-weekend/

all religion, military like all religion, public and sensational like all religion.

They are not reverent any more than Roman Catholics are reverent, for reverence in the sad and delicate meaning of the term reverence is a thing only possible to infidels. That beautiful twilight you will find in Euripides, in Renan, in Matthew Arnold; but in men who believe you will not find it—you will find only laughter and war.

A man cannot pay that kind of reverence to truth solid as marble; they can only be reverent towards a beautiful lie. And the Salvation Army, though their voice has broken out in a mean environment and an ugly shape, are really the old voice of glad and angry faith, hot as the riots of Dionysus, wild as the gargoyles of Catholicism, not to be mistaken for a philosophy.

Professor Huxley, in one of his clever phrases, called the Salvation Army "corybantic Christianity." Huxley was the last and noblest of those Stoics who have never understood the Cross. If he had understood Christianity he would have known that there never has been, and never can be, any Christianity that is not corybantic.[593]

There was a piece in *Quillette* recently that has been niggling at the back of my mind. "Progress and Polytheism," it is entitled. "Could an Ethical West Exist Without Christianity?"[594] The answer, according to its author, is of course, yes, because Stoicism—but this is to make the same mistake Huxley did. Stoics—and I would venture that the majority of my colleagues in academia, if they follow any philosophy at all, are at heart Stoics—are embarrassed by displays such as those Milo makes, not to mention by claims that Christianity is somehow necessary to an enlightened understanding of the world.

Like Harvard psychologist Steven Pinker—whom Quillette author Ben Bassett, "a Ph.D. researcher at Monash University in archeology and ancient history," cites with approval—they want nothing to do

---

[593] http://www.gutenberg.org/files/470/470-h/470-h.htm

[594] https://quillette.com/2018/08/23/progress-and-polytheism-could-an-ethical-west-exist-without-christianity/

with the claim that Christianity brought with it any lasting good. As Bassett summarizes Pinker's position, "the Christian period [before the Enlightenment] was one of moral and political stagnation, thanks in part to its reliance on superstitious 'revelation.'" Why are academics so allergic to Christianity, when, as I pointed out in my *Sightings* article, the very universities at which they teach trace their institutional foundations back to the Middle Ages when theology was queen?[595] Chesterton knew.

> There is only one thing in the modern world that has been face to face with Paganism; there is only one thing in the modern world which in that sense knows anything about Paganism: and that is Christianity. That fact is really the weak point in the whole of that hedonistic neo-Paganism of which I have spoken.

> All that genuinely remains of the ancient hymns or the ancient dances of Europe, all that has honestly come to us from the festivals of Phoebus or Pan, is to be found in the festivals of the Christian Church. If any one wants to hold the end of a chain which really goes back to the heathen mysteries, he had better take hold of a festoon of flowers at Easter or a string of sausages at Christmas.

> Everything else in the modern world is of Christian origin, even everything that seems most anti-Christian. The French Revolution is of Christian origin. The newspaper is of Christian origin. The anarchists are of Christian origin. Physical science is of Christian origin. The attack on Christianity is of Christian origin. There is one thing, and one thing only, in existence at the present day which can in any sense accurately be said to be of pagan origin, and that is Christianity.

> The real difference between Paganism and Christianity is perfectly summed up in the difference between the pagan, or natural, virtues, and those three virtues of Christianity which the Church of Rome calls virtues of grace. The pagan, or rational, virtues are such things as justice and temperance, and Christianity has adopted them. The three

---

[595] They have argued with me about this, too—clearly none of them has ever heard of the universities of Oxford and Cambridge, never mind Paris. Harvard was founded to be the Cambridge of New England. Just saying.

mystical virtues which Christianity has not adopted, but invented, are faith, hope, and charity.

Now much easy and foolish Christian rhetoric could easily be poured out upon those three words, but I desire to confine myself to the two facts which are evident about them. The first evident fact (in marked contrast to the delusion of the dancing pagan)—the first evident fact, I say, is that the pagan virtues, such as justice and temperance, are the sad virtues, and that the mystical virtues of faith, hope, and charity are the gay and exuberant virtues. And the second evident fact, which is even more evident, is the fact that the pagan virtues are the reasonable virtues, and that the Christian virtues of faith, hope, and charity are in their essence as unreasonable as they can be.[596]

My academic colleagues want me—and Milo—to be soberly virtuous. They want him and me to behave with justice and temperance, not exuberant hope. They cannot understand why I spend my time championing someone who dresses up in costume in order to make a serious point—or uses jokes to make intellectually challenging arguments. They see only his antics, never his joy. They hear only his laughter, never his love. They worry about Milo's campy posturing and the effect that it will have on how my own work is received. They think they are being reasonable. I think they are being sticks in the mud.

Perhaps it is impossible for me to help my academic colleagues see what Milo and I are doing with our costumes and jokes. Certainly, they have proved resistant to the arguments I have made about why I have adopted the methodology that I have in my teaching and in my research.[597],[598] But I do not think that this is a reason to stop trying, any more than I think Christianity is dependent on "superstitious 'revelation'" or religion only about being well-behaved. *Hot as the riots of Dionysius, wild as the gargoyles of Catholicism.* Indefensible?

---

[596] https://www.gutenberg.org/files/470/470-h/470-h.htm#chap12

[597] https://home.uchicago.edu/~rfulton/Masterclass.pdf

[598] https://home.uchicago.edu/~rfulton/Professional%20Self%20Portrait.pdf

Yes, if you are a pagan. Not at all if you are willing to give yourself over to faith, hope, and love.

MARY AND MARTHA, OR WHAT I DID IN MY SUMMER VACATION

September 22, 2018

It has been quite the summer.[599] First I learned how to search Twitter and discovered what my academic colleagues have really been saying about Milo and me for the past several years.[600] Then there was the takeover of the Kalamazoo Medieval Congress Facebook group by the SJWs.[601] Then there was Milo's *magnum opus* about the controversy in my field. Then there was getting to see Milo and my friends from Three Kraters in person. There were the invitations to appear on YouTube videos and podcasts.[602]

Then there was the Open Letter that the National Association of Scholars wrote in my support[603]—not to mention the thousand-plus signatures it has received.[604] Then there was the continuing pressure on

[599] https://fencingbearatprayer.blogspot.com/2018/09/report-from-culture-front.html

[600] https://fencingbearatprayer.blogspot.com/2018/08/game-of-threads.html

[601] https://fencingbearatprayer.blogspot.com/2018/07/sjws-converge-on-medieval-studiesin.html

[602] https://fencingbearatprayer.blogspot.com/p/bear-on-air.html

[603] https://fencingbearatprayer.blogspot.com/2018/08/would-you-sign-letter-in-my-support.html

[604] https://www.nas.org/blogs/press_release/nas_supports_a_besieged_academic

the part of my academic colleagues for me to stay quiet.[605] Then there are all the arguments still to be made on the culture front. *A girl might be forgiven for finding it hard to settle down and—as Milo keeps telling me I should—get back to work!* Did I tell you he reminds me of Jesus?

> Now it came to pass as they went, that he entered into a certain town: and a certain woman named Martha, received him into her house. And she had a sister called Mary, who sitting also at the Lord's feet, heard his word.
>
> But Martha was busy about much serving. Who stood and said: Lord, hast thou no care that my sister hath left me alone to serve? speak to her therefore, that she help me.
>
> And the Lord answering, said to her: "Martha, Martha, thou art careful, and art troubled about many things. But one thing is necessary. Mary hath chosen the best part, which shall not be taken from her."—Luke 10:38-42 (Douay Rheims)

It is a tension as old as Christianity itself. Which is better: to serve in the world or to sit still in contemplation? My colleagues in medieval studies who have been most upset with me these past several years would almost certainly answer that it is better to be Martha, actively engaged. That is, after all, how they see themselves: fighting on the front lines of the culture war against the institutional racism, white supremacism, and fascism on which they argue our culture is structurally dependent.

Those who keep urging me to let go of my blogging would most likely insist that it is better to be Mary, removed from the world and its temptations. Except, of course, that what they really mean is, *removed from the temptations to activism of which they disapprove*. Some of the same colleagues advising me to shut up are themselves ::ahem:: quite politically active, just not fans of what Milo and I would say is at stake in the culture wars. Milo is the only one who appreciates what

---

[605] https://fencingbearatprayer.blogspot.com/2018/09/get-thee-to-library.html

is truly at stake. Milo is the one who wants me to be Mary and get back to my proper work, sitting at the feet of the Lord. You'd think I would listen to him, wouldn't you?

The temptations are relentless. Do you know *how much fun* I have been having being out there on the front lines after training for decades to learn the material that I am now being given the opportunity to share? Think Wonder Woman in the trenches given the opportunity to go over the top into No Man's Land. This is what I have been *training for*. This is *my fight. And Milo wants me to sit still?!* If I won't listen to him, perhaps I will listen to Camille Paglia. She knows what it is like to enjoy being in the fray. But she also knows what it is like pretending to be doing work when you aren't. Academics are especially good at this. They call it "presenting at conferences."

> The self-made Inferno of the academic junk-bond era is the conferences, where the din of ambition is as deafening as on the floor of the stock exchange. The huge post-Sixties proliferation of conferences [*Paglia was writing in 1991*], used as an administrative marketing tool by colleges and universities, produced a diversion of professional energy away from study and toward performance, networking, advertisement, cruising, hustling, glad-handing, back-scratching, chitchat, groupthink. Interdisciplinary innovation? Hardly. Real interdisciplinary work is done reading and writing at home and in the library. The conferences teach corporate raiding: academics become lone wolves without loyalty to their own disciplines or institutions; they're always on the trail and on the lookout, ears up for the better job and bigger salary, the next golden fleece or golden parachute. The conferences are all about insider trading and racketeering, jockeying for power by fast-track traveling salesmen pushing their shrink-wrapped product and touting fancy new commercial slogans. The conferences induce a delusional removal from reality....

> Whole careers have gone down the tubes at conferences. Dozens of prominent academics are approaching the moment of reckoning, when they and everyone else will realize they have wasted the best years of their professional lives on cutesy mini-papers and globe-trotting....

What is absurdly called theory today is just a mask for fashion and greed. The conferences are the Alphabet City of addiction to junk, the self-numbing anodyne of rootless, soulless people who have lost contact with their own ethnic traditions. Their work will die with them, for it is based on neither learning nor inspired interpretation. The conferences are oppressive bourgeois forms that enforce a style of affected patter and smarmy whimsy in the speaker and polite chuckles and iron-butt torpor in the audience. Success at the conferences requires a certain kind of physically inert personality, superficially cordial but emotionally dissociated. It's the genteel high Protestant style of the country clubs and corporate board rooms, with their financial reports and marketing presentations. The transient intimacies of the conferences are themselves junk bonds. Dante would classify the conference-hoppers as perverters of the intellect, bad guides, sowers of schism.[606]

No wonder my colleagues in medieval studies were so eager to take over the International Congress on Medieval Studies proposal review![607] *I wonder where Dante would put them?* There is likewise the constant temptation of wanting to belong to what C.S. Lewis called "The Inner Ring," that privileged conversation of "we," the "sensible people," the ones inside.[608] That is, the World to which academics all want to belong, to be excluded from which is to feel oneself damned, cast out into the darkness, made an unperson. A shade. Like, for example, Allen Frantzen.[609] Or me.

Because, of course, the whole point of the existence of the Inner Ring is to exclude. This happens accidentally, if the purpose of the Ring is to encourage real craftsmanship and expertise. But it happens purposefully when the point is to be one of the Inner Ring. After all,

[606] https://www.bu.edu/arion/files/2017/09/Arion-Camille-Paglia-Junkbonds-Corporate-Raiders.pdf

[607] https://www.insidehighered.com/news/2018/07/12/medieval-studies-groups-say-major-conference-trying-limit-diverse-voices-and-topics

[608] https://www.lewissociety.org/innerring/

[609] https://www.chronicle.com/article/Prominent-Medieval-Scholar-s/235014

in Lewis's words, "there'd be no fun if there were no outsiders. The invisible line would have no meaning unless most people were on the wrong side of it. Exclusion is no accident; it is the essence."

The desire to belong, to be one of the Inner Ring has the power to make scoundrels of us all. It is also the most direct route to spending our lives chasing that desire, rather than settling down and doing our own work. To be Conference Marthas, rather than Marys, sitting at the feet of the Lord. There are yet other temptations, of which Milo has been trying to warn me, practiced as he is in braving the No Man's Land of being in the public eye.

There is the temptation to please one's fans by sacrificing one's proper work for something more marketable. There is the temptation to avoid disagreements by talking only with those who already agree with you—or by saying only the things your fans tell you they expect you to say. There is the temptation to keep fighting the same fight over and over again when it would be much better to move on. There is the temptation to feel important because one is involved in much serving—and thus to lose sight of the Lord that we serve. *I don't know how Milo does it.*

Contemplation is hard. It involves sitting still for great stretches of time, thinking thoughts nobody else can appreciate because there is nobody but God to hear. It involves putting yourself on the front line not of attacks from other people, but of your own ignorance—and your own vanity. It is so much easier just to keep talking about things that you already know.

I have greatly enjoyed doing all the podcasts and videos I have recorded this summer. And I have enjoyed the conversations that I have had on my Facebook page and—now that I have some inkling how it works—on Twitter. I enjoy hearing from people who have been reading my blog, and I like the thought that I am helping encourage others who have felt the brunt of the culture wars. But Milo is right. It is not enough to be bustling about all the time, taking care of others. I need to spend some time sitting still again. *I need to remember what it means to be Mary, now that I have had a summer of being Martha for the sake of the Lord.*

AN OPEN LETTER TO THE FACULTY ADVISORY BOARD OF THE NYU STUDENT NEWSPAPER, ON LIES TOLD ABOUT MILO YIANNOPOULOS

November 5, 2018

To:
Yvonne Latty, Clinical Professor of Journalism
Meredith Broussard, Assistant Professor of Journalism
Nanci Healy, Assistant Director of the Center for Student Life

Re: The recent coverage in the Washington Square News of Prof. Michael Rectenwald's invitation for Mr. Milo Yiannopoulos to speak to his class on Halloween

Dear Colleagues,

I read with interest the statement published today by the WSN Editorial Board on their coverage of Milo Yiannopoulos.[610] I understand from the WSN statement of ethics that the students take sole responsibility for the editing of their work, but I am concerned that their statement contains a number of libels against Mr. Yiannopoulos

---

[610] https://nyunews.com/2018/11/04/11-05-ops-house/

presented as facts in support of their coverage.[611] The student editors have also seen fit to run an opinion piece by Ms. Abby Hofstetter which contains an even larger number of libels.[612]

As someone who is well-acquainted with Mr. Yiannopoulos's public statements, I write to draw your attention to these libels, in the hope that you might advise the students about the legal danger they are in. In their editorial, the WSN Editorial Board makes two clearly libelous statements.

1. *"[Mr. Yiannopoulos] makes horrifying statements in order to gain attention, such as when he endorsed the pedophilia within the Catholic Church...."* Mr. Yiannopoulos has never made such a statement. He has spoken in videos easily available on YouTube about his experiences growing up as a gay man, including his experience being sexually abused by two older men when he was between the ages of 13 and 16.[613],[614] He made a public statement about these comments on February 21, 2017, in which he reiterated what he had said in the YouTube videos: he does *not* condone pedophilia and has spent much of his career exposing pedophiles.[615],[616] In his own words:

> I would like to restate my disgust at adults who sexually abuse minors. I am horrified by pedophilia and I have devoted large portions of my career as a journalist to exposing child abusers. I've outed three of them, in fact—three more than most of my critics....

---

[611] https://nyunews.com/about/

[612] https://nyunews.com/2018/11/05/nyu-needs-to-acknowledge-its-anti-semitic-problem/

[613] https://youtu.be/azC1nm85btY

[614] https://youtu.be/LnH67G7vAu4

[615] https://www.breitbart.com/the-media/2017/02/21/full-remarks-milo-delivers-speech-press-conference-amid-video-scandal/

[616] https://www.breitbart.com/politics/2015/09/21/heres-why-the-progressive-left-keeps-sticking-up-for-pedophiles/

I do not believe sex with 13-year-olds is okay. When I mentioned the number 13, I was talking about myself, and the age I lost my own virginity...

I shouldn't have used the word "boy"—which gay men often do to describe young men of consenting age—instead of "young man." That was an error. I was talking about my own relationship when I was 17 with a man who was 29. The age of consent in the UK is 16.[617]

On the very day that he was scheduled to speak to Professor Rectenwald's class, Bombadier Books released Mr. Yiannopoulos's second book *Diabolical*, in which he criticizes Pope Francis and his supporters specifically for their role in the cover-ups of sexual abuse in the Church. He also details in this book his experience of abuse from the age of 13 and how he now understands why he spoke about it in the way that he did in the videos, for which he apologized in the press conference in February 2017:

I haven't ever apologized before. Name-calling doesn't bother me. But to be a victim of child abuse and for the media to call me an apologist for child abuse is absurd... I regret the things I said. I don't think I've been as sorry about anything in my whole life. This isn't how I wanted my parents to find out about this.

As Mr. Yiannopoulos makes clear in *Diabolical*, having spoken with other victims of Father Michael, he now realizes that others received far worse treatment at Father Michael's hands and were more damaged by their experiences than he. In retrospect and with this additional information, Mr. Yiannopoulos now holds the matter to be much more serious than he had originally thought, when he was speaking solely on the basis of his own experiences.

2. *"...and made racist, dehumanizing comments toward Leslie Jones."* Mr. Yiannopoulos has never made a racist or dehumanizing comment about Ms. Leslie Jones. In the review that he published of the movie

---

[617] https://www.breitbart.com/social-justice/2017/02/21/milo-apologizes/

Ghostbusters, he specifically critiqued the character that Ms. Jones portrayed as racist and stereotypical, and he chided the writers of the movie for giving her such a demeaning role. In his words:

> Patty [Ms. Jones's character] is a two dimensional racist stereotype by even the most forgiving measure.

> Patty is the worst of the lot. The actress is spectacularly unappealing, even relative to the rest of the odious cast. But it's her flat-as-a-pancake black stylings that ought to have irritated the SJWs. I don't get offended by such things, but they should....

> The petty, two-dimensional feminist posturing of *Ghostbusters* is demeaning to all four of its leads, particularly when you consider how complex and interesting the film could have been with someone like Joss Whedon at the helm.[618]

When Ms. Jones went on Twitter to complain about the poor ticket sales the movie was receiving, Mr. Yiannopoulos tweeted: "If at first you don't succeed (because your work is terrible), play the victim. EVERYONE GETS HATE MAIL FFS." Ms. Jones reported Mr. Yiannopoulos to Twitter and called one of his fans a "racist b*tch" for saying "how sad that a comedian would want to limit free speech. Lenny Bruce is rolling over in his grave."

Mr. Yiannopoulos responded to Ms. Jones: "Ghostbusters is doing so badly they've deployed @Lesdoggg to play the victim on Twitter. Very sad!" "Barely literate. America needs better schools." At which point, Mr. Yiannopoulos was blocked from linking to her account. To which Mr. Yiannopoulos replied: "Rejected by yet another black dude."[619] It is true that Mr. Yiannopoulos makes critical remarks about the feminist posturing of the movie and that in his Tweets he suggested that Ms. Jones looks like a man, but unless men are not

---

[618] https://www.breitbart.com/tech/2016/07/18/milo-reviews-ghostbusters/

[619] https://www.breitbart.com/social-justice/2016/07/18/ghostbuster-leslie-jones-reports-milo/

human, he did not "dehumanize" her. He explicitly defended her against the racist stereotype she was given to portray.

In her opinion piece, Ms. Abby Hofstetter makes a number of even more libelous assertions. While the WSN Editorial Board claims that Mr. Yiannopoulos "endorsed the pedophilia within the Catholic Church," Ms. Hofstetter calls him a pedophile. In her words: "I was also surprised at how many students I heard excusing Yiannopoulos' racism, anti-Semitism and pedophilia in the name of the First Amendment." This is clear libel. Ms. Hofstetter has stated that Mr. Yiannopoulos has sex with children, an actionable crime.

Ms. Hofstetter supports her assertion of Mr. Yiannopoulos's "racism" with a link to an article about Ms. Jones.[620] She links to an article citing statements that Mr. Yiannopoulos made on a video with Dave Rubin about Jews being prominent in banking and the media to prove his "anti-Semitism."[621] She links to the article that Mr. Yiannopoulos co-authored with Mr. Allum Bokhari on the alt-right as it was in March 2016 as proof that Mr. Yiannopoulos himself is "alt-right."[622]

She uses Mr. Yiannopoulos's marriage to his black husband John (whom she describes as Muslim on the basis of no evidence whatsoever)[623] and his references to his Jewish grandmother[624] as proof of Mr. Yiannopoulos's "racism," and she links to the video where Mr. Yiannopoulos was singing *America the Beautiful* as proof of his

---

[620] https://www.usatoday.com/story/life/books/2017/02/21/leslie-jones-advice-milo-yiannopoulos-stop-feeding-trolls/98190810/

[621] https://forward.com/fast-forward/363722/before-milo-yiannopoulos-backed-sex-with-teens-he-spewed-anti-semitism/

[622] https://www.breitbart.com/tech/2016/03/29/an-establishment-conservatives-guide-to-the-alt-right/

[623] https://www.dailymail.co.uk/news/article-4938912/Milo-gets-married-Hawaii.html

[624] https://forward.com/fast-forward/361705/watch-milo-yiannopoulos-says-hes-a-jew-not-a-nazi/

association with Mr. Richard Spencer.[625] In Ms. Hofstetter's words, Mr. Yiannopoulos is "[a] man who waves his 'blind for love' black Muslim husband and Jewish grandmother around like they signed his permission slip to be hailed by Richard Spencer," insulting both Mr. Yiannopoulos and his husband in one go, while at the same time suggesting that Mr. Yiannopoulos has any control over Mr. Spencer's actions.

Not only does Ms. Hofstetter dismiss both the fact that Mr. Yiannopoulos is married to a black man and that he is ethnically Jewish in order to call him a racist and an anti-Semite, but she also implies that Mr. Yiannopoulos's husband is a pawn in the machinations of a "white supremacist," while insisting that a man who describes himself as an "utterly unreconstructed Zionist" can have his Jewishness stripped from him as a consequence of his politics.[626]

Ms. Hofstetter also claims that Mr. Yiannopoulos is a "white supremacist," a libel for which Mr. Yiannopoulos has rightly been granted a retraction by numerous journalists and publications. The one citation Ms. Hofstetter gets right is that Mr. Yiannopoulos described himself on October 30, 2018, as "the most censored man in America," the day on which Mayor Bill DeBlasio stepped in to cancel his visit to NYU.

I have written at length on my blog about the slurs cast against Mr. Yiannopoulos over the past two years, including the claim that he is in any way an associate of Mr. Richard Spencer. The mutual dislike between Mr. Yiannopoulos and Mr. Spencer is well-documented and public. Any inference that they are "associates" is dishonest in the extreme, as the Tweets Mr. Spencer made on the day of Mr.

---

[625] https://youtu.be/XLNLPIRS62g
[626] https://www.campusreform.org/?ID=11150

Yiannopoulos's shaming for speaking loosely about his own abuse make clear.

> Just finished a video on Milo, uploading now. The guy is totally done. No sane person will defend him. —Richard Spencer @RichardBSpencer (20 Feb 2017)

> #Milo is now irrelevant. He channeled troll culture and the Alt Right. That's over, and thus he's over. It's not like he is a deep thinker. — Richard Spencer @RichardBSpencer (21 Feb 2017)

Not only does Mr. Spencer think Mr. Yiannopoulos is "totally done" and "[not] a deep thinker." He thinks Mr. Yiannopoulos is a Zionist and a cultural degenerate thanks to Mr. Yiannopoulos's friendship with Pamela Geller, herself a Jew and whose name he (Mr. Spencer) can't spell:[627]

> 6/ The fact that Milo and Pamela Gellar have come together reveals what's at the heart of anti-Sharia: Zionism and cultural degeneration. —Richard Spencer @RichardBSpencer (10 Jun 2017)

Ms. Hofstetter argues that NYU needs to "acknowledge its anti-Semitic problem." Given that she has described a man who is close friends with a Jewish woman now under a fatwa for her outspoken defense of Western civilization as "anti-Semitic," it is unclear what anti-Semitic problem Ms. Hofstetter means. Not only is Mr. Yiannopoulos friends with Ms. Geller; as the publisher of her book *Fatwa: Hunted in America* (2017), he is under the fatwa himself as her business associate, in effect risking death for her—hardly the action of an anti-Semite.

To cap it all off, Ms. Hofstetter claims that the talk that Mr. Yiannopoulos live-streamed on Halloween in lieu of his appearance in Professor Rectenwald's class was "riddled with jokes about Anne Frank, pedophilia and suicide." If Ms. Hofstetter watched the video as carefully as she must have in order to glean even a few examples

---

[627] https://youtu.be/RbsEiYKi-2Y

of things she did not find funny, she knows that she is taking them out of context.

Also, Mr. Yiannopoulos did not mention pedophilia, and if he had, it would have been to condemn it as he does in *Diabolical: How Pope Francis Has Betrayed Clerical Abuse Victims Like Me–And Why He Has to Go* (2018). According to the conduct policy published on your About page,

> WSN requires its staff and writers to behave in a professional manner and adhere to industry-standard guidelines for reporting. We seek to find the truth and report it while minimizing the risk of harm, protecting sources and striving for honesty and accuracy in what we publish.

You also note that "WSN will correct articles as soon as possible and provide updated information whenever possible." I hope to see the corrections to the articles above made as soon as possible, particularly those statements libeling Mr. Yiannopoulos with opinions he does not hold and labeling him an actual criminal of the worst kind.

I would hope that your editors would see fit in future to research such claims properly, rather than relying on hearsay and links to uncorroborated reporting.

I would not want for their sloppiness in reporting on this important issue to stand as a reflection on the caliber of education they are receiving at your institution nor on the quality of mentorship you have offered them as their advisors. I trust you share my respect for the gravity of this responsibility.

Yours sincerely,

Rachel Fulton Brown

Associate Professor of History

The University of Chicago

CREDO UT INTELLIGAM

December 26, 2018

It is difficult to describe the crisis I have been living through these past several weeks. *Short version*: Don't call out the Devil if you aren't ready to bout. *Alternative short version*: "Where is the wise? Where is the scribe? Where is the disputer of this world? Hath not God made foolish the wisdom of the world?"[628] There has been much bitterness.

There have been feelings of betrayal.

There have been feelings of being lied to while watching people whom I thought were my supporters fall away. Friends warn me about overreacting. At which I overreact. "Academic freedom means nothing if the faculty do not stand up for it." I believed that. Someone whom I have trusted my entire academic career told me that. I still believe it—but do my colleagues?

"Any sufficiently advanced intelligence is indistinguishable from insanity." I heard someone say that recently on his livestream. Someone whom my friends tell me I should be wary of associating myself with because he has been called the same names I have over the past several years.

---

[628] 1 Corinthians 1:20

❧

Three weeks ago, I found this note tucked behind a drawing that I had posted by my office door.

Dear Dr. Brown.

You are a white nationalist and a detriment to all forms of knowledge. Please resign, as your institution has and will continue to fail to condemn your actions.

You are a violent and malicious threat to academia and to the future. Not only do you profess racist ideologies, but you collude with all sorts of monstrous people who transform your otherwise out-dated and foolish forms of racism into something much worse.

I posted the letter on my social media and my friends got a good laugh out of it. I told my dean and chair about the letter, and the campus police sent an officer round that evening to take a statement from me. Colleagues from around the world wrote to me, expressing dismay that I should be receiving such missives. *And nothing happened.*

"The greatest trick the Devil ever pulled was convincing the world he didn't exist." —Kevin Spacey, in *The Usual Suspects*.

❧

How do you know you aren't crazy when all around you people are telling you that you are seeing things that aren't there? And that you are missing things that are? My friends and I did an episode on Three Kraters Symposium about Vox Day's book on Jordan Peterson.[629],[630] Milo wrote the Foreword.[631] You know what I think about Milo. You can probably guess what I think about Professor Peterson from the posts I did about him this past year.[632]

---

[629] https://youtu.be/mLrE2D7RAuE

[630] *Jordanetics: A Journey into the Mind of the World's Greatest Thinker* (2018)

[631] http://voxday.blogspot.com/2018/11/the-wrong-kind-of-chameleon.html

[632] https://fencingbearatprayer.blogspot.com/p/the-lady-and-logos.html

My friends disagree. We recorded our episode on Peterson the evening of the same day I found the letter tucked behind the Bulbasaur. I gave my statement to the campus police officer minutes before we started recording. Vox Day did a blogpost about our episode and then came over to our YouTube channel to weigh in.[633] My friends disagreed with him, too.

My take on Professor Peterson, short version: He speaks in a way that leaves people guessing. He refuses to define terms and/or offers definitions that shift according to the audience to whom he is speaking. People project onto him what they want to believe he has said, which is why they become so defensive when people like Vox Day and Milo (and me) call him out. Judging from the responses I have seen to our video, some agree with Vox and Milo, even if they don't like either of them. Some insist that Peterson is not a Christian. Others insist that he is. Why should it be so difficult to tell?

My take on Professor Peterson, slightly longer version: His theology, such as it is, derives ultimately from Ludwig Feuerbach.[634] The whole point of Feuerbach's theology is to insist that human beings project themselves onto an imaginary Being they call "God," whom they then imagine works back on them. In much the same way, Professor Peterson's followers project themselves onto Professor Peterson, to whom they look as their father-figure who then tells them what to do.

"When man ceases to worship God he does not worship nothing but worships everything."—G.K. Chesterton (attributed)

"If you drive out explicit theology from public education, you get not *no* theology, but only *bad* theology, theology never properly examined as such."—Rachel Fulton Brown, "Why Milo Scares Students—and Faculty Even More"

---

[633] http://voxday.blogspot.com/2018/12/the-lobster-cult-is-shook.html

[634] https://fencingbearatprayer.blogspot.com/2018/07/if-professor-jordan-b-peterson-said-he.html

Back in the Middle Ages, Anselm of Canterbury prayed to God to help him understand how to find Him:

> Teach me to seek you, and reveal yourself to me, when I seek you, for I cannot seek you, except you teach me, nor find you, except you reveal yourself. Let me seek you in longing, let me long for you in seeking; let me find you in love, and love you in finding.

> Lord, I acknowledge and I thank you that you have created me in this your image, in order that I may be mindful of you, may conceive of you, and love you; but that image has been so consumed and wasted away by vices, and obscured by the smoke of wrong-doing, that it cannot achieve that for which it was made, except you renew it, and create it anew.

> I do not endeavor, O Lord, to penetrate your sublimity, for in no wise do I compare my understanding with that; but I long to understand in some degree your truth, which my heart believes and loves. For I do not seek to understand that I may believe, but I believe in order to understand. For this also I believe, —that unless I believed, I should not understand.[635]

The modern world has no use for such a prayer. In the modern world, Reason is believed to be paramount. It is the argument that the New Atheists use: something that cannot be proven by reason cannot be true, while those who seek in faith are blind. I get this a lot on Twitter these days:

> Have you listened to Gaslit Nation? Rachel's tactics are textbook authoritarian tactics. A seemingly impenetrable fortress of obfuscation, denial, charm, fake experts, conspiracy theories, & blythe nonchalance. I've had enough. Merry Christmas. —Sarah Woods @ArtSciSarah (20 Dec 2018)

> It's also scary: the border wall, the Muslim banning, the transphobia... she's all in, prayers only for blastocysts as she votes against the living trying to get to safety. —D.E.M. @AddieBundren (Dec 20)

---

[635] https://sourcebooks.fordham.edu/basis/anselm-proslogium.asp

It's the impenetrability I find so mystifying. No matter how half-baked, inhumane, or indecent her positions are shown to be, she maintains her self-perception of virtue. Chris Stoop writes about the "pro-life" "fetish." I am interested in the stubbornness of delusion. —Sarah Woods @ArtSarah (Dec 20)

Owen Benjamin has described Professor Peterson as a "wizard," by which he means someone who uses language to affect reality.[636] Vox Day makes a similar argument in his book. Professor Peterson's Eighth Rule is *Tell the Truth—Or, At Least, Don't Lie*. But, as Vox shows, Professor Peterson regularly lies about things he himself has said. Vox gives the example of Peterson's comments on *The Joe Rogan Experience* when he claimed not to have slept for 25 days.[637] I have written about the way in which Peterson claimed not to know Milo when he had been talking about him regularly for the better part of two years. What does Professor Peterson's eighth rule really mean, according to Vox?

The Eighth Principle of Jordanetics: You can speak a new world into existence through lies.

℀

How did we get to the place where those of us arguing in favor of the existence of nations are called racist even when nothing that we say in this context has anything to do with race?[638] How did we get to the place where those of us arguing that abortion is the intentional killing of a living creature are called delusional when the whole point about abortion is that if you don't have one when you get pregnant you will have a baby? How did we get to the place where those of us arguing in favor of Christianity as against other theological traditions are called phobic simply for pointing out the real differences between

---

[636] https://youtu.be/L_zQAlLNX7M

[637] https://youtu.be/9Xc7DN-noAc

[638] https://fencingbearatprayer.blogspot.com/2016/11/i-will-be-wall-for-them.html

the traditions?[639],[640] How did we get to the place where those of us arguing in favor of the virtues of the towns are called white supremacist, again, when nothing in our argument has anything to do with race?[641] The answer is simple: we—by which I mean, "we moderns"—have rejected Revelation.

> "For I do not seek to understand that I may believe, but I believe in order to understand. For this I also believe, —that unless I believed, I should not understand." —Anselm of Canterbury

One of the readers of Vox Day's blog wrote to me and recommended a book he thought I would like: Fr. Seraphim Rose's *Nihilism: The Root of the Revolution of the Modern Age* (1994). The problem, according to Fr. Seraphim, is not with postmodernism or political correctness or any of the fashionable boogeymen of the day. It is with modernity itself and its embrace of nihilism, the conviction that there is no such thing as truth, only "truths" which cannot be proven except empirically. Professor Peterson uses a similar definition of "truth":

> The moral relativists ask: what do you mean by should? Here's how you should act: Act in a way so that things are good for you like they would be for someone you're taking care of. But they have to be good for you in a way that's also good for your family, and they have to be good for you and your family also in a way that's good for society (and maybe even good for the broader environment if you can manage that), so it's balanced at all those levels. And it has to be good for you, your family, and society right now, AND next week, AND next month, AND a year from now, AND ten years from now. It's this harmonious balancing of multiple layers of Being simultaneously, and that's a Darwinian reality, I would say. Your brain is actually attuned to tell you when you are doing that. And the way it tells you is that it reveals that what you're doing is meaningful. That's the sign. Your nervous system is adapted

---

[639] https://fencingbearatprayer.blogspot.com/2016/01/on-anger-righteous-or-otherwise.html

[640] https://fencingbearatprayer.blogspot.com/2016/03/all-cultures-are-not-one.html

[641] https://fencingbearatprayer.blogspot.com/2017/09/bourgeois-is-new-white.html

to do this. It's adapted to exist on the edge between order and chaos. Chaos is where things are so complex that you can't handle it, and order is where things are so rigid that it's too restrictive. In between that, there's a place. It's a place that's meaningful. It's where you're partly stabilized, and partly curious. You're operating in a manner that increases your scope of knowledge, so you're inquiring and growing, and at the same time you're stabilizing and renewing you, your family, society, nature; now, next week, next month, and next year. When you have an intimation of meaning, then you know you're there.... Lies and deception destroy people's lives. When they start telling the truth and acting it out, things get a lot better.[642]

Truth is something you *act on*. You know that it is true when your life improves—"and that's a Darwinian reality." I agree with Professor Peterson that it is important to tell the truth. Based on Milo's and my experience over the past several years, I do not agree with his criterion for determining what is truth—for otherwise why would I be getting hate mail tucked into the Pokémon by my office door? *Hint: Notice how what Professor Peterson is actually suggesting: truth is what makes you fit in because it is the way you achieve "balance."*

I am struggling now with how to make clear the things that I see thanks to my faith. For a time, I believed as others do that Professor Peterson was speaking in a way that pointed, like Anselm's, to God. But the more I listened to him, the more I realized that it was my own faith I was projecting onto him, not something that he himself shared. Vox Day calls Professor Peterson's use of Christianity "his own personal Trojan Horse, with all manner of occult heresies lurking within." Here I am inclined to agree. As I argued last winter, I think at best Professor Peterson is a Pelagian; at worst, well, it remains to be seen.[643]

---

[642] https://en.wikiquote.org/wiki/Jordan_Peterson

[643] https://fencingbearatprayer.blogspot.com/2018/02/who-wants-to-be-heretic.html

The problem is, how do I know? How do I know that I am not now projecting onto him the same kind of lies that others have projected onto Milo and me?

Why do you not know my speech? Because you cannot hear my word. You are of your father the devil: and the desires of your father you will do. He was a murderer from the beginning: and he stood not in the truth, because truth is not in him. When he speaketh a lie, he speaketh of his own: for he is a liar, and the father thereof. But if I say the truth, you believe me not.[644]

Again, back in the Middle Ages, Christians would know.

And if you should ask me how one can know that the visitation is from the devil and not from me, I would answer you that this is the sign:

If it is the devil who has come to visit the mind under the guise of light, the soul experiences gladness at his coming. But the longer he stays, the more gladness gives way to weariness and darkness and pricking as the mind becomes clouded over by his presence within.

But when the soul is truly visited by me, eternal Truth, she experiences holy fear at the first encounter. And with this fear comes gladness and security, along with a gentle prudence that does not doubt even while it doubts, but through self-knowledge considers itself unworthy...

This, then, is how the soul can tell whether she is being visited by me or by the devil: In my visitation she will find fear at the beginning; but in the middle and at the end, gladness and a hunger for virtue.

When it is the devil, however, the beginning is happy, but then the soul is left in spiritual confusion and darkness. Now I have warned you by giving you the sign, so that the soul, if she chooses to behave humbly and prudently, cannot be deluded. The one deluded will be the soul who chooses to travel only with the imperfect love of her own consolation rather than of my affection.[645]

᪥

---

[644] John 8:43-45

[645] St. Catherine of Siena, *Dialogue*, chapter 71, trans. Suzanne Noffke (1980)

Two years ago, writing about the riots that accompanied Milo's attempts to speak truth on college campuses, I argued that we in academia were experiencing a crisis of faith, at which colleagues around the country declared me hateful, not to mention wrong. At that point, I still believed that it was possible to argue against their perceptions of him on the basis of evidence.

Two years and many blogposts later, I have come to the conclusion that my optimism was misplaced. My colleagues in academia—including whoever wrote the letter left by my office door—are no more capable of hearing what I say about Milo (my most "monstrous" associate) than they are of hearing what I say about Mary *because they do not have faith*.[646] They have ears but they *cannot* hear; they have eyes but they *cannot* see. That Twitter thread where Sarah Woods and D.E.M. decided I was delusional?[647]

It went on for weeks, with Ms. Woods arguing that Jesus was a rape baby and Mary the victim of a pedophile, me arguing that the whole point of the Incarnation was that Mary gave her consent.[648] Ms. Woods and I literally inhabit different realities, she one in which Christianity is to blame for the evils of teen pregnancy and the submission of women, myself one in which Christianity is the sole tradition in which women have been recognized as equals with men, made in the image and likeness of God and endowed with free will—thus the doctrine of consent on which Ms. Wood bases her critique of the Annunciation. There is no middle ground, one or the other of us must be wrong.

That thread, too, began *the same day* on which I received the letter by my office door, *the same day* on which my friends and I did our episode about Vox Day's critique of Jordan Peterson. I kept hoping that someone would come to my rescue. I kept hoping that there would

---

[646] https://fencingbearatprayer.blogspot.com/2018/11/satan-be-gone.html

[647] https://twitter.com/RFultonBrown/status/1071063556379066374

[648] https://medium.com/@artscisarah/jesus-was-a-rape-baby-98e652f2d8f8

be some response from my colleagues about the letter that I received, other than sending the campus police officer to take a statement. I kept hoping that I could convince my friends in Three Kraters that what I had seen in Professor Peterson's (lack of) theology was real.

I kept hoping that someone would back me up in my argument on Twitter (although, to be fair, I kept that thread going as much for my own amusement as for the need to practice my arguments; plus, as I told Ms. Wood, I also hoped to keep it going long enough to wish her "Merry Christmas" on the day). Day after day after day. And no help came. Until Christmas. More precisely, until midnight Mass on Christmas Eve, when at last, after weeks going without communion (thanks to a fencing tournament and holiday travel—*I know, big mistake!*), I made it to church. And I was no longer alone.

How do Christians explain to those without faith what it means to see the world as a creature of God? How do we explain the joy that we experience in knowing ourselves to be creatures of God, made in His image and likeness in order to praise and enjoy Him? How do we fight the constant temptation to give into the world and to the pressure to conform to its promises which we know are lies? How do we show them the way to the truth which passes all understanding on whose foundations the world was made?

Milo knows what is at stake. It is the reason he has not given up, despite everything.[649] Because he believes, as I believe, that "the Word became flesh and dwelt among us (and we saw his glory, the glory as it were of the only begotten of the Father), full of grace and truth."[650] *If only there were some way to help others understand what—and whom—it is we see.*

---

[649] https://www.milo.net/49828/milo-my-christmas-message-2018/
[650] John 1:14

2019

2019

HOW TO BE GOD-RIGHT

January 19, 2019

I have had a fair amount of fall-out thanks to the video that I did with my friends about Vox Day's book on Jordan Peterson, *Jordanetics: A Journey into the Mind of Humanity's Greatest Thinker* (2018).[651],[652] If you have watched the video, you know that I agree with Milo (who wrote the Foreword) and Vox in their critique of the Good Professor. Like Milo and Vox, I do not see Jordan as on "our" side.[653] Quite the reverse. I became wary of Professor Peterson about this time last year, after spending over a month trying to make sense of what happened in his interview with Cathy Newman.[654]

I became increasingly suspicious as I watched his interactions with Ben Shapiro and Dave Rubin on their shows, and I lost all faith in him as an ally when he threw Milo under the bus rather than argue with Bari Weiss about whether Milo was "possibly [a racist]." By the time Professor Peterson made his Kavanaugh tweet, the camel was already on the ground, crippled and unable to rise.

---

[651] https://youtu.be/mLrE2D7RAuE

[652] https://voxday.blogspot.com/2018/12/the-lobster-cult-is-shook.html

[653] http://voxday.blogspot.com/2018/06/mailvox-unorthodox-or-enemy.html

[654] https://fencingbearatprayer.blogspot.com/p/the-lady-and-logos.html

I do not think Professor Peterson believes in God by any definition that I would recognize.[655],[656],[657] (*Hint*: If you care more about what Professor Peterson thinks about God than about how God makes Himself visible to the world, you are worshipping an idol. Just saying.) But that is not what this post is about. This post is about fear and how SJWs use it to silence you by making you disavow your friends.[658] "You know Vox is alt-right, don't you?" one of my friends messaged me after watching our video.

Me: "I have heard my Vile Boyfriend described that way, too. Funny that."[659]

My friend: "Your 'vile boyfriend' hasn't come out and actually stated he is alt-right."[660]

Me: "And yet, oddly, he is still friends with Vox. So much so that he wrote a foreword for Vox's book.[661] Twice.[662] In case there is any question: Vox is no more 'alt-right' in the terms you mean than Milo is. They are friends."

My friend: "Yeah. That is odd and troubling. You are clearly ignoring the large swath of Vox's words and ideology because of your fascination with Milo."[663]

Me: "Why? Milo is not a white supremacist, if that is what you are worrying about. Neither is Vox. Nothing Vox says is any more

[655] https://fencingbearatprayer.blogspot.com/2018/07/if-professor-jordan-b-peterson-said-he.html

[656] https://fencingbearatprayer.blogspot.com/2009/06/bears-proof-for-existence-of-god.html

[657] https://fencingbearatprayer.blogspot.com/2008/06/shield-of-faith_29.html

[658] http://voxday.blogspot.com/2017/04/sjw-doesnt-like-being-identified-as-such.html

[659] http://voxday.blogspot.com/2016/09/the-pretty-monstrous-face.html

[660] http://voxday.blogspot.com/2016/08/what-alt-right-is.html

[661] http://voxday.blogspot.com/2018/11/the-wrong-kind-of-chameleon.html

[662] *SJWs Always Lie: Taking Down the Thought Police* (2015)

[663] http://voxday.blogspot.com/2016/11/controlled-opposition-or-media.html

'extreme' than, for example, what Douglas Murray has said [about immigration]. And Douglas Murray tours with Jordan Peterson. I am not 'fascinated' with Milo. I love Milo."

My friend: "You are obsessed. You are obsessed to the point that you cannot see the danger Vox presents to not only your reputation and friendships but your career. I am saying this because you are a friend, and I don't want to see you destroyed because of this."

My friend clearly hasn't been paying attention. *Doesn't he know that warning me that someone is too dangerous to know is simply to make me all the more curious about what it is he has said?*[664] Of course I went and looked.[665] (*Take your time. Vox has been writing about Milo even longer than I have.*[666]) What did I find? Vox and Milo are friends because Vox and Milo are on the same side—God's side.[667] Vox has stood by Milo, again, for even longer than I have, never once feeling the temptation that Professor Peterson did, to claim that he had not "followed Milo that carefully." Even though Milo is gay and Vox is a devout Christian who believes sodomy is a sin. Little did I know, but Vox has been there all along, taking the hits for Milo, when I thought that Milo was all alone before he found John.

Talk about the Voice of God:

> Milo stood by me when I made a media misstep that angered people at *Breitbart*. I stood by Milo when the media attempted to crucify him for his Joe Rogan interview and he lost his book deal with Simon & Schuster. That's what friends and allies do, even when the other individual is flawed, imperfect, or behaves in a suboptimal manner.

---

[664] My friend insists he urged me to go look at Vox's blog so that I would see that all the things he was telling me about Vox were true. The problem is, I don't see what he sees when I read Vox's own words—much as I don't see the things that people say about Milo in what Milo says.

[665] https://voxday.blogspot.com/search?q=milo

[666] http://voxday.blogspot.com/2017/10/buzzfeed-and-stolen-emails.html

[667] http://voxday.blogspot.com/2015/07/paris-in-48-hours.html

And only a fool or a social reject abandons people over mere differences of opinion or the occasional moral failure.[668]

But what about Vox's "words and ideology" that my friend was warning me against? Surely mere friendship should not be enough to make me lose my discretion. Well. Consider what has been said about Milo. Consider how many lies are out there about him. Consider how I have spent the past two and a half years—just like Vox—defending Milo when the whole world was coming for him and calling him names. Names like "white supremacist." Names like "pedophile apologist." Names like "Nazi."

Milo is none of these things, and yet everyone on social media seems to know that these names are true. They aren't. They are lies. Just like the lies spread about Vox. Now, why would that be? Vox knows. Vox wrote the book on it. SJWs always lie—because that is the only way that they can win. They can't win with arguments, not logical ones. So they win, as Vox has shown, with rhetoric, that is, by playing on their opponents' emotions. Above all, they win with fear—making friends afraid to stand with friends lest they get labeled as beyond the pale. They win by making people so afraid that they won't even go look at the arguments people like Vox and Milo are making. They win, as they have since Robespierre inspired the Mountain, with terror—because they cannot win with truth. In Vox's words:

> Rhetoric is all about what emotions you trigger in the other person; when SJWs talk to each other, they try to inflate themselves at the other's expense in order to sort out their position in the SJW hierarchy.... The basic idea is that if you can make the other person feel small or angry, you are winning at SJW rhetoric. This is why SJWs are constantly accusing other people of being mad or upset; it's just another way of them claiming to be winning the conversation.

---

[668] http://voxday.blogspot.com/2017/09/real-alt-right.html

Vox and Milo drive SJWs mad because they refuse to succumb to such tactics. Vox, because he will not back down no matter what names they call him. Milo, because he turns their attacks into a joke. Meanwhile, the cuckservatives are cowering in fear, begging Milo and Vox to stop drawing enemy fire or, alternatively, throwing them under the bus for being "extreme." Are Milo and Vox "extreme"? Extremely effective, yes. Extreme in political terms, no, unless you think believing in human nature, families, nations, and Our Lord Jesus Christ is "extreme."

I was originally taken with Professor Peterson because he defended Milo when Milo was down and he, Professor Peterson, was first coming under fire. But once the world had embraced him, Professor Peterson seemed to forget what he had said, instead nodding along as Ben and Dave declared Milo "irrelevant," eventually succumbing to Bari Weiss's efforts to make Milo untouchable by labeling him a racist. As Milo noted, at that moment, Professor Peterson was speaking "in front of what must have been the wealthiest audience he'd ever addressed." How many of us would not cave at the prospect of winning the world, if only we were willing to distance ourselves from someone whom otherwise we might call friend? "If the world hates you," someone once said,

> know that it has hated me before it hated you. If you were of the world, the world would love its own. But because you are not of the world, I chose you out of the world, therefore the world hates you... If they persecuted me, they will persecute you; if they kept my word, they will keep yours also. —John 15:18-20

As an antidote to Professor Peterson's "12 Rules for Being Really Mediocre," Vox has offered his own "12 Real Rules for Life." I am still somewhat angry at my friend for suggesting that Vox was anything other than a good friend to Milo—especially now that I know how good a friend Vox actually has been—but I am chastened, as I should be, by Vox's Rule No. 3:

> *Be the friend that you want to have.* Smiles are contagious. Loyalty inspires loyalty. Stand by those who stand by you. Give every friend who fails you a second chance. Only abandon those who have repeatedly proven they cannot be trusted and do not wish you well.[669]

SJWs always lie—but real friends are the ones who stand firm when everyone else runs away.[670] By the by, Vox's family would appreciate prayers for their dog.

---

[669] http://voxday.blogspot.com/2018/11/appendix-c.html

[670] http://voxday.blogspot.com/2019/01/bow-down-before-one-you-serve.html

THE MILO TEST

July 2, 2019

My colleagues in academia must be so jealous of me. I am friends with the most fabulous faggot on the planet. You don't believe me? Look, it says so, right here in *The Chronicle of Higher Education!*[671] Sorry, paywall. I like "cheeky paean" as an epithet for "Three Cheers for White Men." And "journalist-turned-troll-turned-pariah" is amazingly mild as a description of Milo. But my favorite line in Tom Bartlett's article has got to be this one:

> There's enough of a mind-meld between the unlikely pair that some scholars suspect that Brown was essentially the co-author of Yiannopoulos's thesis-length investigation/diatribe. In an email, Brown denied any ghostwriting: "Milo wrote it. He interviewed me. He is a talented journalist who knows his craft."

Have you ever read anything *hotter*? I have a "mind-meld" with Milo?! I think I may need to lie down for a little bit. It's true, Milo and I have been in correspondence for almost three years now. Just ask Joe Bernstein. He knows all about the emails that I wrote to Milo back in autumn 2016—about Christianity and its role in Western civilization. Over the years, I have been suggesting books for Milo

[671] https://www.chronicle.com/interactives/20190628-Medieval

to read, and he and I have talked at length about the sex abuse crisis in the Catholic Church. Milo thanked me in the acknowledgements to his first book *Dangerous* (published two years ago July 4th) for "constant intellectual nourishment."

In return, I have mentioned him and his role in my conversion to Catholicism in podcast after podcast over the past two years.[672],[673],[674] It is hardly a secret that Milo and I talk. Nor is it a secret that I have been blogging about him and that he has shared many of my blogposts on his social media. Do my colleagues think perhaps to shame me by suggesting that I might have *gasp* taught Milo something? The reality is far sexier. Milo is not just my student. He is also my teacher.

As much as I have taught him about the history of Christianity, he has taught me about how to write more effectively, both here and in my more scholarly prose. That "constant intellectual nourishment" I have given him? It is returned in spades by the advice that Milo has given me about capturing an audience's attention and turning an argument to have the greatest effect. I was not kidding when I told Bartlett that Milo is a talented journalist who knows his craft. Why do you think Milo has been banned from almost every social media platform there is other than Telegram and Gab?[675],[676]

Nobody in the conservative media ecosystem can command an audience the way Milo can. And it isn't just because he is so beautiful. Have you ever watched the way Milo uses his hands to make a point? Or how he knows just how long to pause before delivering a riposte? Not to mention the richness of his vocabulary. I myself had to look

---

[672] https://youtu.be/WbLqo3Dej_8

[673] https://soundcloud.com/lumenchristi/rachel-fulton-brown-interview

[674] https://www.nationalreview.com/corner/one-gutsy-medievalist/

[675] https://t.me/MiloOfficial

[676] https://gab.com/m

up three words he used in one recent piece[677]—and I am famous for using words nobody else has ever heard of.[678] Milo has also advised me on my hair—have you noticed how much better it looks in my more recent videos?![679]—and he helped me with designing my set for my new course on Unauthorized.tv.[680]

Did I mention that we were friends? Friends don't let friends go on camera without proper preparation! And, no, Milo did not help me with my script—but with our "mind-meld," who knows? Wait, I thought I was supposed to be ghostwriting for him. What an adventure these past three years have been! Just think. This time in 2016, I had only barely heard of Milo. A year later, I was mentioned in the acknowledgments to *Dangerous*. And a year after that Milo wrote *Middle Rages* about me.

Meanwhile, I have somehow found myself—*mirabile dictu*—overcoming my hatred of seeing myself on camera. Two years ago at Summer Nationals, I was asking my friend Ed's advice about being on camera. I even made a few test videos, thinking I wanted to start my own YouTube channel.[681] And here now I am giving lectures about medieval history on my very own television show. Past me would have died of embarrassment before going on camera. Milo has taught me to be beautiful in ways I never imagined I could be, and it isn't just to do with my hair. *Risus et bellum!* Laughter and war. The adventure has only just begun.

---

[677] https://www.milo.net/50638/say-farewell-to-the-klepto-queens-of-the-british-far-right/

[678] hibernacle, ultracrepidarian, Kummerspeck

[679] https://fencingbearatprayer.blogspot.com/p/bear-on-air.html

[680] https://unauthorizedmedievalhistory.blogspot.com

[681] https://www.youtube.com/user/FencingBearatPrayer/

RACHEL FULTON BROWN

ॐ

Rachel Fulton Brown is Associate Professor of History at the University of Chicago, where she has taught since 1994. She is the author of *From Judgment to Passion: Devotion to Christ and the Virgin Mary, 800-1200*, and *Mary and the Art of Prayer: The Hours of the Virgin in Medieval Christian Life and Thought*, as well as co-editor of *History in the Comic Mode: Medieval Communities and the Matter of Person*, all published by Columbia University Press. She writes for the public on her blog *Fencing Bear at Prayer*. She has appeared on numerous videos, podcasts, and radio shows over the past several years, talking about her conversion to Catholicism and her role in the culture wars. She teaches *Medieval History 101: The Unauthorized Version* at Unauthorized.tv. Her engagements with her colleagues in academia have been recounted in *The Chronicle of Higher Education*, *Inside Higher Ed*, *The New York Times*, *The College Fix*, and *First Things*, and have been narrated in full by Milo Yiannopoulos in *Middle Rages* (Dangerous Books, 2019).

9 789527 303573